International Criminal Procedure

International Criminal Procedure

The Interface of Civil Law and Common Law Legal Systems

Edited by

Linda Carter

Professor of Law and Co-Director, Global Center for Business and Development, University of the Pacific, McGeorge School of Law, Sacramento, California, USA

Fausto Pocar

Professor of International Law, University of Milan, Italy and Appeals Judge, International Criminal Tribunals for the former Yugoslavia and for Rwanda

Edward Elgar

Cheltenham, UK • Northampton, MA, USA

Published by
Edward Elgar Publishing Limited
The Lypiatts
15 Lansdown Road
Cheltenham
Glos GL50 2JA
UK

Edward Elgar Publishing, Inc.
William Pratt House
9 Dewey Court
Northampton
Massachusetts 01060
USA

A catalogue record for this book
is available from the British Library

Library of Congress Control Number: 2012950429

This book is available electronically in the ElgarOnline.com
Law Subject Collection, E-ISBN 978 0 85793 958 6

FSC www.fsc.org
MIX
Paper from responsible sources
FSC® C018575

ISBN 978 0 85793 957 9 (cased)

Typeset by Servis Filmsetting Ltd, Stockport, Cheshire
Printed and bound by MPG Books Group, UK

Contents

About the editors

Linda Carter (United States) is a Professor of Law and Co-Director of the Global Center for Business and Development, University of the Pacific, McGeorge School of Law. Professor Carter has lectured and researched international criminal law issues in multiple venues. In 2005, she studied the Gacaca trials in Rwanda and conducted a workshop in Cambodia. In 2007, she served as a Visiting Professional in the Appeals Chamber of the International Criminal Court in The Hague and as a legal researcher at the International Criminal Tribunal for Rwanda. She was a Fulbright Senior Specialist in Senegal in 2009. Since 2003, she has worked with the Brandeis Institute for International Judges, which convenes meetings of judges from all major international tribunals. Prior to entering academia, Professor Carter litigated civil and criminal cases: from 1978 to 1981, she was an attorney in the honors program of the Civil Rights Division of the United States Department of Justice in Washington, D.C., and from 1981 to 1985, she was an attorney with the Legal Defender Association in Salt Lake City, Utah. She is the author of books and articles on domestic and international criminal law and procedure.

Fausto Pocar (Italy) is a Professor Emeritus of International Law at the Faculty of Law, University of Milan. Since 2000, he serves as Appeals Judge of the International Criminal Tribunal for the former Yugoslavia as well as of the International Criminal Tribunal for Rwanda, and has presided over some 20 appeal cases in either tribunal. Judge Pocar has also served as the President of the ICTY from 2005 to 2008. Prior to being a judge, Professor Pocar served from 1984 to 2000 as a member, and for one term as the President, of the Human Rights Committee under the International Covenant on Civil and Political Rights. He has also contributed to several United Nations activities in the field of international law, international humanitarian law and human rights law, including to the elaboration of the General Assembly Resolution on the rights of minorities of 1992. As an academic, Professor Pocar is the author of books and articles on international law, and in recent years has published extensively on criminal law and international criminal justice. A doctor honoris causa in Antwerp and Buenos Aires, he has lectured in many universities in and outside Europe.

Contributors

Guido Acquaviva (Italy)
Chef de Cabinet, Office of the President, Special Tribunal for Lebanon.

Hannah Garry (United States)
Clinical Associate Professor of Law and Director, International Human Rights Clinic, University of Southern California Gould School of Law.

Sigall Horovitz (Israel)
Research Associate, PhD Candidate and Transitional Justice Project Manager, Faculty of Law, Hebrew University of Jerusalem.

Charles Chernor Jalloh (Sierra Leone and Canada)
Assistant Professor of Law, University of Pittsburgh School of Law.

Magali Maystre (Switzerland)
Legal Officer, Appeals Chamber, International Criminal Tribunal for the former Yugoslavia.

Jenia Iontcheva Turner (Bulgaria and United States)
Professor of Law, Southern Methodist University, Dedman School of Law.

Preface

The choice of procedures for international criminal courts is an unusual process, often untethered to any particular national procedure. For the first international criminal court since Nuremberg, the International Criminal Tribunal for the former Yugoslavia, the judges were able to select the applicable procedures. For the International Criminal Court, the Assembly of States Parties decided upon them. Some of the mixed tribunals, such as the Extraordinary Chambers in the Courts of Cambodia, primarily followed a national procedure. With all of the courts, however, choices were necessary. The idea for this book grew from a realization that many of the procedures in international criminal tribunals reflect an interaction of civil law and common law. This interface of procedures is at times a smooth merger and at times an uneasy union. One key ingredient for making well-reasoned decisions is a comprehension of the context from which a procedure is derived. This analysis calls for an understanding of comparative legal systems, their premises and component parts. Civil law and common law are the focus of this book because those are the systems to which the international courts turned. Other legal systems in the world are important as well and could become the basis for international procedures in the future.

This book is intended for anyone interested in the complex and fascinating interaction of civil law and common law procedures in the international criminal courts. Students of international criminal law will gain a basic understanding of the differences between civil and common law systems and an appreciation for the impact of these differences in international criminal proceedings. Lawyers and judges involved in cases in international criminal tribunals may find the analysis of the issues in this book of interest in their work. The issues that we have chosen for discussion are the ones that, in our view, are the most interesting and difficult to meld together from the two legal systems. They include plea bargaining, witness proofing, written and oral evidence, self-representation and the use of assigned, standby and amicus counsel, the role of victims, and the right to appeal. We first created classes in these topics for the LL.M. program in International Crime and Justice, jointly administered by the University of Turin and the U.N. Interregional Crime and Justice

Research Institute (UNICRI), and for an International Criminal Law course at the University of the Pacific, McGeorge School of Law. From our experience in teaching this topic, we believe that the readings will enrich any course in international criminal law or comparative law.

It has been a pleasure to work with our contributing authors and our research assistants. Our contributing authors come from both civil and common law systems, and from different parts of the world. Each one has experience in international criminal tribunals and the issues in this field of law. Their diversity of backgrounds and experiences contributes to the multiple perspectives presented. A special note of appreciation goes to Rebecca Tatum White and Andrew Ducart, law students at Pacific McGeorge School of Law, who devoted many hours to assisting in the completion of the manuscript. We also thank everyone at Edward Elgar Publishing Ltd for their encouragement and support on this project.

Linda Carter
Fausto Pocar

Table of Cases

1. The challenge of shaping procedures in international criminal courts

Fausto Pocar and Linda Carter

I. THE INTERNATIONAL AND HYBRID CRIMINAL COURTS

The progressive and unprecedented advancements in international criminal law since the 1990s have brought about the establishment of a number of criminal courts and tribunals with the participation of the international community, in order to prosecute international offenses, such as war crimes, crimes against humanity and genocide. These judicial bodies are clearly rooted in the precedent set by the Nuremberg and Tokyo Military Tribunals, which were established by the Allied Powers in the aftermath of World War II and were tasked to deal with the same core international crimes which constitute the basis of the current jurisdictions,[1] but they present different features and cannot be regarded as a unity from the legal point of view. While the international military tribunals were established

[1] The London Charter of the International Military Tribunal established three categories of crimes prosecutable at Nuremberg: 1) war crimes; 2) crimes against the peace or crimes of aggression; and 3) crimes against humanity. *See* Agreement for the Prosecution and Punishment of the Major War Criminals of the European Axis, and Charter of the International Military Tribunal, Aug. 8, 1945, 82 U.N.T.S. 279. The first and third categories remain crimes in all the international or mixed tribunals discussed herein. However, the crime of aggression exists only at the ICC and has yet to be applied. The crime of aggression was finally defined at the Review Conference in Kampala in June 2010, but this amendment of the Rome Statute has yet to take effect. Nonetheless, the other two categories of international crimes remain the cornerstone of international criminal law. At Nuremberg, the crime of genocide was included in crimes against humanity, but since the Convention on the Prevention and Punishment of the Crime of Genocide, Dec. 9, 1948, 78 U.N.T.S. 277, which entered into force in 1951, genocide has become the third core crime on which international criminal tribunals focus their jurisdiction. Thus, war crimes, crimes against humanity and genocide are considered the three principal offenses at the ICTY and ICTR.

by occupying powers on the territory of occupied States,[2] recent criminal jurisdictions have been promoted by the entire international community, as represented by the Security Council of the United Nations.

This is in particular the case of the establishment of the International Criminal Tribunal for the former Yugoslavia (ICTY) in 1993 and the subsequent creation of the International Criminal Tribunal for Rwanda (ICTR) in 1994, which rely upon the initiative of the Security Council.[3] This new approach fostered the further proliferation of criminal courts and tribunals under international auspices in the past two decades. First, the creation of these two ad hoc tribunals demonstrated the need for a permanent criminal jurisdiction, and accelerated the adoption of the Statute of the International Criminal Court (Rome Statute and ICC, respectively) in 1998.[4] However, the adoption of the Rome Statute and the operations of the ICC have not limited the establishment of other international criminal jurisdictions and judicial bodies.[5] The international community and the United Nations (UN) in particular have since supported the institution of many judicial bodies, as is illustrated by the establishment of the Special Chamber of the Supreme Court of Kosovo by the United Nations administration in Kosovo (Special Chamber, 2002);[6] the Special Court for Sierra Leone (SCSL, 2002);[7] the Panels with Exclusive Jurisdiction over Serious Criminal Offences in East Timor (Panels, 2000);[8] the Extraordinary Chambers in the Courts of Cambodia (ECCC, 2003);[9] and more recently

---

[2] A phenomenon not entirely new under international law. *See* The Geneva Conventions, Aug. 12, 1949, *e.g.*, Geneva Convention IV relative to the Protection of Civilian Persons in Time of War, art. 67; art. 70, ¶ 1.

[3] *See* UNSC Res. 827, UN Doc S/RES/827 (May 25, 1993) (which established the ICTY); UNSC Res. 955, UN Doc. S/RES/955 (Nov. 8, 1994) (which established the ICTR).

[4] *See* Rome Statute of the International Criminal Court, July 17, 1998, 2187 U.N.T.S. 90.

[5] Fausto Pocar, *The Proliferation of International Criminal Courts and Tribunals*, 2 J. INT'L CRIM. JUST. 304 (2004).

[6] *See* UN Interim Administration Mission in Kosovo (UNMIK) Reg. No. 2002/12 (June 13, 2002), as amended by UNMIK Regulation No. 2008/4 (Feb. 5, 2008) (adopted under UNSC Res. 1244 (June 10, 1999)).

[7] *See* Agreement Between the United Nations and the Government of Sierra Leone on the Establishment of a Special Court for Sierra Leone, UN Doc. S/2000/915 (concluded on Jan. 16, 2002 under UNSC Res. 1315 (Aug. 14, 2000)).

[8] *See* UN Transitional Administration in East Timor (UNTAET) Reg. No. 2000/15 (June 6, 2000), adopted under UNSC Res. 1272 (Oct. 25, 1999).

[9] *See* Agreement Between the United Nations and the Royal Government of Cambodia Concerning the Prosecution Under Cambodian Law of Crimes Committed During the Period of Democratic Kampuchea (concluded on June 6,

the Special Tribunal for Lebanon (STL, 2007).[10] This phenomenon may well continue irrespective of the ICC having come into operation for a variety of reasons, such as bringing perpetrators to justice for having committed crimes before the entry into force of the Rome Statute, or providing support to domestic jurisdictions to allow them to comply efficiently with the complementarity principle and thus to avoid overburdening the ICC with cases that should be better dealt with at the domestic level.[11]

Irrespective of their denomination, these courts and tribunals are all intended to deter future violations of international law and ensure the end of impunity for individual leaders and participants. However, their characterization does present different issues with respect to applicable law and enforcement, and cannot be regarded as uniform from the legal point of view. In this context, the ICTY and ICTR are "purely international tribunals," as they were established by the Security Council pursuant to Chapter VII of the UN Charter and are composed of international judges elected by the General Assembly from recommendations of the Security Council, as well as an independent prosecutor appointed by the Security Council on nomination by the UN Secretary General.[12] As these ad hoc tribunals are entirely international, they apply only international law, primarily customary law, and operate under international standards of fair trial. Furthermore, they adjudicate on cases in the name of the entire international community. The ICC is equally purely international in nature as it was created by a multilateral treaty, which is voluntarily ratified by States and currently has just over 120 States Parties.[13] An Assembly of the States Parties elects the judges as well as an independent prosecutor. However, as previously mentioned, the ICC was established pursuant to the Rome Statute and thus implements mutually agreed upon treaty law. Under Article 21 of the Rome Statute, customary international law may complement the Rome Statute and the Elements of Crimes annexed thereto, yet the ICC interprets and applies primarily its own Statute.

The features of the other above mentioned judicial bodies are quite

---

2003, under UNGA Res. 57/228 (Dec. 18, 2002)) [hereinafter Agreement Between the UN and Cambodia].

10 *See* Agreement Between the United Nations and the Lebanese Republic on the Establishment of a Special Tribunal for Lebanon (concluded under UNSC Res. 1757 (May 30, 2007)), and the Statute (STL Statute) annexed thereto.

11 *See* Pocar, *supra* note 5, at 306.

12 *See supra* note 3.

13 In addition to the States Parties, there remain about 30 nations that have signed the Rome Statute but have yet to ratify it, including the United States and Russia.

distinct from those of the ad hoc tribunals and the ICC. With the possible exception of the SCSL, for the reasons explored below, these mixed judiciaries should not be regarded as purely international institutions and are thus commonly referred to as "hybrid" or "mixed." The Special Chamber of Kosovo and the Panels in East Timor were established as mixed judiciaries functioning within the domestic legal system, although they cooperate with and are regulated by international entities. In accordance with the UN Interim Administration Mission in Kosovo (UNMIK) Regulations, the Special Chamber formed part of the local judiciary.[14] However, in further accordance with these regulations and in an attempt to ensure the impartial and independent implementation of justice, these panels comprised both Kosovar and internationally appointed judges, the latter being in the majority. The same composition existed at the Panels for East Timor, which were incorporated into the East Timorese judiciary and were composed of both national judges and a majority of internationally appointed judges, following a practice commenced by the UN transitional administration in 2001.[15]

A similar arrangement exists for the ECCC, mandated to prosecute the crimes committed by the Khmer Rouge regime during the period of Democratic Kampuchea rule from 1975–79.[16] Like the Special Chamber and the Panels, the ECCC consists of a combination of national and internationally appointed judges, but unlike in Kosovo and East Timor, the national judges in the ECCC form the majority.[17] These Chambers expressly form part of the national judiciary with the purpose of prosecuting crimes under Cambodian criminal law as well as international customary and humanitarian treaty law.[18] Thus, the ECCC is a mixed judicial body and encompasses both national and international law within its domestic jurisdiction.

Similarly, the STL is a mixed judicial body, based on a Security Council Resolution. Like the Special Chamber, the Panels, and the ECCC, the STL has a combination of national and internationally appointed judges and an independent, internationally appointed prosecutor. However, unlike these previously mentioned courts, the STL does not apply substantive international law; it only prosecutes crimes in accordance with

---

14 UNMIK Reg. No. 2000/64 (Dec. 15, 2000).

15 UNTAET Reg. No. 2000/15 (June 6, 2000).

16 Agreement between the United Nations and the Royal Government of Cambodia Concerning the Prosecution Under Cambodian Law of Crimes Committed During the Period of Democratic Kampuchea (June 6, 2003).

17 *Id.* art. 3, ¶ 2(a)–(b).

18 *Id.* art. 1.

the Lebanese Criminal Code relating to crimes of terrorism, and yet it has to conform to international standards of fair trial and due process.[19] Therefore, like the other mixed courts, the STL is incorporated into the domestic judicial system. However, it remains unique because, while it is a domestic court, it sits in The Hague, Netherlands and not in Lebanon itself. It is also worth noting that the STL is the first of the hybrid tribunals to incorporate the defense into the structure of the tribunal as a separate organ of the Court on the same footing as the prosecution.[20] Thus, although the STL was created by a UN Security Council Resolution, like the other mixed courts, it remains a part of the domestic criminal jurisdiction with international participation and supervision.

With respect to internationally focused judiciaries within national jurisdictions, it is also worth mentioning the War Crimes Chamber of the State Court of Bosnia-Herzegovina, which exercises criminal jurisdiction over offenses defined in the Criminal Code of Bosnia and Herzegovina and other laws of Bosnia and Herzegovina, as well as over crimes under international law, including war crimes.[21] Like the previously mentioned judicial bodies, the War Crimes Chamber has both internationally appointed judges and prosecutors, but functions entirely as a part of the domestic legal system. The Section dealing with war crimes has five first-instance court panels composed of three judges each, two appointed by the High Representative for Bosnia-Herzegovina[22] and one nationally appointed. This Court has already issued a number of judgments and is proceeding to try cases, including some referred to Bosnia-Herzegovina by the ICTY

---

19 *See* the Annual Report for the Special Tribunal for Lebanon from 2009–10.

20 Both the SCSL and the ICC also have offices of defense counsel. While these offices are given significant autonomy, they are administratively within the Registry of each Court and not a separate organ as in the STL. Similar to the STL, the attorneys in the Office of the Principal Defender at the SCSL and in the Office of Public Counsel for the Defence at the ICC can protect the defense interests from the beginning of an investigation, appear as duty counsel if there is no appointed counsel, and otherwise assist the defense counsel and the accused. Although the defense operates independently of the UN at the ICTY and ICTR, there is no office of defense counsel as in the other tribunals.

21 The War Crimes Chamber of Bosnia and Herzegovina of the Court of Bosnia and Herzegovina was established by the High Representative for Bosnia and Herzegovina to bring war criminals to justice in a domestic setting, in order to foster the completion strategy of the ICTY. It began operation on March 9, 2005.

22 The Office of the High Representative for Bosnia was created under the General Framework Agreement for Peace, known as the Dayton Peace Agreement, 1995. The High Representative is nominated by the Steering Board of the Peace Implementation Council, and the nomination is endorsed by the UN Security Council, which approved the Dayton Peace Agreement.

pursuant to Rule 11*bis* of the ICTY Rules of Procedure and Evidence (RPE).[23]

Finally, the SCSL is also a mixed tribunal. However, unlike the judiciaries discussed above, it does not function as a part of the national judiciary. The SCSL was established by agreements between the government of Sierra Leone and the UN, in order to prosecute the crimes perpetrated during the civil war which devastated the country between 1991 and 2001.[24] Unlike the ad hoc tribunals, which were created solely by Security Council Resolutions, the SCSL is not a purely international court. The SCSL is more like the above-mentioned mixed courts because it is composed of both national and internationally appointed judges and can prosecute crimes under Sierra Leonean law as well as international war crimes and crimes against humanity.[25] Nevertheless, despite the incorporation of a few selected Sierra Leonean crimes into its Statute, this court remains more international in nature than other mixed courts, and its progress is monitored by the international community through the Security Council.[26]

Whatever their denomination, these mixed courts are essentially national tribunals with strong international participation and supervision.[27] The mere participation of internationally appointed judges does not alter the nature of the jurisdiction they are called upon to exercise, which remains national, with the possible exception of the SCSL. Furthermore, this national characterization is not modified simply because these courts are mandated to apply international law alongside domestic criminal

---

23 ICTY Rules of Procedure and Evidence (ICTY RPE), Rule 11*bis* A, D(iv), and F provide for the determination on the transferability of a case, that the Prosecutor may observe and monitor the national proceedings and that the ICTY retains the authority to revoke the transfer, respectively. *See also* OSCE Mission to Bosnia and Herzegovina, The Processing of ICTY Rule 11*bis* Cases in Bosnia and Herzegovina 7–11 (2010) (this report traces Rule 11*bis* referrals and monitors interactions with the ICTY with respect to these referrals). Rule 11*bis* of the ICTR Rules of Procedure and Evidence (ICTR RPE) provides for the same process of referral of cases to national courts. These Rule 11*bis* referrals are not limited to the domestic courts of the territory of the relevant state.

24 See UNSC Res. 1315 (Aug. 14, 2000).

25 SCSL Statute, arts. 2, 3.

26 SCSL Statute, art. 5 (this article incorporates domestic law with respect to specific crimes such as crimes against girls and offenses relating to wanton destruction of property).

27 In this respect, the denomination also frequently used, referring to these institutions as "internationalized" courts or tribunals, is misleading as it may give the impression that these domestic courts have shed their national jurisdiction and have become "international."

provisions, as it is becoming standard for most domestic jurisdictions also to apply international law, indirectly as persuasive law or directly through its incorporation into the national law. Thus, the designation of the tribunal as international, national, or hybrid may be less important today in regard to the substantive law applied because each is using international law principles. However, the designation has significance in the procedures used in each court, which are discussed in the following sections.

II. THE NEED FOR RULES OF PROCEDURE AND EVIDENCE

The characterization of the above-described judicial bodies as genuinely international or comparable to national courts inevitably affects their RPE. The rules that each of them is called to apply to its proceedings may even be regarded as one of its more significant distinguishing features. The question of determining the RPE which would be applicable to an international or a mixed criminal tribunal was indeed a thorny one before the international institutions which established them or promoted their establishment. In shaping such rules, however, only a few basic conditions had to be taken into account, the remaining issues being a matter of choice in light of factors which will be analyzed hereafter: first, the somewhat obvious consideration that any criminal court needs some form of procedural and evidentiary rules to govern its proceedings; second, the need for any such rules to be inspired by principles of fairness and due process; third, the assessment that the rules should ensure an efficient conduct of investigations, prosecutions and trials within the context in which a court is set up.

The first requirement is self-explanatory. No court proceedings can be conducted in an orderly way in the absence of rules governing all stages of the procedure as well as the admissibility and the criteria for the evaluation of the evidence. Rules may be written or rooted in a court's practice, imposed on a court by legislation or elaborated by the court itself, strict or flexible, allowing for wide or narrow margins of interpretation, but they are necessary in order to ensure that judicial proceedings are correct and predictable.

As to the second requirement, the compliance of procedural rules with fundamental principles of fair trial and due process is also a must in contemporary criminal law. Such principles are enshrined in international legal instruments, in particular in Article 14 of the International Covenant on Civil and Political Rights (ICCPR), which is overall accepted by

States.[28] Arguments sometimes put forward against the need for international courts to comply with such principles, either drawn from the special nature of international and hybrid tribunals or from the consideration that international instruments on human rights provide for obligations of States which would not bind international institutions, are manifestly flawed. On one hand, although the ICCPR is a treaty ratified by States and a source of State obligations, it was adopted by a resolution of the General Assembly of the UN. Especially for the UN-created courts (ICTY, ICTR, SCSL), it would be odd to regard the Covenant as having no binding effect on the organization which promoted and endorsed the principles contained therein. On the other hand, the consideration that the exercise of criminal jurisdiction over international crimes is primarily a prerogative and responsibility of State authorities, which have the primary duty to prevent, prosecute and punish the commission of such crimes on their territory or by their nationals, requires that the complementary exercise of such jurisdiction by international or hybrid courts must conform with the same fair trial conditions that are required and expected from States. Disparities of treatment of similar cases which would result from the non-observance of these conditions would appear manifestly unjustified. Lastly, there is no doubt about the special nature of international and hybrid courts, both when they are ad hoc judicial bodies and when they are given permanent general jurisdiction, since even the latter have in fact special jurisdiction as compared with the general jurisdiction of the State courts and tribunals. However, their special nature cannot be invoked for derogating from generally accepted principles of fair trial; rather, it constitutes a ground for increasing the attention to the observance of such principles, because special jurisdictions are more exposed to disregarding them.[29]

Turning to the third condition, i.e., that any procedure should aim at ensuring efficiency within the context that characterizes the establishment of a particular court, it has to be stressed that it is highly unlikely that a domestic procedure may be suitable to be applied, as such, in an international context. In an international context, a court is facing additional problems which depend on it not being inserted in a stable and organized judiciary, in particular the absence of an executive branch tasked with

---

[28] *See infra* note 46 and accompanying text, noting that there are 167 States Parties to the ICCPR and describing the specific principles.

[29] *See* Human Rights Committee (HRC), General Comment No. 13 (1984), ¶ 4, and General Comment No. 32 (2007), ¶ 14, UN Doc. HRI/GEN/1/Rev. 9. *See also* Manfred Nowak, U.N. Covenant on Civil and Political Rights: CCPR Commentary 309 (2d ed. 2005).

assisting it in the enforcement of its decisions. The distance from the place where the crimes occurred and the language skills of the persons participating in the proceedings – including the judges, the parties and all those who assist in the conduct of a trial – may also raise issues which a domestic jurisdiction will normally not face, except in extraordinary circumstances. Admittedly, these problems may be of less significance if a hybrid court is established within the country of commission of the crimes alongside the domestic judiciary, and even of lesser significance if that court is recognized as forming part of that judiciary. However, even in such cases, some adjustments will be necessary in order to reach satisfactory solutions which would adequately take into account the exigency that a judicial body is able to perform its tasks efficiently within a reasonable time frame, as required by the principle that justice should be exercised without undue delay.

III. CHOICES FOR RULES OF PROCEDURE AND EVIDENCE

When a new court or tribunal is established at the international level or with international participation, the choice for its RPE will have to be made taking into account the factors as described above. Predictability, fairness and efficiency should be the guiding lines and at the same time the considerations and the goals limiting the choice of the model which will inspire the rules to be applied by that court or tribunal. Within the framework of these general principles, however, the margins of choice offered to the drafters of such RPE are rather ample. Three basic options will generally be available: a) adopting a specific domestic model; b) drafting a completely new model; c) blending domestic models. Admittedly, these are not entirely independent options, and there may be some interaction between them. Thus, the adoption of a specific domestic model may require adjustments which may be inspired by other domestic rules or international exigencies. Drafting a completely new model may also occasionally reflect existing domestic or international rules. Blending domestic models will not exclude the insertion of additional rules that do not belong to the domestic systems concerned.

Practice which has developed so far shows a variety of approaches that are closer to one or other option as identified above. However, these approaches also reveal some preference for the option consisting of largely referring to a specific domestic system when a hybrid court is established in order to deal with a country situation, and a preference for the option of blending major domestic systems when purely international tribunals are concerned.

A. Hybrid and Mixed Courts and Tribunals

In the case of hybrid courts it has appeared natural to give special attention to the rules of procedure and evidence already in force in the domestic legislation, with the possible infusion of international principles where appropriate. This is the case of the statute of the ECCC, which declares that:

> The procedure shall be in accordance with Cambodian law. Where Cambodian law does not deal with a particular matter, or where there is uncertainty regarding the interpretation or application of a relevant rule of Cambodian law, or where there is a question regarding the consistency of such a rule with international standards, guidance may also be sought in procedural rules established at the international level.[30]

A similar approach characterizes the statute of the STL, which tasked the judges of the Special Tribunal with adopting RPE, and subsequently amending them, as appropriate. According to the statute:

> In so doing, the judges shall be guided, as appropriate, by the Lebanese Code of Criminal Procedure, as well as by other reference materials reflecting the highest standards of international criminal procedure, with a view to ensuring a fair and expeditious trial.[31]

International practice appears to deviate from this approach when hybrid judicial bodies have been established by international authorities that had full control over the legal system of the country concerned. Except for the War Crime Chamber in Bosnia and Herzegovina, which is fully integrated into the domestic Bosnian legal system and applies the Bosnian Code of Criminal Procedure, in such cases the authority and the court have been given more latitude in adopting the RPE. This is the case of the Special Chamber in Kosovo, where the Special Representative of the Secretary-General declared in the relevant regulation that he himself,

> shall promulgate rules for the conduct of proceedings before the Special Chamber through the issuance of an administrative direction. Such rules shall provide a party with a meaningful opportunity to have his claim adjudicated, including a judicial review of such adjudication, in an impartial and transparent manner within a reasonable period of time and in accordance with norms established under the European Convention on Human Rights and having regard

---

30 Agreement Between the UN and Cambodia, *supra* note 9, art. 12(1).
31 STL Statute, art. 28(2).

> to generally accepted international standards. In cases that are not clearly or expressly covered by such Rules the Special Chamber shall have authority to issue additional Rules of Procedure consistent with these principles.[32]

Similarly, the Special Representative of the Secretary-General in East Timor promulgated Transitional Rules of Criminal Procedure for the Panels by drafting an entirely new set of rules,[33] which establish an adversarial system notwithstanding the presence of an investigative judge, who in fact does not have investigatory functions, but is "empowered to ensure that the rights of every person subject to a criminal investigation and the rights of any alleged victims of the suspected crime under investigation are respected."[34]

With respect to hybrid courts, a further deviation from a reference to a specific domestic model is demonstrated by the SCSL statute, which explicitly endorses as a model the RPE adopted by an international tribunal, the ICTR, though eventually assigning a significant role to domestic legislation. Under the statute:

> The Rules of Procedure and Evidence of the [ICTR] obtaining at the time of the establishment of the Special Court shall be applicable *mutatis mutandis* to the conduct of the legal proceedings before the Special Court.
>
> The judges of the Special Court as a whole may amend the Rules of Procedure and Evidence or adopt additional rules where the applicable Rules do not, or do not adequately, provide for a specific situation. In so doing, they may be guided, as appropriate, by the Criminal Procedure Act, 1965, of Sierra Leone.[35]

B. International Courts and Tribunals

The reference thus made to the Rules of the ICTR leads to consideration of the approach followed so far with respect to purely international courts and tribunals, in particular the ICTY and the ICC. The Statute of the ICTR, indeed, simply accepts the choice made by the ICTY and explicitly endorses its Rules, by stating that:

---

32 UNMIK Regulation No. 2008/4, § 7 (Feb. 5, 2008).

33 *See* UNTAET Regulation No. 2000/30 (Sept. 25, 2000) (as amended by UNTAET Regulation No. 2001/25 (Sept. 14, 2001)), as well as the Democratic Republic of Timor-Leste Government Decree-law No. 13/2005, approving the Criminal Procedure Code and repealing the Transitional Rules of Criminal Procedure.

34 UNTAET Regulation No. 2000/30, § 9(1) (Sept. 25, 2000).

35 SCSL Statute, art. 14. Changes made in the provisions are actually minimal, and depend on the non acceptance by the ICTR judges of some amendments made to the ICTY Rules.

> The Judges of the International Tribunal for Rwanda shall adopt, for the purpose of proceedings before the International Tribunal for Rwanda, the Rules of Procedure and Evidence for the conduct of the pre-trial phase of the proceedings, trials and appeals, the admission of evidence, the protection of victims and witnesses and other appropriate matters of the International Tribunal for the Former Yugoslavia with such changes as they deem necessary.[36]

Thus, the ICTY was the only international tribunal, and indeed also the first one, which was mandated with the adoption of its own RPE, and the only one which had a full choice before it as to the model to follow in this respect. The ICTY Statute simply states that:

> The judges of the International Tribunal shall adopt rules of procedure and evidence for the conduct of the pretrial phase of the proceedings, trials and appeals, the admission of evidence, the protection of victims and witnesses and other appropriate matters.[37]

It was therefore open to the ICTY judges to make any choice with respect to the rules that they deemed the most appropriate to govern the proceedings of the tribunal. Faced with this challenge, and having no real precedent since the Nuremberg and Tokyo tribunals had very rudimentary rules of procedure and all other matters were left to the case-by-case ruling of the Tribunals, the ICTY first, "deemed important to adopt precise and detailed rules to govern the principal aspects of the proceedings and to provide a solid basis to the rights of the defence,"[38] with a view to ensuring a fair and expeditious trial and complying with the basic requirements of predictability, due process, and efficiency. Turning to the issue of adopting an adversarial or inquisitorial model, the ICTY inclined toward a largely adversarial approach, prevailing in *common law* systems, rather than the inquisitorial system prevailing in *civil law* systems in continental Europe and other countries, with some exceptions.[39] In particular, initially it was felt that technical rules for the admissibility of evidence were not necessary in the absence of a jury, that judges should be allowed to order the production of additional evidence *proprio motu*, and that the practice of plea bargaining could find no place in the rules. The number of exceptions increased during the operation of the Tribunal, as the plenary of the judges

---

36 ICTR Statute, art 14.

37 ICTY Statute, art. 15.

38 ICTY, YEARBOOK, 1996, ¶ 57 (1994).

39 ICTY, YEARBOOK, 1999, ¶¶ 71–2 (1994). In this chapter, the terms inquisitorial, non-adversarial, and civil law are used interchangeably. Similarly, the terms adversarial and common law are interchangeable. *See infra* in the subsection on Civil and Common Law Traditions for further discussion of terminology and of civil and common law traditions.

adjusted the rules to the needs that arose in the daily practice. It can easily be said that the ICTY set aside the option of following a specific domestic model, resisted the temptation to follow a completely new model, and followed rather the option of trying to blend two domestic models – the adversarial common law and the inquisitorial civil law – in order to shape the best rules of procedure and evidence for the international Tribunal.

A somewhat different approach was taken for the adoption of the rules of procedure and evidence of the ICC, the only permanent international court potentially entrusted with jurisdiction over all international crimes, irrespective of the place of commission and the nationality of the perpetrator. Unlike in the ICTY, the judges of the ICC were not entrusted with the adoption of their rules. Rather, the rules enter into force only "upon adoption by a two-third majority of the members of the Assembly of States Parties."[40] Judges can, like States Parties and the prosecutor, propose amendments which will have to be adopted by the same majority of States Parties, and only exceptionally can apply such proposals as provisionally operative until the formal adoption occurs. As the rules are negotiated within a political body instead of a restricted group of judges, they tend to be more elaborated and articulated than the rules of the ICTY,[41] and, as a consequence, they also lack the flexibility of the latter. However, like the ICTY rules, they essentially adopt an adversarial system with exceptions inspired by civil law systems. Setting aside the option of following a specific domestic model, they oscillate between the options of establishing a completely new model or of blending domestic models. Looking at them as a whole, they appear to accept more features of civil law procedures than the ICTY rules do, though keeping a basically adversarial system. In other aspects, they try to blend common and civil law models with the addition of elements which do not match entirely either of the two models.

C. Reasons for Choices

The choice of the specific domestic system of the country of operation of the court is clearly rooted for hybrid courts in the aim to deviate as little as possible from the activity of the ordinary judiciary. The consistency with domestic courts prevents an excessive differentiation in the treatment of similar cases by the established special court as compared with the ordinary courts, avoids subjecting the accused and possibly the defense

---

40 ICC Statute, art. 51(1).

41 Notwithstanding the numerous amendments approved in 20 years of activity, the RPE of the ICTY comprise now 155 rules, while the RPE of the ICC are 225.

to an unfamiliar system, and allows for better coordination of the judicial bodies operating in the country concerned. However, one may wonder why aims of this kind seem not to have even crossed the mind of the drafters of the RPE of purely international courts. In particular, the drafters of the RPE in the ICTY do not appear to have discussed the impact that the adoption of a common law accusatorial system could have on the trials of individuals who allegedly committed crimes in countries whose legislation was following the civil law inquisitorial model.[42]

There may be reasons why the issue was not discussed. The ICTY judges may have been more inclined to follow a common law model because of their personal legal background, or simply have regarded an adversarial common law procedure as the more appropriate for exercising jurisdiction by an international court. It should be noted that the Nuremberg and Tokyo trials, although they do not provide many precedential guidelines pertaining to procedure and evidence, were essentially conducted according to common law procedures. Furthermore, in drafting the first set of international rules to ever exist, judges may have been guided by the desire to establish an adversarial procedure as a precedent and model for other international criminal courts that would address situations in other areas of the world. Indeed, the ICTY rules have since been exported to the ICTR and the SCSL and have, though only to some extent, influenced other courts, including the ICC.

Would the adoption of a civil law system closer to the legislation and practice of the States concerned have ensured more fairness to the accused, the victims, and the witnesses, avoiding differentiations in treatment depending on whether the case was dealt with at the international or the domestic level? Would it have made the proceedings of the ICTY more understandable for the people in the Balkans and helped to reduce the inevitable gaps in communication and visibility deriving from trials conducted far away from the place of commission of the crimes? Even more importantly, would the defense of the accused have been more efficient if counsel, frequently coming from the region, had been more familiar with the procedure followed by the Tribunal? It is difficult to give a clear answer to these questions. However, it is likely that at least the cooperation between the domestic courts and the ICTY, which now plays an

---

[42] The Report of the Secretary-General to the Security Council is entirely silent on this point and simply refers any decision on the RPE to the judges of the ICTY: *see* Report of the Secretary-General pursuant to paragraph 2 of Security Council Resolution 808, UN Doc. S/25704 (May 3, 1993), ¶ 83. Likewise, in reporting on the approaches followed in drafting the RPE, the ICTY makes no mention of this issue.

important role in the legacy approaches of the Tribunal, would have been facilitated and may have been hindered by the difficulty to understand and adapt to unfamiliar procedures. Nevertheless, it must be recognized that the blending of traditions has been carried out thoughtfully and with full awareness of the tension between strict adherence to human rights and the efficiency of international criminal justice.[43]

It is less surprising that these issues have not been discussed in the drafting of the RPE of the ICC. Although in theory one could have opted for the adoption of different procedures for different situations in lieu of one system of procedure and evidence, it is evident that such an approach would have been the source of many prospective difficulties in the application of the rules, for the judges sitting in more than one bench, for the accused and the defense, and for any other person involved in the holding of the trial, including the registry which would have been obliged to serve the court under different rules of procedure and evidence. In light of the nature of the crimes subject to the jurisdiction of the court, which may have a transnational dimension, one could even expect litigation on the procedure to be followed in a particular case. These factors could have seriously affected the capacity of the ICC to conduct fair and expeditious trials. Furthermore, it has to be recognized that if, by following one system of procedure and evidence, the ICC faces the same problems that the ICTY has experienced in its relations with the region concerned, it will also ensure the enforcement of a procedure that will be applicable worldwide as more States ratify or accede to the Rome Statute.

The above brief overview of the approaches followed by existing international and hybrid courts and tribunals allows for some provisional conclusions. First, there is no clear consistency as to the choice of models made in shaping rules of procedure and evidence for these courts. Second, hybrid courts tend, with some exception, to adopt rules which are largely or partly influenced by the need to take into account the specific domestic rules in force in the country over whose territory the jurisdiction of the court extends. By contrast, purely international courts tend to rely on rules that do not follow any specific domestic model and rather try to blend the dominant models in the world, i.e., the common law adversarial system and the civil law inquisitorial system. The reliance of hybrid courts on the specific domestic system of the country in which the court operates does not reflect a real choice of a model, but rather adaptations

---

43 *See* Fausto Pocar, *The ICTY's Continuation Strategy: Partnership with Regional Judges and Attorneys, in* Assessing the Legacy of the ICTY 169–70 (Richard H. Steinberg ed., 2011).

and adjustments aimed at rendering the rules of that system suitable for the special jurisdiction of the court. Consequently, one can conclude that only purely international courts and the SCSL made a choice towards an international model, which would not be completely new, and result in the blending of different domestic models.

In this context, a study of the RPE of international courts and tribunals from the angle of the combination of different domestic models mainly implies a consideration of two achievements in the direction of blending the common law adversarial system and the civil law inquisitorial traditions: the substantially identical RPE of the ICTY, ICTR,[44] and SCSL on one hand, and the RPE of the ICC on the other. The solutions adopted by hybrid courts may supplement this study, bearing in mind that they are not motivated by an effort to blend different models, but rather to deviate as little as possible from domestic law.

IV. CIVIL LAW AND COMMON LAW TRADITIONS

As noted earlier, what we commonly refer to as "civil law" is also called an "inquisitorial," "Romano-Germanic," or "non-adversarial" system. In contrast, a "common law" system is viewed as synonymous with an "adversarial" approach. The terminology is imprecise and somewhat misleading. Civil law systems, in fact, have adversarial aspects to them and common law systems have non-adversarial parts. Even more importantly, neither "civil law" nor "common law" is a monolith. There are many variations among civil law and common law systems. For instance, the "civil law" systems of France and Germany evolved differently and, consequently, some procedures differ. Similarly, the evolution of the "common law" systems in the United States and in England and Wales diverged, resulting in differences in their procedures. For our purposes, however, we will use the terminology of "civil law" and "common law" to represent certain fundamental conceptual differences and certain specific procedural implications.

---

44 The identical terms of the text are further reflected in a common interpretation of the Rules, as the ICTY and the ICTR share the Appeals Chamber. Pursuant to Article 13(4) of the ICTR Statute, "the members of the Appeals Chamber of the International Tribunal for the Former Yugoslavia shall also serve as the members of the Appeals Chamber of the International Tribunal for Rwanda." Strictly speaking, the ICTY and the ICTR have separate Appeals Chambers that both sit in The Hague and are composed of the same judges. However, decisions of one Appeals Chamber are obviously persuasive in the other.

It is also important to note that there are legal systems other than civil and common law. Religious-based systems, such as Shari'a law, exist in many countries as do customary law systems, based on historical practices. In this book, we focus on civil and common law traditions because they have formed the basis of the procedures in the international criminal courts. This is not, however, to say that the other legal systems are insignificant or should not be examined when designing future procedural mechanisms in international courts.

Why do we have two major legal systems in the world today? Both civil law and common law systems have roots in Roman law. The civil law tradition, however, is the far older development from Roman law, especially the law related to civil (non-criminal and non-commercial) matters. Other sources for civil law traditions include the Canon law of the Roman Catholic Church and the development of commercial law. Roman law received great attention and revival in the eleventh century, with those efforts centered at the University of Bologna in Italy. The law and methodologies were then disseminated throughout Europe by those who studied in Bologna. Two of the major approaches within civil law that developed are represented by the written codifications of France and Germany. The codes of France and Germany, in turn, have influenced the development of many other civil law systems around the world. The common law tradition is also grounded in Roman law, but is the result of the divergence of legal developments in England after the Norman Conquest of 1066. The isolation of the British Isles allowed the common law system to develop in a different direction from the civil law traditions on the continent. In contrast to the civil law systems on the continent, the law and methodology of the emerging common law system was largely unwritten and developed by the courts. Needless to say, there are many variations today in both civil law and common law systems. The influence, however, of each tradition is reflected throughout the world, with civil law a more dominant approach. Civil law is the basis for approximately two-thirds of the world's legal systems while common law is the basis for only about one-third of national systems.[45]

Although the civil law and common law traditions differ in many respects, systems derived from each tradition have a common grounding in fundamental rights accorded to the accused. Major human rights treaties

---

[45] *Juriglobe*, UNIVERSITY OF OTTAWA, http://www.juriglobe.ca/eng/syst-onu/tab-regroupement.php#civil (last visited June 20, 2012) (the statistics are approximate because there are numerous systems that are a mixture of civil law and common law).

apply in virtually all countries. The International Covenant on Civil and Political Rights (ICCPR) has 167 States Parties.[46] All 47 members of the Council of Europe are parties to the European Convention for the Protection of Human Rights and Fundamental Freedoms (ECHR).[47] The American Convention on Human Rights (ACHR), with 24 States Parties,[48] and the African Charter on Human and Peoples' Rights (ACHPR), with 53 States Parties,[49] similarly embody the basic rights of an accused person.

The fundamental rights from human rights treaties pertain to pretrial, trial, and post-conviction stages. The ICCPR provides, inter alia, that any person charged with a criminal offense shall have the right:[50]

1. To a fair and public hearing by a competent, independent and impartial tribunal established by law
2. To be presumed innocent
3. To be informed promptly and in detail in a language which he understands of the nature and cause of the charge against him
4. To adequate time and facilities for the preparation of his defence and to communicate with counsel of his own choosing
5. To be tried without undue delay
6. To be tried in his presence
7. To defend himself in person or through legal assistance of his own choosing
8. To have legal assistance assigned to him
9. To examine, or have examined, the witnesses against him and to obtain the attendance and examination of witnesses on his behalf
10. To the free assistance of an interpreter

---

[46] *See International Covenant on Civil and Political Rights status as of June 20, 2012*, UNITED NATIONS, http://treaties.un.org/Pages/ViewDetails.aspx?src=TREATY&mtdsg_no=IV-4&chapter=4&lang=en (last visited June 20, 2012).

[47] *See* Treaty Office, *Convention for the Protection of Human Rights and Fundamental Freedoms status as of June 20, 2012*, COUNCIL OF EUROPE, http://conventions.coe.int/Treaty/Commun/ChercheSig.asp?NT=005&CM=8&CL=ENG (last visited June 20, 2012).

[48] *See* Dept. of Int'l Law, *B-32: American Convention on Human Rights "Pact of San Jose, Costa Rica"*, ORG. OF AMERICAN STATES, http://www.oas.org/juridico/english/sigs/b-32.html (last visited June 20, 2012).

[49] *See African Charter on Human and Peoples' Rights*, AFRICAN COMMISSION ON HUMAN AND PEOPLES' RIGHTS, http://www.achpr.org/instruments/achpr/ (last visited June 20, 2012).

[50] ICCPR, art. 14.

11. Not to be compelled to testify against himself or to confess guilt
12. To have his conviction and sentence reviewed by a higher tribunal according to law.

These basic rights are represented in the law and practice of States and also in the statutes of the international criminal tribunals. Although the same rights find a place substantively within all major legal systems, the procedures for implementing those rights differ. The differences procedurally are especially striking with regard to certain of the rights. Those procedural aspects that differ are the focus of the chapters in this book.

V. GOALS OF CRIMINAL JUSTICE SYSTEMS AND CONTROL OF EVIDENCE AT TRIAL

Many of the differences between systems based on the civil law and common law traditions stem from two key foundational characteristics. The first is the dominant goal of a trial. The second is who is in control of the evidence at the trial.

Scholars have commented on a traditional difference in goals between a search for truth and a dispute resolution mechanism. The driving force of a civil law system was viewed as a desire to determine, as closely as possible, the absolute truth of what occurred in a situation.[51] Although a determination of what actually occurred is also important in a common law system, such systems are regarded as elevating resolution of the dispute between the prosecution and defense as the dominant goal.[52] Common law

---

[51] *See* Mirjan Damaška, *Evidentiary Barriers to Conviction and Two Models of Criminal Procedure: A Comparative Study,* 121 U. PA. L. REV. 506, 580 (1973) (describing civil law system as "more committed to the search for truth" than an adversary system). *See also* Mirjan Damaška, *The Competing Visions of Fairness: The Basic Choice for International Criminal Tribunals*, 36 N.C. J. INT'L L. & COM. REG. 365, 369–70 (2011) [hereinafter Damaška, *Competing Visions of Fairness*] (noting a more recent decrease in emphasis on truth with an increase in procedural fairness); Thomas Weigend, *Is the Criminal Process About Truth?: A German Perspective*, 26 HARV. J.L. & PUB. POL'Y 157, 161–2 (2003) (describing traditional emphasis on truth and noting changes due to procedural rights of the accused).

[52] *See* the work of Prof. Mirjan Damaška characterizing the common law as "resolving a conflict." DAMAŠKA, THE FACES OF JUSTICE AND STATE AUTHORITY: A COMPARATIVE APPROACH TO THE LEGAL PROCESS 161 (1991) (contrasting "conflict-solving" proceedings with "policy-implementing" proceedings; also commenting that, given the uncertainty of determining actual truth, it is more accurate to describe a goal of "optimal levels of fact-finding accuracy); and Damaška, *Evidentiary Barriers*, *supra* note 51, at 581 (referring to the "contest" model).

systems are also viewed as placing a greater emphasis on the rights of the accused, which may compromise the search for absolute truth. Civil law systems today, however, also place an increasing emphasis on the rights of the accused.[53] Although the description of a truth focus in civil law systems compared with a dispute resolution focus in common law systems does not do justice to the complexity of the systems today, the two themes are descriptive and explanatory of some of the procedures. For instance, if determining the absolute truth is a priority, then it is preferable to have a system in which as much evidence as possible is admissible so that all relevant facts are known. If resolving the dispute is the dominant goal, then establishing "rules of the game" that regulate what evidence is admissible helps to control the proceeding on the dispute. Civil law systems generally reflect the emphasis on truth finding with fewer restrictive evidence rules than one finds in common law systems, which have more elaborate rules for admission of evidence.

The second difference relates to the approach to who controls the admission of evidence at trial. The two models could be described as judge-centric and party-centric.[54] Most civil law-based systems use a judge-centric approach while most common law-based systems use a party-centric model.

In a judge-centric model, it is the judge, or sometimes a panel of three judges, who determines what evidence is admissible and which witnesses will be called to testify at trial.[55] Prior to trial there will ordinarily be a pretrial investigation by either an investigating judge[56] or a prosecutor,[57]

---

[53] Damaška, *Competing Visions of Fairness*, *supra* note 51, at 369–70.

[54] There are a number of similar characterizations of the two systems. *See, e.g.*, Craig R. Callen, *Cognitive Strategies and Models of Fact-Finding*, *in* CRIME, PROCEDURE AND EVIDENCE IN A COMPARATIVE AND INTERNATIONAL CONTEXT 165 (2008) (describing "judge-driven" and "party-driven" systems); DAMAŠKA, *supra* note 52, at 109, 154 (referring to the systems as one of "party control" or "official control").

[55] Gordon Van Kessel, *European Perspectives on the Accused as a Source of Testimonial Evidence*, 100 W. VA. L. REV. 799, 801 (1998) (describing continental systems in general); Richard S. Frase, *Comparative Criminal Justice as a Guide to American Law Reform: How Do the French Do It, How Can We Find Out, and Why Should We Care?*, 78 CALIF. L. REV. 539, 640 (1990) (describing French system).

[56] FRANCIS PAKES, COMPARATIVE CRIMINAL JUSTICE 75 (2010) (describing the role of the investigating judge in The Netherlands); Renee Lettow Lerner, *The Intersection of Two Systems: An American on Trial for an American Murder in the French Cour D'assises*, 2001 U. ILL. L. REV. 791, 801 (2001) (describing the role of the *juge d'instruction* in serious cases in France).

[57] For example, in Germany, there is no longer an investigating judge; the prosecutor directs the pretrial investigation. PAKES, *supra* note 56, at 75.

who will interview witnesses and collect documents. Like the investigating judge, the civil law prosecutor has a neutral role to collect both inculpatory and exculpatory evidence.[58] The investigatory information is then turned over to the presiding trial judge in a written case file, often called a *dossier*.[59] There is a role at trial for the prosecutor and defense counsel, but their roles are secondary to the judges. The prosecutor and defense counsel can suggest additional witnesses or lines of questioning to the judges.[60] The judges, thus, maintain an active role in conducting the proceedings.

In a party-centric model, it is the prosecution and defense counsel who determine what evidence to present and which witnesses to call.[61] The judge's role is to rule on the admissibility of the evidence proffered by the parties and to regulate the timing of the trial. If there is a jury, the judge also has the role of instructing the jury as the need arises during the trial and at the conclusion of the evidence before the jury begins deliberations.[62] The prosecutor is not in a neutral role in this type of system. Both the prosecution and the defense introduce evidence that supports only their side in the case. The theory is that, by having each side introduce evidence that best supports their theory of the case, the fact finder will have all the evidence necessary to make a determination of the facts.[63]

---

58 Keith A. Findley, *Adversarial Inquisitions: Rethinking the Search for the Truth*, 56 N.Y.L. Sch. L. Rev. 911, 931 (2012) (describing a German prosecutor as a "second judge" who functions in a "neutral, detached, and objective" role). In France, the prosecutor, or *procureur,* is considered to be part of the judiciary, *magistrat*. Jacqueline S. Hodgson, *The French Prosecutor in Question*, 67 Wash. & Lee L. Rev. 1361, 1366 (2010). Note, though, that the inclusion of the *procureur* as part of the *magistrat* has been criticized because the European Court of Human Rights has not viewed the *procureur* as independent and because the *procureur* does not have the independence of the others in the *magistrat*. *See also* Jacqueline Hodgson, French Criminal Justice 65 (2005).

59 Pakes, *supra* note 56, at 88, 94–5; Lerner, *supra* note 56, at 805.

60 Mireille Delmas-Marty & J.R. Spencer, European Criminal Procedures 253, 258 (J.R. Spencer trans., Cambridge University Press, 2002) (1995); Leonardo J. Raznovich, *A Comparative Review of the Socio-Legal Implications of Burden of Proof and Presumptions to Deal with Factual Uncertainty*, 32 Am. J. Trial Advoc. 57, 58 (2008).

61 Delmas-Marty & Spencer, *supra* note 60, at 627; Stephane Bourgon, *Procedural Problems Hindering Expeditious and Fair Justice*, 2 J. Int'l Crim. Just. 526, 530 (2004).

62 *See* Steven M. Warshawsky, *Opposing Jury Nullification: Law, Policy, and Prosecutorial Strategy*, 85 Geo. L.J. 191, 231 (1996); Nancy S. Marder, *The Myth of the Nullifying Jury*, 93 Nw. U. L. Rev. 877, 904 (1999) (describing the United States); Delmas-Marty & Spencer, *supra* note 60, at 500 (describing England).

63 David A. Harris, *The Constitution and Truth Seeking: A New Theory on Expert Services for Indigent Defendants*, 83 J. Crim. L. & Criminology 469,

It is the party-centric aspect that has led commentators to refer to a common law-based trial as a dispute resolution mechanism rather than a search for the absolute truth. With a judge-centric model, in contrast, there is arguably a greater emphasis on determining the truth because the judges are neutrally trying to find out all of the facts on guilt or innocence.

Another ramification of emphasizing either the determination of the truth or dispute resolution is the weight that each system puts on the rights of the accused and on efficiency. Typical common law systems place great emphasis on the fairness of the proceedings to the accused. Evidence illegally obtained is excluded, even if it would assist in determining the truth of what occurred.[64] The accused is given great leeway in representing himself, even if the resulting trial unfairly disadvantages the accused.[65] Self-representation that jeopardizes the fairness of the proceedings is less likely to be tolerated in a civil law system with an emphasis on finding the true facts.[66]

Not only do civil law systems focus on the truth, but they also focus on the efficiency of the proceedings.[67] In contrast, common law trials may take much longer than a parallel civil law trial. The priority on efficiency in a civil law system is enhanced by putting significant control over the admission of evidence in the hands of the judges. With the prosecution and defense counsel determining the presentation of evidence in a common law system, there is less ability to ensure a highly efficient proceeding.

The international criminal courts are not clear whether their priority is truth or dispute resolution. As a result, there is a mixture of approaches. For instance, the extent to which an accused has a right to represent

---

499–500 (1992); Richard E. Myers, *Adversarial Counsel in an Inquisitorial System*, 37 N.C. J. INT'L L. & COM. REG. 411, 414 (2011).

[64] Myers, *supra* note 63, at 413–6 (commenting on "truth-deflecting" practices in adversarial proceedings); Jacqueline S. Hodgson, *Safeguarding Suspects' Rights in Europe: A Comparative Perspective*, 14 NEW CRIM. L. REV. 611, 620 (2011) (discussing exclusion of police interrogations that are not recorded in England and Wales).

[65] *Faretta v. California*, 422 U.S. 806, 834 (1975) (taking the position that the defendant's choice to represent himself must be honored even though he "may conduct his own defense ultimately to his own detriment").

[66] Rachel K. Jones, *Untangling the Right to Self-Representation in the International Criminal Tribunal for the Former Yugoslavia*, 43 GA. L. REV. 1285, 1295 (2009) (describing greater ability to require counsel in serious cases or where the accused's rights are at stake in civil law systems); Michael P. Scharf, *Self-Representation Versus Assignment of Defence Counsel Before International Criminal Tribunals*, 4 J. INT'L CRIM. JUST. 31, 35 (2006) (describing required counsel in France, Belgium, and Germany).

[67] Frase, *supra* note 55, at 627 (describing German and French trials as more streamlined).

himself has generated a number of decisions as the courts try to find the right balance between self-representation and the fairness and efficiency of the proceedings. Issues related to representation of the accused are discussed in Chapter 5. With regard to the neutrality or non-neutrality of the prosecutor, a clearer choice has been made in the ICTY and ICTR than in the ICC. In all three courts, the prosecutor has an independent role and is not part of the judicial function. The ICTY statute is framed much like the common law approach of a non-neutral prosecutor who is investigating to prepare for prosecution if the evidence is sufficient.[68] In contrast, the ICC statute phrases the prosecutor's role in more neutral terms, at least at the outset of the investigation. Article 54 states that the prosecutor shall "[i]n order to establish the truth, extend the investigation to cover all facts and evidence relevant to an assessment of whether there is criminal responsibility under this Statute, and, in doing so, *investigate incriminating and exonerating circumstances equally*."[69] At trial, however, the ICC Prosecutor operates in an adversarial mode. Another example of an area in which the international courts do not clearly reflect a particular focus is in the evidence rules. There are fewer restrictive evidence rules in the international courts than one finds in common law systems and, yet, the procedures are party-centric. It may be, however, that the absence of complex evidence rules is explained more by the absence of a lay jury. The significance of trials without juries is discussed in the next section.

VI. THE USE AND IMPACT OF A LAY JURY

A further difference in systems that has resulted in a divergence on rules of evidence is the presence of a lay jury in common law systems. Civil law systems often have lay jurors in serious cases, but the lay jurors sit with professional judges in deliberating on the case.[70]

---

[68] ICTY Statute, art. 16 provides: "The Prosecutor shall be responsible for the investigation and prosecution of persons responsible for serious violations of international humanitarian law committed in the territory of the former Yugoslavia since 1 January 1991." ICTY Statute, art. 18 provides: "The Prosecutor shall assess the information received or obtained and decide whether there is sufficient basis to proceed."

[69] ICC Statute, art. 54 (emphasis added).

[70] Delmas-Marty & Spencer, *supra* note 60, at 502 (describing mixed courts in some cases in Italy, France, and Germany of both professional judges and lay jurors); John H. Langbein, *Mixed Court and Jury Court: Could the Continental Alternative Fill the American Need?*, 1981 Am. B. Found. Res. J. 195, 195–6 (1981) (describing continental systems in general).

In contrast, a typical common law system utilizes lay jurors who receive no assistance in deliberating on the charges from the judge presiding over the case.[71] When the jury deliberates, they are alone in a room with no judges present. In order to insulate lay jurors from evidence that they may not be able to evaluate fairly, common law systems typically have detailed rules of evidence. By excluding character evidence and hearsay, for example, there is less risk that jurors will place undue weight on evidence that may be of questionable reliability. In contrast, if judges deliberate with the jurors, there is less need for rules of exclusion. The evidence can be admitted, even if the weight should be reduced, because the professional judges can evaluate the strength of the evidence and advise the jurors of that fact.

The common law rules excluding evidence also work to regulate the conduct of the trial. Since the prosecution and defense are striving to put on only evidence that supports their side of the case, the evidentiary rules operate to place a limit on how far the attorneys may go with their presentation of evidence.[72] In a civil law system, that type of regulation is unnecessary because it is the judges in a neutral role who are deciding on the presentation of the evidence. The theory is that the judges will consider all relevant evidence and there is no need to impose limits where the judges are not advocates for either side.[73]

There is no lay jury participation in the international criminal courts. Indeed, it would be difficult to know how to compose a jury for an international court. Where would the jurors come from? For the courts in The Hague, would the jurors come from the affected countries? The transportation and housing costs would be exorbitant. Would the jurors come from The Netherlands? If so, would having jurors only of one nationality detract from the international nature of the tribunals? Perhaps even more difficult is the length of the trials. Jurors would have to remain on the case for years since most of the trials are multi-year proceedings. It would clearly be problematic to design a jury system under these circumstances. As a result of operating without juries, the international courts do not tend to have the elaborate evidentiary systems of the common law. Instead, they have broad admissibility of evidence that the judges evaluate for the probative value and weight.[74]

---

[71] *See* PAKES, *supra* note 56, at 109, 112 (noting that juries in the U.K. and the U.S. decide the cases on their own).

[72] GEORGE FISHER, EVIDENCE 1 (Robert C. Clark et al. eds., 2d. ed. 2008) (discussing reason for evidence rules in U.S. trials).

[73] PAKES, *supra* note 56, at 91 (commenting on minimal rules in non-adversarial systems).

[74] ICTY RPE 89(C) and (D) (admission of relevant evidence and exclusion of

VII. SIGNIFICANT STEPS IN CIVIL AND COMMON LAW SYSTEMS

As discussed above, two key foundational characteristics that lead to differences between civil law and common law systems are 1) what constitutes the dominant goal of a criminal justice system and 2) who controls the admission of evidence. These characteristics, in turn, shape the procedures employed. The emphasis on truth seeking or on dispute resolution leads to different structures. Similarly, the choice of a judge-centric or a party-centric approach to the admission of evidence will greatly influence the procedures. An additional point of comparison to keep in mind is whether the actor is neutral or partisan. A neutral role will require less regulation than a partisan role. In the following subsections, selected procedures will be compared in a) pretrial activities; b) presentation of evidence; and c) appeals. The roles of judges, prosecutor, defense counsel, and victims are all sculpted by the key characteristics of the legal system and the specific procedures that implement them.

A. Pretrial Activities

Civil and common law systems differ in some of their pretrial activities. Two of the major differences involve plea bargaining and interviewing witnesses before trial.

Not only is plea bargaining, or negotiated justice, permitted in common law systems, it is essential to the operation of those systems. It is estimated that about 90 percent of criminal cases in the United States are resolved through a plea bargain.[75] The plea bargain relieves the court system of the expense and time of conducting a trial. The accused pleads guilty to one or more charges and foregoes the right to a trial. There are significant advantages in efficiency and certainty with plea bargaining. Since trials in common law systems can be quite time-consuming, the overall justice system is more efficient by using plea bargaining. There is also a measure of certainty for the prosecution. A conviction is assured whereas there is

---

evidence if "its probative value is substantially outweighed by the need to ensure a fair trial"); ICC Statute, art. 61(4) ("The Court may rule on the relevance or admissibility of any evidence, taking into account, inter alia, the probative value of the evidence and any prejudice that such evidence may cause to a fair trial or to a fair evaluation of the testimony of a witness . . .").

[75] Joseph A. Colquitt, *Ad Hoc Plea Bargaining*, 75 Tul. L. Rev. 695, 700 (2001) (noting that 90 to 95 percent of the criminal cases are resolved by pleas in many U.S. jurisdictions).

a risk of an acquittal at trial. This emphasis on resolving the case is also a logical extension of a dispute resolution model.

In contrast, plea bargaining is not the norm in civil law systems. In part, this stems from the goal of determining the absolute truth. A plea bargain may prevent the truth from being known about some of the charges. If a plea bargain results in a dismissal of some of the charges, the practice also runs counter to the idea in some civil law systems of prosecuting all possible crimes. The idea that an accused can negotiate the terms of justice is antithetical to the underlying concept of a civil law system of holding an accused accountable for everything that he has done and determining the truth of what occurred. Nevertheless, many civil law jurisdictions are now permitting forms of negotiated justice, at least for lesser crimes.[76]

The international criminal courts have encountered the issue whether or not to use a form of plea bargaining. As discussed in Chapter 2, there are different approaches that reflect the practices and concerns of both common law and civil law systems.

Another major pretrial activity is interviewing and preparing witnesses for trial. In a typical civil law system, pretrial contact with witnesses is prohibited to the prosecution and defense.[77] Instead, after the initial investigation and preparatory document (the *dossier*) is prepared, contact with the witnesses is left in the hands of the trial judges.

In the common law system in the United States, pretrial contact with witnesses by the attorneys is not only permitted, but is virtually obligatory.[78] If the prosecution and defense do not meet with the witnesses to interview and prepare them for testifying, they are likely to be viewed as incompetent. The system in England and Wales takes a middle ground

---

[76] Jenia Iontcheva Turner, Plea Bargaining Across Borders, at 73–5, 142 (2009) (describing liberalization of plea bargaining in Germany and Russia); Luca Marafioti, *Italian Criminal Procedure: A System Caught Between Two Traditions*, *in* Crime, Procedure and Evidence in a Comparative and International Context 89–90 (Maximo Langer & Peter Tillers eds., 2008) (describing negotiation of sentences and also a process of an abbreviated trial based only on the case file and defense evidence in exchange for a reduced sentence).

[77] Lerner, *supra* note 56, at 802–3 (describing prohibition of speaking with non-party witnesses pretrial in France in serious cases (prosecution); Rupert Skilbeck, *Frankenstein's Monster Creating A New International Procedure*, 8 J. Int'l Crim. Just. 451, 457 (2010) (noting that in most civil law systems counsel is forbidden from interviewing witnesses).

[78] Restatement (Third) of the Law Governing Lawyers § 116, cmt. B (2012) (setting forth permissible practices in the United States of interviewing witnesses pretrial); Monroe Freedman & Abbe Smith, Understanding Lawyers' Ethics 192–4, § 7.05 (4th ed. 2010).

between the civil law prohibition of witness contact and the United States' open-ended approach. In England and Wales, the solicitors prepare a "proof of evidence" for the barristers, who will try the case, but the barristers do not interview the witnesses pretrial on the content of their testimony.[79] Barristers may, however, speak pretrial with their clients, their experts, and any character witnesses.[80]

The differences in approaches somewhat reflect both the goal of the system and whether the system is judge-centric or party-centric. Arguably, the absolute truth is better protected if the witnesses are not "tainted" by talking with counsel before trial. On the other hand, in a party-centric system as with common law, it is far more necessary for the parties to speak with the witnesses to know whether or not to call them than in a civil law system in which the judge is making that determination.

The international criminal courts have divided on the issue of "witness proofing." This issue is explored in detail in Chapter 3.

B. Presentation of Evidence at Trial

Control of the evidence introduced at trial is one of the major areas of difference between civil law and common law legal systems. In typical civil law systems, the presiding judge determines which witnesses to call and does most of the questioning. Usually, the prosecutor, defense counsel, and victim's representative, if present, may also question, but their questioning is supplementary to the judicial role. In contrast, in a typical common law system, the judge has no role in determining which witnesses to call and ordinarily does no questioning of witnesses. Instead, the prosecutor and defense counsel make the decisions on which witnesses they intend to call and they control the questioning of the witnesses.

The difference between a judge-centric and a party-centric approach to the presentation of evidence has at least three ramifications that result in different procedures. The three consequences are 1) the form of the testimony; 2) the roles of the lawyers and judges; and 3) the participation of victims.

What is the form of the testimony in each system? The systems differ in how oral testimony is presented and also in the prevalence of written evidence. In civil law systems, with a judge, a neutral player, in control,

---

79 Skilbeck, *supra* note 77, at 457–8.

80 *Rules of Conduct for Counsel and Judges: A Panel Discussion on English and American Practices*, 7 Geo. J. Legal Ethics 865, 868 (1994).

witnesses are usually allowed to speak in a narrative.[81] In common law systems, with non-neutral attorneys trying to elicit testimony favorable to their side, the testimony proceeds through questions and answers, which usually precludes a narrative.[82] Witnesses may well be cut off with an admonition to "answer only the question asked." A narrative approach, in contrast, allows the witness more freedom to speak naturally about what occurred.

Similarly, written evidence is more freely admitted in civil law systems where the judges can control the admissibility and can assess the reliability of the evidence. In a common law system, with attorneys presenting partisan evidence, there are greater restrictions on written evidence through restrictive evidentiary rules.

How do the roles of the judges and lawyers differ? Judges in both common law and civil law systems are viewed as neutral. However, their roles are radically different because of the difference in judge-centric versus party-centric approaches. Judges are far more active and involved in the process in a civil law system.[83] The judges have the responsibility to ensure all relevant evidence is presented and to bring out pertinent facts through questioning the witnesses. In a common law system, the judge rules on objections to evidence, may limit the time or number of witnesses that each side may present, and instructs the jury. In the United States, for example, it is rare to see a judge question a witness and even more rare to see a judge ask for an additional witness.[84] The passive role of the judge is

---

[81] William T. Pizzi & Walter Perron, *Crime Victims in German Courtrooms: A Comparative Perspective on American Problems*, 32 STAN. J. INT'L L. 37, 43 (1996) (describing the German system); Gordon Van Kessel, *Adversary Excesses in the American Criminal Trial*, 67 NOTRE DAME L. REV. 403, 424 (1992) (describing civil law trials in general).

[82] PAKES, *supra* note 56, at 88–90 (contrasting the narrative style of witness testimony in France with the question-and-answer format used in British and American trials); WILLIAM T. PIZZI, TRIALS WITHOUT TRUTH 21–2 (1999) (contrasting the pretrial preparation and question-and-answer approach in court to witness testimony in the U.S. with the narrative approach in civil law systems).

[83] Vivienne O'Connor, *Common Law and Civil Law Traditions*, Int'l Network to Promote the Rule of Law Practitioner's Guide 18, 24 (March 2012); PAKES, *supra* note 56, at 88–9 (describing the "archetypal" French system), 94–5 (describing the Dutch system); PIZZI, *supra* note 82, at 141.

[84] Rules of evidence in the United States generally provide for the possibility of a judge questioning or calling witnesses, but it is unusual in practice. *See, e.g.*, FED. R. EVID. 614 (permitting a court to call a witness and to examine any witness); CHRISTOPHER B. MUELLER & LAIRD C. KIRKPATRICK, EVIDENCE 613–4 (4th ed. 2009) (describing the infrequency of judges questioning and calling witnesses; indicating the importance in an adversary system of the judge maintaining an impartial

necessary to ensure an equal balance, or "equality of arms," between the prosecution and defense. The judge should not be seen as favoring one side or the other. The roles of the lawyers for the prosecution and defense are lesser or greater depending upon the role of the judge. In a civil law system, with the judge actively controlling the proceedings, the attorneys are in a position of supplementing what the judge asks the witnesses or determining which witnesses will testify.[85] In a common law system, with the judge in a non-active role regarding evidence, the attorneys play the major role in calling witnesses and questioning them.[86]

How do victims participate in the proceedings in the two systems? With the focus on equality between the prosecution and defense in common law systems, it is not surprising that victims do not ordinarily have a role other than as witnesses called by one of the parties. If the victims were a party or major participant in the trial, the balance would be skewed towards the prosecution and weighted against the defense. This is especially a factor when the decision maker is a lay jury, which is more likely to be influenced by the imbalance than a judge would be. In a civil law system, with a neutral judge in charge of the presentation of the evidence, there is less concern with having an extra party or participant in the proceedings. The judges can control the admission of evidence and can filter the effect of having two parties present evidence against the defendant.

The major international criminal courts are primarily designed as adversarial proceedings. This is the case in the ICTY, ICTR, SCSL, and the ICC. The parties are in charge of calling witnesses, presenting evidence, and questioning the witnesses. The rules do permit the judges to ask questions and even to call witnesses, but the latter option is seldom exercised. As a result, it is predictable that the form of the testimony is largely question and answer, not narrative, and that the attorneys have a major role, with the judges in a lesser role regarding the presentation of evidence. Somewhat more in line with civil law systems, however, there is a greater tolerance of written evidence than in common law systems. Issues related to the admissibility of written evidence are discussed in Chapter 4. One would expect that, with an adversarial system, the victims would be in the role of witnesses rather than participants. This is true in the ICTY, ICTR, and SCSL. The ICC, however, has a different design. Victims are able to have legal representation and may participate in the proceedings, subject

---

position); Pizzi, *supra* note 82, at 109 (describing a somewhat more active role for judges in England and Wales, including asking questions of witnesses and summarizing evidence for the jury).

85 O'Connor, *supra* note 83, at 18; Pizzi, *supra* note 82, at 22–3.

86 Pakes, *supra* note 56, at 90.

to limitations if their participation is too prejudicial to the defendant. This interesting blending of common law and civil law in the ICC is discussed in Chapter 6. In contrast to the other international criminal tribunals, the ECCC and STL are based on civil law models that exist in Cambodia and Lebanon. Although their procedures reflect a certain blending of systems, one predictably finds more civil law procedures in those tribunals. Selected aspects of the ECCC and STL are also discussed in the chapters on written evidence and on victim participation.

C. Appeals

A striking difference between civil law and common law legal systems is the nature of the first appeal from a criminal trial. In many civil law systems, the appeal can be a trial *de novo* of the facts in the case.[87] Moreover, the prosecution ordinarily can appeal as well as the defendant, and even the victim as a civil party may appeal.[88] This means that the appellate court may enter a conviction after an acquittal or make different findings on the facts, including newly-admitted facts.[89] There is usually a subsequent appeal available that is on legal issues only.[90] In common law systems,

---

[87] For a description of French appeals, *see* International Network to Promote the Rule of Law, Intro to Civil Law Legal Systems: INPROL Consolidated Response (09-002) 12 (2009), *available at* http://inprol.org/sites/default/files/publications/2011/cr09002.pdf; Lerner, *supra* note 56, at 813–4 (describing French appeals, but noting that an outright acquittal cannot be appealed. For a description of German appeals, see Delmas-Marty & Spencer, *supra* note 60, at 307–8; 332–3 (noting *de novo review* from a court that hears lesser offenses, but on legal errors only from a higher level court that hears more serious offenses).

[88] Frase, *supra* note 55, at 613 (describing French system); Richard S. Frase & Thomas Weigend, *German Criminal Justice As A Guide to American Law Reform: Similar Problems, Better Solutions?*, 18 B.C. Int'l & Comp. L. Rev. 317, 344, 350 (1995) (describing German system).

[89] George C. Thomas, *Improving American Justice by Looking at the World*, 91 J. Crim. L. & Criminology 791, 815 (2001) (reviewing A Review of Criminal Procedure: A Worldwide Study (Craig M. Bradley ed., 1999)) (stating that the norm in most countries is for the appeals court to correct errors after a rehearing rather than remanding); Anna-Rose Mathieson & Samuel R. Gross, *Review for Error*, 2 Law, Probability & Risk 259, 262 (2003) (noting that civil law prosecutors may appeal an acquittal and examining reasons for the differences in the two systems).

[90] Delmas-Marty & Spencer, *supra* note 60, at 308 (stating that the German appeals courts generally can only rule on questions of law, not questions of fact); Lerner, *supra* note 56, at 813 (stating that the French *Cour D'assises* only hears issues concerning errors of law).

the most typical appeal is on legal errors only. The appeal is not a trial *de novo* of the facts.[91] In the United States, the appeal is based on the record from the trial, not on additional evidence.[92] Moreover, due to the use of a lay jury and the interpretation of the double jeopardy principle (*ne bis in idem*), the prosecution cannot appeal an acquittal; a conviction cannot be entered on appeal. In England and Wales, additional evidence may be admitted on appeal, but only in limited circumstances.[93]

The international criminal courts have not followed either the civil law or common law system in its entirety. Instead, the courts have a combined approach of the two systems. Similar to civil law systems, new evidence may be admitted on appeal under certain circumstances,[94] acquittals can be overturned, and convictions entered on appeal. However, both the ICTY and ICC state that the appeal is *not* a trial *de novo* as one would expect in a civil law system.[95] Different from either civil or common law systems, there is no guarantee of an appeal from a finding of guilt if that conviction is entered on appeal. Another issue that arises from the lack of a second appeal on legal issues in the international criminal courts is what constitutes the appropriate standard of review if the Appeals Chamber is reassessing guilt on the basis of evidence admitted on appeal. The issues related to appeal are discussed in Chapter 7.

---

91 Frase & Weigend, *supra* note 88, at 348; O'Connor, *supra* note 83, at 28.

92 RUSSELL WEAVER ET AL., PRINCIPLES OF CRIMINAL PROCEDURE 422–23 (3d ed. 2008) (noting appeal is based on the trial record); Mathieson & Gross, *supra* note 89, at 260–61 (describing an appeal in the U.S. system as a review of procedural error, such as legal error in failing to grant a motion, and not a review of the decision by the jury; further noting that even extraordinary procedures for handling new facts after a verdict do not occur on appeal—instead they involve a different proceeding of *habeas corpus* or clemency).

93 DELMAS-MARTY & SPENCER, *supra* note 60, at 203 (Court of Appeal can hear evidence but rarely does so); *see also* Jacqueline S. Hodgson, *The Future of Adversarial Criminal Justice in 21st Century Britain*, 35 N.C. J. INT'L L. & COM. REG. 319, 355 (2010) (describing the British process for correcting miscarriages of justice; including a commission recommendation to the Court of Appeal, which may quash the conviction).

94 ICTY RPE, Rule 115(B); ICC Statute, art. 83(2).

95 ICTY Statute, art. 25 provides for appeals on the grounds of "(a) an error on a question of law invalidating the decision; or (b) an error of fact which has occasioned a miscarriage of justice." Art. 25 further provides that the Appeals Chamber "may affirm, reverse or revise" the Trial Chamber decisions. ICC Statute, art. 83(2) provides for appeal on grounds of unfairness that "affected the reliability of the decision or sentence" or on grounds that the decision or sentence was "materially affected by error of fact or law or procedural error." The Appeals Chamber may reverse, amend, or order a new trial.

VIII. SUMMARY AND INTRODUCTION TO INDIVIDUAL CHAPTERS

The procedure in the international criminal courts is an interesting blend of civil and common law procedures. In some ways, the international procedure may improve upon the national courts' procedures. In other ways, the combination may be problematic. One needs to remember that each national procedure is part of a whole system. That procedure may work well within the whole context and, yet, not work well in another context. In each case, it is important to consider the purpose and function of the procedure and how it fits within the pretrial, trial, or appellate context. For example, cross-examination is necessary to test the credibility of witnesses in an adversary system. This assessment of credibility may be primarily accomplished in other ways in a non-adversarial system, such as through the questioning pretrial by an investigating judge. In each case, the same purpose and function are achieved, but in different ways. One cannot assess the value of a procedure, such as cross-examination, without understanding its purpose and its role in a specific system.

Another concern with borrowing procedures is that, in many situations, the cases before the international criminal courts are *sui generis,* or at least have unusual attributes. For instance, victim participation may be common in civil law systems, but it would be extraordinarily rare to find 3,000 victims who claim participation rights in one case. Yet, that is likely to be the case in international criminal cases. The international courts must consider the impact of the unusual or *sui generis* aspect of their cases.

Each chapter in this book discusses one of the interesting and complex aspects of the interface of civil law and common law legal systems. Chapter 2 examines the importation of *plea bargaining or negotiated justice* into the international courts. The chapter explores the rationale for plea bargaining in a national system, especially a common law system; the reasoning for generally not permitting plea bargaining in civil law systems; and an analysis of the propriety of plea bargaining in international criminal courts. Chapter 3 focuses on the issue of *pretrial preparation of witnesses, or "witness proofing,"* and the differing approaches taken in the international courts. The discussion contrasts the pretrial preparation of witnesses in common law systems with the prohibition on meeting with witnesses pretrial in many civil law systems. Chapter 4 analyzes the use of *written and oral evidence* in international criminal procedures. The chapter explores the contrast between the greater use of written documents in civil law systems and the evidentiary rules that preclude many written documents in common law systems; the evolution of the rules on written and oral evidence in the ICTY; and the practice of the ICC in the application of its rules on evidence. Chapter 5 tackles the complex issues concerning *self-representation and the use of amicus, standby, and assigned counsel*, especially when an accused is disruptive. The practices in civil law and common law systems are reviewed and the application of these practices in the procedure before international courts is analyzed. Chapter 6 considers the *role of victims* in the international criminal courts. The contrast between the active victim representation in civil law systems and the victim's role as only a witness in common law systems is examined; the different approaches to victim participation in the international criminal courts are discussed; and the problems raised by victim participation in cases concerning mass crimes are analyzed. Finally, in Chapter 7, issues related to *appeal* are explored. The chapter discusses the fundamental right to appeal from a conviction in two major contexts in the international criminal courts. The first is when an acquittal is reversed on appeal and the second is when new evidence is admitted on appeal. The approaches of common law and civil law systems are reviewed and the practices of the international criminal courts are evaluated. Each chapter contributes to our knowledge of civil and common law differences and similarities, and provides insight into the combination of these legal systems in international criminal procedure.

2. Plea bargaining

Jenia Iontcheva Turner*

I. INTRODUCTION

Over the last two decades, plea bargaining has spread beyond the countries where it originated – the United States and other common law jurisdictions – and has become a global phenomenon. It is spreading rapidly to civil law countries that had previously viewed the practice with skepticism. And it has now arrived at international criminal courts.

While domestic plea bargaining is often limited to non-violent crimes,[1] at the international courts it is possible for even the most serious offenses, including genocide and crimes against humanity. Its use remains highly controversial, and debates about plea bargaining in international courts continue in court opinions and academic commentary: Is it appropriate to offer sentencing concessions to a defendant who pleads guilty to a heinous crime involving thousands of victims? How can the avoidance of a public trial be reconciled with some of the professed goals of international criminal law, including the goal of creating a more accurate historical record of the atrocities and that of providing victims with a voice in the process? Conversely, given the very limited resources and enforcement powers of international criminal courts, could these courts achieve any of their goals effectively without the use of plea bargaining?[2]

The guilty plea of Biljana Plavšić at the International Criminal Tribunal

* Professor of Law, SMU Dedman School of Law. This chapter draws on my previous work in JENIA IONTCHEVA TURNER, PLEA BARGAINING ACROSS BORDERS (2009) and on my collaboration with Thomas Weigend on *Negotiated Justice*, *in* GENERAL RULES AND PRINCIPLES OF INTERNATIONAL CRIMINAL PROCEDURE (Göran Sluiter et al. eds., forthcoming 2012) (on file with author). I would like to thank Jeff Bellin and John Turner for their helpful comments and suggestions, and Amber Reece for her capable research assistance.

1 Civil law countries are more likely to limit plea bargaining to non-violent crimes, although a few states in the United States have also imposed such restriction, TURNER, *supra* note * at 28.

2 *Id.* at 214.

for the former Yugoslavia (ICTY) illustrates some of the potential pitfalls of plea bargaining in international crimes cases. As a co-president of the Serbian Republic in Bosnia and Herzegovina, Plavšić assisted in the campaign of ethnic cleansing against Bosnian Muslims and Croats, which resulted in the killing of more than 50,000 non-Serbs and the expulsion of many more.[3] She was indicted on two counts of genocide and six counts of crimes against humanity. In return for her guilty plea to persecution as a crime against humanity, prosecutors dismissed both genocide counts and five of the lesser crimes against humanity counts.[4] The prosecution recommended a sentence of between 15 and 25 years of imprisonment. But the Trial Chamber sentenced Plavšić to 11, noting that her guilty plea made a significant contribution to uncovering the truth about the crimes and promoting reconciliation in the region.[5] The court's leniency enraged Bosnian Muslims,[6] and their outrage was reignited when, just before her early release for "good behavior," Plavšić publicly renounced her admission of guilt and stated that she had pleaded guilty simply to get a break in her sentence.[7]

Plavšić's case was by no means the only one in which international prosecutors offered to drop serious charges and recommend a more lenient sentence to obtain a defendant's guilty plea. Nor was it the only one in which the defendant offered statements of remorse and the court rewarded them with lenience, but their sincerity and effect on reconciliation remained in question. Finally, Plavšić's case was also one of several in which the defendant received significant sentencing reductions even though he or she did not cooperate with the prosecution in other cases.

Plavšić's guilty plea – and others like it – may help explain why international criminal courts have not fully embraced plea bargaining. Indeed, ICTY judges have on several occasions refused to follow the parties' plea agreements and in some cases have attempted to place limits on charge bargaining. While judges have recognized the potential of plea bargaining to contribute to truth-seeking and reconciliation, particularly when the defendant cooperates with the prosecution in other cases, they have also

---

3 *Prosecutor v. Plavšić*, Case No. IT-00-39&40/1-S, Sentencing Judgement, ¶ 41 (ICTY Feb. 27, 2003) [hereinafter *Plavšić*, Sentencing Judgement].

4 *Id.* ¶ 5.

5 *Id.* ¶ 73.

6 Nancy Amoury Combs, Guilty Pleas in International Criminal Law: Constructing a Restorative Justice Approach 74 (2007).

7 Olivera Simic, *Bringing "Justice" Home? Bosnians, War Criminals, and the Interaction Between the Cosmopolitan and the Local*, 12 German L.J. 1388, 1400 (2011).

remained skeptical of guilty pleas that are rewarded for nothing more than their efficiency.

This skepticism is based in part on the unique features of international criminal justice, especially the horrific nature of the crimes prosecuted and the emphasis on uncovering the truth about these crimes. The resistance to plea bargaining may also be related to the blending of inquisitorial and adversarial approaches at the international courts. The inquisitorial tradition of full and independent judicial inquiry into the facts of the case, which has influenced the procedures of international courts, may help explain why plea bargaining continues to remain controversial in that setting.

This chapter highlights the different approaches to plea bargaining in civil law/ inquisitorial and common law/adversarial systems and how the blending of these traditions has influenced plea bargaining at the international criminal courts. It ends with an overview of the debates concerning plea bargaining in international criminal procedure and some recommendations for making the practice more consistent with the goals of international criminal justice.

II. PLEA BARGAINING AT THE NATIONAL LEVEL

A. Common Law Systems

Plea bargaining has long been a staple of common law criminal justice systems. In the United States, plea bargaining was practiced as early as the mid-nineteenth century, and today more than 90 percent of convictions at the state and federal level result from guilty pleas. Plea bargaining is also used regularly in Australia, Canada, Nigeria, New Zealand, South Africa, and the United Kingdom. In the typical common law plea bargain, the defendant agrees to plead guilty and perhaps cooperate with the prosecution in other cases, in return for reduced charges or the prosecutor's agreement to seek a lower sentence.

Plea bargaining holds two important advantages that help explain its dominance in common law systems and recent spread to new jurisdictions. First, it conserves resources by allowing the parties to negotiate the outcome of a criminal case and eliminate the need for a full trial. Second, in complex, multi-defendant cases, it helps prosecutors obtain critical insider information about criminal networks. As crime becomes more sophisticated and transnational and taxes more of the criminal justice system's resources, plea bargaining is increasingly seen as essential in prosecuting crimes efficiently and successfully.

Despite its rising popularity, plea bargaining remains controversial in the countries where it originated, and commentators continue to call for reform or outright abolition of the practice. Some are concerned that the plea discounts offered as part of bargaining are often so large that they could effectively coerce innocent defendants into pleading guilty.[8] Others argue that the unduly generous concessions of plea bargaining are unfair to victims and undercut the deterrent effect of sanctions.[9] Finally, plea bargains are criticized for interfering with the court's ability to uncover the truth.[10]

To reduce the dangers that a plea bargain may be unfair or factually inaccurate, common law jurisdictions have introduced certain procedural safeguards. For instance, in the United States, at the hearing where the defendant tenders a guilty plea, the court conducts an inquiry to ensure that the plea is voluntary, informed, and factually based. If the parties have agreed that the prosecutor will merely recommend a sentence, then the court may accept or reject that recommendation.[11] Even when the parties agree on a specific sentence, the court may reject the agreement if it is inconsistent with the interests of justice.[12] In some common law jurisdictions, internal regulations also require prosecutors to consult with victims before entering into plea negotiations.[13]

But these safeguards do not go far enough in addressing the various concerns about plea bargaining. Judges only become involved in the plea-bargaining process after the negotiations have ended, by which time the parties have reached an agreement that they are unlikely to want to

---

[8] Stephen J. Schulhofer, *Plea Bargaining as a Disaster*, 101 YALE L.J. 1979 (1992); Albert W. Alschuler, *Implementing the Criminal Defendant's Right to Trial*, 50 U. CHI. L. REV. 931 (1983).

[9] Albert W. Alschuler, *The Changing Plea Bargaining Debate*, 69 CAL. L. REV. 652 (1981); Sarah N. Welling, *Victim Participation in Plea Bargains*, 65 WASH. U. L.Q. 301 (1987).

[10] *E.g.*, Alschuler, *supra* note 8; Schulhofer, *supra* note 8.

[11] The court must, however, advise the defendant that he would not be able to withdraw his guilty plea if the court rejects the recommendation. FED. R. CRIM. P. 11(c)(1)(B), (c)(3)(B).

[12] *See, e.g., id.* 11(c)(3)(C); *see also In re* Morgan, 506 F.3d 705, 711–12 (9th Cir. 2007); Virgin Islands v. Walker, 261 F.3d 370, 375 (3rd Cir. 2001).

[13] Code for Crown Prosecutors—Draft for Public Consultation § 10.2 (Jan. 2009), *available at* http://www.cps.gov.uk/consultations/Code_for_Crown_Prosecutors_%20draft_%20for_public_consultation.pdf; U.S. Department of Justice, U.S. Attorneys' Manual § 9-16.030 (citing Victim and Witness Protection Act of 1982, P.L. 97-291, § 6, 96 Stat. 1256) (stating that United States Attorneys should make reasonable efforts to notify identified victims of, and consider victims' views about, any proposed or contemplated plea negotiations).

upset. They may conceal inconvenient details about the nature of the plea negotiations or even present facts about the case that are inaccurate. The court is unlikely to uncover these gaps and inaccuracies because it is almost entirely dependent on the parties for evidence in the case. It is also unlikely to spot inadequate representation because of the limited exposure to defense counsel during the plea hearing. And since informed advice by counsel is critical to the defendant's ability to tender a knowing and voluntary guilty plea, the lack of oversight undermines the court's ability to ensure that a guilty plea is genuine and factually justified. Further, judges themselves are usually interested in expediting cases and often hold perfunctory hearings that fail to probe meaningfully into the facts of the case or the voluntariness of the guilty plea. In the end, a strong case can be made that the procedural safeguards present in common law systems inadequately protect the fairness and accuracy of plea bargains. This helps explain why plea bargaining, despite its prevalence in common law systems, remains deeply controversial.

B. Civil Law Systems

Until the 1980s, civil law jurisdictions generally regarded plea bargaining as inimical to their traditions of criminal procedure. Plea bargaining was seen as inconsistent with the principle of mandatory prosecution and with the duty of the court to investigate the facts of the case independently. The idea that the parties could resolve the case in an informal and consensual fashion starkly conflicted with the inquisitorial model of detailed judicial inquiry into the substantive truth. From a practical standpoint, the lack of juries and more limited defense rights also made plea bargaining less necessary.

Nonetheless, as civil law countries have faced an increasing number of complex criminal cases and have expanded defense rights, they have sought ways to conserve resources. Modified forms of plea bargaining have gradually come to be accepted. In Germany, practitioners and judges began informally negotiating cases in the 1980s, and the practice grew for several decades before it was formally authorized by legislation. In other countries, such as Italy, France, Russia, and Spain, the legislature took the initiative and introduced limited forms of plea bargaining as part of broader criminal procedure reforms.[14]

---

[14] *E.g.*, TURNER, *supra* note *, at 73, 142 (discussing Germany and Russia); Jacqueline Hodgson, *Guilty Pleas and the Changing Role of the Prosecutor in French Criminal Justice*, *in* THE PROSECUTOR IN TRANSNATIONAL PERSPECTIVE (Eric

Because of the tension between plea bargaining and the inquisitorial tradition, the type of bargaining introduced in civil law countries has been more restrained. The civil law variant of plea bargaining usually applies only to relatively minor, non-violent crimes. Sentence reductions as part of a plea bargain are often capped, and concessions other than sentencing reductions, such as charge reductions or detention conditions, are typically prohibited.[15] Like their common law counterparts, civil law systems require that an admission of guilt be voluntary, informed, and factually based. But civil law judges typically have better tools to ensure that this is the case. They are often involved in the negotiations between the parties and can examine the terms of the bargain before they are final. They have access to the entire investigative file in the case and can independently gather additional evidence if they have doubts about the facts underlying a plea agreement. More generally, they have greater authority to oversee plea agreements, including agreements about the charges.[16]

Civil law systems also continue to favor confessions over guilty pleas. In contrast to guilty pleas, confessions are typically more detailed and do not entirely eliminate the trial process. Instead, courts receiving a confession are expected to continue the proceedings and review the evidence supporting the credibility of the confession.[17] This is consistent with the traditional commitment of continental systems to uncovering the precise truth of the case.[18] For the same reason, continental systems place a greater emphasis on ensuring that admissions of guilt rest on a solid factual basis. Some countries even expressly prohibit in their constitutions a conviction based solely on the suspect's confession.[19] In addition, civil law countries provide for broader disclosure of evidence to the defendant before plea negotiations begin, and many require that a defendant consult with counsel before pleading guilty.[20]

In a number of civil law countries, victims' rights are also considered in the plea bargaining scheme. Victims are often involved at plea hearings,

---

Luna & Marianne Wade eds., forthcoming 2012); Luca Marafioti, *Italian Criminal Procedure: A System Caught Between Two Traditions*, *in* CRIME, PROCEDURE AND EVIDENCE IN A COMPARATIVE AND INTERNATIONAL CONTEXT 81 (Maximo Langer & Peter Tillers eds., 2008).

15 Turner & Weigend, *supra* note *, at *41.

16 *Id.* at *42, 46.

17 *Id.* at *43.

18 *Id.*

19 TURNER, *supra* note *, at 273.

20 Turner & Weigend, *supra* note *, at *43; TURNER, *supra* note *, at 272.

may be consulted before a court approves a plea agreement, and in some cases can veto a plea agreement.[21]

Perhaps because civil law systems have adopted plea bargaining only recently, many of them have not fully implemented procedural mechanisms to deal with the rupture of plea negotiations or the breach of a plea agreement. By contrast, American law is better developed when it comes to provisions for withdrawal of guilty pleas, remedies for breach of a plea agreement, and the regulation of cooperation agreements between the defendant and the prosecution. Some civil law countries have already begun to import some of these provisions, with the objective of making plea bargaining more predictable and attractive to the parties.[22]

Although plea bargaining is being increasingly adopted by civil law jurisdictions, the practice is not yet universal. A number of jurisdictions have opted for simplified trial procedures as an alternative or complement to plea bargaining. Others, such as Japan, encourage confessions and cooperation with the prosecution only tacitly, by regularly rewarding such conduct with more lenient treatment.[23] In short, civil law countries continue to regard plea bargaining with greater skepticism than their common law counterparts. This helps explain the somewhat more restrained form of plea bargaining adopted by international criminal courts, which combine features of both the civil law and common law models.

III. PLEA BARGAINING AT INTERNATIONAL CRIMINAL COURTS

A. The Introduction of Plea Bargaining

As plea bargaining began spreading to an increasing number of domestic jurisdictions in the 1990s, it was perhaps not surprising that it ultimately

---

21 Turner & Weigend, *supra* note *, at *45–6.

22 *See, e.g.*, Bosnian Crim. P. Code § 230(3) (noting that if the court rejects a guilty plea, any statements related to the guilty plea will not be admissible as evidence in the subsequent criminal trial); *id.* § 229(3) ("A plea of not guilty shall never be held against the accused in fashioning a sentence if the accused is found guilty at the trial or subsequently changes his plea from not guilty to guilty."); Bulg. Crim. P. Code § 382(8) (providing that, if a plea agreement is rejected by the court, self-incriminating statements made by the defendant during the plea hearing have no probative value in future trials); *see also* FED. R. EVID. 410.

23 TURNER, *supra* note *, at 171–98; David T. Johnson, *Plea Bargaining in Japan*, *in* THE JAPANESE ADVERSARY SYSTEM IN CONTEXT 140 (Malcolm M. Feeley & Setsuo Miyazawa eds., 2002).

made its way to international criminal courts. All such courts, with the exception of the Extraordinary Chambers in the Courts of Cambodia, provide for the possibility of plea bargaining.[24] But the introduction of plea bargaining was far from predetermined and remains controversial. In fact, three of the courts that allow plea bargaining in their statutes – the International Criminal Court (ICC), the Special Court for Sierra Leone (SCSL, 2002), and the Special Tribunal for Lebanon (STL, 2007) – have yet to resolve a case through plea bargaining. And the two major international tribunals to use plea bargaining extensively – ICTY and the International Criminal Tribunal for Rwanda (ICTR) – have not accepted a negotiated guilty plea since 2007.[25]

When the ICTY and ICTR were established in the early 1990s, neither their statutes nor their rules mentioned plea bargaining. The drafters of the ICTY Rules of Procedure expressly rejected a proposal to allow offers of immunity to suspects who provide substantial cooperation to the prosecution.[26] Both testimonial immunity and plea bargaining were seen as inappropriate in the context of international criminal prosecution.

Yet the Statutes and Rules of the ICTY and ICTR did provide for guilty pleas, and this was a stepping stone to the introduction of plea bargaining.[27] The ICTY received its first guilty plea in May 1996, when

---

[24] Turner & Weigend, *supra* note *, at *31.

[25] Although the ICTY and ICTR are in the process of completing their cases, this does not fully explain the lack of guilty pleas in the last five years. Since 2007, the ICTY has had 13 defendants who have moved into the pre-trial stage and 20 more who were at different trial stages, but none of these defendants has pleaded guilty. ICTY Annual Report 2007, *available at* http://www.icty.org/x/file/About/Reports%20and%20Publications/AnnualReports/annual_report_2007_en.pdf; ICTY Annual Report 2008, *available at* http://www.icty.org/x/file/About/Reports%20and%20Publications/AnnualReports/annual_report_2008_en.pdf; ICTY Annual Report 2009, *available at* http://www.icty.org/x/file/About/Reports%20and%20Publications/AnnualReports/annual_report_2009_en.pdf; ICTY Annual Report 2010, *available at* http://www.icty.org/x/file/About/Reports%20and%20Publications/AnnualReports/annual_report_2010_en.pdf; ICTY Annual Report 2011, *available at* http://www.icty.org/x/file/About/Reports%20and%20Publications/AnnualReports/annual_report_2011_en.pdf.

[26] Judge Antonio Cassese, President of the ICTY, *Statement Made at a Briefing to Members of Diplomatic Missions*, U.N. Doc. IT/29 (Feb. 11, 1994), *reprinted in* An Insider's Guide to the ICTY 649, 652 (Virginia Morris & Michael P. Scharf eds., 1995).

[27] Article 20 of the ICTY Statute and Article 19 of the ICTR Statute stated that "the Trial Chamber shall read the indictment, satisfy itself that the rights of the accused are respected, confirm that the accused understands the indictment, and instruct the accused to enter a plea . . . " The original Rule 62, common to the

Dražen Erdemović pleaded guilty to crimes against humanity for participating in the killing of hundreds of Bosnian Muslims from Srebrenica. His initial guilty plea was apparently not induced by prosecutorial promises of lenient treatment.[28] But because he did not fully comprehend the consequences of his guilty plea, the ICTY Appeals Chamber concluded that the plea was uninformed and therefore invalid. At the same time, in commenting on guilty pleas more broadly, the Appeals Chamber lauded the merits of plea bargaining and concluded that the practice could make a valuable contribution to international criminal justice. Reassured of the acceptability of plea bargaining at the ICTY, Erdemović and the prosecution reached a plea agreement under which Erdemović would plead guilty to the lesser offense of war crimes and the prosecution would recommend a lower sentence to the court. The ICTY found that Erdemović's second guilty plea was sufficiently informed.[29]

Once the ICTY Appeals Chamber displayed its approval of plea bargaining, the practice quickly gained a foothold. In 2000, Stevan Todorović entered a guilty plea that was the product of a negotiated plea agreement. Between 2001 and 2003, 13 more defendants did the same. As of August 15, 2011, the ICTY had convicted 64 defendants, of whom 20 pleaded guilty.[30] The ICTR accepted its first guilty plea, from Jean Kambanda, in 1998.[31] Between 1998 and August 2011, the tribunal convicted 37 more defendants of international crimes, of whom seven pleaded guilty.[32]

The Rome Statute of the International Criminal Court was signed in 1998, at about the same time that the international criminal tribunals began accepting their first guilty pleas. It provided for "proceedings on admission of guilt," a term chosen over "guilty pleas" as a compromise between the civil law and common law traditions.[33] Despite the different

---

ICTY and ICTR Rules of Procedure, also provided that defendants enter a plea of guilty or not guilty at their initial appearance.

28 Combs, *supra* note 6, at 60.

29 Prosecutor v. Erdemović, Case No. IT-96-22-T*bis*, Sentencing Judgement (ICTY Mar. 5, 1998) [hereinafter *Erdemović*, Sentencing Judgement].

30 The number of convicted defendants does not include those whose cases are being appealed. ICTY, Key Figures of ICTY Cases (May 20, 2012), *available at* http://www.icty.org/sections/TheCases/KeyFigures.

31 Prosecutor v. Kambanda, Case No. ICTR-97-23-S, Judgement and Sentence, ¶ 3 (Sept. 4, 1998) [hereinafter *Kambanda*, Judgement and Sentence].

32 This number does not include a guilty plea by a former ICTR witness for giving false testimony to the Tribunal. Also, the number of convictions does not include seven convictions that are currently on appeal. *See Status of Cases*, ICTR, http://www.unictr.org/Cases/tabid/204/Default.aspx (last visited Aug. 15, 2011).

33 Anna Petrig, *Negotiated Justice and the Goals of International Criminal*

phrasing, the effect is still to allow negotiations between the defendant and the prosecution about the disposition of the case. Article 65(5) of the ICC Statute implicitly acknowledges the possibility of such negotiations by noting that "discussions" between the parties about the charges, the admission of guilt, or the sentence will not be binding on the court.[34]

Although the ICC has yet to accept an admission of guilt, it has only recently begun holding its first trials, so it may be too early to predict how likely it is for plea bargaining to develop. Some authors have expressed skepticism that bargaining would thrive at the ICC, given the broad authority of the court to reject agreements between the parties.[35] But others have argued that the court is not likely to be effective in accomplishing its goals unless it begins relying on plea bargains to some degree.[36]

B. Conditions for Valid Plea Agreements

At all international criminal courts, a plea agreement typically consists of some variation of the following exchange: the defendant admits guilt and waives various trial rights in exchange for a reduction of the sentence or the charges.[37] The negotiations occur between the parties, typically before trial, and judges are not involved.

The most common agreements concern sentencing, but agreements about the charges have also been reached a number of times at the ICTY and ICTR. Charge bargains have been more controversial because of concerns that they may obscure the true facts of the case and the full extent of the defendant's culpability. In a dissenting opinion, ICTY Judge Schomburg compared charge bargains to "de facto granting partial amnesty/impunity by the Prosecutor," and criticized them as conflicting with the Tribunals' mission to avoid impunity, to establish the truth, and to promote peace and reconciliation.[38]

The Tribunals' mild skepticism toward charge bargains is consistent

---

Tribunals, 8 CHI.-KENT J. INT'L & COMP. L. 1, 9–10 (2008).

[34] ICC Statute, Article 65(5).

[35] Turner & Weigend, *supra* note *, at *25.

[36] Regina E. Rauxloh, *Plea Bargaining—A Necessary Tool for the International Criminal Court Prosecutor*, 94 JUDICATURE 178, 184 (2011).

[37] *See, e.g.*, Prosecutor v. Blagojević, Case No. IT-02-60-PT, Joint Motion for Consideration of Amended Plea Agreement Between Momir Nikolić and the Office of the Prosecutor 2 (ICTY May 7, 2003); *Plavšić*, Sentencing Judgment, *supra* note 3, ¶ 2.

[38] Prosecutor v. Deronjić, Case No. IT-02-61-S, Sentencing Judgement, Dissenting Opinion of Judge Schomburg, ¶ 11 (ICTY Mar. 30, 2004); *see also id.* ¶¶ 6–7.

with the civil law approach to this issue. Charge bargains are typically disfavored and often prohibited in civil law systems. They are viewed as inconsistent with the rule of mandatory prosecution that still prevails in many civil law countries, as well as with the court's duty to establish to truth of the case. Civil law judges therefore typically have the authority to modify the charges brought by prosecutors, which undermines prosecutors' ability to engage in charge bargains.[39]

Tribunal judges do not have the same power to recharacterize the charges, but they have ample authority to restrain charge bargains in other ways. First, and most obviously, plea agreements – including agreements concerning the charges – are not binding on the court.[40] Second, after charges have been initially confirmed by the pretrial chamber or judge, the prosecutor cannot unilaterally withdraw or alter them without the court's consent. Finally, because judges at the international criminal courts have broad sentencing discretion, they can thwart a charge agreement by imposing a sentence that they believe is more commensurate with the defendant's blameworthiness. For all these reasons, some have argued that charge bargains at the international criminal tribunals are not likely to be effective.[41]

Bargaining at the ICTY and ICTR has also involved concessions other than, on the one hand, guilty pleas and, on the other, reductions of the sentence or charges. A common and well-accepted item of exchange is a commitment by the defendant to cooperate with the prosecution in other proceedings. Such cooperation is expressly envisioned as a mitigating factor by the ICTY and ICTR Rules pertaining to sentencing.[42] Although the prosecution has great influence in ensuring that substantial cooperation will be credited by the court, international courts will assess the value of the cooperation independently and may depart from the prosecutor's recommendations on the issue.[43] This is consistent with the civil law influence on the Tribunals and with the greater responsibility and authority of judges to investigate and determine the facts of the case.

---

39 *E.g.*, TURNER, *supra* note *, at 105–6.

40 ICTY Rules of Procedure and Evidence (ICTY RPE), Rule 62*ter*; ICTR Rules of Procedure and Evidence (ICTR RPE), Rule 62*bis*.

41 Nancy Amoury Combs, *Procuring Guilty Pleas for International Crimes: The Limited Influence of Sentencing Discounts*, 59 VAND. L. REV. 69, 79 (2006).

42 ICTY RPE, Rule 101(B)(ii); ICTR RPE, Rule 101(B)(ii).

43 Prosecutor v. Jelisić, Case No. IT-95-10-A, Appeal Judgement, ¶ 126 (ICTY July 5, 2001); *see also* Prosecutor v. Momir Nikolić, Case No. IT-02-60/1-A, Judgement on Sentencing Appeal, ¶ 96 (ICTY Mar. 8, 2006) [hereinafter *Momir Nikolić*, Judgement on Sentencing Appeal].

Other concessions that have been exchanged are not specifically authorized by the Tribunals' Statutes or Rules. These include: withdrawal of defense motions,[44] waivers of appeal,[45] the dropping of certain factual allegations,[46] recommendations as to imprisonment location,[47] and promises not to refer a case to national authorities.[48] Courts have not always been able to deliver on some of the prosecutorial promises on that list, and this has led to skepticism of the plea bargaining procedure by defendants.[49]

Plea agreements, at least at the Tribunals, must be in writing and must be disclosed to the court in a public session.[50] At all three international criminal courts discussed here, agreements are not binding on the court.[51] Instead, the court will review the agreements, to ensure that they are voluntary[52] and fair[53] and to verify that they are consistent with the "interests of justice," including the interests of victims.[54] Placing the ultimate authority to review and approve the agreement with the court is consistent with both civil and common law approaches to plea bargaining.

To ascertain whether an agreement is consistent with the interests of justice, international criminal courts may call victims to testify at the plea hearing or at the sentencing hearing following the guilty plea. The ICTY and ICTR have not relied on victim testimony when reviewing plea

---

44 *E.g.*, Prosecutor v. Todorović, Case No. IT-95-9/1-S, Sentencing Judgement, ¶ 6 (ICTY July 31, 2001) [hereinafter *Todorović*, Sentencing Judgement].

45 *E.g.*, Prosecutor v. Obrenović, Case No. IT-02-60/2-S, Sentencing Judgement, ¶ 15 (ICTY Dec. 10, 2003) [hereinafter *Obrenović*, Sentencing Judgement].

46 *E.g.*, Prosecutor v. Momir Nikolić, Case No. IT-02-60/1-S, Sentencing Judgement, ¶ 61 (ICTY Dec. 2, 2003) [hereinafter *Momir Nikolić*, Sentencing Judgement].

47 Prosecutor v. Bisengimana, Case No. ICTR-00-60, Judgement and Sentence, ¶ 187 (Apr. 13, 2006); Prosecutor v. Nzabirinda, Case No. ICTR-01-77, Judgement and Sentence, ¶ 97 (Feb. 23, 2007) [hereinafter *Nzabirinda*, Judgement and Sentence].

48 *Nzabirinda*, Judgement and Sentence, *supra* note 47, ¶¶ 42–6; Prosecutor v. Zelenović, Case No. IT-96-23/2-S, Decision on the Prosecution's Motion to Withdraw the Motion Under Rule 11*bis* (ICTY May 8, 2007).

49 Nancy Amoury Combs, *Obtaining Guilty Pleas for International Crimes: Prosecutorial Difficulties*, *in* THE PROSECUTOR IN TRANSNATIONAL PERSPECTIVE (Eric Luna & Marianne Wade eds., 2012).

50 At the ICTY and ICTR, in a showing of good cause, the court will allow the parties to disclose the agreement in a closed session.

51 ICC Statute, Article 65(5); ICTY RPE, Rule 62*ter*; ICTR RPE, Rule 62*bis*.

52 *Todorović*, Sentencing Judgement, *supra* note 44, ¶ 16.

53 *Momir Nikolić*, Sentencing Judgement, *supra* note 46, ¶ 49.

54 *E.g.*, *Obrenović*, Sentencing Judgement, *supra* note 45, ¶ 19.

agreements, but the ICC Statute specifically allows the court to involve victims in the proceedings on admission of guilt.[55]

When faced with an agreement that it believes may not be consistent with the interests of justice, an ICC trial chamber has two options. It may refer the case to proceed under the ordinary trial procedure.[56] Alternatively, if it believes that "a more complete presentation of the facts of the case is required in the interests of justice, in particular the interests of the victims, [it] may: (a) Request the Prosecutor to present additional evidence, including the testimony of witnesses . . . ."[57] This "additional evidence" procedure reduces the efficiency of plea bargaining, but it arguably helps to protect the interests of the international community and of victims in compiling a detailed and accurate record of the crimes. It also reflects the influence of the civil law approach, which emphasizes the duty of the court to fully investigate and document the facts of the case.

C. Conditions for Valid Guilty Pleas

In choosing to forego a trial, a defendant waives a number of other important rights – the right to be presumed innocent until guilt has been established beyond a reasonable doubt, the right to confront and cross-examine adverse witnesses, the right to compel witnesses to appear on his behalf, and the right to testify or to remain silent at trial. The decision to waive these rights is a momentous one, and the court must ensure that it is entered freely and knowingly.

At all international criminal courts, therefore, judges must examine the validity of guilty pleas. At the ICTY and ICTR, a guilty plea must be voluntary, informed, unequivocal, and based on sufficient factual basis to be accepted.[58] At the ICC, the requirements are generally the same, with several notable exceptions which are discussed later in the chapter.[59] The inquiry into the defendant's admission of guilt to ensure that it is

---

55 ICC Statute, Article 65(4); *see also id.* Article 68(3) ("Where the personal interests of victims are affected, the Court shall permit their views and concerns to be presented and considered at stages of the proceedings determined to be appropriate by the Court and in a manner which is not prejudicial to or inconsistent with the rights of the accused and a fair and impartial trial.").

56 *Id.* Article 65(4)(b).

57 *Id.* Article 65(4)(a).

58 ICTY RPE, Rule 62*bis*; ICTR RPE, Rule 62(B)(iii).

59 Specifically, unlike the ICTY and ICTR Rules, the ICC Statute requires the judge to verify the factual basis for a guilty plea independently of the parties' agreement on the facts, and requires consultation with counsel before tendering a guilty plea, but does not require the guilty plea to be unequivocal.

informed, voluntary, and factually based is consistent with both the civil law and common law approaches to this question. It also supports the Tribunals' goals to provide fair trials and serve as a criminal procedure model for national systems.

Guilty pleas must be voluntary

ICTY and ICTR case law has elaborated on the meaning of some of the requirements for a valid guilty plea. ICTY and ICTR Rules do not provide a definition of "voluntariness." But in *Prosecutor v. Erdemović*, the Appeals Chamber explained that for a guilty plea to be voluntary, the accused must be "mentally fit to understand the consequences of pleading guilty" and must not be "affected by any threats, inducements or promises."[60] A defendant is deemed to be mentally fit and competent to plead guilty when he is able "to participate in the proceedings (in some cases with assistance) and sufficiently exercise the identified rights, i.e. to make his or her defence."[61] Being "merely depressed over being isolated while in detention," for example, is not sufficient to render a defendant incompetent to plead guilty.[62]

In general, the threshold for an involuntary guilty plea cannot be met simply by pointing to ordinary pressures attendant to the criminal process. For example, when an ICTY trial chamber suggested to a defendant that it might reject his guilty plea to lesser charges because it did not appear to be factually based, this did not render involuntary his subsequent guilty plea to more serious charges.[63] Similarly, a guilty plea was found voluntary even though the defendant was isolated in detention and consulted only with assigned defense counsel, rather than a counsel of his choice, before pleading guilty.[64] The same ruling held that when the defendant pleaded guilty in the hope that he would avoid life imprisonment, but this was not explicitly stated in the plea agreement, and he was later sentenced to a life

---

60 Prosecutor v. Erdemović, Case No. IT-96-22-A, Joint Separate Opinion of Judge McDonald and Judge Vohrah, ¶ 8 (ICTY Oct. 7, 1997) [hereinafter *Erdemović*, Joint Separate Opinion of McDonald and Vohrah].

61 Prosecutor v. Stanisić, Case No. IT-03-69, Decision on Stanisić Defence's Motion on the Fitness of the Accused to Stand Trial with Confidential Annexes, ¶ 9 (ICTY Apr. 27, 2006); *see also Erdemović*, Joint Separate Opinion of McDonald and Vohrah, *supra* note 60, ¶¶ 10–12.

62 Prosecutor v. Kambanda, Case No. ICTR 97-23-A, Judgement, ¶ 62 (Oct. 19, 2000) [hereinafter *Kambanda*, Judgement].

63 Prosecutor v. Babić, Case No. IT-03-72-A, Judgement on Sentencing Appeal, ¶¶ 8–12 (ICTY July 18, 2005) [hereinafter *Babić*, Judgement on Sentencing Appeal].

64 *Kambanda*, Judgement, *supra* note 62, ¶¶ 57, 64.

term by the court, the guilty plea was still voluntary.[65] Finally, if a defendant affirms in the plea agreement or at the plea hearing that he is pleading guilty of his own free will, he will generally have difficulty later showing that his plea was coerced.[66]

This raises the question whether international criminal courts will consider a guilty plea to be involuntary if it is submitted under the threat of a much more severe sentence upon conviction at trial. In common law systems such as the United States, such a scenario does not render a guilty plea involuntary.[67] Yet in some civil law jurisdictions, such as Germany, threats of a disproportionately harsher sentence upon conviction at trial would invalidate a subsequent admission of guilt.[68]

Although both civil law and common law systems require that guilty pleas be voluntary, their definitions of voluntariness differ somewhat. Common law countries tend to treat defendants as autonomous agents who are able to decide for themselves whether to accept a particular plea bargain, even if the difference between a guilty plea and a conviction after trial is extraordinary. By contrast, civil law countries tend to take a more paternalistic approach and limit the types of bargains that can be offered to defendants. In Italy, France, Russia, and Germany, for example, plea bargains are limited to relatively minor crimes carrying a lower sentence.[69] A number of civil law countries also limit the sentencing discount that can be offered to induce defendants to waive their right to trial.[70] So far, the international tribunals appear to have approached voluntariness along

---

65 *Id.* ¶ 63.

66 *Babić*, Judgment on Sentencing Appeal, *supra* note 63, ¶¶ 8–12; *Kambanda*, Judgement, *supra* note 62, ¶¶ 57, 64.

67 *See* Brady v. United States, 397 U.S. 742 (1970); Bordenkircher v. Hayes, 434 U.S. 357 (1978).

68 BGH GSSt 1/04, Mar. 3, 2005 ("It is unlawful to pressure the accused into a confession by threatening him with an inappropriately severe sentence or by promising him advantages not provided for by the law, to promise the accused a more lenient sentence in exchange for waiving his right to appeal . . . ."); BGH 4 StR 84/04, Urteil v. 16.9.2004 (reversing judgment and ordering new trial of defendant who was threatened with pretrial detention if he refused to confess and persisted in filing motions to subpoena witnesses located abroad); BGH StR 411/04, Beschluss v. 12.1.2005 (holding that a proposed plea discount of about 50 percent, from a sentence of six to seven years to a sentence of three years and six months, was unlawful, because it was an unwarranted reward for a confession and might unduly coerce a defendant into confessing); BGH StV 2004, 470 (5 StR 579/03) (holding that a two-thirds discount, from six years to two years, is unlawful because it may coerce a defendant to plead guilty).

69 Turner & Weigend, *supra* note *, at *41; Turner, *supra* note *, at 75, 142.

70 Turner & Weigend, *supra* note *, at *41.

the lines of the common law model, but it is still possible that future international courts, particularly the ICC, will take the approach of civil law jurisdictions and view voluntariness as a more demanding requirement.

One indication that the ICC may take this approach is that it already requires consultation with defense counsel to ensure that admissions of guilt are voluntary.[71] No such requirement exists at the ICTY and ICTR[72] or in common-law jurisdictions, where defendants can waive their right to counsel before pleading guilty.[73] The ICC approach is instead consistent with that of civil law jurisdictions, which limit the ability of defendants to represent themselves in certain cases, where self-representation is unlikely to be in the defendants' best interests.[74]

Guilty pleas must be informed

For the guilty plea to be valid, it must also be informed. The ICTY Appeals Chamber has explained that this means that "the accused must understand the nature of the charges against him and the consequences of pleading guilty to them."[75] The ICC Statute uses similar language in describing the requirement.[76] As the ICTY has elaborated, the court must ensure that the defendant understands the key elements of the crime to which he is pleading guilty[77] and appreciates the difference between alternative charges.[78] In *Prosecutor v. Erdemović*, the ICTY Appeals Chamber

---

71 ICC Statute, Article 65(1)(b) (requiring that an admission of guilt be made "voluntarily . . . after sufficient consultation with defence counsel").

72 In practice, however, all defendants who have pleaded guilty at the tribunals have been represented by attorneys.

73 *E.g.*, Iowa v. Tovar, 541 U.S. 77 (2004); R v. Hardy, 79 Alta. L.R. (2d) 211 (Alta. Q.B., Dec. 14, 1990).

74 Turner & Weigend, *supra* note *, at *43.

75 *Erdemović*, Joint Separate Opinion of McDonald and Vohrah, *supra* note 60, ¶ 8(b). Although the quote is from a Separate Opinion, at least four judges concurred in this description of the standard for determining whether a guilty plea is informed. Judge Li disagreed with the conclusion that Erdemović's guilty plea was uninformed, but it was not clear whether he disagreed with the legal standard itself. Prosecutor v. Erdemović, Case. No. IT-96-22, Separate and Dissenting Opinion of Judge Li (ICTY Oct. 7, 1997).

76 ICC Statute, Article 65(1) (". . . the Trial Chamber shall determine whether: (a) The accused understands the nature and consequences of the admission of guilt").

77 *Momir Nikolić*, Sentencing Judgement, *supra* note 46, ¶ 12. (The trial chamber "may inquire into the accused's understanding of the elements of the crime or crimes to which he has pled guilty to ensure that his understanding of the requirements of the crime reflects his actual conduct and participation as well as his state of mind or intent when he committed the crime.").

78 *Erdemović*, Joint Separate Opinion of McDonald and Vohrah, *supra* note

invalidated a guilty plea to crimes against humanity because the defendant had not been adequately informed that a crime against humanity is a more serious crime than war crimes (with which he was also charged) and that it carries a more serious punishment.[79]

The court must also ensure that the defendant understands the rights he is waiving by pleading guilty.[80] As noted earlier, these include the right to require the prosecution to prove the charges beyond a reasonable doubt at a public trial, the right to prepare a defense against these charges, the right to be tried without undue delay, the right to confront adverse witnesses and obtain defense witnesses, and the right not to be compelled to testify against oneself.[81] It is now standard practice for plea agreements at the ICTY and ICTR to list the rights that defendants are waiving.

The court must also confirm that the defendant understands that the agreement is not binding on the court, and that the defendant may receive a sentence up to the maximum available at the international criminal courts – life imprisonment. Trial chambers often do admonish defendants of these potential consequences, but have not done so consistently.[82] If a defendant affirms that he understands the charges and the sentencing consequences of the charges, this is likely to be sufficient to show that the guilty plea is informed.[83]

International courts have not addressed the question of whether the defendant must be given access to all evidence material to his defense before a guilty plea. In the United States, the Supreme Court has held that a guilty plea may be informed even when the prosecution did not disclose evidence that could be used to impeach some of its witnesses.[84] But in other common law jurisdictions, defendants receive such information,[85]

60, ¶ 14 (explaining that defendant must understand "the nature and distinction between the alternative charges and the consequences of pleading guilty to one rather than the other").

79 *Id.* ¶¶ 26–7.

80 *Id.* ¶ 15.

81 These waivers are commonly included in written plea agreements between the prosecution and the defense. *E.g.*, Prosecutor v. Deronjić, Case No. IT-02-61-PT, Plea Agreement, ¶ 13 (ICTY Sept. 29, 2003).

82 Julian A. Cook, III, *Plea Bargaining at The Hague*, 30 YALE J. INT'L L. 473 (2005) (criticizing ICTY plea colloquy procedures as inadequate and arguing that judges ought to ask more questions and provide more information to defendants to ensure that guilty pleas are voluntary and knowing).

83 *Kambanda*, Judgement, *supra* note 62, ¶ 72; Prosecutor v. Serushago, Case No. ICTR 98-39-S, Sentencing Judgement, ¶¶ 6–8, 35 (Feb. 5, 1999).

84 United States v. Ruiz, 536 U.S. 622 (2002).

85 *E.g.*, New Zealand Criminal Disclosure Act 2008, No. 38 § 12; New South Wales Criminal Procedure Amendment (Pre-Trial Disclosure) Act 2001, No. 7, §§

and in civil law jurisdictions, defendants receive *all* material evidence in the case against them before they have to make a decision whether to admit guilt and waive trial.[86]

It is likely that the international criminal courts will opt for broader disclosure, at least of exculpatory evidence and certain other evidence material to the defense. The courts' rules already require the prosecution to disclose exculpatory evidence "as soon as practicable"[87] and to allow the defense to inspect documents, books, and other tangible objects which are material to its case.[88]Although the international courts have not fully adopted the civil law approach of providing all evidence in the investigative file to defendants before they admit guilt, broad disclosure of all material evidence would be consistent with the international courts' goal of uncovering the truth and providing an accurate record of the crimes.

Guilty pleas must be unequivocal

The ICTY and ICTR have also adopted the requirement, imported from common law jurisdictions such as the United Kingdom and Malaysia, that the guilty plea must not be equivocal.[89] As the ICTY Appeals Chamber explained, this means that the guilty plea "must not be accompanied by words amounting to a defense contradicting an admission of criminal responsibility."[90] In determining whether a plea is equivocal, the court may examine whether the plea was qualified by statements that appear to present a legal defense to the crime.[91] The court may specifically question the defendant as to his intention to raise any defenses, such as duress or insanity.[92] This requirement is consistent with international

---

47C–47E; Criminal Procedure and Investigations Act 1996 (Eng.) § 3, *as amended by* Criminal Justice Act 2003 (Eng.); R v. Director of Public Prosecutions, *ex parte* Lee [1999] 2 All ER 737; R v. Stinchcombe, (1991) 68 C.C.C. (3d) 1 (S.C.C.).

86 TURNER, *supra* note *, at 116, 152.

87 ICTY RPE, Rule 68; ICTR RPE, Rule 68; ICC Statute, Article 67(2).

88 ICTY RPE, Rule 66; ICTR RPE, Rule 66; ICC RPE, Rule 77.

89 *Erdemović*, Joint Separate Opinion of McDonald and Vohrah, *supra* note 60, ¶¶ 28–30.

90 *Id.* ¶ 8 (italics added). Judge Stephen and Judge Liu also joined this part of the opinion. Judge Cassese filed a Separate Opinion in *Erdemović*. He turned to international law for guidance and similarly concluded that the guilty plea must be voluntary, informed, and unequivocal to be valid. But he noted further that the guilty plea must be supported by facts to be accepted by the court.

91 *Id.* ¶ 31.

92 *Momir Nikolić*, Sentencing Judgement, *supra* note 46, ¶ 52; *see also* Prosecutor v. Banović, Case No. IT-02-65/1-S, Sentencing Judgement, ¶ 17 (ICTY Oct. 28, 2003) [hereinafter *Banović*, Sentencing Judgement].

human rights law and helps to protect innocent defendants from pleading guilty.[93]

Guilty pleas must be factually based

The guilty plea must also rest on a sufficient factual basis. At the ICTY and ICTR, the court must verify that "there is a sufficient factual basis . . . either on the basis of independent indicia or on lack of any material disagreement between the parties about the facts of the case."[94] In other words, the court can establish factual basis resting solely on the parties' agreement. This rule effectively allows the parties to engage in "fact bargaining," whereby they could agree to a set of facts different from the real facts of the case. In practice, trial chambers have usually conducted an independent inquiry into the facts and have required that evidence other than the parties' agreement support the guilty plea.[95] Nonetheless, the ICTY and ICTR have recognized that a factual basis inquiry "do[es] not call for the same scrutiny of facts by a Chamber as in a trial situation where the Prosecutor has the usual burden of proof."[96]

At the ICC, the Statute provides that the factual basis for the plea cannot be based simply on an agreement between the parties about the facts. Instead, the court is expected to review the charging documents, the parties' agreement, any materials presented by the prosecutor which supplement the charges and which the accused accepts, and any other evidence, such as the testimony of witnesses, presented by the prosecutor or the accused.[97] Judges may call on the prosecutor to present additional evidence if they believe "that a more complete presentation of the facts of the case is required in the interests of justice, in particular the interests of the victims."[98]

---

93 *See* Kwiatkowska v. Italy, no. 52868/99, ECtHR (Nov. 30, 2000); Prosecutor v. Erdemović, Case. No. IT-96-22, Separate and Dissenting Opinion of Judge Cassese, ¶ 11 (ICTY Oct. 7, 1997).

94 ICTY RPE, Rule 62*bis*(iv); ICTR RPE, Rule 62(B)(iv).

95 Alan Tieger & Milbert Shin, *Plea Agreements in the ICTY: Purpose, Effects, and Propriety*, 3 J. INT'L CRIM. JUST. 671 (2005); *see also* Prosecutor v. Deronjić, Case No. IT-02-61-A, Judgement, ¶¶ 16–19 (ICTY July 20, 2005); Prosecutor v. Mrđa, Case No. IT-02-59-S, Sentencing Judgement (ICTY Mar. 31, 2004); *Momir Nikolić*, Sentencing Judgement, *supra* note 46, ¶ 52.

96 *See e.g.*, Prosecutor v. Ntakirutimana, Case No. ICTR-96-10-T, ICTR-96-17-T, Decision on the Prosecutor's Motion for Judicial Notice of Adjudicated Facts Rule 94(B) of the Rules of Procedure and Evidence, ¶ 26 (Nov. 22, 2001).

97 ICC Statute, Article 65(1)(c).

98 *Id.*, Article 65(4).

The ICC requirement that admissions of guilt be accompanied by a more complete presentation of the facts appears to be influenced by the civil law approach, which attaches great importance to uncovering the precise truth in criminal cases and creating an authoritative record of events.[99] Although the more probing inquiry may undermine to some degree the efficiency of plea bargaining, it advances the court's goal of revealing the truth about massive and systemic international crimes. Given the special significance of transparency and truth-seeking in international crimes cases, the ICC has arguably struck a more appropriate balance in this respect than its predecessor international courts.

D. Sentencing Consequences of Guilty Pleas

The international criminal courts' rules and statutes make no mention of the sentencing consequences of a guilty plea. But judges have generally accepted that if plea bargaining is to continue, defendants must receive a more lenient sentence in return for admitting their guilt. In most plea-bargained cases, therefore, judges have followed the parties' agreement and reduced the defendant's sentence accordingly.

Courts have not articulated a consistent justification for the sentence reductions awarded to defendants who plead guilty. At the domestic level, guilty pleas are typically rewarded because of their practical benefits in conserving resources of the criminal justice system. This rationale for crediting guilty plea is also mentioned at the international level,[100] but is not given as a primary reason for plea-related sentencing reductions.[101] More frequently, guilty pleas are described as deserving of credit because they advance other key goals of international criminal courts: helping to

---

[99] *See, e.g.*, Elisabetta Grande, *Dances of Criminal Justice: Thoughts on Systemic Differences and the Search for the Truth*, *in* Crime, Procedure and Evidence in a Comparative and International Context 146–7 (John Jackson et al. eds., 2008); Thomas Weigend, *Is the Criminal Process About Truth?: A German Perspective*, 26 Harv. J.L. & Pub. Pol'y 157, 167–73 (2003).

[100] *See, e.g.*, Prosecutor v. Deronjić, Case No. IT-02-61-S, Sentencing Judgement, ¶ 234 (ICTY Mar. 30, 2004) [hereinafter *Deronjić*, Sentencing Judgement]. The contribution of guilty pleas to the efficient operation of the courts is credited as cooperation by the defendant, which is explicitly contemplated by the courts' statutes as a mitigating factor. *See* Prosecutor v. Simić, Case No. IT-95-9/2-S, Sentencing Judgement, ¶ 84 (ICTY Oct. 17, 2002).

[101] *Momir Nikolić*, Sentencing Judgement, *supra* note 46, ¶¶ 67, 151; Prosecutor v. Dragan Nikolić, Case No. IT-94-2-A, Judgement on Sentencing Appeal, ¶ 51 (ICTY Feb. 4, 2005) [hereinafter *Dragan Nikolić*, Judgement on Sentencing Appeal].

establish the truth,[102] encouraging other perpetrators to come forward and accept responsibility,[103] and contributing to reconciliation in war-torn societies by showing the defendant's remorse and contrition.[104] It should be noted, however, that not all decisions have embraced each of these rationales for guilty pleas. Some have held that international courts should not be awarding sentencing reductions merely for efficiency purposes,[105] that a guilty plea is not necessarily an indication of contrition,[106] and that the contribution of guilty pleas to the discovery of the truth is not always positive.[107]

On the whole, ICTY and ICTR defendants who have pleaded guilty have received, on average, a less than 30 percent sentencing discount. This is smaller than the typical discount for guilty pleas in several major national legal systems.[108] The differential also varies from defendant to defendant, and it has increased over time.

---

102 *E.g.*, *Banović*, Sentencing Judgement, *supra* note 92, ¶ 68.

103 *E.g.*, *Dragan Nikolić*, Judgement on Sentencing Appeal, *supra* note 101, ¶¶ 55–6.

104 *Id.*; *Deronjić*, Sentencing Judgement, *supra* note 100, ¶ 236; *Plavšić*, Sentencing Judgement, *supra* note 3, ¶ 76.

105 *Momir Nikolić*, Sentencing Judgement, *supra* note 46, ¶ 67.

106 *E.g.*, Prosecutor v. Jelisić, Case No. IT-95-10-T, Judgement, ¶ 127 (ICTY Dec. 14, 1999). In *Kambanda*, the Trial Chamber considered the guilty plea as a mitigating factor, but it also found that Kambanda had "offered no explanation for his voluntary participation in the genocide; nor [had] he expressed contrition, regret or sympathy for the victims in Rwanda, even when given the opportunity to do so by the Chamber, during the pre-sentencing hearing of 3 September 1998." *Kambanda*, Judgement and Sentence, *supra* note 31, ¶ 51. This was given as one of the reasons why, ultimately, Kambanda was sentenced to life imprisonment (the highest possible sentence), despite his guilty plea. *Kambanda*, Judgement, *supra* note 62, ¶ 118.

107 *Momir Nikolić*, Sentencing Judgement, *supra* note 46, ¶¶ 60–2.

108 England, Italy, and Russia, for example, set a discount of about one-third of either the expected or the maximum sentence or the statutory maximum for the charged offense. *See* SENTENCING GUIDELINES COUNCIL, REDUCTION IN SENTENCE FOR A GUILTY PLEA 5–6 (2007), *available at* http://sentencingcouncil.judiciary.gov.uk/docs/Reduction_in_Sentence_for_a_Guilty_Plea_-Revised_2007.pdf; Nicola Boari & Gianluca Fiorentini, *An Economic Analysis of Plea Bargaining: The Incentives of the Parties in a Mixed Penal System*, 21 INT'L REV. L. & ECON. 213, 216 (2001); UGOLOVNO-PROTSESSUAL'NYI KODEKS ROSSIISKOI FEDERATSII [UPK RF] [Criminal Procedure Code] § 316(7) (Russ.). In the United States, where courts place no limits on plea discounts, discounts are often significantly larger. *See, e.g.*, Russell D. Covey, *Fixed Justice: Reforming Plea Bargaining with Plea-Based Ceilings*, 82 TUL. L. REV. 1261 (2008).

E. Consequences of Rejection of Guilty Pleas and Breach of Plea Agreements

The international criminal courts have yet to develop clear and consistent rules on the consequences of a rejection or withdrawal of a guilty plea and of a breach of a plea agreement.

If the court invalidates a guilty plea, the case proceeds to trial, unless the parties renegotiate and the defendant enters a new, valid guilty plea, as occurred in *Prosecutor v. Erdemović*.[109] But if the court rejects a plea agreement, at least at the ICTY and ICTR, the defendant may not withdraw his guilty plea. Because the trial chambers inform the defendant, before he pleads guilty, that the court is not bound by the agreement, the defendant is expected to be on notice that the court might reject the agreement. The ICC Statute similarly provides that the court is not bound by the agreement, so it is likely that the ICC will adopt a similar approach and refuse to allow a defendant to withdraw his guilty plea even if the court rejects the agreement.

If the guilty plea is invalidated by the court or withdrawn by the defendant, it is not clear whether any statements that the defendant has made in the course of the negotiations or at the plea hearing can be introduced into evidence at trial. One ICTY decision, in dictum, and an ICTY Practice Manual suggest that such statements would be inadmissible,[110] but there has been no authoritative pronouncement on this point. The text of the ICC Statute similarly fails to resolve this question: it provides merely that if the court rejects an admission of guilt, it must consider the admission as not having been made.[111] Whether this provision means that accompanying statements by the defendant are also nullified is unclear.

The approach to this question may depend on whether the courts view plea bargaining from a more inquisitorial or adversarial perspective. As Mirjan Damaška has observed:

> when the admission is treated on the analogy to the guilty plea [as it is in common law systems], it resembles a contract and its withdrawal can easily be justified in the contractual mode: one side has performed while the other has

---

[109] *Erdemović*, Sentencing Judgement, *supra* note 29, ¶¶ 7–8.

[110] Prosecutor v. Blagojević, Case No. IT-02-60-T, Decision on Vidoje Blagojević's Expedited Motion to Compel the Prosecution to Disclose its Notes from Plea Discussions with the Accused Nikolić & Request for an Expedited Open Session Hearing, n.25 (ICTY June 13, 2003); ICTY Manual on Developed Practices § VII, ¶ 72 at 69 (2009), *available at* http://www.icty.org/x/file/About/Reports%20and%20Publications/manual_developed_practices/icty_manual_on_developed_practices.pdf.

[111] ICC Statute, Article 65(3).

> not. But the closer an admission comes to a confession [as in civil law systems], the more difficult it becomes to withdraw or disregard it, because it is in the nature of reliable incriminating evidence.[112]

On the other hand, one could argue that, regardless of whether the admission is treated as a confession or a guilty plea, basic principles of fairness demand that if the court rejects an admission of guilt as invalid, the defendant's waiver of fundamental rights is null and void, must be stricken from the record, and cannot result in any prejudice to him.[113]

None of the international criminal courts has addressed the consequences of a breach of a plea agreement. It is possible that international courts would follow the United States model and award either rescission (treating the guilty plea as not having been made and returning the parties to their original positions) or specific performance (enforcing the plea agreement as negotiated by the parties).[114] When the breach is the fault of the prosecution, international courts might also consider a range of sanctions and remedies available for prosecutorial misconduct, such as a stay of proceedings, sentence reductions, adverse inferences from the evidence, or disciplinary proceedings against the responsible prosecutor.

IV. THE DEBATE OVER PLEA BARGAINING AT INTERNATIONAL CRIMINAL COURTS

Plea bargaining remains more controversial and less common at the international than at the national level. Several reasons account for the skepticism toward plea bargaining in international criminal courts. First, the granting of concessions to defendants accused of international crimes is perceived as unseemly given the heinousness and large scale of the crimes in question. Plea bargaining is seen to dilute the moral message that international courts aim to send – that the international community is outraged and will bring to justice those responsible for the crimes committed. Second, plea bargaining is viewed as interfering with the goal of uncovering the truth about international crimes. Finally, plea bargaining is said to disrespect victims' interests in a public trial and in a sentence

---

112 Mirjan Damaška, *Negotiated Justice in International Criminal Courts*, 2 J. Int'l Crim. Just. 1018, 1038 (2004).

113 Fabricio Guariglia & Gudrun Hochmayr, *Article 65: Proceedings on Admission of Guilt*, *in* Commentary on the Rome Statute of the International Criminal Court 1230 (Otto Triffterer ed., 2008).

114 Santobello v. New York, 404 U.S. 257 (1971).

proportionate to the defendant's blameworthiness. Advocates of the practice counter that plea bargaining is not inherently at odds with the goals of international criminal justice and that if properly structured and administered, a limited form of plea bargaining may provide important benefits to international criminal courts.

The merits of the first major objection to plea bargaining – that it is unfit to use in the heinous crimes that international courts handle – depends heavily on the steepness of the plea discount. If negotiations lead to a sentence of a mere few years' imprisonment for a crime against humanity or genocide, the system will have failed. A sentence that is disproportionately low would conflict with the retributive goal of imposing on the offender the punishment he deserves and expressing commensurate outrage at his actions.[115] Overly lenient dispositions resulting from plea bargains would also reduce the deterrent effect of international criminal justice, which depends on the swiftness, likelihood, and severity of punishment.[116] International criminal courts already face difficulties on all three scores: they are neither swift nor very successful in apprehending and prosecuting suspects, and their baseline sentences are by many estimates too low. Reducing these sentences further as part of plea bargaining dilutes a deterrent effect that is already in question.

Plea bargains that result in sentences that are not excessively lenient, however, can at least take credit for increasing the swiftness and the likelihood of punishment. One way in which they do so is by allowing prosecutors to obtain convictions in the face of evidentiary difficulties. International prosecutors encounter enormous challenges in gathering evidence. The crimes committed are often systemic, widespread, and complex. Investigations tend to take place in territories plagued by violent conflict or other security risks, and national authorities are often unwilling or unable to help ICC investigators. Witnesses, too, are frequently afraid to testify. Given these difficulties, prosecutors may legitimately prefer a plea bargain resulting in a lower sentence to the risk of an acquittal after trial of a defendant whom they believe to be guilty. Plea bargaining can also provide prosecutors with indispensable inside knowledge

---

[115] Prosecutor v. Bralo, Case No. IT-95-17-S, Sentencing Judgement, ¶ 22 (ICTY Dec. 7, 2005) [hereinafter *Bralo*, Sentencing Judgement]; *see also* Prosecutor v. Aleksovski, Case No. IT-95-14/1-A, Judgement, ¶ 185 (ICTY Mar. 24, 2000) ("An equally important factor is retribution. This is not to be understood as fulfilling a desire for revenge but as duly expressing the outrage of the international community at these crimes.").

[116] Raymond Paternoster, *How Much Do We Really Know About Criminal Deterrence?*, 100 J. Crim. L. & Criminology 765, 769 (2010).

that helps them succeed in other cases against more culpable, high-level offenders.[117]

More broadly, plea bargaining frees up resources that can be used to prosecute a greater number of offenders. Given the high costs, complexity, and length of international trials, this is an important practical consideration. Although efficiency, in and of itself, is not ordinarily viewed as a point of emphasis in international criminal justice,[118] it is a means to achieving the broader goal of punishing and deterring international crimes. The ICTY has expressly recognized this point:

> Substantial human and practical benefits flow from a plea of guilty, particularly one tendered at an early stage in the proceedings. Victims and witnesses who have already suffered enormous psychological and physical harm are not required to travel to the Hague to recount their experiences in court, and potentially re-live their trauma. In addition, scarce legal, judicial and financial resources that would otherwise be expended in preparing for and conducting a lengthy and expensive trial may be redeployed in the interests of securing the wider objectives of the Tribunal.[119]

A recent study of the pace of ICTR and ICTY cases shows that cases resolved by guilty pleas take, on average, half as long as cases resolved by trial.[120] Plea bargaining, by freeing up resources to investigate and prosecute more defendants, probably does increase the swiftness and likelihood of punishment. According to a number of studies, the probability and immediacy of punishment are in fact more influential deterrent factors than the severity of punishment.[121] And although plea bargaining may result in more lenient (and thus less proportionate) punishments than full trials do, it ensures at least some level of retribution for a great number of persons who would otherwise evade punishment altogether.[122]

A second major objection is that plea bargaining undermines the educative function of international criminal law. International criminal trials are said to serve the important purpose of reinforcing the rule of law.

---

117 Mark Harmon, *Plea Bargaining: The Uninvited Guest at the International Criminal Tribunal for the Former Yugoslavia*, *in* THE LEGAL REGIME OF THE ICC: ESSAYS IN HONOUR OF PROF. I.P. BLISHCHENKO 163, 171–7 (José Doria et al. eds., 2009).

118 *E.g.*, *Dragan Nikolić*, Judgement on Sentencing Appeal, *supra* note 101, ¶ 51; *Momir Nikolić*, Judgement on Sentencing Appeal, *supra* note 43, ¶ 67.

119 *Bralo*, Sentencing Judgement, *supra* note 115, ¶ 64.

120 Jean Galbraith, *The Pace of International Criminal Justice*, 31 MICH. J. INT'L. L. 79 (2009).

121 Paternoster, *supra* note 116, at 821.

122 *See* COMBS, *supra* note 6, at 129–30.

They send the message that atrocities, even when committed by those in power, will not be ignored and will be judged. Because of this emphasis on the rule of law, advocates of international criminal justice often find truth commissions or various civil or informal legal mechanisms of dealing with atrocities to be inadequate.[123] Plea bargaining is similarly seen by some to dilute the moral message that international criminal courts send.

It is true that bargaining does not offer the same educational effect as a trial. Its abbreviated inquiries into the facts and the lack of witness testimonies deprive the national and international communities of a powerful and dramatic reminder of the value of the rule of law. Nonetheless, by producing a conviction, a plea bargain still reinforces the basic notion that the rule of law reaches those most responsible for international crimes, even when they are high political and military leaders. And when formerly powerful leaders admit guilt before the Tribunals, they "send[] a powerful message about the legitimacy" of the tribunals and their functions.[124]

International criminal courts have also stressed the importance of protecting the rights and interests of victims. This emphasis on victims' interests likely reflects, at least in part, the influence of the civil law approach to criminal justice, in which victims have stronger rights of participation in criminal cases. But it is also influenced by human rights jurisprudence, which emphasizes the right of victims of human rights atrocities to receive full judicial remedies for the wrongs done to them.[125]

Trials at international courts are said to serve survivors of the crimes by helping them and their communities achieve a sense of closure. One author has called them "an enormous national psychodrama, psychotherapy on a nationwide scale."[126] Trials provide a forum for victims to tell their stories and to have the wrongs done to them formally acknowledged.[127]Against this background, plea bargaining seems an unpalatable alternative from a victim's perspective – it shortcuts the trial proceedings and the healing

---

123 *Cf. Momir Nikolić*, Judgement on Sentencing Appeal, *supra* note 443 ¶ 67 ("[The Tribunal's] very raison d'etre is to have criminal proceedings such that the persons most responsible for serious violations of international humanitarian law are held accountable for their criminal conduct – not simply a portion thereof.").

124 *Plavšić*, Sentencing Judgement, *supra* note 3, ¶ 76.

125 *See* Darryl Robinson, *The Identity Crisis of International Criminal Law*, 21 Leiden J. Int'l L. 925 (2008); Sonja Starr, *Rethinking "Effective Remedies": Remedial Deterrence in International Courts*, 83 N.Y.U. L. Rev. 693 (2008).

126 Mark J. Osiel, *Ever Again: Legal Remembrance of Administrative Massacre*, 144 U. Pa. L. Rev 463, 471 (1995) (quoting French historian Emmanuel Le Roy Ladurie).

127 *Developments in the Law – The Promises of International Prosecution*, 114 Harv. L. Rev. 1957, 1970–71 (2001).

function they may provide for victims, and it reduces the punishment imposed on offenders.[128]

But advocates of plea bargaining note that the tension between victims' interests and plea bargaining is not always so strong. First, international criminal courts can allow victims to participate in plea hearings and express their views on proposed plea bargains. The ICC legal framework already includes some provisions allowing for greater victim participation at the proceedings on admission of guilt.[129] Courts can also encourage the types of guilty pleas that are more likely to be valuable to victims – unequivocal, detailed, and accompanied by genuine and voluntary expressions of remorse.[130] Moreover, at least in the eyes of some victims, avoiding trial testimony may be a benefit. A plea bargain spares these victims the inconvenience of traveling to another country to testify, the concern about their and their family's safety, and the ordeal of facing the defendant, reliving the trauma they experienced, and possibly having their credibility questioned during cross-examination.[131] Plea bargains also benefit all victims by ensuring a speedier completion of the proceedings and facilitating any compensation claims they may have, and thus allowing them to move forward with their lives.[132]

In addition to protecting victims' interests, international criminal courts also aim to promote peace and reconciliation in the region where the crimes took place. This is a goal that is unique to criminal trials at the international level and was used to justify the creation of modern international criminal tribunals.[133] By locating individual responsibility for crimes, international criminal trials aim to end accusations aimed at entire groups and thus break a cycle of conflict.[134]

---

[128] Janine Natalya Clark, *Plea Bargaining at the ICTY: Guilty Pleas and Reconciliation*, 20 EUR. J. INT'L L. 415, 431 (2009).

[129] *See supra* note 52 and accompanying text.

[130] *Cf. Plavšić*, Sentencing Judgement, *supra* note 3, ¶ 77 (citing expert's opinion that such admissions of guilt are more likely to provide closure for victims); Clark, *supra* note 128, at 433 ("[G]uilty pleas are more likely to promote reconciliation when defendants do not simply express remorse but also demonstrate through their actions that they are genuinely sorry for what they have done, for example, by revealing where the remains of their victims are buried."); Turner & Weigend, *supra* note *.

[131] *See, e.g.*, *Momir Nikolić*, Sentencing Judgement, *supra* note 46, ¶ 150; *Kambanda*, Judgement and Sentence, *supra* note 31, ¶ 54.

[132] Turner & Weigend, *supra* note *, at *49.

[133] *See, e.g.*, *Momir Nikolić*, Sentencing Judgement, *supra* note 46, ¶¶ 58–60, 82.

[134] Prosecutor v. Blaškić, Case No. IT-95-14-PT, Decision on the Objection of the Republic of Croatia to the Issuance of Subpoenae Duces Tecum, ¶ 154 (ICTY July 18, 1997).

Proponents of plea bargaining argue that guilty pleas can also contribute to this goal of international criminal justice. When defendants plead guilty, they accept individual responsibility for their actions and help reveal the truth in relation to the crimes charged. By helping establish the truth, guilty pleas contribute to the healing and reconciliation process.[135] The expression of remorse that typically accompanies a guilty plea also promotes reconciliation.[136] As a witness commented on the guilty plea of Miroslav Deronjić, "The Bosnian Muslims in the community that I have spoken to, felt relieved because he admitted his guilt. This is a positive thing and can heal the wounds of the community provided that he is punished adequately."[137]

But the effect of guilty pleas on reconciliation is not straightforward. When pleas are accompanied by significant sentencing discounts, they are controversial among victims and often stir further resentment rather than reconciliation.[138] Even when accompanied by statements of remorse, such guilty pleas are often seen as disingenuous and motivated purely by the sentencing reductions. For guilty pleas to have a positive effect on reconciliation, therefore, they may have to be accompanied by remorseful actions and not mere statements in order to receive a sizable sentencing discount. Courts may choose to grant such sentencing reductions only when the defendant has taken reparative steps beyond a guilty plea – by

---

135 *E.g.*, Prosecutor v. Babić, Case No. IT-03-72-S, Sentencing Judgement, ¶¶ 68–70 (ICTY June 29, 2004); Prosecutor v. Mrđa, *supra* note 95; *Plavšić*, Sentencing Judgement, *supra* note 3, ¶ 77.

136 *Plavšić*, Sentencing Judgement, *supra* note 3, ¶¶ 75–7; *Momir Nikolić*, Sentencing Judgement, *supra* note 46, ¶ 72 ("Through the acknowledgment of the crimes committed and the recognition of one's own role in the suffering of others, a guilty plea may be more meaningful and significant than a finding of guilt by a trial chamber to the victims and survivors . . . . [A]n admission of guilt from a person perceived as 'the enemy' may serve as an opening for dialogue and reconciliation between different groups. When an admission of guilt is coupled with a sincere expression of remorse, a significant opportunity for reconciliation may be created.").

137 *Deronjić*, Sentencing Judgement, *supra* note 100, ¶ 238; *see also Obrenović*, Sentencing Judgement, *supra* note 45, ¶ 112 (quoting statement from a Bosnian Muslim from Srebrenica that "the confessions have brought me a sense of relief I have not known since the fall of Srebrenica in 1995"); *Momir Nikolić*, Sentencing Judgement, *supra* note 46, ¶ 147 (quoting mayor of Srebrenica as saying, "Only by recognizing and admitting the real and whole truth about the crime of July 1995 and other crimes in BH can trust be rebuilt among the citizens of BH.").

138 *Deronjić*, Sentencing Judgement, *supra* note 100, ¶¶ 238–9; Prosecutor v. Dragan Nikolić, Case No. IT-94-2-S, Sentencing Judgement, ¶ 245 (ICTY Dec. 18, 2003) [hereinafter *Dragan Nikolić*, Sentencing Judgement]; Clark, *supra* note 128, at 431–3.

surrendering voluntarily, cooperating with the prosecution in other cases, revealing information beyond that already known to the prosecution, or taking other conciliatory actions toward victims.[139] International courts may also have to conduct more active outreach work in victim communities to explain the justifications for plea bargains.[140]

International criminal courts have also committed to providing fair trials and following procedures that can serve as a model for criminal justice systems around the world. Advocates of plea bargaining argue that the practice is consistent with international human rights law because of the procedural safeguards that international courts have introduced to ensure that a guilty plea is voluntary, informed, and factually based.[141] Critics counter that courts have not adequately addressed the problem that guilty pleas may be coerced through excessive sentencing discounts and that defendants do not always receive sufficient information to waive their rights to trial knowingly and intelligently.[142] Defendants may also suffer unfairness when they plead guilty with the expectation of receiving a sentence reduction, but the court refuses to follow the parties' agreement as to the sentence.[143] Since the court is not bound by the agreement, a defendant who pleads guilty is effectively throwing himself on the mercy of the judges. And although defendants receive notice, before they plead guilty, that the agreement is not binding on the court, this does not entirely eliminate the underlying fairness concern.

Finally, plea bargaining has a complicated relationship with the goal of establishing an accurate record of international crimes. International criminal tribunals have recognized that guilty pleas contribute to the establishment of the truth. Indeed, this is one of the reasons for the substantial weight that guilty pleas carry in mitigation.[144] When defendants plead guilty, they may reveal inside information that would otherwise not surface during a trial – for example, how a leadership structure worked or why certain crimes were committed. By accepting responsibility, defend-

---

139 *Cf.* Clark, *supra* note 128, at 433.

140 *Id.*

141 Human rights jurisprudence generally affirms the legality of plea bargains, as long as the waiver of trial is voluntary, unequivocal, and informed. Kwiatkowska v. Italy, *supra* note 93; Deweer v. Belgium, no. 6903/75, §§ 50–4, ECtHR (Feb. 27, 1980) (holding the defendant's waiver of his trial rights involuntary when the prosecutor had threatened the defendant with a heavy fine and with closing down his business if he chose a trial instead of accepting the settlement offered by the prosecution).

142 *See, e.g.*, Cook, *supra* note 82.

143 *Cf.* Rauxloh, *supra* note 36, at 181.

144 *See supra* note 99 and accompanying text.

ants can also help prevent inaccurate revisionist accounts of history.[145] Once political and military leaders admit their guilt openly in court, "[d]enial of the commission of the crime may no longer be an option for those who have convinced themselves that the Tribunal is biased or that its judgements are based on weak or even false evidence."[146]

Prosecutors and courts must nonetheless remain aware of the risk that plea bargains could undermine the goal of compiling a precise record by omitting facts and failing to test them rigorously through an adversarial procedure. It is always possible that "[n]either the public, nor the judges themselves [will] come closer to know the truth beyond what is accepted in the plea agreement."[147] Charge bargains are especially problematic in this respect:

> If the prosecutor makes a plea agreement such that the totality of an individual's criminal conduct is not reflected or the remaining charges do not sufficiently indicate the gravity of offenses committed by the accused, questions will inevitably arise as to whether justice is in fact being done. The public may be left to wonder about the motives for guilty pleas, whether the conviction in fact reflects the full criminal conduct of the accused and whether it establishes a credible and complete historical record.[148]

As the *Momir Nikolić* Trial Chamber emphasized, it is especially important for international courts to supervise charge bargains and ensure that important facts are not omitted or distorted in the effort to resolve a case consensually.[149] The stricter oversight of charge bargains is consistent with civil law approaches to criminal procedure, and more importantly, with the international criminal courts' goal to establish the truth and provide an accurate record of the crimes.

In summary, the propriety of plea bargaining at international criminal courts continues to be debated and depends greatly on the form that the practice takes. Certain types of plea bargains may interfere with victims' interests and with the truth-seeking, retributive and deterrent goals of the courts. Others may advance these goals, or at the very least avoid conflicting with them. To maximize the value of plea bargains, courts must consider their design carefully.

In this respect, the ICC Statute is an advancement over the ICTY and ICTR Rules on plea bargaining. The ICC Statute emphasizes the

---

145 *See, e.g.*, *Deronjić*, Sentencing Judgement, *supra* note 100, ¶¶ 257–60.
146 *Momir Nikolić*, Sentencing Judgement, *supra* note 46, ¶ 70.
147 *Dragan Nikolić*, Sentencing Judgement, *supra* note 138, ¶ 122.
148 *Momir Nikolić*, Sentencing Judgement, *supra* note 46, ¶ 65.
149 *Id.* ¶¶ 64–5.

importance of gathering ample facts to support an admission of guilt and the duty of judges to review the facts independently. This approach strengthens the historical record that plea bargains produce and enhances the fairness of plea bargaining to defendants and victims. The ICC expressly entrusts judges with the responsibility of ensuring that plea bargains are consistent with the interests of justice and of victims. It also provides for the possibility of victim participation at the proceedings on admission of guilt and allows them to make their views on particular plea bargains known. Further, the ICC provides that an admission of guilt may be tendered only after consultation with defense counsel, thus increasing the likelihood that the admission will be voluntary and informed.

The ICC's approach to plea bargaining therefore has great potential to advance the court's broader goals. But many other ideas merit consideration at the ICC and any other international criminal courts that rely on plea bargaining.

For example, courts may wish to elaborate on the voluntariness standard and furnish examples of the kinds of pressure that may render a guilty plea involuntary. It is important to resolve conclusively whether threats of substantially greater punishment or promises of extraordinarily lenient sentences might render guilty pleas involuntary. If the answer is yes, then international criminal courts ought to take steps to prevent such involuntary pleas (for example, by setting a fixed ceiling on plea discounts and by strictly supervising charge bargains).

It would also be helpful for international criminal courts to determine what kind of evidence defendants must receive before they can tender an informed guilty plea. Consistent with the emphasis on truth-seeking, transparency, and fairness, international criminal courts ought to require that defendants have access to all material evidence in their case before they plead guilty.

International criminal courts may also apply a presumption that defendants have to accept responsibility for their actions in order to receive a sentencing reduction. Guilty pleas should therefore be unequivocal to be valid, as the Rules of the ICTY and ICTR provide. In addition, before awarding any significant sentencing discounts, courts may require evidence of remorse that goes beyond mere statements and includes actions that suggest contrition. Such a requirement can help ensure that guilty pleas, even when accompanied by significant sentencing discounts, still contribute to reconciliation in the region affected by the crimes in question.

Finally, judges ought to actively use the tools provided by the ICC Statute and call for additional presentation of evidence when reviewing admissions of guilt. This practice would enhance the contribution of admissions of guilt to the discovery of the truth and the presentation of an accurate record, which remains a central goal of international criminal courts.

Considering approaches such as these should encourage policymakers to rethink the role of plea bargaining in international criminal law and design procedures that are fair, efficient, and consistent with the goals of international criminal justice.

3. Witness proofing

Hannah Garry*

I. INTRODUCTION

The practice of witness proofing has been one of the more polarizing procedural issues litigated before international criminal tribunals.[1] Generally speaking, this practice encompasses preparation of witnesses for giving testimony by the parties to a case. Much of the debate over proofing has centered on *who* should be allowed access to witnesses pre-testimony and *what* should be the nature of their interaction with the witnesses before giving evidence at trial.

However, witness proofing has not always been so controversial in international criminal law. With the establishment of the International Criminal Tribunal for the former Yugoslavia (ICTY) in 1993 and International Criminal Tribunal for Rwanda (ICTR) in 1994, parties practiced proofing as a matter of course without challenge for the first decade. It was not until

* Clinical Associate Professor of Law and Director, International Human Rights Clinic, University of Southern California Gould School of Law. Professor Garry has previously served as a Legal Officer for the Appeals Chamber at the ICTY and ICTR as well as a Legal Advisor to the ECCC. She also served as Deputy Chef de Cabinet at the ICTY during the presidency of Judge Fausto Pocar. She thanks Siyuan An, Lisa Foutch and Alisa Randell for their assistance with researching and proof-reading this chapter.

[1] *See, e.g.,* Ruben Karemaker, B. Don Taylor III & Thomas Wayde Pittman, *Witness Proofing in International Criminal Tribunals: A Critical Analysis of Widening Procedural Divergence*, 21 LEIDEN J. INT'L L. 683 (2008); Kai Ambos, *'Witness Proofing' Before the International Criminal Court: A Reply to Karemaker, Taylor, and Pittman*, 21 LEIDEN J. INT'L L. 911 (2008); Ruben Karemaker, B. Don Taylor III, and Thomas Wayde Pittman, *Witness Proofing in International Criminal Tribunals: Response to Ambos*, 21 LEIDEN J. INT'L L. 917 (2008); Wayne Jordash, *The Practice of 'Witness Proofing' in International Criminal Tribunals: Why the International Criminal Court Should Prohibit the Practice*, 22 LEIDEN J. INT'L L. 501 (2009); Sergey Vasiliev, *Proofing the Ban on 'Witness Proofing': Did the ICC Get It Right?*, 20 CRIM. L.F. 193 (2009); WAR CRIMES RESEARCH OFFICE, AM. UNIV. WASHINGTON COLL. OF LAW, WITNESS PROOFING AT THE INTERNATIONAL CRIMINAL COURT (2009).

2004, in the ICTY's *Limaj et al.* case, that the practice was first contested by the defense on grounds that it breached fair trial rights.[2] The Trial Chamber flatly rejected the motion, noting in particular the longstanding and widespread practice of witness proofing at the Tribunal and in adversarial jurisdictions generally.[3]

In stark contrast, Chambers in the *Lubanga* case, the first trial before the International Criminal Court (ICC), prohibited the practice in 2006,[4] finding that the ICC's Statute "moves away from the procedural regime of the ad hoc tribunals."[5] In its place, they authorized the practice of "witness familiarization," a process that retains some aspects of witness proofing practiced by the ICTY and ICTR, but only allows for the Court's Victims and Witnesses Unit (VWU) to have direct contact with the witnesses before they testify.[6] While parties in a case may meet with witnesses before giving testimony, they may only do so through the VWU, and the nature of their contact is limited for purposes of acquainting themselves.[7]

Subsequently, Trial Chambers at the ICTY, ICTR and Special Court for Sierra Leone (SCSL), as well as the ICTR Appeals Chamber, repeatedly affirmed the practice in response to defense challenges to proofing relying upon the ICC *Lubanga* decisions. Meanwhile, Chambers in other ICC cases have so far followed the *Lubanga* approach. Similarly, although no judicial pronouncement has been made on the question, parties before the Extraordinary Chambers in the Courts of Cambodia (ECCC) do not practice witness proofing.[8] This is in line with Cambodian procedural

---

[2] Prosecutor v. Limaj et al., Case No. IT-03-66-T, Decision on Defence Motion on Prosecution Practice of "Proofing" Witnesses, 1 (ICTY Dec. 10, 2004) [hereinafter *Limaj et al.*, Decision on Witness Proofing].

[3] *Limaj et al.*, Decision on Witness Proofing, *supra* note 2, at 2.

[4] Prosecutor v. Lubanga Dyilo, Case No. ICC-01/04-01/06, Decision on the Practices of Witness Familiarisation and Witness Proofing, at 19–22 (Nov. 8, 2006) [hereinafter *Lubanga*, Pre-Trial Chamber Decision].

[5] Prosecutor v. Lubanga Dyilo, Case No. ICC-01/04-01/06, Decision Regarding the Practices Used to Prepare and Familiarise Witnesses for Giving Testimony at Trial, ¶ 45 (Nov. 30, 2007) [hereinafter *Lubanga*, Trial Chamber Decision].

[6] *Lubanga*, Pre-Trial Chamber Decision, *supra* note 4, at 21–2; *Lubanga*, Trial Chamber Decision, *supra* note 5, ¶¶ 53–7.

[7] Prosecutor v. Bemba Gombo, Case No. ICC-01/05-01/08, Victims and Witnesses Unit's Amended Version of the "Unified Protocol on the Practices Used to Prepare and Familiarise Witnesses for Giving Testimony at Trial" Submitted on 22 October 2010, ¶¶ 30–31 (Dec. 7, 2010) [hereinafter Amended Unified Protocol of 7 December 2010].

[8] *See generally* ECCC Internal Rules (Rev. 8) (Aug. 3, 2011), Rules 24, 50, 55, 60, 80, 84, 91 (regarding procedures for investigations and interviewing witnesses by investigative judges and submission of the case file to the Trial Chamber, which

law, which is directly applied in these hybrid tribunal proceedings[9] and has its roots in the French civil law tradition.[10] Finally, it remains to be seen whether witness proofing will be allowed at the Special Tribunal for Lebanon (STL).[11]

In the face of this clear divide, this chapter seeks to understand the differences in approach to witness proofing among today's international criminal tribunals. Given that tribunals largely look to national legal systems in formulating their procedural law, Part II begins by contrasting witness preparation by parties in criminal cases in adversarial or common law systems with the prohibition on meeting with witnesses pre-testimony in a number of other national legal systems, especially inquisitorial or

---

reflects the civil law model, and makes witness proofing unnecessary). *See also* Rupert Skilbeck, *Frankenstein's Monster: Creating a New International Procedure*, 8 J. INT'L CRIM JUST. 451 (2010); RUTH MACKENZIE ET AL., THE MANUAL ON INTERNATIONAL COURTS AND TRIBUNALS 227–8 (2d ed. 2010).

9 *See generally* Law on the Establishment of the Extraordinary Chambers in the Courts of Cambodia for the Prosecution of Crimes Committed During the Period of Democratic Kampuchea, with inclusion of amendments as promulgated on 27 October 2004 (NS/RKM/1004/006), Art. 33 (new) (stipulating that Cambodian procedural law applies to proceedings before the ECCC and guidance may be sought in international procedure where local law does not govern a specific matter).

10 Skilbeck, *supra* note 8, at 453; MACKENZIE ET AL., *supra* note 8 at 227–8.

11 At the time of the writing of this chapter, no formal decision on witness proofing had been issued by the STL. It remains to be seen whether Chambers will allow it, given the particular blend of adversarial and inquisitorial procedures in its rules. *See* Explanatory Memorandum by the Tribunal's President on the Rules of Procedure and Evidence, ¶ 4 (Nov. 25, 2010); STL Statute, S/RES/1752 (2007), Art. 28(2) (stipulating that Judges of the STL shall adopt rules of procedure and evidence guided by international criminal procedure and the Lebanese Code of Criminal Procedure as appropriate); STL Rules of Procedure and Evidence (STL RPE), as amended (Feb. 8, 2012), Rule 149 (providing that in the event of a lacunae in the rules, a Chamber shall apply provisions of the Lebanese Code of Criminal Procedure in accordance with the highest standards of international criminal procedure). There is no explicit mention of the practice found in the STL's Statute, Rules or Practice Directions; however, parties to a case are responsible for investigation with direct contact with witnesses during that process under the supervision of a Pre-trial Judge. Furthermore, parties may lead and question witnesses at trial. What is clear at this point is that the VWU is responsible for witness familiarization prior to giving testimony, and the STL Code of Professional Conduct for Counsel Appearing Before the Tribunal provides rules regulating witness proofing "if allowed." *See* STL RPE, as amended (Feb. 8, 2012), Rules 50(B)(ii), 60, 68, 77, 88, 89, 91, 92, 95, 110, 112, 113, 145, 146, 150; STL Code of Professional Conduct for Counsel Appearing Before the Tribunal, STL-CC-2011-01, (Feb. 28, 2011), ¶ 6(h) ("Counsel shall . . . if allowed to proof a witness, avoid exercising improper influence over the witness's recollection of events.").

civil law systems. Part III then provides an overview of the adaptation of national approaches into the procedural framework of international criminal tribunals, particularly the ICTY/ICTR and ICC. Part IV proceeds to critique these approaches from a human rights perspective, noting the rights at stake and the extent to which each upholds those rights. Finally, Part V concludes by way of offering some preliminary observations.

II. WITNESS PROOFING IN NATIONAL LEGAL SYSTEMS

A survey of witness proofing in national criminal legal systems reveals that there is a broad spectrum of approaches as well as varying terms and definitions describing the practice. In addition, there is lack of agreement on whether the practice should be allowed in the first place and, if so, to what extent.[12] The reason for this disagreement stems in part from fundamental differences in perspective over the role and purpose of witness testimony and the rules surrounding its production and presentation at trial.[13]

In general, it may be concluded that some form of witness proofing whereby there is "discussion on the substance of the testimony to be given by a witness is either allowed or encouraged" between the parties and the prospective witnesses in systems that are more adversarial in nature.[14] In

---

[12] *Lubanga*, Pre-Trial Chamber Decision, *supra* note 4, ¶¶ 36–37; Prosecutor v. Bemba Gombo, Case No. ICC-01/05-01/08, Partly Dissenting Opinion of Judge Kuniko Ozaki on the Decision on the Unified Protocol on the Practices Used to Prepare and Familiarise Witnesses for Giving Testimony at Trial, ¶ 14 (Nov. 24, 2010) [hereinafter Ozaki Dissenting Opinion].

[13] Kai Ambos, *"Witness Proofing" Before the ICC: Neither Legally Admissible nor Necessary*, *in* THE EMERGING PRACTICE OF THE INTERNATIONAL CRIMINAL COURT 606 (Carsten Stahn & Göran Sluiter, eds., 2009).

[14] Ozaki Dissenting Opinion, *supra* note 12, ¶ 14 (citing *New South Wales Barristers' Rules 2001* (NSW) Rules 43, 44 (Austl.); *Crown Policy Manual—Witness 2005* (Can.); *Law Society of Upper Canada, Rules of Professional Conduct 2000*, Rules 4.03, 4.04 (Can.); *The Crown Prosecution Service—Pre-Trial Witness Interviews, Guidance for Prosecutors* (Eng. & Wales); The Rt. Hon. The Lord Goldsmith QC, *Pre-Trial Witnesses Interviews by Prosecutors Report 2004* (Eng. & Wales); RESTATEMENT (THIRD) OF LAW GOVERNING LAWYERS: INTERVIEWING AND PREPARING A PROSPECTIVE WITNESS § 116 (2000) (U.S.); Legal Practitioners Act—Rules of Professional Conduct in the Legal Profession (1980) 67:5 O.G. § 20 (Nigeria); Rules of Conduct and Client Care for Lawyers 2008 reg. 13.10 (N.Z.); Rules of Criminal Procedure, Rules of the Supreme Court, No. 32 of 1948, art. 191-3 (Japan)). *See also* Prosecutor v. Haradinaj et al., Case No. IT-04-84-T, Decision on Defence

these systems, witnesses are understood to belong to the parties to the proceedings.[15] As such, the parties are primarily responsible for calling and questioning witnesses in support of the presentation of their cases,[16] while the judge acts as a neutral umpire maintaining order and fairness in the courtroom.[17] In these systems, "in-court oral testimony of witnesses plays a central role in the evaluation of the evidence"[18] and the critical means for determining reliability and credibility of witness testimony is through cross-examination by the opposing side.[19] Consequently, the decision-maker, often a lay jury, is "unlikely to believe a witness who goes *off piste* during the course of giving evidence" especially because the decision-maker may not have the ability to seek further clarification.[20] The underlying belief of the adversarial or common law approach is that the best means for ascertaining truth is through this competitive presentation and cross-examination of evidence by opposing parties before a neutral decision-maker exposed to the evidence for the first time.[21] As a result, in such a system, witness proofing is deemed to be of critical importance such that failure to exercise it would be unethical and contrary to the best interests of the client.

While the common purposes of witness proofing in adversarial jurisdictions are to refresh a witness's memory and check the witness's evidence for relevance, accuracy and completeness prior to testifying, there is divergence in the rules governing proofing and providing safeguards from

---

Request for Audio-Recording of Prosecution Witness Proofing Sessions, ¶ 17 & n. 69 (ICTY May 23, 2007) [hereinafter *Haradinaj et al.*, Decision on Witness Proofing Sessions] (noting that Australia, Canada, India, Pakistan, South Africa, Tanzania, England and Wales and the United States of America permit witness preparation by parties); Ambos, *supra* note 13, at 605; Albin Eser, *Procedural Structure and Features of International Criminal Justice: Lessons from the ICTY*, *in* The Legacy of the International Criminal Tribunal for the Former Yugoslavia 127 (Bert Swart, Alexander Zahar & Göran Sluiter, eds., 2011); Vladimir Tochilovsky, *The Nature and Evolution of the Rules of Procedure and Evidence*, *in* Principles of Evidence in International Criminal Justice 177 (Karim A.A. Khan, Caroline Buisman & Christopher Gosnell, eds., 2010).

15 Ambos, *supra* note 13, at 605; Eser, *supra* note 14, at 127.

16 John D. Jackson & Sarah J. Summers, The Internationalisation of Criminal Evidence: Beyond the Common Law and Civil Law Traditions 122–3 (2012).

17 Stephanos Bibas & William W. Burke-White, *International Idealism Meets Domestic Criminal Procedure Realism*, 59 Duke L. J. 637, 695 (2010).

18 Ozaki Dissenting Opinion, *supra* note 12, ¶ 14.

19 Bibas & Burke-White, *supra* note 17, at 700–701.

20 Skilbeck, *supra* note 8, at 458–9.

21 *See generally* Jackson & Summers, *supra* note 16, at 127–9.

improper conduct during the sessions.[22] For example, in England and Wales, there is a "formal separating of pre-trial and trial functions between solicitors and barristers."[23] A barrister as in-court advocate is strictly forbidden from speaking with a witness prior to giving evidence[24] "save for a pep-talk in order to familiarize the witness with the procedure and to calm the nerves."[25] That said, under new procedures, a barrister may conduct video-taped preparatory sessions where exceptional circumstances require it and certain safeguards are followed.[26] In addition, solicitors in a case are allowed to "see proposed defence witnesses to prepare a proof of evidence from which the court advocate will work" and may also interview prosecution witnesses.[27] When attorneys are interviewing a witness regarding the substance of forthcoming testimony, they may not train or practice with the witness.[28] On the other hand, witness familiarization, which involves simply informing witnesses about the layout of the court and procedure at trial so as to prevent them from being taken by surprise, is welcome.[29]

In contrast, in the United States, there is no clear distinction with respect to which advocates may meet with witnesses before they testify. Furthermore, witness proofing encompasses a wide range of measures including substantive discussion of forthcoming testimony, rehearsal and witness familiarization techniques.[30]

The only exception to this variance in approach on proofing in common

---

22 *Lubanga*, Pre-Trial Chamber Decision, *supra* note 4, ¶ 12; *Lubanga*, Trial Chamber Decision, *supra* note 5, ¶¶ 39–42; Ozaki Dissenting Opinion, *supra* note 12, ¶ 14. *See also* Ambos, *supra* note 13, at 606–11.

23 Ambos, *supra* note 13, at 606 (citing *inter alia* F. LYALL, AN INTRODUCTION TO BRITISH LAW 42 (2d ed. 2002)).

24 Code of Conduct of the Bar of England & Wales, 8th ed., Oct. 31, 2004, as amended in 2012, ¶ 705; Written Standards for the Conduct of Professional Work, § 6.3 (implementing the Code of Conduct of the Bar of England & Wales), *available at* http://www.barstandardsboard.org.uk/regulatory-requirements/the-code-of-conduct/written-standards-for-the-conduct-of-professional-work/.

25 *See* Skilbeck, *supra* note 8.

26 *Id.* at 457–8.

27 *Id.*; *see generally* Solicitors Regulation Authority Code of Conduct, Oct. 6, 2011, Chap. 5, *available at* http://www.sra.org.uk/solicitors/handbook/code/content.page.

28 Code of Conduct of the Bar of England & Wales, 8th ed., Oct. 31, 2004, as amended in 2012, ¶ 705(a); Crown Prosecution Service, Code of Practice, February 2008, *available at* http://www.cps.gov.uk/victims_witnesses/resources/interviews.html#a01; R v. Momodou, [2005] EWCA Crim 177, ¶ 61.

29 *Momodou supra* note 28, ¶ 62.

30 *See* RESTATEMENT (THIRD) OF THE LAW GOVERNING LAWYERS §116(1) and cmt. b (2000) (allowing for witness preparation before testifying and stipulating that permissible techniques include:

law systems appears to be the rule that measures taken during witness proofing will be prohibited that have the potential to taint or influence the evidence, such as witness coaching; manipulating the evidence; or encouraging a witness to testify in a way that will obscure or distort the truth.[31] What exactly those measures are, however, varies by jurisdiction.

On the other hand, national legal systems based in the inquisitorial or civil law tradition largely do not allow for the discussion of evidence or even contact between witnesses and the parties before testimony.[32] Some legal systems of mixed legal traditions, not strictly based in the civil law, are included in this group on the understanding that such practice is either unethical or unlawful.[33] This is due to the fact that in such systems, witnesses do not belong to the parties but are "witnesses of the Court or the truth."[34] Under the inquisitorial framework, both inculpatory and exculpatory evidence is gathered and led by an investigative judge who thoroughly interviews and questions witnesses prior to their

---

Discussing the role of the witness and effective courtroom demeanor; discussing the witness's recollection and probable testimony; revealing to the witness other testimony or evidence that will be presented and asking the witness to reconsider the witness's recollection or recounting of events in that light; discussing the applicability of law to the events in issue; reviewing the factual context into which the witness's observations or opinions will fit; reviewing documents or other physical evidence that may be introduced; and discussing probable lines of hostile cross-examination that the witness should be prepared to meet. Witness preparation may include rehearsal of testimony. A lawyer may suggest choice of words that might be employed to make the witness's meaning clear).

[31] Ozaki Dissenting Opinion, *supra* note 12, ¶ 14. *See, e.g.*, Code of Conduct of the Bar of England & Wales, 8th ed., October 31, 2004, as amended in 2012, ¶ 705; Solicitors Regulation Authority Code of Conduct, *supra* note 27; Crown Prosecution Service, Code of Practice, February 2008, *supra* note 28; *Momodou supra* note 28, ¶ 61; American Bar Association Model Rules of Professional Conduct (2010), Rule 3.3(a)(3) and 3.4(b) (prohibiting a lawyer from presenting evidence known to be false and stating that lawyers must not "falsify evidence, counsel or assist a witness to testify falsely . . ."). *See also* Shannon M. Awsumb, *Avoiding a Career-Ending Mistake: The Line Between Witness Preparation and Coaching*, THE HENNEPIN LAWYER, Feb. 20, 2007.

[32] Bibas & Burke-White, *supra* note 17, at 696. SEE Skilbeck, *supra* note 8.

[33] *Lubanga*, Pre-Trial Chamber Decision, *supra* note 4, ¶ 37 (noting that the witness proofing advanced by the prosecution would be unethical or unlawful in countries such as Brazil, Spain, France, Belgium, Germany, Scotland, and Ghana); *Haradinaj et al.*, Decision on Witness Proofing Sessions, *supra* note 14, ¶ 17 & n. 69 (noting that Argentina, Austria, Belgium, Cameroon, Chile, Croatia, Denmark, France, Germany, Italy, The Netherlands, Norway, Peru, Serbia, Spain, Sweden and Switzerland do not use witness proofing).

[34] Ambos, *supra* note 13, at 605.

testimony.[35] Subsequently, the statements taken from witnesses in the investigative stage are included in the case file as highly probative evidence and are read by the trial judges prior to their testimony "thus logically rendering witness proofing by the parties unnecessary and irrelevant."[36] At trial, witness testimony does not play as central a role for evaluating the evidence as it does in the adversarial framework, judges lead the questioning,[37] and cross-examination is not a common practice.[38] In this context, the judges "will be far less bothered by the demeanour and poise of the witness than by the truths perhaps revealed"[39] particularly as a result of "helpful spontaneity" during trial testimony.[40] Under the inquisitorial approach, this focus on neutral judges actively and methodically gathering evidence and leading the questioning of witnesses at trial is perceived as the best means for arriving at the truth.[41]

III. WITNESS PROOFING IN INTERNATIONAL CRIMINAL PROCEEDINGS

A. The Differing Approaches

1. The ICTY, ICTR and SCSL

In the beginning, the procedural framework of both the ICTY and ICTR was largely adversarial or common law in nature[42] and, in that context, witness proofing was widely practiced.[43] However, in the absence of deci-

---

35 Bibas & Burke-White, *supra* note 17, at 695.

36 Ozaki Dissenting Opinion, *supra* note 12, ¶ 20.

37 *See* Skilbeck, *supra* note 8.

38 Ambos, *supra* note 13, at 606.

39 *See* Skilbeck, *supra* note 8.

40 Ambos, *supra* note 13, at 613.

41 Bibas & Burke-White, *supra* note 17, at 695.

42 Robert Cryer et al., An Introduction to International Criminal Law and Procedure 428 (2d ed. 2010); Bibas & Burke-White, *supra* note 17, at 694; Jackson & Summers, *supra* note 16, at 122. It is important to note that over the years, the procedural framework for the *ad hoc* tribunals has been amended to incorporate more rules that have civil law aspects. *See, e.g.*, Daryl Mundis, *From "Common Law" Towards "Civil Law": The Evolution of the ICTY Rules of Procedure and Evidence*, 14 Leiden J. Int'l L. 367 (2001); Fausto Pocar, *Common and Civil Law Traditions in the ICTY Criminal Procedure: Does Oil Blend with Water?*, 49 S.C.L.R. (2d) 439–41 (2010); Tochilovsky, *supra* note 14, at 161–74.

43 Prosecutor v. Karemera et al., Case No. ICTR-98-44-AR73.8, Decision on Interlocutory Appeal Regarding Witness Proofing, ¶¶ 8–10 (May 11, 2007) [hereinafter *Karemera et al.*, Appeal Decision on Witness Proofing]; *Limaj et al.*, Decision

sions from Chambers or explicit rules on the procedure,[44] the exact definition or parameters of the practice remained unclear.[45] This changed with the rendering of the first decision on witness proofing in 2004 by the ICTY Trial Chamber in *Limaj et al.*, followed by further decisions on witness proofing in cases before the ICTY, ICTR and SCSL.

In *Limaj et al.*, the Trial Chamber did not expressly define witness proofing or its exact parameters when affirming the practice as one that is "widespread . . . in jurisdictions where there is an adversary procedure."[46] Nevertheless, it may be inferred that the Chamber considered that proofing entails a detailed meeting or series of meetings by the prosecution or defense with witnesses who are going to testify at trial.[47] Those meetings are specifically directed towards: 1) "identifying fully the facts known to the witness that are relevant to the charges in the actual Indictment"; 2) comparing a witness' recollection of relevant facts with earlier statements given by the witness during investigations in order to examine any "deficiencies and differences" between the two; 3) identifying any additional recollections which are to be disclosed to the other party; and 4) preparing a witness to cope adequately with the stress of international criminal proceedings.[48]

Two years later, in *Milutinović et al.*, another ICTY Trial Chamber considered a challenge to witness proofing. When assessing the merits of the motion, the Chamber analyzed witness proofing as composed of two

---

on Witness Proofing, *supra* note 2, at 2; Prosecutor v. Karemera et al., Case No. ICTR-98-44-T, Decision on Defence Motions to Prohibit Witness Proofing, ¶¶ 9–15 (Dec. 15, 2006) [hereinafter *Karemera et al.*, Decision on Witness Proofing]; *Haradinaj et al.*, Decision on Witness Proofing Sessions, *supra* note 14, ¶ 8.

44 *Karemera et al.*, Appeal Decision on Witness Proofing, *supra* note 43, ¶ 8; Prosecutor v. Milutinović et al., Case No. IT-05-87-T, Decision on Ojdanić Motion to Prohibit Witness Proofing, ¶ 5 (ICTY Dec. 12, 2006) [hereinafter *Milutinović et al.*, Decision on Witness Proofing].

45 *See, e.g.*, *Haradinaj et al.*, Decision on Witness Proofing Sessions, *supra* note 14, ¶ 8 (noting that with respect to the ICTY, "[d]espite the fact that the practice of proofing witnesses, by both the Prosecution and the Defence, has been in place since the inception of the Tribunal, there is no set definition of proofing at the Tribunal").

46 *Limaj et al.*, Decision on Witness Proofing, *supra* note 2, at 2.

47 *Id.*

48 *Id.* at 2–3. The Chamber noted that proceedings at the ICTY could be particularly stressful for witnesses due to "the cultural differences encountered by most witnesses . . . when brought to The Hague and required to give a detailed account of stressful events, which occurred a long time ago, in a formal setting, and doing so in response to structured precise questions, translated from a different language." *Id.* at 3.

distinct parts: "[t]he practice of witness familiarisation and then the practice of a party reviewing a witness' evidence prior to his/her testimony."[49] This bi-furcated definition was drawn from a previously rendered decision in the ICC *Lubanga* case. The Trial Chamber appeared to accept that witness proofing consists of "a series of arrangements to familiarise the witnesses with the layout of the Court, the sequence of events that is likely to take place when the witness is giving testimony, and the different responsibilities of the various participants at the hearing."[50] However, the Chamber rejected the approach taken by the ICC that witness familiarization should be limited to the Tribunal's Victims and Witnesses Section rather than conducted by the parties to a case.[51] With respect to the practice of "discussions between a party and a potential witness regarding his/her evidence," the Chamber also rejected the approach taken by the ICC in prohibiting it.[52] However, the Chamber stressed that these discussions are to be a "genuine attempt to clarify a witness' evidence" that does not amount to "'rehears[ing], practis[ing], or coach[ing] a witness.'"[53]

Finally, in *Haradinaj et al.,* the ICTY Trial Chamber expressly defined proofing. Although noting that "there is no set definition of proofing at the Tribunal,"[54] the Chamber broadly defined the practice as "a meeting held between a party to the proceedings and a witness, usually shortly before the witness is to testify in court, the purpose of which is to prepare and familiarize the witness with courtroom procedures and to review the witness's evidence."[55]

The question of the definition of witness proofing was explicitly addressed by the ICTR for the first time in 2006 in the *Karemera et al.* case. When affirming the practice, the Trial Chamber articulated its definition as follows:

> [p]rovided that it does not amount to the manipulation of a witness' evidence, this practice may encompass preparing and familiarizing a witness with the proceedings before the Tribunal, comparing prior statements made by a witness, detecting differences and inconsistencies in recollection of the witness, allowing

---

49 *Milutinović et al.*, Decision on Witness Proofing, *supra* note 44, ¶ 4. The Trial Chamber divided witness proofing into these two separate practices following the lead of the ICC Pre-Trial Chamber in *Lubanga. Id.*

50 *Id.* ¶ 6 (quoting the *Lubanga* Pre-Trial Chamber Decision, *supra* note 4, ¶ 15).

51 *Id.* ¶ 10.

52 *Id.* ¶¶ 16, 20–22.

53 *Id.* ¶ 16 (quoting Article 705 of the Code of Conduct of the Bar Council of England and Wales).

54 *Haradinaj et al.*, Decision on Witness Proofing Sessions, *supra* note 14, ¶ 8.

55 *Id.*

> a witness to refresh his or her memory in respect of the evidence he or she will give, and inquiring and disclosing to the Defence additional information and/or evidence of incriminatory or exculpatory nature in sufficient time prior to the witness' testimony.[56]

With respect to witness familiarization as a component of witness proofing, the Chamber also noted the definition in *Lubanga*.[57] However, like the *Milutinović et al.* Trial Chamber, the Chamber rejected the holding in *Lubanga* that familiarization should be limited to the Witnesses and Victims Support Section of the Tribunal.[58] The Chamber also made clear that witness proofing does not allow for training, coaching or tampering with the evidence against an accused when dismissing the defense allegation that the prosecution had, in that case, been putting to a witness "the exact questions to be asked during his or her testimony" which was "not in conformity with established practice."[59]

On interlocutory appeal, the *Karemera* Appeals Chamber affirmed the Trial Chamber's definition of witness proofing as being in line with the approach previously sanctioned by the Appeals Chamber in the *Gacumbitsi* case whereby the Chamber found that discussing prior statements and the content of forthcoming testimony is not *per se* inappropriate.[60] In its decision, the Chamber also concluded that "'[i]t is not inappropriate *per se* for the parties to discuss the content of testimony and witness statements with their witnesses, unless they attempt to influence that content in ways that shade or distort the truth'" such as by coaching a witness.[61]

Finally, the SCSL considered and upheld the practice of witness proofing in the *Sesay et al.* case. In its decisions, the Trial Chamber consistently relied on the definition of proofing found in the ICTY's *Limaj et al.* case.[62]

---

56 *Karemera et al.*, Decision on Witness Proofing, *supra* note 43, ¶ 15.

57 *Id.* ¶ 4 (quoting the *Lubanga* Pre-Trial Chamber Decision, *supra* note 4, ¶ 15).

58 *Id.* ¶ 10 (citing the *Milutinović et al.* Decision on Witness Proofing, *supra* note 44, ¶ 10).

59 *Id.* ¶¶ 21–4.

60 *See* Gacumbitsi v. The Prosecutor, Case No. ICTR-2001-64-A, Judgment, ¶ 74 (July 7, 2006) [hereinafter *Gacumbitsi*, Appeals Judgment] (rejecting the defense's argument that a witness' testimony lacked credibility because the witness was allegedly coached and holding that discussing the content of testimony and witness statements with a witness prior to giving testimony is not *per se* inappropriate).

61 *Karemera et al.*, Appeal Decision on Witness Proofing, *supra* note 43, ¶ 9 (quoting *Gacumbitsi*, Appeals Judgment, *supra* note 60, ¶ 74).

62 *See, e.g.*, Prosecutor v. Sesay et al., Case No. SCSL-04-15-T, Decision on the Gbao and Sesay Joint Application for the Exclusion of the Testimony of Witness TF1-141, ¶¶ 30, 33 (Oct. 26, 2005) [hereinafter *Sesay et al.*, Decision on Exclusion of Testimony]. *See also* Wayne Jordash, *The Practice of 'Witness Proofing' in*

In sum, given that the ICTY and ICTR share the same Appeals Chamber,[63] witness proofing is now a firmly accepted practice in both Tribunals following the Appeals Chamber's affirmation of the practice in 2007 in the *Karemera et al.* case. Furthermore, the definition and parameters of the practice have been clarified through judicial examination to encompass meeting(s) between the parties to a case and prospective witnesses who will give evidence at trial. Those meetings may consist of measures to familiarize a witness with the organization of the proceedings as well as to substantively discuss the forthcoming testimony of the witness.

With respect to familiarization, logistical matters are covered such as: the layout of the Court, the roles of the various participants in the proceedings and the sequence of events that are to take place in the hearings. As for substantive discussion of the witness' testimony, it may involve: 1) refreshing a witness' memory with respect to evidence to be given; 2) comparing a witness' prior statements; 3) detecting any differences or inconsistencies in the witness' recollection; 4) asking the witness about any additional information and/or evidence of an incriminatory or exculpatory nature; and 5) disclosing any new information to the defence in a timely manner prior to the witness' testimony.[64]

However, witness proofing seems to preclude putting "to the witness the exact questions to be asked during his or her testimony."[65] More generally, it does not involve any measures that could improperly influence the content of the witness testimony "in ways that shade or distort the truth"[66] such as those that would effectively "train, coach or tamper a witness before he or she gives evidence"[67] and thereby "amount to the manipulation of the witness' evidence . . . ."[68] The SCSL has followed the same approach to witness proofing although nothing in the jurisprudence specifically addresses whether putting to the witness the questions to be asked during testimony is permissible.

International Criminal Tribunals: Why the International Criminal Court Should Prohibit the Practice, 22 LEIDEN J. INT'L L. 501, 509–10 (2009).

63 Statute of the International Criminal Tribunal for Rwanda, Art. 13, Jan. 31, 2010.

64 *Karemera et al.*, Appeal Decision on Witness Proofing, *supra* note 43, ¶ 4 (quoting *Karemera et al.*, Decision on Witness Proofing, *supra* note 43, ¶ 15).

65 *Id.* ¶ 23.

66 *Id.* ¶ 9 (quoting *Gacumbitsi*, Appeals Judgment, *supra* note 60, ¶ 74).

67 *Id.* ¶ 12.

68 *Id.* ¶ 4 (quoting *Karemera et al.*, Decision on Witness Proofing, *supra* note 43, ¶ 15).

2. The ICC

In contrast to the ad hoc criminal Tribunals, ICC Chambers have explicitly prohibited many aspects of witness proofing as defined in the ICTY and ICTR jurisprudence and do not allow for direct contact between parties to a case and prospective witnesses pre-testimony.

The ICC first addressed the issue of witness proofing in depth in 2006 during its inaugural trial in the *Lubanga* case, when the prosecution informed the Pre-Trial Chamber in a status conference that it would be conducting proofing sessions with a witness in the coming week.[69] The prosecution was requested to refrain from undertaking any proofing until the Chamber determined whether it was permissible.[70] Subsequently, the Pre-Trial Chamber rendered its decision on the matter, first addressing the specific question of what is meant by witness proofing, noting that national jurisdictions use various terminology "in connection with those practices followed to prepare a witness to give oral testimony before a court."[71]

Ultimately, the Pre-Trial Chamber settled on a narrower definition of witness proofing than that applied in the ad hoc jurisprudence. According to the Chamber, proofing consists of meetings between parties and prospective witnesses encompassing the following practices: 1) allowing a witness to read his/her statement and refresh his/her memory with respect to the evidence he/she will give; 2) putting to the witness questions that a party intends to ask in the order in which they will be asked during the witness's testimony; and 3) inquiring about any further information that the witness may potentially give at trial, incriminatory or exculpatory.[72] That definition excludes other measures such as: 1) providing the witness an opportunity to become acquainted with those who will examine him/her in Court; 2) familiarizing the witness with the courtroom, proceedings and participants in the proceedings; 3) reassuring the witness about his/her role in the proceedings; 4) discussing matters related to safety and security with the witness; 5) reinforcing the witness's obligation to tell the truth during testimony; and 6) explaining the process of examination-in-chief, cross-examination and re-examination.[73] With regard to these other measures, the Pre-Trial Chamber held that they constitute a separate practice, which it labeled "witness familiarisation."[74]

---

69 *Lubanga*, Pre-Trial Chamber Decision, *supra* note 4, ¶ 1.
70 *Id.* ¶ 2.
71 *Id.* ¶ 12.
72 *Id.* ¶ 17.
73 *Id.* ¶ 14.
74 *Id.* ¶ 23.

Having established that distinction, the Pre-Trial Chamber turned to consider the admissibility of both witness proofing and witness familiarization, as it had defined them. In the end, it concluded that witness proofing is not authorized in ICC proceedings under the Statute, Rules or Regulations of the Court or under any other applicable law outlined within the ICC's Statute.[75] In contrast, witness familiarization is in fact *mandated* under specific provisions of the Statute and Rules of the Court.[76] Furthermore, under a plain reading of the Statute and Rules and in light of their object and purpose, the Court's VWU should, in consultation with the relevant party, be solely responsible for witness familiarization.[77]

Subsequently, the prosecution raised the issue of witness proofing again before the Trial Chamber who agreed with the Pre-Trial Chamber's decision. This was despite the fact that the prosecution stressed that, contrary to the Pre-Trial Chamber's definition of witness proofing, it "would not constitute a rehearsal of the questions that would be asked in court."[78] Rather, witness proofing would constitute:

> providing written statements to a witness a few days prior to their testimony; meeting with the witness at that time to remind the witness of their duty to tell the truth; discussing with the witness during this meeting information which may inform a decision about the protection of the witness; addressing the area of the witness statement that will be dealt with in Court; and showing the witness any potential exhibits for his comment prior to testimony.[79]

The Chamber first agreed with the Pre-Trial Chamber in separating out witness familiarization measures from "the practice of substantive preparation of a witness for their in-court testimony."[80] Furthermore, it found the Pre-Trial Chamber's outline of witness familiarization measures to be appropriate and clarified further the process of assisting witnesses to fully understand the court proceedings.[81] It also emphasized that familiarization should be undertaken by the VWU so long as it works "in consultation with the party calling the witness, in order to undertake the practice . . . in the most appropriate way" with respect to any special characteristics or vulnerabilities of the witness.[82] In addition, the Chamber noted that

---

75 *Id.* ¶¶ 28, 33–4, 42.
76 *Id.* ¶¶ 20–23.
77 *Id.* ¶¶ 24–27.
78 *Lubanga*, Trial Chamber Decision, *supra* note 5, ¶ 14.
79 *Id.* ¶ 48.
80 *Id.* ¶ 28.
81 *Id.* ¶¶ 30–2.
82 *Id.* ¶¶ 33–4.

two of the measures within the prosecution's definition of witness proofing were already appropriately provided for in this familiarization process – reminding witnesses of their obligation to tell the truth and the implementation of any necessary protective measures.[83]

With respect to substantive preparation of a witness for giving testimony, or witness proofing, the Chamber agreed with the Pre-Trial Chamber that there is no legal basis for it generally before the ICC, and that prohibited it in the *Lubanga* proceedings.[84] It nevertheless concluded that one aspect of proofing should be part of the witness familiarization process: provision of past statements made by a witness to that witness prior to giving in-court testimony.[85] However, the Chamber stressed that provision of these statements should be transmitted by the VWU after receiving them from the party calling the witness and shall be "for the sole purpose of refreshing memory"[86] such that there shall not be "any discussion on the topics to be dealt with in court or any exhibits which may be shown to a witness in court."[87] In addition, while "witnesses will be allowed to meet the advocates who are to examine them in court" during familiarization, it will only be "under the supervision of the staff of the VWU . . . [and] the VWU will not facilitate any further contact between the witness and the party calling him or her until their [sic] testimony is complete."[88]

Finally, the Chamber concluded that the prohibition of witness proofing does not apply to expert witnesses[89] such that "discussion between the parties and their experts may take place at any stage prior to calling the witness."[90] The Chamber agreed with the prosecution that "the importance of lack of rehearsal and the need for spontaneity do not apply" to expert witnesses, and that it would be helpful for the parties "to meet their experts in conference to discuss the relevant scientific and technical issues" "thereby leading to a focussed and accurate presentation of the evidence" at trial.[91] As such, in the *Lubanga* case, parties were allowed to

---

[83] *Id.* ¶ 49.

[84] *Id.* ¶¶ 35–45, 57.

[85] *Id.* ¶ 50.

[86] *Id.* ¶¶ 55, 57.

[87] *Id.* ¶ 51.

[88] Prosecutor v. Lubanga Dyilo, Case No. ICC-01/04-01/06-1351, Decision Regarding the Protocol on the Practices to Be Used to Prepare Witnesses for Trial, ¶ 5 (May 23, 2008) [hereinafter *Lubanga*, Decision Regarding Protocol to Prepare Witnesses for Trial].

[89] Prosecutor v. Lubanga Dyilo, Case No. ICC-01/04-01/06, Transcript of Jan. 16, 2009 Hearing at 29:3–11 (Jan. 16, 2009) (No. ICC-01/04-01/06-T-104-ENG).

[90] Amended Unified Protocol of 7 December 2010, *supra* note 7, ¶ 32.

[91] Prosecutor v. Lubanga Dyilo, Case No. ICC-01/04-01/06, Transcript of Jan.

jointly proof expert witnesses or separately where joint instruction was not possible.[92]

Subsequent to the Trial Chamber's decision in *Lubanga,* Trial Chamber II implicitly adopted that approach in the *Katanga and Ngudjolo* case[93] "by adopting Unified Protocols for witnesses' familiarisation in which no provisions for witnesses' preparation by the parties, or proofing" were included.[94] In addition, Trial Chamber III in the *Bemba* case explicitly adopted the *Lubanga* approach.[95] While other Trial Chambers have made some adjustments to the *Lubanga* approach for their specific proceedings through adoption of Unified Protocols for preparing witnesses for trial, these have been limited to relatively minor variations or added clarifications to the *Lubanga* approach.[96]

In sum, the current approach taken by Trial Chambers at the ICC is as follows. Witness proofing, defined as a party meeting with its witness to discuss substantively that witness' evidence by, for example, examining any past witness statements that will be dealt with in court or any potential exhibits that may be submitted during the witness' testimony (but not rehearsing the questions that will be asked of the witness in court), is prohibited.[97] On the other hand, the VWU is allowed to meet with witnesses for purposes of witness familiarization, which commences once a "witness arrives in the Netherlands, or at the location of testimony where different from the seat of the Court, prior to giving evidence."[98] During

---

16, 2009 Hearing at 28:22–25; 29:3–11 (Jan. 16, 2009) (No. ICC-01/04-01/06-T-104-ENG).

[92] Prosecutor v. Lubanga Dyilo, Case No. ICC-01/04-01/06, Decision on the Procedures to be Adopted for Instructing Expert Witnesses, ¶ 12 *et seq.* (Dec. 10, 2007) (finding that Regulations 44 (2) and (4) and 54 (m) of the Court, ICC-BD/01-01-04 (May 26, 2004) allow for the Trial Chamber to direct the instruction of expert witnesses jointly or separately by the participants in a case).

[93] Prosecutor v. Katanga & Ngudjolo, Case No. ICC-01/04-01/07-1134, Decision on a Number of Procedural Issues Raised by the Registry, ¶ 18 (May 14, 2009) [hereinafter *Katanga & Ngudjolo*, Decision on Procedural Issues].

[94] Prosecutor v. Bemba Gombo, Case No. ICC-01/05-01/08, Decision on the Unified Protocol on the Practices Used to Prepare and Familiarise Witnesses for Giving Testimony at Trial, ¶ 34 (Nov. 18, 2010) [hereinafter *Bemba*, Decision on Unified Protocol].

[95] *Id.*

[96] *See generally Lubanga*, Decision Regarding Protocol to Prepare Witnesses for Trial, *supra* note 88; *Katanga & Ngudjolo*, Decision on Procedural Issues, *supra* note 93; *Bemba*, Decision on Unified Protocol, *supra* note 94.

[97] *Lubanga*, Trial Chamber Decision, *supra* note 5, ¶¶ 51–7.

[98] Amended Unified Protocol of 7 December 2010, *supra* note 7, ¶ 28.

that process, the party calling the witness is not allowed to meet with the witness unsupervised outside of court until after testimony is given.[99] Witness familiarization consists of the following measures intended for preparing witnesses:

(a) Assisting the witness to understand fully the court's proceedings, its participants and their respective roles;
(b) Reassuring witnesses about their role in proceedings before the court;
(c) Ensuring that witnesses clearly understand that they are under a strict legal obligation to tell the truth when testifying;
(d) Explaining to the witnesses the process of examination;
(e) Discussing matters relating to the security and safety of witnesses in order to determine the necessity of applications for protective measures;
(f) Providing witnesses with an opportunity to acquaint themselves [briefly] with the people who may examine them in court;
(g) "Walking witnesses through" the courtroom and its procedure prior to the day of their testimony in order to acquaint them with the layout of the court, and particularly where the various participants will be seated and the technology that will be used in order to minimize any confusion or intimidation.[100]

During familiarization, the VWU will also "make available to the witness a copy of any witness statement they may have made in order to refresh their memory"[101] as well as "any document or information generated or provided by the witness when giving any of his/her previous statements"[102] as provided by the calling party, but may not discuss the statements or information substantively with the witness.[103] Consequently, "[t]he VWU will not be in a position to answer any legal or factual questions that might arise in relation" to the statements and must "remind the witness that any such questions should be ventilated in Court."[104] Finally, the prohibition against witness proofing or meeting with witnesses at any stage prior to

---

99 *Id.* ¶¶ 30, 31, 104. After a witness gives testimony, a Chamber may still prevent that witness and the calling party from meeting if the circumstances of the case require it. *Id.* ¶ 104.

100 *Lubanga*, Trial Chamber Decision, *supra* note 5, ¶ 53.

101 *Id.* ¶ 55.

102 Amended Unified Protocol of 7 December 2010, *supra* note 7, ¶ 83.

103 *Id.* ¶¶ 91–3.

104 *Id.* ¶ 92.

giving testimony in order to substantively discuss their evidence generally does not apply to expert witnesses.[105]

B. The Rationales for the Approaches

So how is it that Chambers at the ICTY, ICTR, SCSL and ICC have arrived at such different positions on witness proofing in international criminal proceedings, thereby mirroring the variance found in national legal systems? As reflected in the various holdings just summarized, the different choices made by Chambers at the tribunals on these two issues flow from their perception of their hybrid procedural framework as being more adversarial or inquisitorial in nature. Indeed, there is an "underlying 'system dimension' of proofing" and, as noted previously, the rules and underlying philosophies of the adversarial and inquisitorial systems divide sharply with respect to the production, presentation and primary purpose of witness testimony as evidence.[106] Consequently, in order to understand the various rationale offered by tribunals in support of these two approaches, it is important to note how they perceive themselves procedurally and how this then results in them being at odds on the following interrelated issues: 1) *who* should be allowed to be in contact with witnesses pre-testimony; and 2) *what* should be the nature of their contact.

1. Who may contact witnesses

On the first issue, as detailed previously, Chambers at the ICTY, ICTR and SCSL have concluded that *parties* to a case may engage with witnesses. In contrast, at the ICC, any such direct contact by parties with witnesses is strictly prohibited; instead, only VWU officers may meet with witnesses directly.[107]

Justification for the ICTY/ICTR/SCSL approach is based primarily on the nature of their procedural framework and the understanding that "[i]t is widespread practice in jurisdictions where there is an adversary procedure" for parties, as those responsible for leading evidence at trial and to whom witnesses "belong," to meet with potential witnesses beforehand.[108]

---

105 *Id.* ¶¶ 32, 35.

106 Ambos, *supra* note 13, at 606.

107 *Lubanga*, Trial Chamber Decision, *supra* note 5, ¶¶ 53, 55–6. However, the VWU may arrange for brief, supervised meetings between witnesses and the parties for purposes of allowing witnesses to know ahead of time who will be examining them in court. Amended Unified Protocol of 7 December 2010, *supra* note 7, ¶¶ 30, 31, 69–73.

108 *Limaj et al.*, Decision on Witness Proofing, *supra* note 2, at 2 (cited with

In this context, parties have both a right[109] and a duty to hold these meetings.

In previous cases, the ICTY Appeals Chamber has looked to specific provisions in the Statute and Rules explicitly giving the prosecution the power to question potential witnesses during investigations as a legal basis for proofing.[110] These include: Article 18(2) of the ICTY Statute, which gives the prosecution "the power to question suspects, victims and witnesses";[111] Rule 39 of the ICTY Rules of Procedure and Evidence (RPE), which allows the prosecution in conducting an investigation to "summon and question suspects, victims and witnesses";[112] and Rule 54 of the ICTY RPE, which allows a Judge or Trial Chamber to issue an order or subpoena as may be necessary for the preparation or conduct of the trial,[113] including to require a prospective witness to attend at a designated place and time in order to be interviewed by a party.[114] On the basis of these provisions, the ICTY Appeals Chamber concluded that "both sides have the right to interview" witnesses on grounds that "[w]itnesses to a crime are the property of neither the Prosecution nor the Defence" but are shared between them.[115] Both parties may have a legitimate need for interviewing a witness in order to procure important information for building their cases, and each party has the right to do so in order to avoid the opposing party having an unfair advantage at trial.[116] Finally, not only do parties have this right, but the Appeals Chamber found that "it would be contrary to the duty owed by counsel to their client to act skillfully and

---

approval in *Sesay et al.*, Decision on Exclusion of Testimony, *supra* note 62, ¶ 30; *Milutinović et al.*, Decision on Witness Proofing, *supra* note 44, ¶¶ 16, 18–19; *Karemera et al.*, Decision on Witness Proofing, *supra* note 43, ¶¶ 13, 15); *Haradinaj et al.*, Decision on Witness Proofing Sessions, *supra* note 14, ¶ 17.

109 *Karemera et al.*, Decision on Witness Proofing, *supra* note 43, ¶ 9 (finding that the practice of witness proofing "is in accordance with the Appeals Chamber's finding that each party has the right to interview a potential witness").

110 *See, e.g.*, Prosecutor v. Mrksić, Case No. IT-95-13/1-AR73, Decision on Defence Interlocutory Appeal on Communication with Potential Witnesses of the Opposite Party (ICTY July 30, 2003) [hereinafter *Mrksić*, Decision on Communication with Potential Witnesses].

111 ICTY Statute, Art. 18(2).

112 ICTY RPE, Rule 39.

113 *Id.*, Rule 54.

114 Prosecutor v. Krstić, Case No. IT-98-33-A, Decision on Application for Subpoenas, ¶ 10 (ICTY July 1, 2003).

115 *Mrksić*, Decision on Communication with Potential Witnesses, *supra* note 110.

116 Prosecutor v. Halilović, Case No. IT-01-48-AR73, Decision on the Issuance of Subpoenas, ¶¶ 12–15 (ICTY June 21, 2004).

with loyalty" to participate in a trial without first knowing what witnesses will say.[117] As such, it would be *unethical* for a party to fail to meet with prospective witnesses before they give evidence. This reasoning clearly is based in the adversarial systems' philosophy that the best means for ascertaining truth is through presentation and cross-examination of evidence by opposing parties bringing their case on a "fair playing field" before an impartial decision-maker exposed to the evidence for the first time.

Furthermore, the ICTY/ICTR Chambers have allowed contact between parties and witnesses on grounds that there are several safeguards in place to mitigate any risk of improper influence by a party on the forthcoming testimony of a witness. First, under the Tribunals' rules, "intentionally seeking to interfere with a witness's testimony is prohibited,"[118] and there are "clear standards of professional conduct" that govern when counsel meet with witnesses.[119] Second, through careful cross-examination, an opposing party may "explore the impact of preparation on the witness's testimony and use this to call into question the witness's credibility."[120] Third, where evidence of any impropriety comes to light, the Tribunals' rules allow for Chambers to take appropriate action through initiating contempt proceedings and excluding tampered evidence.[121] As noted previously, most adversarial models of justice at the national level have similar safeguards in place and have considered that witness preparation for trial is so important that this outweighs any potential for abuse of the proofing process.

In contrast, the ICC approach has been based, primarily, on a belief that from a systemic perspective, the ICC procedural framework requires no direct contact between witnesses and parties pre-testimony. Indeed, the *Lubanga* Trial Chamber found that under the ICC Statute, certain provisions depart from that of the more adversarial model found in the ad hoc Tribunals,[122] towards a mixed model that features more civil law

---

117 *Karemera et al.*, Appeal Decision on Witness Proofing, *supra* note 43, ¶ 10 (citing Prosecutor v. Krstić, Case No. IT-98-33-A, Decision on Application for Subpoenas, ¶ 8 (ICTY July 1, 2003)).

118 *Id.* ¶ 13

119 *Limaj et al.*, Decision on Witness Proofing, *supra* note 2, at 3; *Karemera et al.*, Decision on Witness Proofing, *supra* note 43, ¶¶ 16, 24.

120 *Karemera et al.*, Appeal Decision on Witness Proofing, *supra* note 43, ¶ 13.

121 *Id.*

122 *Lubanga*, Trial Chamber Decision, *supra* note 5, ¶ 45 (reasoning that under the ICC procedural framework, the prosecution is tasked with investigating both exculpatory and incriminatory evidence; the Bench is allowed to have greater intervention; and victims are allowed to participate). *See also Lubanga*, Pre-Trial Chamber Decision, *supra* note 4, ¶ 26 & nn. 29–30 (noting its past decisions

notions, "introducing additional and novel elements to aid the process of establishing the truth."[123] Consequently, "the procedure of preparation of witnesses before trial is not easily transferable into the system of law created by the ICC Statute and Rules."[124] Underlying this conclusion is the ICC's understanding as to whom the witnesses "belong" in a criminal proceeding. As stated by the *Lubanga* Pre-Trial Chamber, the no-contact rule for parties "is consistent with the principle that witnesses to a crime are the property neither of the Prosecution nor of the Defence . . . but [are] *witnesses of the Court,*"[125] a principle directly found in inquisitorial national systems.

As such, a further reason for the no-contact rule is an ethical one. The *Lubanga* Pre-Trial Chamber found that under the object and purpose of the ICC Statute and Rules, only the VWU should be allowed direct access to a witness in order to ensure "thorough and *objective* preparation of witnesses."[126] In this way, any risk of witnesses being exposed to a biased interpretation of ICC applicable law or of witness' testimony being improperly influenced in some way is minimized as much as possible.[127] This is important according to the *Lubanga* Trial Chamber in order to preserve "helpful spontaneity during the giving of evidence by a witness" which is "of paramount importance to the Court's ability to find the truth."[128] Again, this emphasis on eliminating any potential risk of taint of witness testimony so as to preserve its objectivity and spontaneity for ascertaining truth is grounded in the inquisitorial approach.

---

regulating parties' contact pre-confirmation hearing with witnesses that the other party intends to rely upon at the hearing, and Rule 140 of the ICC Rules, which refers to "question the witness" or "examine the witness" with respect to the parties' questioning of witnesses at trial rather than "examination-in-chief," "cross-examination" and "re-examination").

123 *Lubanga*, Trial Chamber Decision, *supra* note 5, ¶ 45.

124 *Id.*

125 *Id.* ¶ 26 (emphasis added). *See also id.* ¶ 34. While the ICTY Appeals Chamber has also confirmed that witnesses are not property of one party over the other, it has stated that they are shared between the parties such that each has the right to interview all witnesses in a case. *Mrksić*, Decision on Communication with Potential Witnesses, *supra* note 110.

126 *Lubanga*, Pre-Trial Chamber Decision, *supra* note 4, ¶ 27 (emphasis added).

127 *Id.*

128 *Lubanga*, Trial Chamber Decision, *supra* note 5, ¶ 52.

2. The nature of witness contact

Turning to the second issue, what should be the nature of interaction with witnesses before testifying, the ICTR Appeals Chamber has approved of witness proofing and stipulated that the practice broadly involves preparation of witnesses to testify at trial both with respect to the substance of their testimony as well as with respect to certain logistical matters surrounding the proceedings.[129] As in the United States, the exact measures to be taken or number of meetings to be held[130] for purposes of proofing are largely left to the discretion of the parties according to the circumstances required by a particular case, except that they may not compromise or manipulate the evidence of a witness leading to distortion of the truth.[131] One such prohibited measure explicitly highlighted by the ICTR is that of rehearsing or practicing with a witness the exact questions to be asked during testimony at trial,[132] similar to the approach found in England and Wales.[133]

ICTY and ICTR Trial Chambers have reasoned that witness proofing, broadly defined, is appropriate first, because it upholds certain rights of the defense, including the rights to an expeditious and fair trial. On the right to an expeditious trial, one ICTY Trial Chamber reasoned that the essence of witness proofing is a "genuine attempt to clarify a witness' evidence" in order to facilitate a smooth and orderly trial[134] which, as in adversarial systems generally, is led by the parties. As such, witness proofing allows for: 1) identifying in full all of the facts known to the witness that are relevant to the indictment given that earlier interviews took place during the investigative phase before confirmation of the indictment by investigators with a different professional perception on what is relevant; 2) refreshing the witness's recollection given that interviews with investigators often take place long before giving evidence at trial; and 3) identifying any deficiencies and differences in a witness's recollection as compared to earlier statements thereby enabling the witness to provide a "more accurate, complete, orderly and efficient presentation of the evidence" at trial.[135]

---

129 *Karemera et al.*, Appeal Decision on Witness Proofing, *supra* note 43, ¶ 9.

130 *Limaj et al.*, Decision on Witness Proofing, *supra* note 2, at 3.

131 *Karemera et al.*, Appeal Decision on Witness Proofing, *supra* note 43, ¶¶ 4, 9.

132 *Karemera et al.*, Decision on Witness Proofing, *supra* note 43, ¶ 23.

133 Code of Conduct of the Bar of England & Wales, 8th ed., October 31, 2004, as amended in 2012, ¶ 705(a); Crown Prosecution Service, Code of Practice, *supra* note 28; *Momodou*, *supra* note 28, ¶ 61.

134 *Milutinović et al.*, Decision on Witness Proofing, *supra* note 44, ¶ 16.

135 *Limaj et al.*, Decision on Witness Proofing, *supra* note 2, at 2; *see also Karemera et al.*, Decision on Witness Proofing, *supra* note 43, ¶ 17; *Milutinović et al.*, Decision on Witness Proofing, *supra* note 44, ¶ 20.

As for the defense's right to a fair trial, the ICTR Appeals Chamber in *Karemera et al.* noted that the practice of witness proofing by Chambers is permissible under Rule 89(B) of the Tribunal's Rules, which "generally confers discretion on the Trial Chamber to apply 'rules of evidence which will best favour a *fair* determination of the matter before it.'"[136] Specifically, witness proofing was found to facilitate fairness because it provides notice to the defense of any different or additional recollections of a witness compared to earlier statements made during the investigative phase so as to avoid undue surprise.[137] Witness proofing therefore fulfills disclosure obligations[138] and allows for the defense to prepare sufficiently for cross-examination.[139] This emphasis on upholding fairness in particular reflects the adversarial law understanding that it is necessary at trial to establish a fair playing field on which two competing parties lead evidence and verify the authenticity of that evidence through rigorous cross-examination as they work to prove their case.

ICTY and SCSL Chambers have further justified witness proofing as necessary for protecting the rights of witnesses. Chambers have noted that proofing assists witnesses in "cop[ing] with the process of giving evidence" before international tribunals, in a way that is different from the support provided by the Victims and Witnesses Section.[140] Through proofing sessions, witnesses are prepared to: face cultural differences; provide a detailed account of facts occurring long ago; testify about stressful events; give evidence in a structured and formal setting; testify with the use of translators; and deal with the overall stress of the proceedings generally.[141] Again, this emphasis on helping witnesses to cope with the stress of adversarial proceedings generally is also found in the system in England and Wales,[142] which allows for barristers as in-court advocates to meet with

---

[136] *Karemera et al.*, Appeal Decision on Witness Proofing, *supra* note 43, ¶ 8 (emphasis added).

[137] *Limaj et al.*, Decision on Witness Proofing, *supra* note 2, at 2; *see also Karemera et al.*, Decision on Witness Proofing, *supra* note 43, ¶ 17; *Milutinović et al.*, Decision on Witness Proofing, *supra* note 44, ¶ 20.

[138] *Karemera et al.*, Decision on Witness Proofing, *supra* note 43, ¶¶ 11–12.

[139] *Id.* ¶ 18.

[140] *Limaj et al.*, Decision on Witness Proofing, *supra* note 2, at 3. *Cf. Milutinović et al.*, Decision on Witness Proofing, *supra* note 44, ¶ 10; *Karemera et al.*, Decision on Witness Proofing, *supra* note 43, ¶ 10.

[141] *Limaj et al.*, Decision on Witness Proofing, *supra* note 2, at 3; *Sesay et al.*, Decision on Exclusion of Testimony, *supra* note 62, ¶ 33. *See also Milutinović et al.*, Decision on Witness Proofing, *supra* note 44, ¶ 9.

[142] *Momodou*, *supra* note 28, ¶ 62.

witnesses before giving testimony for this purpose as an exception to the general rule against such meetings.[143]

Finally, it was reasoned by the *Karemera et al.* Trial Chamber that widespread practice of proofing is "justified by the particularities of these proceedings that differentiate them from national criminal proceedings."[144] For example, as just noted, witnesses before international tribunals often must give testimony in stressful circumstances given cultural, legal and linguistic differences; furthermore, many witnesses must testify about quite traumatic events occurring long ago.[145] In addition, the factual complexity of proceedings at the international tribunals and the difficulties in gathering evidence results in the fact that:

> crimes charged in the indictment occurred many years ago and, in many cases, witness interviews took place a long time ago; matters that were relevant during the course of the investigations may need to be reviewed in light of the case that the Prosecution intends to present; . . . [and] the duration of the proceedings and the time elapsed between prior testimonies may require further interviews with a witness before he or she testifies and reduce the effect of surprise to the Defence in cases where the witness recollects elements that were not previously disclosed.[146]

On the other hand, the ICC Trial Chambers have so far rejected witness proofing as a proper practice before the ICC with respect to most witnesses,[147] insofar as it consists of any substantive discussion with witnesses regarding their forthcoming testimony.[148] Interestingly, however, the ICC has adopted witness familiarization measures often found in adversarial systems as part of the proofing process, so long as only the VWU has direct contact with the witnesses and does not discuss with the witness any prior statements or documentation obtained by parties during the investigation stage.[149] Such witness familiarization has been justified under the Court's rules, even at the risk of tainting the witness's testimony at trial, because they stipulate that the Court "take appropriate measures to protect the safety, physical and psychological well-being, dignity and

---

143 *See* Skilbeck, *supra* note 8.

144 *Karemera et al.*, Decision on Witness Proofing, *supra* note 43, ¶ 8.

145 *Limaj et al.*, Decision on Witness Proofing, *supra* note 2, at 3; *Sesay et al.*, Decision on Exclusion of Testimony, *supra* note 62, ¶ 33. *See also Milutinović et al.*, Decision on Witness Proofing, *supra* note 44, ¶ 9.

146 *Karemera et al.*, Decision on Witness Proofing, *supra* note 43, ¶ 17.

147 As noted earlier, expert witnesses are excluded from this rule.

148 *Lubanga*, Trial Chamber Decision, *supra* note 5, ¶¶ 51–7.

149 *Id.* ¶¶ 53–7; Amended Unified Protocol of 7 December 2010, *supra* note 7, ¶¶ 91–3.

privacy of victims and witnesses."[150] In so doing, the VWU is encouraged to "work in consultation with the party calling the witness" given that it is "likely to have greater insight into the background and particular facets of the witness."[151] Furthermore, familiarization is allowed because it prevents "the witness from finding himself or herself in a disadvantageous position, or from being taken by surprise as a result of his or her ignorance of the process of giving oral testimony before the Court,"[152] a reason proffered in favor of familiarization in England and Wales particularly with respect to the adversarial nature of its criminal proceedings.[153]

Witness proofing is prohibited at the ICC on the basis that "it could lead to a distortion of the truth and may come dangerously close to constituting a rehearsal of in-court testimony."[154] However, the *Lubanga* Trial Chamber was not convinced that it is practically feasible to take steps to mitigate the danger of rehearsal.[155] Consequently, the Chamber would be prevented from hearing the "totality of an individual's recollection" given that "[a] rehearsed witness may not provide the entirety or the true extent of his memory or knowledge of a subject."[156] Similarly, drawing upon a civil law premise, the Chamber noted that proofing could diminish the spontaneity of the testimony, which could "be of paramount importance to the Court's ability to find the truth."[157] Finally, the *Lubanga* Trial Chamber found that the "pro-active role" of Judges under the ICC's procedural framework would help to prevent witnesses from being "re-victimized" by giving testimony or from being improperly influenced during the trial.[158]

In sum, the inquisitorial law "concept of witness as a witness of the Court or, as some may say, of the truth, prohibits not only the evidence related preparation of this witness but even his/her much more general familiarization by one party" at the ICC.[159] However, unlike in a purely inquisitorial model, the ICC allows for familiarization of a witness even at the risk of tainting the forthcoming evidence, which it mitigates by having familiarization conducted according to detailed regulations by the VWU

---

150 *Lubanga*, Pre-Trial Chamber Decision, *supra* note 4, ¶ 21(ii).
151 *Lubanga*, Trial Chamber Decision, *supra* note 5, ¶ 34.
152 *Lubanga*, Pre-Trial Chamber Decision, *supra* note 4, ¶ 20.
153 *Momodou*, *supra* note 28, ¶ 62.
154 *Lubanga*, Trial Chamber Decision, *supra* note 5, ¶ 51.
155 *Id.*
156 *Id.*
157 *Id.* ¶ 52.
158 *Id.*
159 Ambos, *supra* note 13, at 602.

as a neutral third party. This approach results from the explicit requirements under the ICC Statute and Rules for upholding the rights of witnesses and is a prime example of the ICC's *sui generis* approach to criminal procedure.[160]

IV. AN INTERNATIONAL HUMAN RIGHTS CRITIQUE

The previous sections have laid out the ICTY/ICTR/SCSL approach to witness proofing as compared to the ICC approach and their underlying rationale flowing from their mixed adversarial and inquisitorial procedural structures. It is also important to examine the soundness of each from an international human rights perspective. All international and hybrid criminal tribunals are obligated under their Statutes, either explicitly or implicitly, to respect certain international human rights norms codified in the 1966 International Covenant on Civil and Political Rights (ICCPR) while exercising their criminal jurisdiction.[161]

In the context of witness proofing, the rights of two key players in a criminal trial are at stake: the defendant and the witnesses. Article 14 of the ICCPR provides for the following defense rights that pertain to the issue of witness proofing specifically: 1) the right to a fair trial; 2) the right to adequate time for preparation of a proper defense; 3) the right to be tried without undue delay; 4) the right to effective assistance of counsel; and 5) the right to examine or have examined witnesses brought either for or against the defense.[162] Furthermore, Articles 6, 9 and 17 of the ICCPR protect individual rights that are relevant for witnesses who testify in international criminal proceedings: 1) the right to life; 2) the right to liberty and

---

160 Fatou Bensouda, *The ICC Statute—An Insider's Perspective on a* Sui Generis *System for Global Justice*, 36 N.C.J. INT'L L. & COM. REG. 277, 285 (2011).

161 *See, e.g.*, Updated Statute of the International Criminal Tribunal for the Former Yugoslavia, Arts. 20–22, Sept. 2009; Statute of the International Criminal Tribunal for Rwanda, Arts. 19–21, *as amended* Jan. 31, 2010; Statute of the Special Court for Sierra Leone, Art. 17, Jan. 16, 2002; Rome Statute of the International Criminal Court, Arts. 64, 67–68, July 17, 1998, 2187 U.N.T.S. 38544 (entered into force July 1, 2002) [hereinafter ICC Statute]; Law on the Establishment of the Extraordinary Chambers in the Courts of Cambodia, Arts. 33(new), 35(new), *with inclusion of amendments as promulgated on* Oct. 27, 2004, NS/RKM/1004/006; Statute of the Special Tribunal for Lebanon, Arts. 15–17, 21, 28, June 10, 2007.

162 International Covenant on Civil and Political Rights (ICCPR), Arts. 14(1), (3)(b)–(d), (3)(e), *adopted* December 16, 1966 (entered into force Mar. 23, 1976).

security of person; and 3) the right to be free from arbitrary or unlawful interference with privacy, family, honor and reputation.[163]

Turning first to protection of witness's rights, both the ICTY/ICTR/SCSL and ICC approaches to witness proofing seek to address the physical and psychological needs of witnesses before, during and after giving evidence at trial. Safety and privacy are addressed by discussing with the witness any need to apply to a Chamber for protective measures. Psychological well-being and dignity are addressed by explaining and acquainting a witness with the details of an international criminal trial, including: the courtroom setting; participants and their respective roles; the structure and format of the trial; technology; translation and any other issues that might contribute to overall stress in giving evidence before an international criminal tribunal. Furthermore, care is taken to discuss with witnesses any cultural differences, trauma or stress that they may experience when testifying about difficult and complicated past events.

However, the ICC approach, drawing from the inquisitorial model, seems limited in its ability to fully care for the physical and psychological needs of a witness given the prohibitions on direct contact with witnesses by the parties and on discussion about the substance of the prospective testimony. This is due to the presence of adversarial procedures in the ICC's mixed framework for production and presentation of evidence whereby the parties are still primarily responsible for calling witnesses and leading their questioning at trial.[164] For example, with respect to protective measures, it could prove difficult to assist a witness with an application to the relevant Chamber where the prospective testimony is the basis for the application. While the VWU is supposed to liaise with the party calling the witness on such matters, there is potential for oversight due to lack of communication or understanding.

In addition, it is not clear if the ICC approach effectively assists a witness in dealing with the psychological stress of testifying about extremely traumatic events occurring long ago. This is especially true when considering that a number of witnesses are so-called "vulnerable" witnesses. They may be victims of charged international crimes such as rape, they may be minors, or they may come from very different cultural and educational backgrounds.[165] Again, it would seem difficult to address potential trauma or any potential misunderstanding caused by

---

[163] ICCPR, Arts. 6, 9, 17.

[164] ICC Statute, Art. 69(2)–(3); ICC Rules of Procedure and Evidence (ICC RPE), Rule 140(2). JACKSON & SUMMERS, *supra* note 16, at 140–41.

[165] *See* WAR CRIMES RESEARCH OFFICE, AM. UNIV. WASHINGTON COLL. OF LAW, WITNESS PROOFING AT THE INTERNATIONAL CRIMINAL COURT 1, 5, 38–9 (2009).

a witness's background without going into the substance of his or her forthcoming testimony. Furthermore, one might query whether giving the witness his or her past statements without discussing them is sufficient for assisting that witness with recall at trial. If not, there is a danger, in a predominately adversarial system for calling and examination of witness testimony at trial, that perfectly relevant testimony is thrown out on the basis that it comes across as not credible. Finally, with the emphasis at the ICC on spontaneous testimony, there is a risk that questioning could quickly become a form of re-traumatization for a witness, threatening his or her privacy and dignity. This danger is especially relevant during the adversarial, cross-examination phase. While it is true that more proactive Judges found at the ICC may help to mitigate such questioning, the same Judges may unwittingly be the cause of the questioning or fail to effectively deter it without a full understanding of the witnesses' background because *they were called by the parties*. Consequently, "the opportunity for a witness to tell his/her story to the party calling him/her prior to giving evidence in Court may prove comforting, or at least, serve as a very beneficial, substantive preparation for what will occur in Court."[166]

As for defense rights, it is important to note that the exercise of witness proofing such as at the ICTY/ICTR/SCSL has potential to lead to infringement of defense rights, particularly, the rights to a fair trial, time to prepare a proper defense and to a trial without undue delay.[167] Indeed, under the adversarial procedures found for production and presentation of evidence at the ICTY/ICTR/SCSL, witness proofing has, at times, resulted in: "late proofing" just before trial;[168] late disclosure of "new material, and a failure to provide signed statements of new or changed evidence";[169] several disclosures of new material from proofing sessions bringing a witness's testimony in line with other prosecution evidence in a case;[170] "excessive proofing" of some witnesses either in the number or duration of sessions;[171] discrepancies between proofing notes disclosed by the prosecution to the defense and in-court testimony

---

166 Ozaki Dissenting Opinion, *supra* note 12, ¶ 24.

167 Ambos, *supra* note 13, at 614.

168 *Milutinović et al.*, Decision on Witness Proofing, *supra* note 44, ¶ 21.

169 *Limaj et al.*, Decision on Witness Proofing, *supra* note 2, at 3; *Milutinović et al.*, Decision on Witness Proofing, *supra* note 44, ¶ 21; *see also Karemera et al.*, Decision on Witness Proofing, *supra* note 43, ¶ 19.

170 *Karemera et al.*, Appeal Decision on Witness Proofing, *supra* note 43, ¶ 12.

171 *Limaj et al.*, Decision on Witness Proofing, *supra* note 2, at 3.

of witnesses;[172] and "admission of evidence outside of the scope of the Indictment."[173]

The ICC's approach may better contribute to fairness and efficiency at trial. This approach is an absolute safeguard against the prosecution using proofing unfairly by influencing or manipulating its case against the defense such that "rather than promoting the establishment of truth" actually counteracts it.[174] Further, it prevents the prosecution from conducting a "*de facto* delayed investigation,"[175] whereby the defense is overwhelmed with newly disclosed information from proofing sessions just prior to or even during trial. Although a Chamber may mitigate such unfairness by allowing the defense further time to review the new disclosures, or decide to exclude the additional information at trial, this may still result in infringement on the defense's right to a trial without undue delay.

That noted, the ban on witness proofing by the ICC also has the potential to undermine fairness and efficiency of international criminal proceedings, particularly where oral testimony is central to the proceedings as at the ICTY/ICTR/SCSL, and is primarily led by the parties. In this context, it is worth pointing out that while a ban on witness proofing prevents the parties from unfairly manipulating proceedings, it may nevertheless lead to an inability to identify improper influence on witnesses by non-parties to a case. This situation arose in the *Lubanga* case with the use of "intermediaries" who assisted the ICC with the logistics of locating and contacting witnesses during investigations.[176] As argued by one author:

> a competent and honest Prosecutor allowed to proof witnesses due to testify – and recording such sessions – would have found out, and alerted Judges and the Defence about, any suggestion that some intermediaries had exerted improper influence on witnesses, thus benefiting the search for the truth and saving the court time and resources.[177]

In addition, emphasis on having spontaneous testimony and probing the totality of an individual's recollection in the search for truth may increase the "likelihood that the evidence given by the witness will be

---

172 *Haradinaj et al.*, Decision on Witness Proofing Sessions, *supra* note 14, ¶ 2.

173 *Karemera et al.*, Decision on Witness Proofing, *supra* note 43, ¶ 19.

174 Eser, *supra* note 14, at 127.

175 Ozaki Dissenting Opinion, *supra* note 12, ¶ 23.

176 Guido Acquaviva, *The* Lubanga *Trial Comes to an End—Reflections on the First Conviction by the International Criminal Court*, J. Int'l Crim Just at 3, Advance Access published online August 8, 2012, doi:10.1093/jicj/mqs047.

177 *Id.* at 4.

incomplete, confused and ill-structured."[178] Why? Because of the reality of international criminal proceedings where: 1) witnesses often give their initial statements during the investigative phase long before the indictment is confirmed and the trial commences; and 2) those statements are taken by investigators who may have a very different professional perception as compared to the attorney at trial on what is relevant for a case.[179] Consequently, in these circumstances, witness proofing is crucial for refreshing the witness's recollection; identifying differences between a witness's present-day recollection as compared to earlier statements made long ago; identifying in full all the relevant facts known to a witness vis-à-vis the confirmed indictment; and avoiding undue delay caused by the party calling the witness not knowing what the witness is going to say.[180] Otherwise, a party "must utilize the skill of using non-leading questions to take the witness through their evidence as if blind-folded, but with the added difficulties of translation and, perhaps, a significant cultural chasm."[181]

Furthermore, witness proofing may prove particularly helpful for preparing witnesses to deal with the "magnitude and complexity" of international criminal proceedings, wherein they are asked to testify with respect to international crimes and modes of liability that often "necessitate the review of a large number of complicated and detailed exhibits, which may include various types of documents, audio-video records, different kinds of communications from governments or other entities, maps, and pictures."[182] In addition, witnesses in international criminal proceedings are often giving evidence not only in a criminal justice process that is foreign to them but also while having to use translation services. In the face of these challenges that flow from the nature of international criminal trials, proofing can assist the "smooth conduct of the proceedings by enabling a more accurate, complete, methodical and efficient presentation of the evidence."[183]

---

178 Ozaki Dissenting Opinion, *supra* note 12, ¶ 21.

179 *Limaj et al.*, Decision on Witness Proofing, *supra* note 2, at 2; *see also Karemera et al.*, Decision on Witness Proofing, *supra* note 43, ¶ 17; *Milutinović et al.*, Decision on Witness Proofing, *supra* note 44, ¶ 20.

180 *But see* Acquaviva, *supra* note 176, at 4 ("In general, and despite initial fears by many, decisions to bar proofing have arguably not had a great impact on the quality of the evidence led at trial or the length of the examination of witnesses" in the *Lubanga* case.), Advance Access published online August 8, 2012, doi:10.1093/jicj/mqs047.

181 Skilbeck, *supra* note 8, at 459.

182 Ozaki Dissenting Opinion, *supra* note 12, ¶ 22.

183 *Id. But see Lubanga*, Pre-Trial Chamber Decision, *supra* note 4, ¶ 34 & n. 38

Finally, the ICC approach may hinder the rights of the defense to effective assistance of counsel, to examine the witnesses brought against him or her, and to prepare a proper defense. Because the ICC approach prevents the defense from having notice of any different or additional recollections of a witness compared to earlier statements made during the investigative phase, it may not have time to prepare sufficiently for examination of witnesses on the basis of this new exculpatory or inculpatory information. While a Chamber may prevent any injustice in such a scenario by adjourning in order to allow the defense sufficient time to respond, this then results in delay of proceedings. Furthermore, under the ICC approach, defense witnesses may be deemed to lack credibility in the giving of evidence, or that evidence may be rejected for failure to be probative or relevant.

V. CONCLUDING OBSERVATIONS

From a human rights perspective, it would seem that the ICC's approach of banning witness proofing, insofar as it consists of direct pre-testimony contact between witnesses and parties and substantive discussion of the evidence, applies a hammer where a scalpel would suffice. As intimated earlier in this chapter, a number of problems with witness proofing have clearly developed over the years at the ICTY/ICTR/SCSL in the practice of witness proofing impacting negatively on defense rights in particular. However, it is important to note that these issues resulted from *how* proofing was conducted by the prosecution rather than the practice itself. Similarly, in none of those cases was proofing found to allow or lead to unfair coaching, training or otherwise influencing the evidence of a witness by definition.[184]

While the ICC approach eliminates the possibility of such prejudice to defense rights or unethical behavior resulting from the use of witness proofing, it may nevertheless still lead to infringement of those same rights by prohibiting the practice, as detailed previously. Indeed, as acknowledged by the defense in the ICTR *Karemera et al.* trial, witness proofing serves to assist the defense in better preparing its cross-examination and

---

(dismissing this argument by the Prosecution on grounds that under the principles of complementarity or universal jurisdiction, national legal systems with jurisdiction over international crimes have not changed their approach to witness proofing as an unethical or unlawful practice).

[184] *See, e.g.*, *Limaj et al.*, Decision on Witness Proofing, *supra* note 2, at 1, 3; *Karemera et al.*, Decision on Witness Proofing, *supra* note 43, ¶¶ 17–24.

expedites the proceedings.[185] In addition, the ICC approach could jeopardize effective protection of the rights and interests of witnesses in its proceedings, particularly vulnerable witnesses. Consequently, on balance, it would appear that the ICC approach has the potential to undermine more rights than it upholds.

The reason for this result, it seems, is because although the ICC procedural framework does perhaps reflect more of a blending of the common and civil law than the ICTY, ICTR or SCSL,[186] it is still primarily adversarial in nature when it comes to the procedure for submission and examination of evidence at trial.[187] At the ICC, similar to the ad hoc Tribunals: (1) oral evidence is central to the proceedings;[188] (2) witnesses are, for the most part, called by the parties;[189] and (3) in-court evidence results primarily from the questioning of the witnesses by the parties and Judges.[190] Consequently, "such a system . . . is different from the practice of many civil law jurisdictions, where witnesses have been thoroughly questioned by a judge (*juge d'instruction*) mandated to instruct the case, and where statements produced by such examination are automatically included in the case file, as highly probative evidence at the trial stage."[191] As noted previously, such a system is found in the ECCC and, logically, witness proofing is not found to be necessary before that tribunal.[192] Therefore, in this context, contrary to the view of the ICC *Lubanga* Trial

---

185 *Karemera et al.*, Decision on Witness Proofing, *supra* note 43, ¶ 18.

186 *Lubanga*, Trial Chamber Decision, *supra* note 5, ¶ 45 (reasoning that under the ICC procedural framework, the prosecution is tasked with investigating both exculpatory and incriminatory evidence; the Bench is allowed to have greater intervention; and victims are allowed to participate). *See also Lubanga*, Pre-Trial Chamber Decision, *supra* note 4, ¶ 26 & nn. 29–30 (noting its past decisions regulating parties' contact pre-confirmation hearing with witnesses that the other party intends to rely upon at the hearing, and Rule 140 of the ICC Rules, which refers to "question the witness" or "examine the witness" with respect to the parties' questioning of witnesses at trial rather than "examination-in-chief," "cross-examination" and "re-examination.").

187 Ozaki Dissenting Opinion, *supra* note 12, ¶ 20. *See also* JACKSON & SUMMERS, *supra* note 16, at 140–41.

188 ICC Statute, Art. 69(2).

189 ICC Statute, Art. 69(3).

190 ICC RPE, Rule 140(2).

191 Ozaki Dissenting Opinion, *supra* note 12, ¶ 20.

192 *See generally* ECCC Internal Rules (Rev. 8) (Aug. 3, 2011), Rules 24, 50, 55, 60, 80, 84, 91 (regarding procedures for investigations and interviewing witnesses by investigative judges and submission of the case file to the Trial Chamber, which reflects the civil law model, and makes witness proofing unnecessary). *See also* Skilbeck, *supra* note 8; MACKENZIE ET AL., *supra* note 8, at 227–8.

Chamber,[193] transposition of the more adversarial approach to witness proofing at the *ad hoc* Tribunals to ICC proceedings may well have been quite appropriate.

In conclusion, an alternative approach that the ICC could have taken would have been to allow witness proofing as necessary for its more adversarial approach to production and presentation of evidence at trial, but actively and systematically to regulate the practice in such a way as to avoid abuse of the process by the parties or better safeguard against any risk of taint or unethical tampering of the evidence.[194] Instead, through this "pick and mix" approach to building a new hybrid international criminal justice system, there is a danger that the ICC, with respect to the issue of witness proofing, has "a system that contains none of the checks and balances that bring order to a national system."[195] Only time will tell whether the ICC's prohibition of witness proofing within its procedural framework leads to the infringement of defense and witness rights described above and, if so, whether ICC Chambers are able to find ways to prevent that infringement, perhaps through a more inquisitorial approach to collecting and leading the evidence at trial. It is suggested that careful attention should be paid to the application of this approach at the ICC and adjustments made where necessary for ensuring full respect for the rights of defendants and witnesses in the process.

---

193 *Lubanga*, Trial Chamber Decision, *supra* note 5, ¶ 45.

194 *See, e.g.*, Ozaki Dissenting Opinion, *supra* note 12, ¶¶ 26–7 (suggesting the following safeguards: creating clear guidelines that provide a definition and detailed guidance on the practice of proofing, including a list of recommended, acceptable, and prohibited conduct, together with a strict code of conduct applicable to all counsel; video-audio recording of proofing sessions; allowing the presence of a neutral third-party at proofing sessions such as someone from the VWU; fixing a cut-off date for witness proofing before trial; or training counsel on the purpose of witness proofing).

195 *See* Skilbeck, *supra* note 8.

4. Written and oral evidence

Guido Acquaviva*

I. INTRODUCTION

This chapter mainly focuses on the system of rules regulating the admission of evidence into the trial record in international criminal proceedings.[1] Particular reference will be made to the practices of the main international criminal courts and tribunals – the International Criminal Tribunal for the former Yugoslavia (ICTY), the International Criminal Tribunal for Rwanda (ICTR), the Special Court for Sierra Leone (SCSL), the International Criminal Court (ICC) – as well as certain unique facets of the Extraordinary Chambers in the Courts of Cambodia (ECCC) and the Special Tribunal for Lebanon (STL).

As mentioned in the Introductory chapter of this volume, legal systems based on the common law tradition (adversarial systems) developed strict sets of exclusionary rules for the admission of evidence, for instance limiting the admission of written statements and hearsay in criminal proceedings. These rules were premised, inter alia, on the assumption that, in the courtroom, juries should generally be exposed only to first-hand knowledge of the events in question. This allows a sort of "duel" of the parties who, through strictly regulated examination and cross-examination procedures, are able to present evidence which will lead to a conviction only if guilt is demonstrated beyond reasonable doubt.[2] In essence, according to

---

* LLM (Tulane Law School), PhD (University of Padova). Chef de Cabinet, Office of the President, Special Tribunal for Lebanon. The opinions expressed in this article are those of the author and do not necessarily reflect those of the Special Tribunal.

[1] International criminal procedure, as this volume shows, is generally understood as including the law of evidence which in some domestic systems (mainly common law ones) would instead be considered as a separate area.

[2] In common law, the many exclusionary evidence rules have the practical result of leading to a significant use of oral testimony. It is often contended that the principle of "immediacy" in civil law systems has a similar effect. Mirjan Damaška, *Evidentiary Barriers to Conviction and Two Models of Criminal Procedure: A*

the pure common law tradition, nothing really counts as "evidence" until and unless it is heard orally at trial.[3]

Systems of criminal procedure stemming from the civil law tradition vary widely. For the purposes of this chapter, however, these systems have been historically premised on the assumption that judges – and not jurors – are called to be the fact-finders, and that they will generally be guided by the "intimate conviction" (from the French expression "*conviction intime*"), their inner belief that guilt has been established by the prosecuting authorities. In practical terms, of course, the standard of proof "beyond reasonable doubt" has come to be seen as essential in the civil law tradition, too.[4] Nonetheless, in their quest for the truth, judges in these systems have traditionally been afforded greater latitude in admitting and assessing both oral and written evidence than in common law systems,[5] although this has been changing in recent times.[6] Civil law judges (even lay judges, who are required in some systems to decide on allegations of the most serious crimes) have historically been the adjudicators of both procedure and substance. This means that they will see all of the evidence, even that against which a party raises admissibility issues. Common law judges, on the other hand, routinely exercise their duty of "screening" the

---

Comparative Study, 121 U. PA. L. REV. 506, 517 (1973) (tracing the historical origins of such approach).

[3] John R. Spencer, *Introduction*, *in* EUROPEAN CRIMINAL PROCEDURES 21 (Mireille Delmas-Marty & John R. Spencer eds., 2002).

[4] See, for instance: Cour de cassation [Cass.] [Supreme Court for Judicial Matters] crim., Jan. 24, 2007, judgment n. 06-82.769 (Fr.) (rejecting the arguments that the appellate court had convicted despite reasonable doubt); Cassazione Sezione Penale, Nov. 24, 2003, n. 45276 (*Andreotti et al.*) (It.).

[5] See Section 244 of the German Code of Criminal Procedure, which reads, in part: "In its search for the truth, the Court shall extend the taking of evidence to any fact or means of proof relevant to the decision." Section 258 of the Austrian Code of Criminal procedure provides in part: "The court shall examine the evidence carefully and conscientiously with regard to its trustworthiness and conclusiveness separately and as a whole. Judges shall not decide upon the question of whether or not a particular fact has been proven according to formal [or statutory] rules of evidence, but only according to their own conclusions drawn on the basis of their careful examination of all of the evidence on the record." All translations of non-English case law and legislation are the author's own.

[6] John R. Spencer, *Evidence*, *in* EUROPEAN CRIMINAL PROCEDURES, *supra* note 3, at 600–602. An extreme exception to the regime of free evidence is provided by the Dutch Code of Criminal Procedure, which requires that a conviction be based only on a list of enumerated "legal means of gathering evidence" (Articles 338 and 339). A brief account of the evolution of the systems in the civil law tradition is JOHN HENRY MERRYMAN & ROGELIO PÉREZ-PERDOMO, THE CIVIL LAW TRADITION 125–33 (2007).

evidence in order for jurors – the fact-finders – not to come in contact with evidence deemed unreliable or of unjust origin.[7]

Contemporary international criminal tribunals have witnessed an evolution of at least part of the law applicable to the presentation, admission, and evaluation of evidence.[8] Two issues are here essential to understand: (i) the general rules on the admission of evidence, and (ii) the dichotomy between oral and written evidence.

As regards the first issue, from their inception the ad hoc tribunals have relied on the traditional civil law approach of not burdening fact-finders with strict rules of evidence, doing without most of the complexities of the exclusionary rules so essential to common lawyers and, progressively, to most contemporary civil law systems. However (and this is the second issue), regarding the admission of evidence, the ICTY and the ICTR originally tended to follow a typical common law approach in clearly favoring oral evidence over written documents or statements.[9] While the former assumption has essentially remained unchanged, the latter has undergone significant developments since the time the Rules of Procedure and Evidence (RPE) were first drafted.[10] The ICTY Appeals Chamber has aptly observed that "while the system under which the Tribunal's rules of evidence operates is predominantly adversarial, the jurisprudence – and the Rules themselves – have recognized from the beginning the necessity, and desirability, of certain features which do not accord with a strictly adversarial criminal procedure."[11] Paramount amongst these features is

---

[7] When a jury trial is waived and a bench trial is conducted, the judge becomes the trier of fact and will also have the task of determining whether the evidence is both relevant and admissible. This is premised on the assumption that, unlike jurors, professional judges are conceptually able to distinguish the two tasks. The same assumption forms the basis of international criminal trials, where no juries exist.

[8] As discussed in the *Introduction* to this volume, ICTY and ICTR Rules of Procedure and Evidence (RPE) are adopted and amended by judges themselves; it is therefore common (especially in the field of evidence) that a solution is first suggested as a jurisprudential development and then is refined and adopted as a full-fledged rule by the Plenary of judges. This process is more complicated at the ICC, where the RPE are adopted by the Assembly of State Parties.

[9] The original Rule 90(A) of the ICTY RPE read: "Witnesses shall, in principle, be heard directly by the Chambers." The ICTR never modified this rule, which is therefore formally still valid.

[10] Rule 89(F) of the ICTY RPE now reads: "A Chamber may receive the evidence of a witness orally or, where the interests of justice allow, in written form." Various specific rules added over the years detail how this can be done.

[11] Prosecutor v. Prlić et al., Case No. IT-04-74-AR73.6, Decision on Appeals Against Decision Admitting Transcript of Jadranko Prlić's Questioning into Evidence, ¶ 40 (ICTY Nov. 23, 2007) [hereinafter *Prlić* Decision].

that of admitting written evidence, including previous statements of witnesses, with the aim of expediting trials by shortening the presentation of evidence in the courtroom.

One final overarching note is in order. International criminal tribunals consider it axiomatic that they should, and indeed are bound to, respect international human rights standards.[12] In interpreting this body of law, international criminal tribunals have often made recourse to the decisions of the European Court of Human Rights (ECtHR), especially in the field of evidence. This is not, of course, because ECtHR rulings are per se binding on these jurisdictions, but rather because they deal with cases from different jurisdictions applying a variety of different procedural rules through the prism of a provision (Article 6 of the Convention for the Protection of Human Rights and Fundamental Freedoms) which is very similar to the catalogue of fair trial rights enshrined in the 1966 International Covenant on Civil and Political Rights (ICCPR) and in these tribunals' founding instruments.[13]

The following sections describe the main characteristics of the regime for the admission of evidence before international criminal tribunals (Section II). Without attempting to be exhaustive, this chapter then proceeds to outline how witnesses are heard before these judicial institutions (Section III), and further how other types of information are submitted into the trial record (Sections IV, V and VI).

II. GENERAL RULES AND PRINCIPLES ON ADMISSION OF EVIDENCE

A. Historical Precedents

For the purpose of international criminal proceedings, evidence can be defined as all information that is admitted by a Chamber as tending to prove or disprove – in a broad sense – allegations contained in the document setting out the charges against the accused (usually referred to as an "indictment"). Importantly, as hinted earlier, international criminal tribunals are

---

12 Rep. of the Secretary-General Pursuant to Paragraph 2 of Security Council Resolution 808, UN Doc. S/25704 (1993), ¶ 106. See also Article 23(3) of the ICC Statute. On the consequences for breach of human rights by international tribunals, see Guido Acquaviva, *Human Rights Violations Before International Tribunals: Reflections on the Responsibility of International Organizations*, 20 Leiden J. Int'l L. 613 (2007).

13 *Prlić* Decision, *supra* note 11, ¶ 51.

not endowed with juries, and thus judges are called to assess the admissibility of evidence as well as its significance for the ultimate findings.

The post-WWII international military tribunals (the International Military Tribunal (IMT) and the International Military Tribunal for the Far East (IMTFE)) had extremely lax rules of evidence, which allowed judges to exercise a very broad discretion in admitting evidence, oral or written.[14] During the Nuremberg trial, various judges modified their own attitudes towards the admission and testing of evidence – something made possible by the flexible and somewhat vague nature of the rules in question. Justice Robert H. Jackson, U.S. Chief Counsel for the Prosecution at Nuremberg, wrote after the trial:

> On the Continent, as you know, cross-examination is very little used by members of the bar. [...] In fact, there was no Russian equivalent for the term 'cross-examination.' The French made little attempt to use cross-examination. Most of the cross-examining was done by the British, who are adept at it, or by the Americans. The Soviets at first hesitated – and then apparently they found it to be great fun, and cross-examined everybody.[15]

However, despite witness evidence and various examples of masterful examination and cross-examination, there is no denying that at Nuremberg most of the pivotal evidence relied upon was *written* evidence, and specifically documents prepared by the German themselves to record their campaigns and operations.[16] It is against the backdrop of these precedents that one should understand contemporary international practice.

B. Contemporary Rules and Practice

The ICTY, ICTR and STL RPE provide that "[a] Chamber may admit any relevant evidence which it deems to have probative value,"[17] subject

---

[14] Article 19 of the IMT Charter provided that "[t]he Tribunal shall not be bound by technical rules of evidence. It shall adopt and apply to the greatest possible extent expeditious and non-technical procedure, and shall admit any evidence which it deems to be of probative value." Article 13 of the IMTFE added that "[a]ll purported admissions or statements of the accused are admissible."

[15] Robert Jackson, *Nuremberg Trial of the Major Nazi Leaders*, 70 N.Y. St. B.A. Rep. 147, 157 (1947).

[16] "There is no count in the Indictment that cannot be proved by books and records. The Germans were always meticulous record keepers, and these defendants had their share of the Teutonic passion for thoroughness in putting things on paper." (2 Trial of the Major War Criminals Before the International Military Tribunals 102 (1947)).

[17] Rule 89(C) of the ICTY RPE; Rule 89(C) of the ICTR RPE; Rule 149(C) of the STL RPE.

to a number of constraints and restrictions.[18] Similarly, the ICC Statute provides that the parties may submit evidence relevant to the case, and that the Court may rule on the relevance or admissibility of any evidence, taking into account its probative value.[19] The corresponding provision in the Internal Rules of the ECCC (the hybrid court that most closely follows the civil law approach) is even more explicit in providing that "[u]nless otherwise provided . . . all evidence is admissible. The Trial judges shall weigh all such evidence independently in deciding whether guilt has been proven beyond a reasonable doubt."[20]

The inescapable conclusion is that contemporary international criminal tribunals have followed the example set by the post-World War II tribunals – and traditional civil law codes – in avoiding complex technical rules of evidence. To the common law trained reader, such a situation poses a number of questions: is there no barrier to admitting evidence before international criminal tribunals? How do the judges – and parties themselves – manage to sift through the huge amount of material that could be admitted to the record? How can fact finders be satisfied of the reliability of the evidence presented by the parties?

At the outset, it is important to clarify that the absence of a detailed regime of evidence (such as comprehensive exclusionary rules) does not necessarily signify that there are no rules at all in this area. As the provisions quoted above demonstrate, and as will be seen in the next pages, international criminal tribunals work with a very limited set of explicit technical rules regulating the admission of evidence, but they do possess a functioning system in this respect, albeit framed in rather general terms. The aim of this Section is to cover the main aspects of this system.

C. Admission of Evidence and Exclusionary Rules

The first substantive rule of evidence guiding judges of international criminal tribunals is, as hinted above, that a Chamber may admit *any relevant information* as evidence, taking into account its probative value.[21]

---

18 Rules 89–98 of the ICTY and ICTR RPE.

19 ICC Statute, Article 69(3) and (4). *See also* ICC Rule 63(2).

20 Rule 87(1) of the ECCC Internal Rules. On the peculiar nature of these Internal Rules, see Guido Acquaviva, *New Paths in International Criminal Justice? The Internal Rules of the Cambodian Extraordinary Chambers*, 6 J. INT'L CRIM. JUSTICE 129 (2008).

21 Articles 19 and 20 of the IMT Charter, Article 13(a) and (b) of the IMTFE Charter, Rule 89(C) of the ICTY RPE, Rule 89(C) of the ICTR RPE, Article 69(4) of the ICC Statute, Article 21(2) of the STL Statute, Rule 149(C) of the STL RPE.

This essentially means that a Trial Chamber, when ruling on the admission of evidence (oral or otherwise) will make a preliminary assessment of the likely probative value of the evidence in question vis-à-vis the charges contained in the indictment – while, of course, a final assessment of the probative value of each piece will only be made at the end of the trial, upon a full record. A rule of this type clearly affords judges enormous discretion, which is nonetheless tempered by exceptions and limitations (further discussed below).

Despite these restrictions, however, the general principle stands: international criminal judges are generally allowed great flexibility with respect to the admission of evidence, and their evaluation of what is relevant and what has probative value is largely left unchecked until the judgment is rendered. In this respect, they are in a position similar to German judges, who are required by Section 244 of their Code to search for the truth through any relevant means of proof – of course within the boundaries of carefully crafted principles.

As a corollary of this discretion, *international criminal tribunals are not bound by any national rules of evidence*, including the various exclusionary rules developed by most contemporary systems of criminal law and procedure.[22] This means that, in theory, each international criminal tribunal has its own self-contained system for the admission of evidence. In practice, however, the various courts and tribunals follow some shared rules and general principles, which form the kernel of what is developing as a body of international criminal procedure,[23] including the law dealing with evidence admission and evaluation.

The exclusion of domestic rules of evidence also means that documents

---

These articles generally refer to "evidence" rather than information – while technically information becomes evidence only after being admitted into the record.

[22] Rule 89(A) of the ICTY RPE, Rule 89(A) of the ICTR RPE, Rule 89(A) of the SCSL RPE, Rule 63(5) of the ICC RPE. The STL is an exception in this respect, since it provides that, in case of a lacuna, judges may apply provisions of the Lebanese Code of Criminal Procedure "consistent with the highest standards of international criminal procedure." (Rule 149(A) of the STL RPE).

[23] This international criminal procedural law appears to be developing a common set of basic due process guarantees that each international judicial body called to examine individual criminal responsibility is required to follow. In a similar vein, see Stefania Negri, *The Principle of "Equality of Arms" and the Evolving Law of International Criminal Procedure*, 5 INT'L CRIM. L. REV. 513 (2005) and works cited therein. On the meaning of "general rules and principles" in this field, see *inter alia* Sergey Vasiliev, *General Rules and Principles of International Criminal Procedure: Definition, Legal Nature, and Identification*, *in* INTERNATIONAL CRIMINAL PROCEDURE: TOWARDS A COHERENT BODY OF LAW 19 (Göran Sluiter et al. eds., 2009).

or other exhibits that would formally have been inadmissible in certain national legal systems might nonetheless be legitimately considered by international judges in order to assess the guilt or innocence of an accused. For instance, phone communications intercepted in contravention of the domestic legislation of various states of the former Yugoslavia have been admitted into the trial record of ICTY proceedings.[24] Similarly, the ICC has held that search and seizure operations undertaken in violation of domestic procedures do not per se render the evidence gathered inadmissible.[25]

This liberal approach to the admission of evidence essentially leads international criminal tribunals to postpone the moment when evidence is scrutinized. Such a careful analysis is carried out not at the time the evidence is tendered (as in common law jurisdictions), but rather when the evidence as a whole is evaluated in its context, i.e., at the time of the final judgment, when the full record of the case is available. Various authors have suggested that the use of some exclusionary rules of evidence from the common law tradition would make international criminal trials fairer, shorter and more efficient[26] – but to date such critiques have not been heeded.[27]

The only general exclusionary rule requires that judges in all contemporary courts and tribunals exclude evidence obtained by methods which cast substantial doubt on its reliability or if its admission is contrary to, and would seriously damage, the integrity of the proceedings, e.g., by being contrary to the basic legal instruments of these courts and/or in violation of established human rights.[28] This appears to be a sort of "baseline" rule, which focuses on the results which judges of international criminal tribunals are required to ensure (integrity of the proceedings; fairness and protection of the rights of the accused), rather than providing specific

---

24 *See, e.g.*, Prosecutor v. Brđanin, Case No. IT-99-36-T, Decision on the Defence "Objection to Intercept Evidence" (ICTY Oct. 3, 2003); Prosecutor v. Haraqija & Morina, Case No. IT-04-84-R77.4, Decision on Astrit Haraqija and Bajrush Morina's Joint Request for Reconsideration of the Trial Chamber's Decision of 4 September 2008 (ICTY Sept. 24, 2008).

25 Prosecutor v. Lubanga, Case No. ICC-01/04-01/06, Decision on Confirmation of Charges, ¶¶ 74–8 (Jan. 29, 2007).

26 *See, e.g.*, Peter Murphy, *No Free Lunch, No Free Proof – The Indiscriminate Admission of Evidence is a Serious Flaw in International Criminal Trials*, 8 J. INT'L CRIM. JUSTICE 539 (2010).

27 For a defense of the main features of the present system, see among others CHRISTINE SCHUON, INTERNATIONAL CRIMINAL PROCEDURE: A CLASH OF LEGAL CULTURES 136 et seq. (2010).

28 Rules 89(D) and 95 of the ICTY RPE, Rule 95 of the ICTR RPE, Article 69(4) and (7) of the ICC Statute. *See also* Rule 149(D) of the STL RPE.

instructions on the type of evidence that should be excluded from the trial record. To this general principle, one should add that international criminal tribunals have excluded evidence gathered in *serious* violation of their own procedures, such as those rules requiring counsel to be present during suspect interviews.[29]

In essence, these provisions mitigate the consequences of not adhering to strict exclusionary rules that have evolved – often due to constitutional and due process requirements – in various common law traditions.[30] For example, intercepted communications gathered illegally under the national laws of a country or evidence collected during a (domestically) unlawful search and seizure operation which are likely to be inadmissible in a common law system would still be inadmissible if such procedural violations had substantial detrimental effects on the rights of the accused. Thus, international judges are called to appraise carefully on a case-by-case basis the effects of the methods used to gather evidence upon the internationally recognized rights of the defendant and, through such appraisal, rule on the exclusion of exhibits. As hinted above, this is how several civil law systems operated decades ago, even though it should be recognized that these systems – at least in countries subject to the ECtHR – are now trending towards enforcing stricter exclusionary rules.

The final check in relation to the admission of potentially unreliable evidence before international criminal tribunals is provided by yet another feature derived from civil law systems: the requirement that the verdict of innocence or guilt be contained in a reasoned judgment.[31] Unlike the simple finding by common law juries that an accused is "guilty" or "not guilty," international criminal judgments tend to be rather lengthy, because trial judges must duly explain their assessment of the relevance and probative value of the (main) evidence, as well as their own reasoning in reaching the verdict.[32] Even though judges are not required to articulate

---

29 *See, e.g.*, Prosecutor v. Bagosora et al., Case No. ICTR-98-41-T, Decision on Prosecutor's Motion for the Admission of Certain Materials Under Rule 89(C), ¶ 21 (Oct. 14, 2004).

30 The traditional common law view has actually historically been that courts should not be concerned with *how* the evidence was obtained, and that evidence is admissible if relevant. *See* Kuruma Son of Kaniu v. The Queen [1955] AC 197, 203 (PC). As is well-known, this is not the position in the U.S. (*see* Mapp v. Ohio, 367 U.S. 643 (1961)).

31 A reasoned judgment is however often required in common law systems when no jury trial takes place. *See, e.g.*, Taito v. R, [2002] UKPC 15, ¶ 18.

32 Problems however abound. This is for instance what the Trial Chamber stated in the *Milutinović* judgment (a 1,700-page long ruling, still under appeal): "The Prosecution chose to present a case founded upon a multitude of alleged

every step of their reasoning for each specific finding,[33] what triers of fact are encouraged to do, for instance, is to discuss *why* they rely on certain parts of a witness' testimony, while they reject other parts as not credible.[34] The same applies to documents, in particular those bearing directly on the guilt or innocence of the accused. This is not dissimilar to what civil law systems provide, and actually human rights bodies tend to require, when mandating judges to give reasons for their decisions.[35]

Keeping in mind these basic overarching principles and rules, let us now consider how evidence – starting with oral testimony – is actually admitted during proceedings before international criminal tribunals.

III. ORAL EVIDENCE

International tribunals have undoubtedly heeded the European Court of Human Rights' prescription that "all the evidence must normally be produced at a public hearing, in the presence of the Accused, with a view to adversarial argument,"[36] something aimed at ensuring that the defense is able to effectively challenge the case against the accused. This is in line with the requirement of the ICCPR (Article 14(e)), and enshrined in all of the international courts' founding instruments, that an accused must be able to "examine, or have examined, the witnesses against him or her." Importantly, Article 14 has been interpreted as requiring not only equality between prosecution and defense in obtaining, leading and challenging evidence, but also that each accused "must have the right to act diligently and fearlessly in pursuing all available defences."[37] As discussed above,

---

events in [13] separate municipalities .... The Prosecution led evidence from a small number of people in relation to each of the municipalities, but invited the Chamber to make wide-ranging findings about the perpetration of crimes and the movement of hundreds of thousands of people and the murders of many hundreds of people .... The net effect is that the Chamber had the very onerous task of carefully considering whether the witnesses presented were sufficiently reliable to enable such wide-ranging conclusions to be based on their evidence." Prosecutor v. Milutinović et al., Case No. IT-05-87-T, Judgement (Volume 1 of 4), ¶ 45 (ICTY Feb. 26, 2009) [hereinafter *Milutinović*, Trial Judgement].

33 *See* Prosecutor v. Musema, Case No. ICTR-96-13-A, Appeal Judgement, ¶ 18 (Nov. 16, 2001).

34 *See, e.g.*, Prosecutor v. Krajišnik, Case No. IT-00-39-A, Appeal Judgement, ¶150 (ICTY Mar. 17, 2009).

35 Garcia Ruiz v. Spain [GC], no. 30544/96, ¶ 26, ECtHR 1999-I (Jan. 21, 1999).

36 *See, e.g.*, A.M. v. Italy, no. 37019/97, ¶ 25, ECtHR 1999-IX (Mar. 14, 2000).

37 *General Comment No. 13: Equality before the courts and the right to a fair and public hearing by an independent court established by law (Art. 14)*, ¶ 11.

such considerations must necessarily inform the interpretation and application of the evidence rules of international criminal tribunals.

For these and other reasons – in both common law and civil law criminal trials, as well as in proceedings before international criminal tribunals – preference is currently given to *oral* evidence presented through examination and cross-examination of witnesses before the fact-finders.[38] This is despite the fact that in recent years the scientific basis for preferring eyewitness testimony as the most reliable form of evidence in criminal proceedings has been strongly criticized, and largely proven wrong.[39]

Nonetheless, by and large the presentation of oral evidence before international criminal tribunals has undoubtedly taken the form that is typical in adversarial proceedings – namely, the examination and subsequent cross-examination of witnesses, called first by the prosecution and then by the defense.[40] This procedure appears to be best suited to ensuring equality of arms between the parties since it requires, for instance, the prosecution to present the results of its investigation in a public courtroom and it allows the accused to challenge before an impartial fact-finder the charges leveled against him.[41] Under this model, leading questions by the party calling the witness are banned, though this prohibition does not apply during cross-examination[42] or when questions are posed by the judges

---

[38] While the traditional English view enshrined in Myers v. Director of Public Prosecution [1965] AC 1001 (HL), requiring oral evidence in all cases, has been gradually replaced by statutes allowing hearsay and records created in the course of business, it is still true that the most important evidence is presented at an oral hearing. Thus, it is interesting that countries traditionally identified with the civil law tradition have been increasingly embracing the adversarial system of evidence presentation. See Article 111 of the Italian Constitution, amended in 1999, now stating: "In criminal law proceedings, the formation of evidence is based on the principle of adversary hearings. The guilt of the defendant cannot be established on the basis of statements by persons who, out of their own free choice, have always voluntarily avoided undergoing cross-examination by the defendant or the defence counsel."

[39] This point has been convincingly made in Nancy A. Combs, Fact-finding Without Facts: The Uncertain Evidentiary Foundations of International Criminal Convictions 14–20 (2011) (but see also 63–105 for problems specifically affecting international criminal tribunals).

[40] This section does not deal with *expert* testimony, which follows somewhat different rules. In general on the topic, see Avi Singh, *Expert Evidence*, *in* Principles of Evidence in International Criminal Justice 599 (Karim A. A. Khan et al. eds., 2010).

[41] *See* Michele Caianiello, *First Decisions on the Admission of Evidence at ICC Trials*, 9 J. Int'l Crim. J. 385, 389 (2011).

[42] *Id.* at 394. The main modification of this model at the ICC in respect to the one adopted by the ad hoc tribunals is that legal representatives of victims are participants and therefore are given time to question witnesses themselves.

themselves.[43] While, theoretically, Article 64(8)(b) of the ICC Statute gives the Presiding Judge of the Trial Chamber ample discretion over the procedure to be followed in the presentation of evidence, practice thus far has overwhelmingly followed the adversarial model – even if, in order to avoid the appearance of favoring one legal culture over another, certain terms (such as "cross-examination") do not even appear in the ICC Statute or Rules.[44] Moreover, all international criminal tribunals foresee the possibility of live testimony through video-link from another location,[45] despite the fact that this might make it harder for the participants in the courtroom and the judges to assess the demeanor of the witness testifying.[46]

The fact that the regime of oral testimony before international criminal tribunals is grounded in the common law tradition more than in others is also borne out by the fact that ICTY, ICTR, SCSL and STL allow the accused to testify at his own trial.[47] This is generally not allowed in civil law systems, where the accused may of course make statements, but never as a witness proper (i.e., under solemn declaration). Civil law systems in fact prefer not putting defendants to the choice of testifying as witnesses, with the perceived consequent risk of creating an incentive to lie.[48]

The features described thus far would suggest that, in evidence-related matters, contemporary international tribunals follow the main facets of adversarial common law. Nonetheless, a few variations make the system

---

[43] Prosecutor v. Lubanga, Case No. ICC-01/04-01/06, Decision on Judicial Questioning (Mar. 18, 2010).

[44] K. Ambos, *International Criminal Procedure: "Adversarial", "Inquisitorial" or Mixed?*, 3 Int'l Crim. L. Rev. 1, 20 (2003). On the application of the adversarial model at the ICC, see for instance, Prosecutor v. Katanga & Ngudjolo, Case No. ICC-01/04-01/07, Directions for the Conduct of the Proceedings and Testimony in Accordance with Rule 140 (Nov. 20, 2009).

[45] *See, e.g.*, Rule 81*bis* of the ICTY RPE; Prosecutor v. Nahimana et al., Case No. ICTR-99-52-T, Decision on Prosecutor's Application to Add Witness X to Its List of Witnesses and for Protective Measures (Sept. 14, 2001). As for the ICC, see Rule 67(1).

[46] The U.K. House of Lords has however stated that "[i]mprovements in technology enable . . . evidence to be tested as adequately if given by [video conferencing] as it could be if given in court." Polanski v. Condé Nast Publications Ltd. [2005] UKHL 10.

[47] *See* STL Rule 144(D). The other tribunals, including the ICC, do not have specific provisions on this – but the right to testify has been considered inherent in the general system of evidence.

[48] On the relationship between this issue and the right to silence before international criminal tribunals, see William Schabas, The International Criminal Court: A Commentary on the Rome Statute 813–14 (2010).

of international criminal procedure somewhat different from those stemming out of the pure common law tradition.

First, when following international criminal proceedings one cannot fail to note that *judges are generally more active* in intervening and posing questions to the witnesses, and even calling witnesses.[49] This naturally changes depending on the composition of the bench, and the personal inclination of each judge, but it undoubtedly creates the impression that the fact-finders are much more involved than in ordinary jury trials (and, of course, there is no jury to "impress"). At the ICC, for instance, Rule 140 of the Rules of Procedure and Evidence explicitly provides that the prosecution and the defense have the right to question witnesses about relevant matters related to the witness's testimony and its reliability, the credibility of the witness and other relevant matters, but then adds that the Chamber also has the right to question a witness both before or after the witness is questioned by those participants. This occurs frequently. Only two of the hybrid tribunals (the ECCC and STL) foresee a somewhat more civil law-oriented approach to questioning witnesses, with the possibility of judges taking the lead in the examination. At the ECCC, the Trial Chamber shall hear the witnesses and the civil parties in the order it considers useful.[50] Article 20(2) of the Statute of the STL provides that "[u]nless otherwise decided by the Trial Chamber in the interests of justice, examination of witnesses shall commence with questions posed by the presiding judge, followed by questions posed by other members of the Trial Chamber, the Prosecutor and the Defence."

Second, in contrast to traditional common law systems, *hearsay evidence* is admissible before international criminal tribunals. ICTY case law has defined hearsay as a statement (oral or written) made otherwise than in the proceedings in which it is being tendered, but nevertheless being tendered in those proceedings in order to establish the truth of the matter asserted.[51] The ICTY Appeals Chamber has clarified that establishing the reliability of hearsay evidence is of paramount importance, exactly because of the fact that hearsay evidence is admitted as substantive

---

49 ICTY and ICTR Rule 98; ICC Regulations of the Court, Regulation 44(4).

50 Rule 91 of the ECCC Internal Rules.

51 A few variations of this definition exist. *See, e.g.*, Prosecutor v. Aleksovski, Case No. IT-95-14/1-AR73, Decision on Prosecutor's Appeal on Admissibility of Evidence, ¶ 14 (ICTY Feb. 16, 1999) [hereinafter *Aleksovski* Decision]; *Milutinović*, Trial Judgement, *supra* note 32, ¶ 38. Various common law systems have recently also changed attitude towards hearsay. *See, e.g.*, Dushkar Kanchan Singh v. the Queen [2010] NZSC 161, ¶ 23 (referring to the New Zealand Evidence Act of 2006, which, inter alia, allows prior out of court statements by witnesses).

evidence in order to prove the truth of its contents.[52] In order to be admissible, hearsay evidence must be reliable for the purpose of proving the truth of its contents, in the sense of being voluntary, truthful and trustworthy.[53] More generally, international criminal tribunals have adhered to the human rights principle according to which unacceptable infringements of the rights of the defense occur when a conviction is based solely, or in a decisive manner, on the depositions of a witness whom the accused has had no opportunity to examine or to have examined either during the investigation or at trial.[54] This principle has become essential to understanding the admission and evaluation of evidence even beyond the area of hearsay *stricto sensu*, as will become clearer in the next pages.

Third, international criminal procedure has at times allowed – or at least not explicitly banned – the use of *anonymous witnesses*, i.e., witnesses who testify without having to disclose their identity or other identifying personal information to the accused. This is clearly a major exception to the basic tenets of adversarial procedures and, it should be noted, this type of heightened protection has so far been granted *only in one case* before the ICTY. In the *Tadić* case, a majority of a Trial Chamber granted some witnesses anonymity based on Rule 75 of the ICTY RPE. As anonymity strongly affects the accused person's ability to defend himself or herself, the Trial Chamber identified a number of criteria that must be fulfilled before it can be granted: (i) there must be real fear for the safety of the witness or his family; (ii) the testimony of the particular witness must be important to the case; (iii) the Chamber must be satisfied that there is no *prima facie* evidence that the witness is untrustworthy; (iv) any relevant witness protection program must be ineffective or non-existent; and (v) the anonymity is strictly necessary.[55] Despite these stringent criteria, the *Tadić* decision has been much criticized[56] and it has not been followed in later

---

52 *Aleksovski* Decision, *supra* note 51, ¶ 15.

53 Prosecutor v. Kordić, Case No. IT-95-14-2, Appeal Judgement, ¶ 283 (ICTY Dec. 17, 2004) (restating the principle).

54 In addition to the *A.M.* case cited *supra* note 36, the principle was espoused in Saïdi v. France, no. 14647/89, ¶¶ 43–4, ECtHR (Sept. 20, 1993) and Unterpertinger v. Austria, no. 9120/80, ¶¶ 31–3, ECtHR (Nov. 24, 1986). On the application of this principle by the ICTY, see for instance *Prlić* Decision, *supra* note 11, ¶ 53.

55 Prosecutor v. Tadić, Case No. IT-94-1-T, Decision on the Prosecutor's Motion Requesting Protective Measures for Victims and Witnesses, ¶¶ 62–6 (ICTY Aug. 10, 1995).

56 *See e.g.*, Natasha A. Affolder, Tadić, *The Anonymous Witness and the Sources of International Procedural Law*, 19 MICH. J. INT'L L. 445 (1997); Monroe Leigh, *Witness Anonymity is Inconsistent with Due Process*, 91 AM. J. INT'L L. 80 (1997).

case law of the ad hoc tribunals. When the ICC Statute was negotiated, no agreement could be reached on the question of allowing anonymous witness testimonies; thus, the ICC Statute and the Rules do not contain any specific provisions either barring or admitting such practice.

The STL Rules do grant the possibility for the Pre-Trial Judge to question anonymous witnesses. In the STL President's explanatory memorandum, Rule 93 has been justified by the extraordinary nature of terrorist criminality.[57] More concretely, STL Rule 93 establishes that where, at any stage of the proceedings, there is a serious risk that a witness or a person close to the witness would lose his life or suffer grave physical or mental harm as a result of his identity being revealed, and ordinary measures for the protection of witnesses would be insufficient to prevent such danger,[58] the Pre-Trial Judge may question the witness in the absence of the parties (including legal representatives of victims). In questioning such a witness, participants are given the opportunity to convey questions to the witness through the Pre-Trial Judge, and a provisional transcript of the witness's answers is given to them in order to allow the posing of additional questions. STL Rule 159 explicitly underlines that a Chamber may exclude statements of anonymous witnesses if their probative value is substantially outweighed by the need to ensure a fair trial, and that a conviction may never be based solely, or to a decisive extent, on such statements.

The use of anonymous witnesses, and in general of *ex parte* evidence, at trial does not really follow the common law *vs.* civil law divide. For instance, the United Kingdom has introduced legislation related to its fight against terrorism that allows detention of foreign nationals on the basis of witness statement and other evidence not disclosed to the individual detained.[59] Other countries have introduced similar provisions, for instance in cases of sexual violence trials; others allow statements given to the police or investigating magistrates to be read into the trial record, without confrontation, when circumstances so require. In this respect, the

---

[57] STL RPE Explanatory Memorandum, Nov. 10, 2009, ¶ 35, *available at* www.stl-tsl.org.

[58] Virtually all contemporary international criminal tribunals provide for a non-exhaustive list of measures available to protect witnesses and ensure they are allowed to provide evidence in a secure environment. These include: (i) expunging names and identifying information from the tribunal's public records, (ii) non-disclosure to the public of any records identifying the victim or witness, (iii) the giving of testimony through image- or voice-altering devices or closed circuit television, (iv) assignment of a pseudonym, and (v) closed sessions. An extreme form of protection is relocation of a witness, coupled with in-court protective measures.

[59] See the facts of the case in A. and Others v. UK, no. 3455/05, ECtHR (Feb. 19, 2009).

ECtHR has forcefully stated that where full disclosure of the evidence against a person is not possible (due to national security interest or serious witness intimidation), such restriction on the rights of the accused are nonetheless to be "counterbalanced in such a way that each applicant still had the possibility effectively to challenge the allegations against him."[60] The STL Rule in this respect is certainly an exception to the general trend of disallowing anonymous witnesses; it remains to be seen how judges of that Tribunal will be able to apply it in practice abiding by the overarching obligation to ensure a fair trial.

This principle, as seen above, is now at the basis of the procedural system developed by international criminal tribunals, where normally the accused are able to confront witnesses testifying about their alleged criminal conduct[61] – but providing that, if exceptions are established, the evidence thus presented must be corroborated and cannot form the sole basis for conviction. Understanding this principle essential to both common law and civil law countries, *i.e.*, that no one can be convicted solely on the basis of evidence which he had no opportunity to test, allows us also to move into the regime used by international criminal tribunals to admit written evidence into the trial record.

IV. WRITTEN STATEMENTS

While oral evidence was – and to a large extent still is – an extremely important type of evidence before international criminal tribunals, as time has progressed and cases have become more complex, the disadvantages of unnecessarily time-consuming live testimony (often recounting events that have been already discussed in other cases before the same tribunal) have become apparent. In particular, oral evidence has been deemed increasingly unnecessary in interrelated international criminal cases, which deal with the same (or extremely similar) factual bases.

The ICTY and ICTR have therefore introduced over the years a series of provisions to facilitate the admission of written statements of witnesses,[62]

---

60 *Id.* ¶ 218. See also the UK House of Lords ruling in R v. Davis, [2008] UKHL 36, ¶ 25 (Lord Bingham of Cornhill) endorsing the ECtHR approach that "no conviction should be based solely or to a decisive extent upon the statements or testimony of anonymous witnesses. The reason is that such a conviction results from a trial which cannot be regarded as fair."

61 This is similar to a long-held position of the U.S. Supreme Court. *See* Turner v. Louisiana, 379 U.S. 466 (1965).

62 These are non-contemporaneous statements generally produced by a party

while at the same time striving to maintain the adversarial nature of the system and ensuring the fairness of the proceedings. This section discusses the mechanisms for admitting such statements before the ad hoc tribunals (including the SCSL and the STL), and the safeguards embedded in them.

Overall, it must be pointed out that on various occasions tribunals have clarified that less weight is attributed to written statements than to oral evidence presented in court.[63] More importantly, no conviction can be based solely on uncorroborated written statements (or other written evidence, for that matter) if the accused had no opportunity to cross-examine the witness in question.[64] This is an essential principle intended to guarantee that an accused will always be able to challenge the evidence on which a conviction against him might be based.[65] The first of these new Rules (ICTY and ICTR Rules 92*bis*) provides that witness statements (gathered pursuant to certain formal requirements meant to ensure their reliability) or transcripts of previous testimony can be admitted at trial. The Chamber *may*, however, require the witness in question to be present for cross-examination (or questioning by the judges), and *must* do so if the statement or transcript relates to the acts and conduct of the accused as charged in the indictment.[66] Evidence of an accused's "acts and conduct" may, for example, establish (a) that the accused physically perpetrated any of the crimes charged; or (b) that he planned, instigated or ordered the crimes charged; or (c) that he otherwise aided and abetted those who actually did commit the crimes in their planning, perpetration or execution of those crimes; or (d) that he was a superior to those who actually did commit the crimes and (i) he knew or had reason to know that those crimes were about to be or had been committed by his subordinates, and (ii) he

---

for submission at trial; their regime, though formally somewhat different at the ICTY and ICTR, is in practice applied very similarly. *See* Chris Gosnell, *Admissibility of Evidence*, *in* PRINCIPLES OF EVIDENCE, *supra* note 40, at 403–04.

63 *See, e.g.*, Prosecutor v. Naletilić, Case No. IT-98-34-T, Judgement, ¶ 12 (ICTY March 31, 2003).

64 Prosecutor v. Martić, Case No. IT-95-11-A, Appeal Judgement, fn. 486 (ICTY Oct. 8, 2008).

65 See also the application of the principle in Prosecutor v. Galić, Case No. IT-98-29-AR73.2, Decision on Interlocutory Appeal Concerning Rule 92*bis*(C), ¶¶ 13–15 (ICTY June 7, 2002) and *Prlić* Decision, *supra* note 11, ¶¶ 53, 59 (ICTY, Nov. 23, 2007).

66 This of course creates problems if the statement is from the accused himself or from a co-accused who elect not to testify at trial. On this issue, see Sara Luzzati, *On the Admissibility of Statements Made by the Defendant Prior to Trial: Remarks on the ICTY Appeals Chamber's Decisions in* Halilović *and* Prlić et al., 8 J. INT'L CRIM. JUSTICE 221 (2010).

failed to take reasonable steps to prevent such acts or to punish those who carried out those acts.[67] Under normal circumstances, witness statements will be admitted without requiring an opportunity for cross-examination if they repeat the evidence of "live" witnesses or if they provide background information that is not pivotal to the prosecution case.

At the ICTY, if a witness is present in court, his previous statements can be admitted even for matters relating to the acts and conduct of the accused, provided that he is *available* for cross-examination and any questioning by the judges, and he *attests* that the statement accurately reflects his other declaration and what he would say if examined.[68] For common law lawyers used to the "show" of witnesses in court, this ICTY rule, adopted in 2006, provides one of the most vivid illustrations of the shift in approach in evidence presentation.[69] On the basis of this provision, examination-in-chief is now of much less significance at the ICTY (because it is usually superseded by mere attestation that a previous statement is accurate), while cross-examination and re-examination are the source of the bulk of the evidence presented before the court. The effect of this is often that the spectators to the proceedings cannot really follow the cross-examination because – unlike the judges – they have not had the chance of perusing the previous statements of the witness in question prior to the hearing. More importantly, the party calling the witness will try to

---

[67] The language "acts and conduct of the accused" – though by now established as a fundamental feature of the procedures at the ICTY, ICTR, SCSL, and STL – is unsatisfactory. What the provision in question is meant to ensure, as discussed earlier, is that no conviction be based on untested evidence. Thus, what appears critical is that, under the circumstances of each case, judges are prevented from considering untested statements containing information essential to the prosecution case – whether or not these relate to the acts and conduct of the accused. Statements regarding the accused's conduct might, for instance, be favorable to the accused and against the prosecution case theory. On the other hand, facts unrelated to the acts and conduct of the accused per se can be pivotal to the prosecution case.

[68] ICTY Rule 92*ter*, codified from the case law previously developed (mainly through Prosecutor v. Milošević, Case No. IT-02-54-AR73.4, Decision on Interlocutory Appeal on the Admissibility of Evidence-in-Chief in the Form of Written Statements (ICTY Sept. 30, 2003)).

[69] Several common law jurisdictions nowadays allow a past (or prior) recollection recorded exception to the hearsay rule (*see, e.g.*, U.S. Federal Rules of Evidence 803(5)). A written statement of a witness is admissible under this exception if the witness is present in court, testifies that the statement was accurate when made, and also that he or she has insufficient recollection to testify "fully and accurately" about the matter recorded. The main difference in this case appears to be that before the ICTY (and the STL) there is no need to show that the statement must be used due to memory loss.

have him recount the most important portions of the evidence during re-examination, thus making this part of the evidence longer than one would otherwise expect – and undermining the very essence of cross-examination as the testing ground for examination-in-chief. In a sense, the procedure ensuing after the adoption of Rule 92*ter* is more similar to what occurs in many traditional civil law systems, where the judge already has an understanding of the evidence to be provided by witnesses (through a case file provided by the investigating judge) and the questioning in court merely serves the purposes of testing this information.

Two additional rules provide for the exceptional admission of previous statements. One is ICTY Rule 92*quater* (similar to Rule92*bis*(C) of the ICTR Rules) which deals with a statement (or transcript) of a witness who has died, can no longer be traced, or who is unable to testify orally owing to a bodily or mental condition after providing a statement for the trial, but before appearing in court.[70] Such statements may be admitted even if they relate to the acts and conduct of the accused, but – under the general rule discussed above – it would appear that they could never form the sole basis for a conviction. Sufficient independent corroboration would be required in order to ensure that the accused's right to test the evidence against him is safeguarded.

ICTY Rule 92*quinquies* provides that, in the interests of justice, a Chamber may admit a written statement or a transcript if the witness (i) has failed to give evidence; (ii) the failure to give evidence has been materially influenced by improper interference, including threats, intimidation, injury, bribery, or coercion; and (iii) reasonable efforts have been made to secure from the witness all material facts known to the witness, by ensuring the necessary protective measures or by other means. This Rule addition was prompted by cases in which trial proceedings were marred by suspicions that witnesses were modifying their testimony or refusing to provide evidence due to improper influence or outright intimidation. In such cases, previous statements are allowed into the record not just to impeach the witness, but for their content. Nonetheless, it would seem that – just like in the case of statements of deceased witnesses – this type of evidence could never form the sole basis for a conviction, because they can never be adequately tested by the accused.

At the ICC, the opportunities for introducing written statements are

---

70 Similarly, see also Rule 158 of the STL RPE, which provides that "[e]vidence in the form of a written statement, any other reliable record of what a person has said, written or otherwise expressed, or transcript of a statement by a person who has died, who can no longer with reasonable diligence be traced, or who is for good reason otherwise unavailable to testify orally may be admitted . . . ."

somewhat reduced, and the presumption is still that witnesses will give evidence by way of in-court testimony.[71] If the witness is not present in court, a recording or a transcript of the witness's evidence may be admitted if both the prosecution and defense had an opportunity to examine the witness during the recording[72] – even if the statement goes to prove the acts and conduct of the accused.[73] Otherwise, the witness must be present in court in order to be available for questioning.

Another (somewhat marginal) case is when the ICC Prosecutor identifies a "unique opportunity to take testimony or a statement from a witness." In certain instances, under the control of the Chamber, such a statement could be admissible, even if the opposing party was not present when it was taken.[74] The rationale of this approach is clearly that of ensuring the preservation of evidence which could otherwise be lost. However, the ICC regime does not appear to allow the admission of statements that were gathered in situations when the defense was not present or where the witness is not available for questioning in court. Since the ICC does not possess a specific provision for statements of deceased witnesses, it would seem that the general rules on non-admission would apply to such circumstances, too.

In sum, both the ad hoc tribunals and the ICC foresee the possibility, typical of traditional civil law systems, of introducing previous statements of witnesses into the trial record, providing exceptions to the orality principle discussed above. The ICC regime is, contrary to what one might expect, more adversarial than that of the ICTY, the STL and even the ICTR, in that it drastically limits the use of written evidence when the opposing party had no opportunity to test it. Of course, there is no strict requirement that this testing needs to occur during the trial proper, since it can be done in the pre-trial stages of the proceedings (during which ICC defense teams are already active), as long as accused and counsel have a real opportunity to challenge the evidence in question during its gathering.

The other contemporary international criminal tribunals have added a number of exceptions in order to expedite proceedings, and allow written statements or previous transcripts in various circumstances. Instead of

---

71 See, for instance, Prosecutor v. Lubanga, Case No. ICC-01/04-01/06-1140, Decision on Various Issues Related to Witnesses' Testimony During Trial, ¶ 41 (Jan. 29, 2008) (related to video-link testimony but expressing a general principle).

72 Rule 68(a) and (b) of the ICC RPE.

73 Prosecutor v. Katanga & Ngudjolo, Case No. ICC-01/04-01/07, Decision on Prosecutor's Request to Allow the Introduction into Evidence of the Prior Recorded Testimony of P-166 and P-219, ¶ 19 (Sept. 3, 2010).

74 Article 56 of the ICC Statute.

restricting the type of evidence that is in principle admissible, they impose a heavier burden on the judges at the stage when they will be evaluating the value and relevance of this evidence to the case as a whole, since at that moment the rules on reliability and corroboration will have to be carefully applied.

V. OTHER DOCUMENTARY EVIDENCE

While witness statements and transcripts of previous proceedings are generally gathered and prepared in view of future litigation, a variety of *other documents* may be relevant in criminal trials, such as minutes of meetings, military orders, newspaper articles, forensic and medical reports, personal diaries, photographs and so on.[75] Such material often amounts to tens of thousands of pages tendered into evidence, especially at the ICTY. Indeed, the trend has been that of an exponential increase in the submission of documents before the judges, such that the ICTY is now inundated with this type of evidence.[76] Parties have made somewhat less use of exhibits at the ICTR and ICC, probably owing to the smaller number of documents generated during the conflicts in question and the more limited temporal scope of each case there. In any event, lengthy documents, such as books or other compilations of material, are not usually admitted in full, but rather a selection is usually made of the passages relevant for the given trial.[77]

The general rule at the ad hoc tribunals is that a party may only request the admission of exhibits that have been included on its list of exhibits, filed before the beginning of each phase of trial proceedings proper (although exceptions can be made upon a showing of good cause). This ensures that appropriate notice is given to the opposing party.

As to the modalities of presenting exhibits before contemporary international criminal tribunals, generally speaking the preference is that, as

---

[75] On this topic generally, see Marc Nerenberg & Wibke Timmermann, *Documentary Evidence*, *in* PRINCIPLES OF EVIDENCE, *supra* note 40, at 443.

[76] While in the first ICTY case, *Tadić*, a total of 386 exhibits were admitted, the number had already risen to 1,268 in the 2001–2003 trial of *Galić* and then to more than 3,800 in the *Krajišnik* case (2004–2006). *See* the table in Chris Gosnell, *The Changing Context of Evidentiary Rules*, *in* PRINCIPLES OF EVIDENCE, *supra* note 40, at 221.

[77] Prosecutor v. Krajišnik, Case No. IT-00- 39-T, Decision on Admission of Material Sought by the Chamber and Other Exhibits, ¶13 (ICTY July 14, 2006); Prosecutor v. Milutinović et al., Case No. IT-05-87-T, Order on Procedure and Evidence, ¶ 6 (ICTY July 11, 2006).

in traditional common law practice, the party tendering evidence must do so through a witness who is either the author of that piece of evidence, or who can otherwise speak to its origins or content. However, due to what is considered a necessity for the efficient management of complex trials at international criminal tribunals, documentary evidence that is shown to be relevant can be admitted directly from the "bar table."[78]

In both cases, it is of course necessary to allow the opposing party an opportunity to challenge the content of the document and its origin – whether by cross-examination of a relevant witness, or by oral or written arguments.[79] However, it is clear that challenging evidence is more difficult when documents are simply tendered from the bar table. The safeguard in this respect is that judges should exercise exceptional caution when assessing, at the moment of the judgment, the probative value of exhibits submitted in this fashion.

The appropriate way to admit and evaluate documentary evidence was spelled out by the ICTY Trial Chamber in the *Milutinović* case, where thousands of documents were tendered. The Chamber stated that it:

> considered the source of the documents, to the extent known, and did not admit a document if there were substantial doubts as to its authenticity. The Chamber carefully scrutinized the thousands of documents that were tendered, some of which were adduced through a witness, some from the bar table, and others by agreement of the parties. However, the Chamber did not automatically accept the statements contained in admitted documents to be an accurate portrayal of the facts. The Chamber evaluated each and every document admitted into evidence within the context of the trial record as a whole.[80]

VI. JUDICIAL NOTICE

An additional way employed by several international criminal tribunals to shorten the presentation of evidence in the courtroom is to allow

---

[78] Prosecutor v. Prlić et al., Case No. IT-04-74-T, Decision Adopting Guidelines for the Presentation of Defence Evidence, ¶ 35 (ICTY Apr. 24, 2008); Prosecutor v. Karadžić, Case No. IT-95-5/18-T, Decision on the Prosecution's First Bar Table Motion (ICTY Apr. 13, 2010); Prosecutor v. Lubanga, Case No. ICC-01/04-01/06-1981, Decision on the Admission from the "Bar Table" (June 24, 2009); Prosecutor v. Katanga & Ngudjolo, Case No. ICC-01/04-01/07, Decision on the Prosecutor's Bar Table Motions (Dec. 17, 2010).

[79] Prosecutor v. Milošević, Case No. IT-02-54-T, Decision on Prosecution Motion for Admission of Witness Statement of Investigator Bernard O'Donnell (ICTY Feb. 12, 2004).

[80] *Milutinović*, Trial Judgement, *supra* note 32, ¶ 56 (internal citations omitted).

Chambers to take judicial notice not just of facts of common knowledge,[81] but also of "adjudicated facts or of the authenticity of documentary evidence from other proceedings of the Tribunal relating to matters at issue in the current proceedings."[82] The procedure has the advantage of dispensing not only with the need of calling additional witnesses or admitting documents to prove a certain fact, but also of assessing the probative value (and in certain instances, even of the relevance) of this evidence. This outcome is premised on the consideration that the fact already adjudicated was thoroughly discussed by another Chamber in another case.

The problematic feature of this procedure – which is generally absent in domestic systems, whatever their tradition – should be evident: the defendant might be faced with a finding made in another case, before different judges and regarding another accused, over which he or she had no control. The case law of the ICTY and of the ICTR has therefore carefully detailed the conditions for this type of judicial notice. Thus, the findings in question must (i) be factual (as opposed to legal characterizations); (ii) be distinct, concrete and identifiable; (iii) have been made during a contested trial (not a plea agreement) and thus form part of a final judgment; (iv) be without any direct bearing on the criminal responsibility of the accused in the case where they are submitted; (v) not be the subject of (reasonable) dispute between the parties in the present case; and (vi) not negatively affect the right of the accused to a fair trial.[83] This last condition allows a Chamber wide discretion in not admitting, for instance, a large amount of adjudicated facts proposed by the prosecution should such an approach endanger the fairness of the proceedings. It is moreover clear that no judicial notice can be taken of facts related to the acts, conduct and mental state of the accused.[84] Moreover, and more

---

81 ICTY Rule 94(A); ICTR Rule 94(A); SCSL Rule 94(A); ICC Rule 69(6); STL Rule 160(A).

82 ICTY Rule 94(B); ICTR Rule 94(B); SCSL Rule 94(B); STL Rule 160(B) ("adjudicated facts from other proceedings of the Tribunal or from proceedings of national and international jurisdictions relating to matters at issue in the current proceedings, to the extent that they do not relate to acts and conduct of the accused that is being tried"). The ICC does not possess a similar provision.

83 *See* Prosecutor v. Krajišnik, Case No. IT-00-39-PT, Decision on Prosecution Motions for Judicial Notice of Adjudicated Facts and for Admission of Written Statements of Witnesses Pursuant to Rule 92*bis* (ICTY Feb. 28, 2003); Prosecutor v. Hadžihasanović, Case IT-01-47-T, Final Decision on Judicial Notice of Adjudicated Facts (ICTY Apr. 20, 2004).

84 *See, e.g.*, Prosecutor v. Dragomir Milošević, Case No. IT-98-29/1-AR73.1, Decision on Interlocutory Appeal Against Trial Chamber's Decision on

importantly, the general understanding is that an adjudicated fact admitted does not constitute definite proof in later proceedings, but is rather a mere *presumption* that the fact in question is proven. The opposing party is therefore free to challenge it during its case through arguments and evidence.

Controversially, through this mechanism, the ICTR has taken judicial notice of the existence of the genocide in Rwanda.[85] However, most instances of judicial notice are rather less problematic, and relate to background facts and/or patterns of criminal behavior that are not directly relevant to the individual criminal responsibility of the accused in question.[86]

VII. CONCLUSION

In the presentation of evidence, international criminal courts and tribunals follow an adversarial approach, tempered by certain principles of civil law origin. It has been remarked that no single national system could by itself provide for how international trials should be conducted due to the "peculiarities and difficulties of unearthing and assembling material for war crimes prosecutions," which call for judicial flexibility.[87] Indeed, despite the fact that most civil law systems today are adding

---

Prosecution's Motion for Judicial Notice of Adjudicated Facts and Prosecution's Catalogue of Agreed Facts, ¶ 16 (ICTY June 26, 2007) (and cited references).

[85] Prosecutor v. Karemera et al., Case No. ICTR-98-44-AR73(C), Decision on Prosecutor's Interlocutory Appeal of Decision on Judicial Notice, ¶ 35 (June 16, 2006) ("The fact of the Rwandan genocide is a part of world history, a fact as certain as any other, a classic instance of a 'fact of common knowledge.'").

[86] *See, e.g.*, Prosecutor v. Željko Mejakić, Case No. IT-02-65-PT, Decision on Prosecution Motion for Judicial Notice pursuant to Rule 94(B) (ICTY Apr. 1, 2004) (admitting, inter alia, adjudicated facts related to the "historical, geographical and political background to the conflict in Yugoslavia up to the disintegration of the federation in the 1990s" and the takeover of various towns by Bosnian-Serb formations, "eventually resulting in the displacement of thousands of non-Serbs"); Prosecutor v. Prlić et al., Case No. IT-04-74-PT, Decision on Motion for Judicial Notice of Adjudicated Facts Pursuant to Rule 94(B) (ICTY Mar. 12, 2006) (admitting, inter alia, adjudicated facts related to the background to the conflict but also to the humanitarian conditions in various towns and municipalities in Bosnia-Herzegovina during the indictment period and the relationship between the Croatian army and Bosnian Croat forces fighting there).

[87] Prosecutor v. Kovačević, Case No. IT-97-24-AR73, Separate Opinion of Judge Shahabuddeen, Decision Stating Reasons for Appeals Chamber's Order of 29 May 1998, pp. 4–5 (ICTY July 2, 1998).

strict sets of exclusionary rules and other rules on the admission and evaluation of evidence typical of common law adversarial approaches, international criminal trials still follow the somewhat older tradition of a flexible and "liberal" approach to the admission of evidence typical of inquisitorial systems, an approach essentially unhindered by specific and technical rules. The need to "shield" a jury from possibly tainted evidence, which created the impetus for devising and refining traditional exclusionary rules at common law, simply does not exist at the international level. The ad hoc tribunals (ICTY and STL in particular, and to a lesser extent ICTR and SCSL) further witnessed a shift away from the original preference for oral evidence in order to expedite proceedings and secure otherwise unavailable evidence through the admission of written statements. Moreover, the judges' role in conducting the examination of witnesses, at times limiting the autonomy of the parties in how evidence is presented, increases the perception that international criminal trials are not fully "adversarial." Such an approach is probably due to the institutional objectives of striving to find the "truth" and of safeguarding the victims' interests[88] by avoiding oppression through unnecessarily harsh cross-examination techniques, similarly to several domestic systems where victims of rape or other serious crimes are granted enhanced protection status.

The main safeguards developed for the lack of detailed exclusionary rules and the admissibility of written evidence consist in the requirements that (i) judges issue their verdicts through reasoned opinions and that (ii) in entering a conviction beyond reasonable doubt, they are banned from relying solely or decisively on evidence which the accused has had no opportunity to test. However, problematic features persist. Notwithstanding the protections developed by international criminal tribunals to ensure that only relevant and reliable evidence is tendered and that a suitable degree of publicity is guaranteed during trial, international judges tend to be flooded with irrelevant and unreliable evidence. This may in turn lead to lengthy delays[89] and, at times, unfair treatment of the accused facing an uphill struggle in understanding the contours of the case

---

[88] Mirjan Damaška, *What Is the Point of International Criminal Justice?*, 83 Chi.-Kent L. Rev. 329 (2008).

[89] In this sense, it is noteworthy that Articles 21 and 28 of the STL Statute require this Tribunal to "confine the trial, appellate and review proceedings strictly to an *expeditious hearing* of the issues raised by the charges, or the grounds for appeal or review, respectively. It shall take *strict measures to prevent any action that may cause unreasonable delay*" and to adopt Rules of Procedure and Evidence "with a view to ensuring a fair and *expeditious* trial." *Id.* (emphasis added).

mounted against them. These are challenges international judges must face in order to guarantee lasting legitimacy of the proceedings before them and, ultimately, of the process of international criminal justice as a whole.

5. Self-representation and the use of assigned, standby and amicus counsel

Charles Chernor Jalloh*

I. INTRODUCTION

On July 3, 2001, former Yugoslav President Slobodan Milošević, who was on trial for his alleged role in perpetrating international crimes in the Balkans, informed the Trial Chamber of the International Criminal Tribunal for the former Yugoslavia (ICTY) that he did not want a lawyer to represent him during future proceedings.[1] The Trial Chamber allowed Milošević to continue in this manner, but also appointed *amicus curiae* to assist the Court.[2] As Milošević's health began to diminish, the ICTY faced difficult questions about if and when to assign counsel to represent the accused, and in so doing, restricting Milošević's right to defend himself.

* LL.B., B.C.L. (McGill), M.St. International Human Rights Law (with distinction) and Chevening Scholar (Oxford); Assistant Professor, University of Pittsburgh School of Law, U.S.A.; formerly Legal Advisor to the Office of the Principal Defender and court-appointed duty counsel to former Liberian President Charles Taylor, Special Court for Sierra Leone; Associate Legal Officer in Trial Chamber I, UN International Criminal Tribunal for Rwanda and Visiting Scholar, Office of the Public Counsel for Defence, International Criminal Court. E-mail: jallohc@pitt.edu.

I am grateful to the editors for their helpful comments which improved the quality of this chapter. I also acknowledge, with gratitude, Professor J. Jan Osei-Tutu, FIU College of Law, for serving as a good sounding board and for her usual support. I am indebted to Samuel Derrick, my summer 2011 research assistant, for his excellent help despite the short deadlines that I often imposed upon him. Kirk Knutson assisted with locating materials, while LaTi Wells did a last round edit and helped with the footnotes. I thank them both for their hard work.

1 Prosecutor v. Milošević, Case No. IT-99-37-I, Written Note by the Accused, Registry pp. 3371–72 (ICTY July 3, 2001); Prosecutor v. Milošević, Case No. IT-99-37-I, Initial Appearance, Transcript pp. 1–2 (ICTY July 3, 2001).

2 Prosecutor v. Milošević, Case No. IT-02-54, Order Inviting Designation of *Amicus Curiae* (ICTY Aug. 30, 2001) [hereinafter *Milošević*, Order Inviting Designation of *Amicus Curiae*].

The ICTY's handling of these problems, as well as Milošević's subsequent death before the completion of his trial, thrust unresolved questions of international criminal procedure into the spotlight.[3]

Since then, many defendants before the ICTY and other international criminal courts have tried to follow Milošević's lead and represent themselves. Others, failing to gain permission to continue without legal counsel, have attempted to emulate Milošević's other lead and disrupt the trial proceedings as much as possible. The evolving body of international criminal law has responded to these challenges by developing procedures to deal with defendants who either want to represent themselves or who create large and continuous disruptions of court proceedings.

This chapter discusses the various roles played by counsel in international criminal trials where defendants choose to represent themselves, or to be disruptive and/or to otherwise engage in obstructionist behavior. It demonstrates that much like U.S. criminal law, in international criminal law, accused persons have the fundamental right to represent themselves in person or through legal assistance of their own choosing. That said, while the right to self-representation sounds good in theory, in practice, it is fraught with difficulties. It is the type of right that defendants should invoke sparingly, if at all, especially considering that they usually stand accused of some of the worst crimes in the legal lexicon.

A review of leading cases shows that by conveniently borrowing from U.S. common law in some cases, and continental European civil law in others, international criminal courts have failed to develop a single or unified approach to defendants' right to represent themselves. This has not helped the accused persons who have sought to use, and sometimes, abuse the right for political purposes. It is submitted that since no self-representing defendant in an international trial has yet succeeded in securing an acquittal, by choosing to exercise the right to self-representation, even legally trained defendants who lack the distance, ability and experience challenging prosecution evidence in complex criminal trials risk helping prosecutors pave the way to their own convictions.

The chapter is organized as follows. Section II provides the background on the right to self-representation and the role of assigned, standby and amicus counsel in international criminal proceedings. Section III examines common law and civil law approaches to the right of self-representation. The focus, although not exclusively, is on the U.S. Supreme Court jurisprudence which offered helpful precedent on how to interpret the right of

---

[3] Joanne Williams, *Slobodan Milošević and the Guarantee of Self-Representation*, 32 Brook. J. Int'l L. 553, 554–5 (2007).

self-representation in the early international criminal tribunal cases.

Section IV discusses the main circumstances under which national courts using these principles appoint counsel to represent the accused, even against his objections, so long as his conduct threatens to derail the integrity of the trial process. This part then assesses how well these principles have been transposed to and applied in international criminal courts. It is suggested that, in national jurisdictions, limited wiggle room is typically afforded to obstructionist defendants bent on undermining their own trials. By contrast, in some international courts, disruptive defendants seem to engage in contumacious conduct without immediately receiving meaningful sanction such as forfeiture of the right to represent themselves in court. This has caused unacceptable delays in many important cases, and has impelled a shift away from the common law's deference towards an accused's right to defend himself in person in favor of the civil law which is less hesitant to qualify the defendant's rights so as to maintain the overall continuity and integrity of the proceedings.

Finally, in Section V which constitutes the Conclusion, the key findings are summarized and there are some final observations. The general improvement we see in international criminal tribunals' ability to smoothly handle self-representing, disruptive or uncooperative defendants is noted. While defendants should always retain the right to choose whether to be represented by counsel, or to appear *pro se*, the attempts by some high profile accused in various tribunals to turn the courtroom into a platform to advance ethnic political agendas, to badger witnesses and victims, and to transform the dignified search for some justice into political theater undermines both the legal and moral justifications for the right. If this trend continues, as international criminal law matures, the tendency will be for the right to be increasingly curtailed over time.

II. THE RIGHT TO SELF-REPRESENTATION AND THE ROLE OF COUNSEL IN INTERNATIONAL CRIMINAL TRIALS

International courts employ three main tools to maintain control over proceedings in cases involving uncooperative or disruptive defendants: (1) standby counsel, (2) court-assigned counsel and (3) *amicus curiae*. Standby counsel is a lawyer appointed by the court to assist an accused who is asserting the right of self-representation.[4] This attorney, who may be designated

4 Although the idea of standby counsel was first discussed in the International

at the court's own initiative, generally assists the defendant to properly prepare and present his case by, for example, helping him understand and navigate basic courtroom procedures.[5] The lawyer is literally on "standby" ready to step in at short notice should the court order him to take over the defense case in exceptional circumstances. For instance, where the defendant engages in disruptive behavior or other conduct requiring his removal from the courtroom, falls ill for an extended period of time, or is otherwise unable to continue participating in the proceedings.

The key is that, once appointed, a "standby" lawyer can only provide assistance if and to the extent requested by the self-representing defendant, who still enjoys the core right and bears primary responsibility to lead and present his own defense. A self-representing accused, including one taking advantage of the assistance offered by standby counsel, may still seek legal advice from a lawyer of his own choosing at his own expense.

Sometimes, the term "duty counsel" is used to refer to a standby lawyer, who may be an employee of the tribunal, who can be asked to provide initial legal advice and assistance to an accused pending the appointment of counsel or if he elects to represent himself. This includes assisting with summary procedures such as representing the accused during his arraignment or stepping in to represent the defendant's interest when he is not present in court either of his own volition or when the court has ordered his removal.

Court assigned counsel is imposed by order of the court, usually over the defendant's objections, and given the responsibility to ensure the defense of the accused person. International tribunals usually assign attorneys to represent accused persons in circumstances where the chamber considers that this is in the best interests of justice because of the defendant's substantial and persistent obstruction of the proceedings which threatens the fair and expeditious conduct of the trial or the proper administration of justice.

The role of a court-assigned lawyer must be distinguished from that of what we might call administratively appointed counsel, who is normally selected and appointed to represent an indigent or partially indigent

---

Criminal Tribunal for Rwanda in Prosecutor v. Barayagwiza, Case No. ICTR-97-19-T, Decision on Defense Counsel Motion to Withdraw, ¶¶ 18–22 (Nov. 2, 2000) [hereinafter *Barayagwiza*, Decision on Defense Counsel Motion to Withdraw], a detailed discussion of the concept was later given in the ICTY case of Prosecutor v. Šešelj, Case No. IT-03-67-PT, Decision on Prosecution's Motion for Order Appointing Counsel to Assist Vojislav Šešelj with His Defence, ¶¶ 12–30 (May 9, 2003) [hereinafter *Šešelj*, Decision on Prosecution's Motion Appointing Counsel].

5 *Šešelj*, Decision on Prosecution's Motion Appointing Counsel, *supra* note 4, ¶ 30.

person by a tribunal administrator (usually the registrar or his delegate), after full consultations with the defendant. Although the case law is often inconsistent in the terminology used, the distinction between *court-assigned* counsel and administratively *appointed counsel* is not only semantic, it is critical both for reasons of principle and practice. In principle, except where the defendant's previously chosen counsel is appointed by the court as standby counsel to continue to represent the accused, he is the court's chosen lawyer representing the defendant in the proceedings rather than the defendant's choice of legal representative.

In practice, depending on the reasons why counsel is being imposed, the lawyer forced upon an accused may not necessarily receive any instructions from the "client" or gain his cooperation on the presentation of the defense case. Whether the defendant instructs or refuses to instruct counsel has serious implications for the type and effectiveness of the defense that the lawyer can mount to counter the prosecution case. It therefore usually raises ethical concerns for the attorney regarding the propriety of representing a defendant who might prove to be uncooperative.

Whereas in the case of counsel administratively assigned by the registrar or the principal defender, the lawyer, who will usually have been selected from the list of counsel taking into account the wishes of the accused, typically enjoys the cooperation of his client. He therefore can seek, receive and act on instructions from the defendant on how best to counter the prosecution's allegations.

The consequence of a lawyer's appointment to represent an accused by the court, instead of by administrative decision of the registrar, also impacts who can terminate counsel. Depending on the stage of the case, usually only during the pre-trial phase, lawyers administratively appointed to represent the accused can be replaced, for example at the defendant's request, simply by withdrawing counsel and replacing him with another.

For practical reasons, because lawyers are generally expected to represent the defendants to the finality of the case, the chances that counsel will be replaced at the accused's request decreases dramatically as the case progresses towards trial and becomes extremely difficult once trial has begun. Provided, of course, that there is no breakdown in the counsel-client relationship. On the other hand, attorneys appointed to represent a defendant by order of the court can only be replaced by fiat of judicial decision. Furthermore, assuming that there is no serious breakdown in the lawyer-client relationship, the likelihood that a court will countenance an administrative change of appointed counsel diminishes dramatically once the trial has opened. It is usually only allowed in the most exceptional circumstances where there is no serious threat of or disruption to the smooth continuation of the proceedings.

The third procedural device used is *amicus curiae*, or "friend of the court,"[6] which as specifically employed in international criminal trials is a creative option that the Tribunals have developed to ensure a particular (defense) perspective is presented during the trial or appeal phase of a case. The *amicus* counsel's duty is to assist the court in any manner counsel deems appropriate to ensure a fair trial and proper determination of the case before the court, for example, by making oral or written submissions on any procedural, evidentiary or substantive issue that could have been properly raised in response to the prosecution case or by bringing to the chamber's attention any exculpatory or mitigating evidence in favor of the accused.[7] The appointment of an *amicus* lawyer usually takes place in situations where the defendant has resisted, or indicated that he will resist, the assignment or appointment of counsel to represent him because he insists he prefers to represent himself personally.

Crucially, the *amicus*, whose main function is to assist the court in its task of rendering credible justice rather than to represent the defendant[8] as such, may or may not receive any cooperation from the accused. He operates independently of the accused although he presents arguments intended to advance the accused's position in the case. The chamber at its discretion may terminate the *amicus curiae* appointment.[9] Termination can also occur where, for example, the accused complains that the conduct of such counsel shows that he is biased against the defendant or had already formulated conclusions as to guilt.

These three procedural devices have been used, singly and in some cases in combination, to varying degrees of success by, not just the ICTY, which has been a pioneering but also well criticized court in this area, but also other ad hoc mechanisms such as the International Criminal Tribunal for Rwanda (ICTR), the Special Court for Sierra Leone (SCSL), the Special Tribunal for Lebanon (STL or Lebanon Tribunal), and even in the nascent practice of the permanent International Criminal Court (ICC).[10] In making decisions regarding use of standby, *amicus*, or court-appointed

---

[6] BALLENTINE'S LAW DICTIONARY 69 (3d ed. 1969).

[7] *Milošević*, Order Inviting Designation of *Amicus Curiae*, *supra* note 2, ¶ 1.

[8] Prosecutor v. Milošević, Case No. IT-02-54, Reasons for Decision on the Prosecution Motion Concerning Assignment of Counsel, ¶ 3 (ICTY Apr. 4, 2003) [hereinafter *Milošević*, Reasons for Decision on the Prosecution Motion Concerning Assignment of Counsel].

[9] *See* Prosecutor v. Milošević, Case No. IT-02-54, Transcript of Record at 10–14 (ICTY Oct. 10, 2002).

[10] The STL has not actually held a trial yet, but provisions of the rules of the Court reflect awareness of this issue. This observation is mentioned further below.

counsel to self-representing or disruptive defendants, international criminal courts are not simply flying blind. There is statutory language drawn from universal and regional human rights instruments commonly shared by nearly all of these tribunals that help to guide, and at the same time, shape or limit their rulings and approaches.

The International Covenant on Civil and Political Rights (ICCPR) states in Article 14(3)(d) that everyone shall be guaranteed the right:

> [t]o be tried in his presence, and to defend himself in person or through legal assistance of his own choosing; to be informed, if he does not have legal assistance, of this right; and to have legal assistance assigned to him, in any case where the interests of justice so require, and without payment by him in any such case if he does not have sufficient means to pay for it.

The ICTY in Article 21(4)(d) and the ICTR in Article 20(4)(d) adopt nearly the same language in their respective statutes,[11] as does the SCSL in Article 17(4)(d). The European Convention on Human Rights (ECHR) similarly grants all criminal defendants the right "to defend himself in person or through legal assistance of his own choosing."[12] The American Convention on Human Rights (ACHR) guarantees "the right of the accused to defend himself personally or to be assisted by legal counsel of his own choosing."

Interestingly, the African Charter on Human and Peoples' Rights (ACHPR) diverges from the European and American Conventions by granting a relatively broader right to a defense of which the role of counsel is only but one component. Article 7(c) of the ACHPR provides each individual "the right to defense, including the right to be defended by counsel of his choice." That article on its face suggests that the defendant, at least in principle, is also guaranteed the lawyer of his choice. This is a much more expansive understanding of the scope of the right to counsel when public funds are being used than under the emerging jurisprudence of the international criminal tribunals which qualifies that right.

Beyond the ACHPR, only two other ad hoc courts diverge from the nearly identical statutory provisions of the other tribunals. Although Article 67(d) of the Rome Statute of the International Criminal Court similarly enshrines the accused person's right "to conduct his defense in person or through legal assistance of the accused's choosing," it explicitly qualifies the enjoyment of that right.[13] Therefore, if the accused

---

11 The ICTR statute reads "himself or herself" rather than only "himself."

12 The European Convention on Human Rights, Rome, 4.X.I. 1950, art. 6, Dec. 10, 1948.

13 The fair trial rights of the accused are set out in Article 67, whereas Article

is present in court but "continues to disrupt the trial," the chamber "may remove the accused" after "other reasonable alternatives" have been exhausted.[14] However, in such instances, the judges are obliged to provide alternate means for the accused "to observe the trial and instruct counsel from outside the courtroom."[15] That said, recognizing the exceptional nature and potential negative impact of such a measure on the fairness and ultimate outcome of the proceedings, barring defendants from court and ordering alternative forms of participation is strictly limited to the duration necessary for the trial's return to normalcy (Article 63(2)).

Similarly, while Article 16(4)(d) of the Statute of the STL grants defendants the right to "be tried in his or her presence, and to defend himself or herself in person or through legal assistance of his or her own choosing," that tribunal's Rules of Procedure and Evidence (RPE) states that "[t]he Pre-Trial Judge or a Chamber may impose counsel present or otherwise assist the accused in accordance with international criminal law and international human rights where this is deemed necessary in the interests of justice and *to ensure a fair and expeditious trial*"[16] (emphasis added). This final provision appears to be the key difference between the rules of the STL and the other ad hoc penal tribunals.[17]

Essentially, the Lebanon Tribunal introduces a second qualifying phrase to the right to defend oneself, thereby granting the judges greater leeway to restrict the enjoyment of that right. Similarly, under the Rome Statute scheme discussed above, the chamber may limit the exercise of this broad right on the basis of the authority explicitly conferred by the primary statute rather than the subordinate rules of procedure and evidence as envisaged under the STL.

---

63 discusses trial presence. *See* Rome Statute of the International Criminal Court, U.N. Doc. A/CONF.183/9, arts. 63, 66, July 1, 2002.

[14] *Id.* art. 63.

[15] *Id.*

[16] Special Tribunal for Lebanon Rules of Procedure and Evidence (STL RPE), Rev. 1, June 10, 2009, Rule 59F, Assignment of Counsel.

[17] IT/32/Rev. 45, ICTY Rules of Procedure and Evidence (ICTY RPE), amended Dec. 8, 2010, states in Rule 45*ter* "The Trial Chamber may, if it decides that it is in the interests of justice, instruct the Registrar to assign a counsel to represent the interests of the accused." The ICTR Rules of Procedure and Evidence (ICTR RPE), amended Oct. 1, 2009, Rule 45*quater* is identical to the ICTY rule. The SCSL Rules of Procedure and Evidence (SCSL RPE), amended May 28, 2010, states in Rule 45(B)(ii) that the defense office shall provide "legal assistance as ordered by the Special Court in accordance with Rule 61, if the accused does not have sufficient means to pay for it, as the interests of justice may so require."

Be that as it may, the language contained in the ICTY and ICTR Statutes seems simple and clear enough. It is, after all, essentially the same language used in at least three international Conventions defining the human rights of suspects and accused persons.[18] Unfortunately, international criminal courts have not found the application of this language easy or satisfying. The problems the pioneer ICTY and ICTR have experienced in dealing with disruptive and self-representing defendants is at least partially responsible for the change in statutory or regulatory language employed by the ICC and other tribunals such as the STL.[19]

There are many aspects to the question of how to appropriately handle these types of situations, most of which have been faced by an international court at least once. Issues that have arisen include handling requests to appear *pro se* at various stages of trial,[20] determining the extent of responsibilities and powers of standby and *amicus* counsel,[21] allowing standby or *amicus* counsel to take over the case when a defendant is removed from court or absent,[22] pre- and mid-trial requests for a change

---

18 The ICCRP, ECHR, and ACHR referenced previously.

19 Michael Scharf, *Chaos in the Courtroom: Controlling Disruptive Defendants and Contumacious Counsel in War Crimes Tribunals*, 39 Case W. Res. J. Int'l L. 155 (2006-07); Mark Ellis, *The Saddam Trial: Challenges to Meeting International Standards of Fairness with Regard to the Defense*, 39 Case W. Res. J. Int'l L. 171 (2006–07).

20 Prosecutor v. Krajišnik, Case No. IT-00-29-T, Decision on Admission of Documents Tendered by Mr. Krajišnik (ICTY Aug. 31, 2005); Prosecutor v. Norman, Case No. SCSL-04-14-T-125, Decision on the Application of Samuel Hinga Norman for Self-Representation Under Article 17(4)(d) of the Statute of the Special Court (June 8, 2004) [hereinafter *Norman*, Decision on the Application of Samuel Hinga Norman for Self-Representation]; Prosecutor v. Gbao, Case No. SCSL-04-15-T-285, Decision on Appeal Against Decision on Withdrawal of Counsel (Nov. 23, 2004).

21 Prosecutor v. Milošević, Case No. IT-02-54-AR73.7, Decision on Interlocutory Appeal of the Trial Chamber's Decision on the Assignment of Defense Counsel (ICTY Nov. 1, 2004) [hereinafter *Milošević*, Decision on Interlocutory Appeal of the Trial Chamber's Decision on the Assignment of Defense Counsel]; Prosecutor v. Karadžić, Case No. IT-95-5/18-AR73, Decision On Radovan Karadžić's Appeal from Decision on Motion to Vacate Appointment of Richard Harvey (ICTY Feb. 12, 2010); Prosecutor v. Šešelj, Case No. IT-03-67-AR73.3, Order Concerning Appointment of Standby Counsel and Delayed Commencement of Trial (ICTY Oct. 25, 2006).

22 Prosecutor v. Karadžić, Case No. IT-95-5/18-T, Decision on Appointment of Counsel and Order on Further Trial Proceedings (ICTY Nov. 5, 2009) [hereinafter *Karadžić*, Decision on Appointment of Counsel and Order on Further Trial Proceedings].

to either standby or appointed counsel,[23] disruption caused by retained counsel,[24] the extent of public legal resources and advice that should be given to self-represented defendants,[25] and other related issues as well.

In making decisions regarding the scope of counsel's role in a trial, international courts are forced to balance many different, and sometimes conflicting, rights. These include the right of the defendant to a fair trial, the right to an expeditious trial, the rights of all those participating in the trial, including the accused and the victims, as well as the seemingly conflicting absolute right to counsel and equally fundamental right to refuse the assistance of counsel.[26] In addition, all of these specific rights are viewed within the context of the broad and amorphous concept of "interests of justice" as indicated by the statutory provisions above.[27]

Central to this discussion, as several appellate courts in some national jurisdictions have emphasized, the court must walk a thin line between improperly allowing a defendant to proceed *pro se*, thereby violating the right to counsel, and improperly requiring the defendant to proceed with counsel, thereby violating his right to defend himself.[28] When considering what role standby counsel and/or *amicus curiae* will have, this line becomes even more difficult to tread because standby counsel could violate either of the defendant's rights by acting either too little or too much during the course of a trial. Defendants in the United States, for example, have appealed trials in which they appeared *pro se* claiming both that standby counsel interfered too much and violated their right to defend themselves,[29] and that a court's use of standby or appointed

---

23 Prosecutor v. Nyiramasuhuko, Case No. ICTR-97-21, Decision on Ntahobali's Motion for Withdrawal of Counsel (Jun. 22, 2001).

24 Prosecutor v. Taylor, Case No. SCSL-2003-01-T, Prosecution Opening Statement, Transcript of Record (June 4, 2007) [hereinafter *Taylor*, Transcript of Record]; Scharf, *supra* note 19, at 164.

25 *Šešelj*, Decision on Prosecution's Motion Appointing Counsel, *supra* note 4; Prosecutor v. Janković, Case No. IT-96-23/2-PT, Decision Following Registrar's Notification of Radovan Stanković's Request for Self-Representation (ICTY Aug. 19, 2005).

26 Nina Jørgensen, *The Problem of Self-Representation at International Criminal Tribunals: Striking a Balance Between Fairness and Effectiveness*, 4 J. INT'L CRIM. JUST. 64, 69 (2006).

27 Göran Sluiter, *Fairness and the Interests of Justice*, 3 J. INT'L CRIM. JUST. 9, 12 (2005).

28 United States v. Frazier-El, 204 F.3d 553, 559 (4th Cir. 2000) (quoting Fields v. Murray, 49 F.3d 1024, 1029 (4th Cir. 1995) (en banc) (quoting Cross v. United States, 893 F.2d 1287, 1290 (11th Cir.1990))).

29 McKaskle v. Wiggins, 465 U.S. 168 (1984).

counsel was insufficient and violated their right to the protections of counsel.[30]

Considering the frequency with which the landmark U.S. Supreme Court decision in *Faretta v. California*,[31] which established the right to self-representation in the United States, is cited by every international tribunal,[32] these same problems are likely to, and in many cases do, arise.

The bad news for international criminal justice is that all of these competing rights and interests make it nearly impossible to create hard and fast rules for the role of counsel at any particular trial.[33] The good news is that the balancing of so many interests allows international courts a great deal of leeway to learn from past trials and tribulations and tweak their assessment of these rights thereby redefining the appropriate role of counsel in specific factually and legally complex international criminal trials. As they tend to construe the text of the fair trial provisions contained in their instruments in a manner that accords with the letter but also the spirit of the rights enshrined by international human rights, these relatively new tribunals have breathed life into otherwise vague human rights provisions. They have done so in light of the problems and experiences garnered from the long experience with concrete criminal trials at the national level.

The international law, however, also has a license for further leeway that most national jurisdictions recognizing the right to self-representation do not. The procedures of international criminal law are usually conceived of as a blend of two major Western legal traditions, in particular, the common law/Anglo-American law and civil law or Continental/Romano-Germanic systems.[34] While the right to represent oneself is almost unanimously

---

30 Clark v. Perez, 510 F.3d 382 (2d Cir. 2008).

31 Faretta v. California, 422 U.S. 806 (1975).

32 Prosecutor v. Šešelj , Case No. IT-03-67-PT, Decision on Assignment of Counsel, ¶ 15 (ICTY Aug. 21, 2006) [hereinafter *Šešelj*, Decision on Assignment of Counsel]; *Milošević*, Decision on Interlocutory Appeal of the Trial Chamber's Decision on the Assignment of Defense Counsel, *supra* note 21, ¶ 11; *Barayagwiza*, Decision on Defense Counsel Motion to Withdraw, *supra* note 4, (Gunawardana Concurring); Prosecutor v. Gbao, Case No. SCSL 2004-15-T, Prosecution's Submissions to Gbao's Appeal from Decision on Withdraw of Counsel of 6 July 2004, ¶ 25 (Sept. 22, 2004).

33 In fact, the RPE at the ICTY have been amended over 40 times since 1993 to account for shifts in the Court's attempt to balance fairness and expediency. Fausto Pocar, *Common and Civil Law Traditions in the ICTY Criminal Procedure: Does Oil Blend with Water?*, 2009 INT'L ASS'N OF PROCEDURAL L. 3–4, *available at* http://www.iapl2009.org/documents/4bFaustoPocar.pdf.

34 Gideon Boas, *Self-Representation Before the ICTY*, 9 INT'L CRIM. JUST. 53 (2011); Michael Scharf & Christopher Rassi, *Do Former Leaders Have an*

recognized by the countries operating with a predominantly common law legal system, countries with a mostly civil law orientation do not always recognize such a right.[35] There are various reasons for this, but for our purposes, the most relevant seems to be that many civilian systems mandatorily assign defense counsel in criminal cases because it is deemed to be in the best interests of justice for the accused to be assisted by counsel.[36]

Different civil law traditions structure the mandatory assignment of a lawyer in criminal cases in different ways.[37] For some, like Italy, counsel must always be present; whereas, for others such as Germany, this requirement of counsel is confined only to cases where the accused is charged with serious crimes.[38] Other civil law countries occupy an intermediate twilight zone between these two extremes, for instance in the practice of criminal courts in France and Belgium,[39] counsel will be imposed, but only if the accused does not initially choose one.

This discrepancy in the general attitudes of "inquisitorial" civil law systems, compared to "adversarial" common law systems, require a kind of broad, big-picture balancing.[40] Thus, while international criminal procedure is still a work in progress, the international penal tribunal must seek to reconcile underlying philosophical differences between the national legal principles that form the basis of the procedural decisions and rules defining the role of the parties, especially the accused and his counsel, in a criminal trial.[41]

To understand how the role of counsel is defined at the international level, therefore, appears to require an understanding of two intertwined balancing processes. The first is the balancing of the uneven blend of common and civil law principles that have resulted in the emergence of a mixed system of international criminal procedure while providing a credible institutional mechanism for prosecuting the types of heinous

---

International Right to Self-Representation in War Crimes Trials?, 20 OHIO ST. J. ON DISP. RESOL. 3, 15 (2004).

35 *Šešelj*, Decision on Assignment of Counsel, *supra* note 32, ¶ 20.

36 Prosecutor v. Milošević, Case No. IT-02-54-T, Reasons for Decision on Assignment of Defence Counsel, ¶ 50 (Sept. 22, 2004) [hereinafter *Milošević*, Reasons for Decision on Assignment of Defence Counsel].

37 *Šešelj*, Decision on Assignment of Counsel, *supra* note 32, ¶ 21; *Šešelj*, Decision on Prosecution's Motion Appointing Counsel, *supra* note 4, ¶ 16.

38 *See* German Code of Criminal Procedure, s. 140.

39 *See* French Code de Procedure Penal, arts. 274, 317.

40 For a discussion of the different types of truths sought, *see* SALVATORE ZAPPALÀ, HUMAN RIGHTS IN INTERNATIONAL CRIMINAL PROCEEDINGS 16 (2003).

41 *See Milošević*, Reasons for Decision on Assignment of Defence Counsel, *supra* note 36, ¶ 50.

and large-scale crimes for which available national legal remedies are, for whatever reason, either unavailable or inadequate.[42] The second is the balancing of the aforementioned considerations raised by the largely adversarial criminal trials likely taking place a considerable distance from the scene of the alleged crimes on a very public and visible stage involving high profile and usually astute defendants.

By first recognizing and considering each of these complex balancing processes and the situations in which they arise at the international level, it will hopefully be possible to clearly (re)define the lines for the appointment of counsel. It will also hopefully be possible to gain a new understanding of the best practices available to international penal courts with respect to standby, *amicus*, or assigned counsel in specific cases where a defendant chooses to defend himself personally or is disruptive.

III. COMMON LAW AND CIVIL LAW PERSPECTIVES ON THE RIGHT TO SELF-REPRESENTATION AND APPOINTMENT OF COUNSEL

The use of counsel in the common and civil law systems diverge rather noticeably. This has been attributed to the differing theories of trial used in each system. In the civil law system, where the judge acts in an investigatory role, finding his own route to the truth, counsel is not as essential as a guarantor of defendant's rights.[43] In the common law system, on the other hand, where the judge is deemed a neutral arbiter or referee between two supposedly equal adversaries, counsel bears primary responsibility for protecting the rights of his accused client by exploring every recognized avenue to ensure that he receives due process and that the trial is conducted fairly.[44] It may therefore not seem unusual that the right to forgo the assistance of counsel and represent oneself is a common feature of common law systems where the role of counsel is a considerably more important facet of a fair trial.

Civil law systems generally do not recognize a defendant's right to conduct his own defense, despite that, or perhaps because, defense counsel plays a much less significant role in determining the outcome of the trial.

---

[42] *See* Pocar, *supra* note 33, for a discussion of the benefits from mixing common and civil procedural norms into a unique international system.

[43] Rosemary Byrne, *The New Public International Lawyer and the Hidden Art of International Criminal Trial Practice*, 25 CONN. J. INT'L L. 243, 249 (2010).

[44] *Id.* at 261.

In addition to the routine and mandatory assignment of counsel in serious criminal cases, another explanation seems to be that in the civilian system, judges are simply applying comprehensive statutory provisions. There is little room for interpretation about what the law is or what the law should be. In contrast, the common law tradition is typically assumed to rest upon judges interpreting community norms and using their discretion to apply general principles found in previous precedent. Because there is a greater likelihood of policy considerations and discussion of how the law *should* be read in a common law court, especially due to the jury's role in adjudicating felony level offenses, there is a greater emphasis placed upon defendant autonomy. The defendant could theoretically persuade the judge and the jury to see things a particular way.

Furthermore, in common law systems, counsel – primarily through cross-examination of witnesses – effectively contributes to shaping the facts and outcome of the trial as ultimately determined by the jury. At the same time, with his professional legal training, the competent defense lawyer is in most cases best able to advise his client who, for all intents and purposes, may exercise his legal right to hold the prosecution to proof of the charges beyond a reasonable doubt by not introducing any evidence in return. In the civil law tradition, there is a much smaller persuasive aspect to a criminal trial, and the need to preserve defendant autonomy is minimized given the seemingly mechanical application of law to fact which is emphasized. Since international courts have so far adopted a system that is essentially adversarial rather than inquisitorial in nature, the common law emphasis on individual autonomy has so far largely prevailed in international criminal trials focused on ensuring fair trials.[45]

In civil law systems, the presence of counsel is not necessarily seen as divesting the defendant of his right to speak in court on his own behalf due to the assistance being rendered by the lawyer. Whereas common law courts tend to take the view that the presence of counsel overrides the rights of the individual to directly participate so long as his lawyer, the expert so to speak, is present and representing him in court. In addition, it may be that the extremely technical rules governing the admissibility of evidence, a significant characteristic of common law trials that have been largely abandoned in international criminal trials, also dampens the idea of direct defendant participation in procedurally complex trials.

These differences aside, it may be helpful to at this stage consider the principles shaping the common law rules on use of standby and *amicus*

---

[45] *Milošević*, Order Inviting Designation of Amicus Curiae, *supra* note 2.

counsel, before assessing how they compare to the "interests of justice" principles frequently invoked in international criminal trials.

In *R v. Woodward*, an early case addressing this issue in the United Kingdom, the English Court of Criminal Appeal held that a defendant had a right to present his own defense to a jury, and counsel could not legally be forced upon him against his will.[46] This brief opinion highlights two key considerations. First is the explicit reference to the jury, to whom the defense case will be presented. Second is the defendant's will, which may not be violated by the court's appointment of counsel upon him.

These same two considerations reappeared in the Supreme Court of the United States 40 years later in the landmark *McKaskle v. Wiggins* case, in which the Supreme Court established the limits upon standby counsel action during a trial. The *McKaskle* court indicated that standby counsel could autonomously take whatever action he deemed appropriate, provided that two important limitations are respected. First, the accused must maintain actual control over the case presented, and secondly, the participation of standby counsel does not go so far as to taint the jury's perception that the accused is conducting or controlling his own defense.[47]

In the leading *Faretta* case, the U.S. Supreme Court recognized the importance of individual autonomy at two distinct places in the majority opinion. To begin with, the court held that since the individual alone would bear the penalties and consequences for the effectiveness of the defense, the decision on how to proceed is rightfully placed in his hands.[48] Second, because a defendant is presumed innocent, the right to autonomous control over his defense cannot be stripped away, otherwise he would become "imprisoned in his privileges."[49]

The Supreme Court of Canada similarly identified respect for individual autonomy as the basis for its conclusion that an adversarial system requires allowing the defendant to control his own defense in *R v. Swain*.[50] The respect for individual autonomy recognized by the British, American and Canadian courts is a frequently cited basis for common law decisions restricting the role of counsel at a defendant's request. It is the Ontario Court of Appeals, however, that perhaps provided the most colorful and illuminating statement on the nature of the common law system when it stated as follows in *Phillips v. Ford Motor Company*:

---

46 R v. Woodward [1944] 1 KB 118 (1944) 29 Cr. App. R. 159.

47 McKaskle v. Wiggins, *supra* note 29, 177–9.

48 Faretta v. California, *supra* note 31, 834.

49 *Id* at 815.

50 R v. Swain (1990) 5 C.R. (4th) 253 (S. Ct. Can.).

> A trial is not intended to be a scientific exploration with the presiding judge assuming the role of a research director; it is a forum established for the purpose of providing justice for the litigants.[51]

This quotation helps to underline one of the major differences between the common and civil law systems. It would not be surprising to find a civil law judge stating that a trial *is* intended to be a scientific exploration for the truth. It in this way underscores the most basic distinction between the two different legal traditions. In the common law system the goal of a criminal trial is to dispense justice, although that may be variedly defined, while in the civil law system the goal of such proceedings is to establish the truth.[52]

This fundamental philosophical difference becomes clearer following an examination of civil law systems, and the codes which govern them. As a general rule, there is much less importance placed on the notion of a defendant's autonomy in the civil law tradition. In comparing France to the United States, for example, there are generally greater limitations placed upon plea bargaining in France.[53] The pre-trial investigatory process is not nearly as restricted by defendant's rights, and evidence is much more rarely excluded from trial.[54] The emphasis on an efficient finding of truth in France is not limited to pre-trial procedure, however.

In France, written briefs submitted to the bench are of much greater importance than in the United States.[55] This is because in civilian systems, the trial does not play the central role in criminal justice that it does in the common law.[56] Due to the extensive pre-trial judicial investigation and the emphasis on written submissions to the court, the trial does not play nearly as large a role in deciding the outcome of the case.[57] Rather than being a forum within which to hear and evaluate all the evidence, the trial

---

51 Phillips v. Ford Motor Company, (1971) 18 D.L.R. (3d) 641 (Ontario Ct. App.).

52 Byrne, *supra* note 43, at 255.

53 Edward Tomlinson, *Non-Adversarial Justice: The French Experience*, 42 MD. L. REV. 131, 161 (1983). Also, this is generally true of most civil law systems, and was one of the aspects of the civil law that was adopted by the ICTY from the beginning. Pocar, *supra* note 33, at 3.

54 Tomlinson, *supra* note 53.

55 Jean-François Poudret & Sébastien Besson, COMPARATIVE LAW OF INTERNATIONAL ARBITRATION 559 (2d ed. 2011).

56 Tomlinson, *supra* note 53.

57 Pre-trial written submissions are starting to play a larger role in international trials, but still do not reach the same level of thoroughness as a civil law dossier. Pocar, *supra* note 33, at 7.

is merely another means by which the judge obtains further evidence that has not already been presented. This all demonstrates the court-centric rather than party-centric emphasis the civil law system employs.

Yet, as important as it is, this difference should not be overstated. In fact, even the common law acknowledges and tries to address the tensions that lead the civilian system to its more pragmatic approach. For instance, as Chief Justice Burger observed in dissent in *Faretta*, the trial judge in a common law court is not simply an "automaton"[58] to ensure adherence to technical rules but also someone responsible for ensuring that justice, in its broadest sense, is achieved in every criminal trial in which public confidence in the system is not undermined. He thus warned that the criminal justice system should not be perverted and transformed into an "instrument of self-destruction"[59] by essentially providing a rope for frustrated or foolish defendants to hang themselves in society's full view, or worse, with its complicity or acquiescence.

The decreased focus on defendant autonomy and increased focus on the independent inquiry of the court is exemplified by the civil law rules regarding the assignment of counsel. Consider the German Code of Criminal Procedure, which after broadly defining when the assignment of counsel is mandatory, goes on to stipulate:

> In other cases the presiding judge shall appoint defense counsel upon application or ex officio if the assistance of defense counsel appears necessary because of the seriousness of the offence, or because of the difficult factual or legal situation, or if it is evident that the accused cannot defend himself, particularly where an attorney has been assigned to the aggrieved person pursuant to Sections 397a and 406g subsections (3) and (4).[60]

This provision grants the judge a great deal of discretion in assigning defense counsel to the accused, even in situations where counsel is not already mandatory.[61] The judge's authority to impose counsel upon a criminal defendant also seems to stem out of the civil law's focus on truth-finding over resolution-seeking. The resolution-seeking court must preserve respect for individual autonomy in order to guarantee confidence from the parties involved that both sides were given a fair chance to present their positions, and the winner was more convincing. The

---

58 Faretta v. California, *supra* note 31, 836.

59 *Id.*

60 The American Series of Foreign Penal Codes, German Code of Criminal Procedure, art. 140 (NYU 1965).

61 *See, e.g.*, *Šešelj*, Decision on Assignment of Counsel, *supra* note 32, ¶ 15.

truth-seeking court is less concerned with the perceptions of the parties involved in any particular case, and more concerned with the general aim for accurate decisions in most instances.

The greater discretion of judges to impose defense counsel against the wishes of an accused in civilian systems can also be attributed to the more active role the judge takes during the course of a criminal trial. Because the judge is personally questioning witnesses and making decisions about the direction a trial will go, appointing counsel has significant benefits to the judge in executing his responsibilities. In a common law system, the judge's role as a "neutral" arbiter certainly gets easier when dealing with counsel rather than the defendant directly. This is because of the increased power the judge wields over counsel through sanctions, penalties and fines, which have less impact upon the accused.[62]

In the civil law system, however, the assignment of counsel is more than just convenient for judges. Because the judge is charged with the responsibility of establishing what happened, requiring counsel from both sides to assist allows the judge greater certainty about both the facts of the case and the decision the court will reach. It seems to follow that both the underlying goals and the structure of each criminal justice system dictates the divergences in appointing counsel between the common and civil law traditions.

In any case, given the not entirely compatible goals of truth and justice, then, it is up to the international criminal law to shape a shared system of criminal procedure and professional roles that reflect the values of both the civil and common law.[63] Of course, both truth and justice play an extremely important role in international criminal law given the reasons behind its implementation. This body of law is taking center stage, although rather too ambitiously, was initially couched as a way to "end impunity" for some of the worst crimes which are otherwise not prosecuted in national courts.[64] As if that grand objective is not enough, the international community also envisaged that the creation of these courts would also help to establish a historical record and thereby foster national healing and reconciliation in countries torn apart by age-old ethnic animosities and violent crimes committed on a vast scale.[65]

In order to achieve the goals of ending impunity and fostering national

---

[62] Scharf, *supra* note 19, at 161.

[63] Byrne, *supra* note 43.

[64] *See* Rome Statute of the International Criminal Court, UN Doc. A/CONF. 183/9, Preamble.

[65] *See* U.N. Resolution 955, S/RES/955, Establishing the ICTR and attaching its Statute, ¶ 6 (Nov. 8, 1994).

healing, both truth and justice are vital factors. The displaying of facts about the crimes that the guilty have committed is vital to allowing countries to learn and perhaps even, with the passage of time, move past atrocities. In this sense, the civil law focus on finding and proclaiming absolute truth in regards to an individual's actions is seemingly more desirable in order to facilitate a country's acceptance of the legitimacy of international proceedings. This is all the more so because international criminal law essentially treads on the toes of states in an area that was classically deemed their exclusive preserve: the exercise of criminal jurisdiction which is both an attribute and a function of sovereignty.

Alternatively, a focus on justice bears just as much importance for the goals of international justice and the perceptions that surround it. It is important that international tribunals not lose legitimacy in making decisions by being perceived as "western" or "winner's" justice only. In order to avoid this perception, fairness to the defendant and respect for the defendant's autonomy during trial is essential. It therefore becomes clear that for an international penal court to even have the hope that it will accomplish its tall primary and secondary goals, the process and procedure of trial must maintain a focus on capturing both truth and justice. In order to do that, a blending and melding of common and civil law concepts and methods in concrete cases seems paramount.[66]

IV. APPLICATION OF COMMON LAW AND CIVIL LAW APPROACHES IN THE INTERNATIONAL CRIMINAL TRIBUNALS

Any international court could be faced with numerous potential decisions regarding the role of counsel in any given trial. Questions such as the amount of time or resources a defendant will have to prepare for trial, or how much funding he will be allowed to hire a defense team. However, the most frequent and most significant decisions that face international criminal tribunals tend to center around three major questions:

(1) Will or should the court appoint counsel for the defendant, or allow him to conduct his own defense?

---

[66] Although, on the other hand, unlike customary law or Islamic legal traditions, the more prevalent common and civil law systems are typically associated with the West. For a case-specific discussion of this idea, see Linda Carter, *Justice and Reconciliation on Trial: the* Gacaca *Proceedings in Rwanda,* 14 NEW ENG. J. INT'L & COMP. L. 41 (2008).

(2) Will or should the court appoint standby counsel and or *amicus curiae*, and if so, what role should they be given?
(3) What is the appropriate response in emergency situations when the defendant (and/or his counsel) is either absent or so disruptive that they need to be removed from court?

These questions have already been confronted by both the growing body of international criminal law and the numerous national jurisdictions many times over. Each of them can be analyzed at the international level by considering the balancing of interests by the court, as well as the goals and procedures employed by common and civil law systems at the national level.

In considering the first question, that is, whether the court should permit the defendant to represent himself or to appoint counsel to act on the accused's behalf, if necessary even against his opposition, the *Milošević* trial seems once again a good place to begin although it set a precedent on self-representation that has come under scathing criticism over time.[67] In allowing Milošević's initial request to represent himself, the judges, as discussed at the outset of this chapter, seemed primarily concerned with respecting the defendant's rights and guaranteeing that there was no question that the tribunal was granting him a fair trial.[68] The Trial Chamber, in an August 30, 2001, ruling, reasoned that Milošević's assertion of the right was both timely and unequivocal, and that Article 21(4)(d) guaranteed his right to conduct his own defense.[69] The judges then appointed three *amicus curiae* to ensure that Milošević's right to defend himself was not interfered with by the court.

Still, the appointment of *amici* was not the end of the court's decision regarding the role of counsel in that case. The judges had to confront the question about what should be done about Milošević's right to self-representation on at least three subsequent occasions. The prosecutor, who had urged the court to appoint defense counsel over Milošević's wishes in their initial ruling, waited just over a year to again urge the Trial Chamber to take action.[70] In an oral ruling on December 18, 2002,

---

[67] *See* Boas, *supra* note 34, at 55 (criticizing the ICTY approach to self-representation, first developed in *Milošević*, "a poor legal ruling," that has led to a "less than satisfactory" and "farcical" results in later case law).

[68] *Milošević*, Reasons for Decision on the Prosecution Motion Concerning Assignment of Counsel, *supra* note 8, ¶ 3.

[69] *Id.*

[70] *Milošević*, Reasons for Decision on Assignment of Defence Counsel, *supra* note 36, ¶ 7.

the Trial Chamber again rejected the prosecutor's request, but promised to keep the matter under review.[71] In September 2003, the prosecution again sought a hearing to address how the court should proceed in light of the disruptions to the trial posed by Milošević's poor health.[72] The judges, faced with this issue for the third time, issued a ruling reducing the number of days the court would sit to three per week, giving him time to rest and recover in between days in court.[73] Finally, after further disruptions, numerous submissions from the prosecutor and *amici* counsel, and health evaluations by three different physicians, the chamber decided in an oral ruling on September 2, 2004, that Milošević's health required them to appoint defense counsel so that the trial could proceed.[74]

At each of these four points of the trial, the Trial Chamber sought to balance a number of considerations in its determination of whether or not to assign counsel for Milošević. In its explanation of the reasons for the oral ruling on December 18, 2002, the court provided two primary justifications for refusing to impose counsel on Milošević. The judges felt that, since the ICTY was essentially operating on the adversarial model for its trials, it was necessarily required to follow accepted common law rules regarding the use of counsel at trial.[75] The judges cited the U.S. Supreme Court decision in *Faretta*, and reasoned that depriving the defendant of his right to represent himself would effectively be depriving him of the right to put forth his own defense.[76] The chamber, in reaching this conclusion, drew parallels between the American common law system and the rules established by the ICCPR and ECHR, as well as the statute for the ICTY itself.[77]

They thus determined that, as a matter of principle, the ICTY rules established an adversarial system in order to preserve the rights of the defendant and ensure a just trial occurred. Interestingly, they largely ignored case law from the civil law system which might have been incorporated into their reasoning to reach a more reasonable and balanced result as between the rights of the accused and the right of the tribunal to render credible justice.

The Trial Chamber's second explanation for their ruling attempted to be pragmatic. They ruled that if they imposed counsel on Milošević, and he

---

71 *Id.* ¶ 8.
72 *Id.* ¶ 9.
73 *Id.* ¶ 10.
74 *Id.* ¶ 1.
75 *Id.* ¶ 45.
76 *Id.*
77 *Id.* ¶¶ 22–32.

then refused to cooperate, they would either have to cut the defendant out of the trial altogether or relegate assigned counsel to a role no greater than that of the *amici* counsel.[78] The judges noted that they already had three lawyers assisting the court, and did not want to raise fairness concerns by denying Milošević the right to participate in his trial.[79] While one could legitimately question whether the chamber was too deferential towards the defendant, considering that other interests such as those of the victims and justice were also at stake, in civil law systems, which ironically would have imposed counsel at this stage, the accused is still typically allowed to participate in the trial by intervening to cross-examine witnesses after counsel and the judge are finished with their questions.[80] It follows that, instead of capitulating to the defendant's threat that he would not participate if counsel was imposed upon him, the chamber could have offered him a limited right to speak in court, on a case-by-case basis, with the leave of the presiding judge. This could have been conditioned on the provision that he would undertake to comport himself with the orders of the court. Interestingly, this approach was later used in other ICTY cases.

In any event, the balancing of interests had changed for the court by September 2004. In that decision, the Trial Chamber highlighted its fundamental duty to ensure a fair and expeditious trial. The court determined that allowing Milošević to proceed without counsel jeopardized the completion of the trial in a reasonable period of time, if at all.[81] After granting concession after concession so that Milošević could exercise a right the court considered fundamental to the adversarial process, the judges finally reached the conclusion that the overall fairness of the trial needed to take precedence over guarantees of fairness to the defendant personally.

Perhaps as a signal of the shift from an absolute to a qualified right of self-representation, and away from common law towards civil law principles, the *Milošević* Trial Chamber's September 2004 decision stopped citing U.S. case law, and instead supported their ruling with citations to the *Barayagwiza* case decided by the ICTR, and the *Norman* case from the SCSL.[82] Although also coinciding with the change to the composition of the Milošević bench around the same time, because of Presiding Judge Richard May's resignation for reasons of ill health, this other international

78 *Id.* ¶ 38.

79 *Id.* ¶¶ 3–4.

80 Wolfgang Schomburg, *The Role of the International Criminal Tribunals in Promoting Respect for Fair Trial Rights*, 8 Nw. U. J. Int'l Hum. Rts. 1, 51 (2009).

81 *Milošević*, Reasons for Decision on Assignment of Defence Counsel, *supra* note 36, ¶¶ 65–6.

82 *Id.* ¶¶ 40–41.

tribunal case law helped the judges to justify their decision to curtail Milošević's right to represent himself in the greater "interests of justice."

In *Barayagwiza*, the ICTR did not have to decide whether to appoint defense counsel, but rather whether to let assigned counsel withdraw from the case. The defendant, Barayagwiza, had proclaimed that the ICTR lacked the degree of independence and impartiality required to hold a fair trial, and refused to attend court because the proceedings were in his view a sham.[83] He had also instructed his assigned counsel not to attend the trial, or any of the court proceedings on his behalf.[84] This had prompted assigned counsel to file a motion to withdraw, in their argument, due to their ethical obligation to follow the instructions of their client in decisions about presenting the defense.[85]

The ICTR Trial Chamber unanimously ruled that assigned counsel did not only owe a duty to the defendant, but also to the tribunal as well.[86] Part of assigned counsel's greater duty towards the court included to ensure a fair and expeditious trial, and to defend their client's interests in an adversarial trial, with or without instructions on how to do so.[87] The judges reasoned that given the gravity of the charges, they had a higher duty to ensure the protection of the defendant's rights particularly given what was at stake for him.[88] Consequently, their obligation to protect the rights of the defendant and to maintain the overall fairness of the proceedings trumped Barayagwiza's assertion of the right to control his defense. In fact, they felt that this duty even trumped the duty of defense counsel – who were also officers of the court – to listen exclusively to Barayagwiza.[89]

In a compelling concurring opinion to the denial of counsel's request to withdraw, Judge Gunawardana relied on U.S. case law to suggest what might have been the better solution. He would have allowed assigned counsel to withdraw and appoint standby counsel for Barayagwiza instead.[90] This would have avoided the entangling of obligations between the defendant's counsel as lawyers for the accused and the duties that they owed the court in their capacity as defense counsel. This would have also

---

[83] *Barayagwiza*, Decision on Defense Counsel Motion to Withdraw, *supra* note 4, ¶ 12.
[84] *Id.*
[85] *Id.* ¶ 17.
[86] *Id.* ¶ 21.
[87] *Id.*
[88] *Id.* ¶ 23.
[89] *Id.* ¶ 24.
[90] *Id.* (Gunawardana, J., concurring).

permitted counsel in court to represent Barayagwiza to proceed along the best course of action, even in light of contrary orders from the defendant. In his view, the interests of justice dictated that the independence of standby counsel be preserved over the ethical obligations of appointed counsel.[91]

The *Norman* case before the SCSL involved a defendant attempting to follow in Milošević's footsteps and proceed to trial without counsel. The Trial Chamber of the SCSL, however, rejected Norman's request to proceed on his own for two main reasons. The first was the timing of Norman's request, which was made on the first day of trial. The court ruled that granting that defendant's request to represent himself before the tribunal would require an enormous delay in the proceedings to both give him time to prepare, and then to conduct the trial with him unrepresented by counsel.[92] The second reason offered was that Norman was not in the case alone as he was jointly being tried with two others. In those circumstances, the SCSL Trial Chamber determined that permitting Norman to proceed without any assistance of counsel would result in extreme unfairness to his two co-defendants, who both had retained counsel for the trial.[93]

In reaching this conclusion, the court considered a number of factors including the necessity of counsel to a fair and expeditious trial, the extreme complexity of the case in question, the public interest in having the trial continue in an expeditious manner, and the potential disruption of the proceedings arising from Norman's request.[94] In the end, the chamber determined that Norman would be required to accept standby counsel if he wanted to proceed in conducting his own defense.[95] The interests of justice, they held, required that the judges not allow Norman to continue entirely without any legal assistance.[96]

The SCSL is also the site of one of the more recent decisions on this topic, which occurred at the outset of the *Taylor* case in June 2007. The accused, former President of Liberia, Charles Taylor, did not appear in court on the day of the prosecution's opening statement.[97] Taylor did not believe that his defense team had been given adequate time, resources,

---

91 *Id.*
92 *Norman*, Decision on the Application of Samuel Hinga Norman for Self-Representation, *supra* note 20, ¶¶ 17–20.
93 *Id.* ¶¶ 13–16.
94 *Id.* ¶ 26.
95 *Id.* ¶ 32.
96 *Id.* ¶ 30.
97 *Taylor*, Transcript of Record, *supra* note 24.

or personnel by the SCSL to hold a fair trial. He therefore dismissed his entire defense team, refusing to allow them to represent him in court, and wrote a letter announcing his intention to represent himself.[98]

In response to what it later termed a "boycott" of the proceedings, the chamber ordered that lead counsel remain to represent the accused Taylor in his absence.[99] Taylor's defense counsel, much like Barayagwiza's lawyers at the ICTR, retorted that it would be unethical for him to purport to represent Taylor without instructions and against his former client's wishes. Although he was wrong on the law, he did not relent from this position, even after he was threatened with potential contempt of court if he departed the courtroom in violation of the chamber's order to remain.[100]

Left without defense counsel and without a defendant, the court appointed duty counsel from the Office of the Principal Defender, a lawyer employed by the SCSL Defense Office, to temporarily take over the defense case for the duration of the opening statement.[101] Consistent with that tribunal's practice, duty counsel had been attached to the case, but only in a limited role prior to that moment.[102] This raised the question of equality of arms and how the sole staff member of a poorly resourced Defense Office in The Hague Sub-Office of the SCSL could face an army of prosecutors to assist the accused during his self-representation.

Ultimately, Trial Chamber II did not permit Taylor's request to conduct his own defense. In a June 25, 2007, ruling, the judges determined that a defendant choosing to represent himself had to be present in court in order for the right to be validly asserted.[103] The court refused to allow Taylor to choose when to appear before them, and instead required that a new defense team be composed to handle his defense case.[104] This decision raised concerns about what judges should do in such circumstances where the absence of a defendant is apparently predicated on the belief that he would not get a fair trial, but at the same time, was clearly not spurious because it was a protest of the tribunal registrar's decision not to afford

---

98 *Id.*

99 *Id.*

100 *Id.*

101 *Id.*

102 For example, duty counsel, as the Head of the Hague Sub-Office of the Principal Defender in the SCSL, did not have access to disclosure materials from the prosecution, nor was he involved in the defense strategy prior to the events of June 4, 2007. In the interest of transparency, this author was the Court appointed counsel for Taylor.

103 *Taylor*, Transcript of Record, *supra* note 24.

104 *Id.*

him an adequate defense team and the chamber's refusal to give counsel sufficient time to prepare his case before the trial opened. In other words, at what point is a supposedly self-representing defendant like Taylor allowed to boycott court proceedings without risking termination of his prima facie right to defend himself in person?

In the end, the Trial Chamber, with great reluctance, delayed the trial by almost five full months to give the newly assigned defense team adequate time to review the disclosure and prepare their client's defense before the first prosecution witnesses were called to the stand.[105] The irony was that had the same judges given the defense counsel and the accused three additional months to prepare for the opening of the prosecution case, that major delay in the opening of the trial could have been easily avoided.

Taken together, this sampling of four important cases from the ad hoc tribunals demonstrate the various ways that international penal courts have weighed the decision whether or not to assign counsel over the defendant's wishes. Each court eventually made the decision to impose some form of counsel based on the interests of justice. The *Milošević* court at the ICTY initially fretted over preservation of the defendant's rights but later became very concerned with the expediency of the trial and the undue delay that allowing him to continue without counsel would cause. In *Barayagwiza*, the ICTR was primarily concerned with balancing the defendant's rights against ensuring the trial's inherent fairness and continuity. In the *Norman* case at the SCSL, the judges considered the expediency of the trial, its overall fairness given his two co-defendants at trial, and various other factors. Yet in *Taylor*, a different group of SCSL judges simply assumed that the defendant was seeking to manipulate the proceedings – as the prosecutors had insisted. They therefore qualified his right to represent himself absent further deliberation or the opportunity for him to clarify his position. The chamber could have, for example, invited him to show cause why counsel should not be imposed on him. That would have given him an opportunity to be heard before this fundamental right is taken away. At the same time, this might have been the right result as there had already been enough delays in that trial. The chamber also saved scarce resources and moved the process forward when it ordered appointment of competent counsel, which was what Taylor really wanted.

In the end, unlike the ICTY in *Milošević*, the stance taken by the SCSL and ICTR trial chambers in *Taylor* and *Barayagwiza* were similar. Each chamber basically determined that the defendants were boycotting the proceedings, after choosing to absent themselves from the trial, concluding

105 *Id.*

that their decisions to terminate counsel and to not instruct them were an attempt to obstruct the proceedings.

The difference between these decisions and the rulings of national courts faced with similar situations seems, at least partially, like a striking reflection of the larger goals of international criminal justice and the influence of civil law thinking. Consider the recent multi-accused case of *R v. Iqbal* before the English Court of Appeal Criminal Division during which one defendant became dissatisfied with his appointed counsel.[106] He requested a change of counsel, but did not provide the court with a substantial reason to justify his decision. The court ended up requiring that Iqbal, if he wanted to dispense with counsel, represent himself during the trial.[107]

This ruling stands in stark contrast to the SCSL decision in *Norman*. The U.K. court was not apparently concerned with the unfairness to Iqbal's five co-defendants. Rather, it cited as the primary consideration the risks of allowing intentional delays of trial by approving unjustified changes to assigned counsel. Additionally, the appeals court actually considered the interests of the five represented co-defendants as a reason to allow him to continue without counsel.[108] Because the other defendants would be represented, there was less danger from Iqbal unduly slowing or disrupting the course of the trial. It seems plausible that the *Norman* trial chamber could have reasonably reached a similar conclusion, considering that it had also ordered that he be assisted, during courtroom proceedings, by the court-appointed counsel.

A second interesting contrast with the balancing process at the international level is the case of *U.S. v. Vernier*, which was recently heard before the Court of Appeals for the Fifth Circuit. In that case, the defendant Vernier told a third party that he intended to disrupt his trial and make a political statement.[109] Unfortunately for his plan, the court denied his request to proceed to trial without representation.[110] This decision highlights the importance to the ICTY of maintaining the appearance of a just trial in the *Milošević* case. Milošević had also commented to the media about the legitimacy of both the tribunal and his upcoming trial. Between his comments, his health, and the considerably larger stage from which the trial would be conducted, the threat of disruption from Milošević was as great if not greater than the threat of disruption posed by Vernier.

There are several possible explanations for the greater leniency that the

106 R v. Iqbal [2011] EWCA Crim 1294.
107 *Id.* at 17.
108 *Id.* at 30.
109 United States v. Vernier, 381 F. App'x 325 (5th Cir. 2010).
110 *Id.* at 327.

ICTY demonstrated towards Milošević as compared to the Fifth Circuit with Vernier. The goals of the court shift based upon what is at stake for each respective defendant. The *Milošević* Court was considering charges of genocide and crimes against humanity, some of the worst crimes of which a person can be accused. The *Vernier* Court was dealing with a defendant accused of car-jacking resulting in death,[111] which is serious, but relatively less so. As the scale of crime becomes less severe, the court's concern with maintaining the continuity of the trial and refusing to allow the defendant's tactics to unnecessarily delay justice become greater.

Additionally, unlike the Fifth Circuit Court of Appeals, international tribunals are always concerned with maintaining the appearance of legitimacy for their verdicts. Besides the Milošević case being the first major test case in which the issue of self-representation confronted international criminal tribunal judges, it seems to become even more important for them to respect the rights of the defendant. At the same time, the countervailing consideration is that they not allow the accused to manipulate the ground rules in order to undermine victims' confidence in the process and ultimately to avoid facing justice.

The relative leniency may partly be a function of international criminal trials being expected to operate at a higher level of respect for defendant rights vis-à-vis domestic trials since they are also often intended to serve as models of fairness for national courts. Strict concern to ensure compliance with the fair trial provisions mandated by international human rights law, such as those found in ICCPR Article 14, appears to push judges to treat defendants with greater sensitivity. The careful balancing required of international criminal tribunals, therefore, result in what could appear as greater leeway than one would find granted within a domestic appellate court.

A final basis for comparison comes in the form of *Clark v. Perez*, heard by the U.S. Second Circuit Court of Appeals in 2008. In that case, the appeals court allowed the defendant Clark to represent herself during the trial.[112] The judge warned her, however, that if she was disruptive during the course of the trial, she would be removed from the court and the trial would continue in her absence.[113] On the first day of trial, Clark explained to the jury that she did not believe the court or the trial was legitimate, and therefore would not participate.[114] After she departed the court, the trial continued in its entirety with no one seated at the table for the defense.[115]

---

[111] Although, Vernier was sentenced to prison for life.
[112] Clark v. Perez, *supra* note 30.
[113] *Id.* at 386.
[114] *Id.* at 387.
[115] *Id.*

The judge did not appoint anyone to represent Clark's interests, but did allow the defendant to follow the remainder of the trial through a radio transmission to her holding cell.[116]

Proceeding with the trial while no one represented the defendant is an option the ICTR never even considered in *Barayagwiza*, and with good reason. The goals of the international penal court could not have been fulfilled had Barayagwiza been convicted without being either present or represented. Beyond the obvious detriment to the overall fairness of the trial, to the extent that such tribunals contribute in this way, there is limited possibility to help foster national healing or reconciliation when the court simply rehashes the crimes of the accused and convicts him without anyone at court trying to present his or at least the other side of the story.

This type of rationale is similar to that of civil law systems which are willing to override the accused person's wishes through the imposition of counsel wherever deemed necessary. In a way, it may represent the meeting point with the common law system given Chief Justice Burger's admonition in *Faretta* that criminal justice systems should not permit themselves to be used by defendants, who against all common sense forgo the assistance of counsel as a way to achieve self-destruction, or as Justice Blackmun put it in his dissent in the same case, as a vehicle for "personal or political self-gratification."[117]

Sometimes, preserving fairness means restricting the autonomy of the defendant as the court did in *Barayagwiza*. At other times, as in *Milošević*, the international courts defer to the defendant's wishes to a far greater extent than one would expect to see on the national level. The most distinct and noticeable difference in the decisions reviewed above is the willingness of the national courts to allow defendants to dig their own grave, so to speak. In *Iqbal*, the court responded to the defendant's frivolous complaints by requiring him to go through trial alone. The *Perez* court let the trial proceed without any defense being presented at all, simply because that was the way the defendant wanted it. These kinds of problematic decisions may be justifiable at the municipal level, but not so at the international level given that the defendants in the latter setting are often charged with heinous international crimes such as genocide, crimes against humanity and war crimes.

One possible noteworthy exception to this observation can be found in the Statute of the Lebanon Tribunal, which, going against the grain of the ICTR's *Barayagwiza* ruling and international criminal tribunal

---

116 *Id.*

117 Faretta v. California, *supra* note 31.

experience, allows for the possibility of trials in absentia.[118] This is an exception to the general rule, and in practice, may prove to be so problematic that the international community might choose to abandon the strategy. The Statute does, however, provide several checks to ensure that a modicum of fairness is maintained. The accused must have been given notice of the trial proceedings going on without him, and counsel must have been appointed either by defendant or the Court.[119] In the result, whether the accused is present or not, the STL Statute does not allow for a *Perez* situation where the defense table in the courtroom remains empty.

Additionally, the STL RPE guarantee that if an absent defendant appears before the conclusion of the trial, he is automatically granted the right to have a retrial if certain preconditions are fulfilled.[120] This said, this right is only guaranteed once.[121] The provision for trials in absentia reflects the civil law tradition more strongly than any previous international court.[122]

Furthermore, the use of trials in absentia was included as part of the

---

118 Article 22(1) of the Statute for the STL reads: The Special Tribunal shall conduct trial proceedings in the absence of the accused, if he or she:

(a) Has expressly and in writing waived his or her right to be present;

(b) Has not been handed over to the Tribunal by the State authorities concerned;

(c) Has absconded or otherwise cannot be found and all reasonable steps have been taken to secure his or her appearance before the Tribunal and to inform him or her of the charges confirmed by the Pre-Trial Judge.

While the above requirements of the statute appeared to be cumulative, Rule 106(A) of the RPE, adopted by the judges on March 20, 2009, essentially reproduced the content of Article 22. However, it introduced two significant amendments imposing a "a reasonable time" requirement for the handing over of a suspect and the phrase "or" was introduced obviously to permit the STL to proceed with an in absentia trials where only one of the three requirements enshrined in the statutory provision are met. The question is whether the United Nations and Lebanon, the drafters of the statute, should have amended the statute in this way instead of the judges stepping into the arena of legislators and doing so themselves. *See* Statute of the STL, *available at* http://www.stl-tsl.org/en/documents/statute-of-the-tribunal/statute-of-the-special-tribunal-for-lebanon; (STL RPE, *available at* http://www.stl-tsl.org/images/RPE/RPE_EN_November_2010_Modified.pdf (as amended Nov. 10, 2010 and corrected Nov. 29, 2010). For the first application of these provisions deciding to proceed with *in absentia* trials against four suspects, see Prosecutor v. Ayyash et al., Case No. STL-ll-OI/I/TC, Decision to Hold Trial *in Absentia* (Feb. 1, 2012).

119 Statute for the STL, S/RES/1757 (2007), art. 22 (2).

120 STL RPE, STL/BD/2009/01/Rev., Rule 108 (amended Nov. 10, 2010).

121 *Id.*

122 U.N Secretary-General, *Report of the Secretary-General on the Establishment of a Special Tribunal for Lebanon*, ¶ 8, S/2006/893 (Nov. 15, 2006).

Special Tribunal because Lebanon's domestic legal system follows the civil law tradition, and the STL reflects those practices.[123] However, the prospect of in absentia trials has already been the subject of significant criticism. Indeed, based on rulings by the Human Rights Committee and the European Court of Human Rights, there are strong grounds to argue that the STL provision is a violation of human rights norms – an argument that the tribunal judges will likely resist.[124]

There is also concern that the provisions for providing notice to the accused and for granting a retrial are insufficient to protect the rights guaranteed by the ICCPR,[125] and that the legitimacy of the STL will, if given effect in the cases that are eventually tried, subsequently erode both abroad and within Lebanon.[126] Such conclusions are probably speculative at this point in the absence of actual trials in that court. Nevertheless, even in the first cases in which this controversial in absentia trial regime was approved recently, the appointment of permanent counsel to represent the accused was deemed necessary. In fact, this occurred the very next day, although it is uncertain how the eight assigned lawyers will mount a defense for suspects with whom they can presumably not communicate.[127]

Each of the above tribunal decisions demonstrates the importance the international courts place on maintaining the perception of complete fairness and a just trial. At the national level, whether it is the right to have counsel or the right to defend oneself, courts are far more likely to restrict the autonomy of the defendant to ensure the trial progresses forward without disruption. The international courts, given the wider perspective the goals of an international trial require them to take, are much more concerned with the appearance of fairness. Part of the reason is undoubtedly because they do have to establish their legitimacy, and are widely seen

---

123 *Id.* ¶ 32.

124 Chris Jenks, *Notice Otherwise Given: Will In Absentia Trials at the Special Tribunal for Lebanon Violate Human Rights?*, 33 FORDHAM INT'L L.J. 57 (2009).

125 It is worth noting that the STL is not purely an "international" court in the same way as the ICTY or ICTR, because it was created by an agreement with the country of Lebanon. This explains some of the divergence from the rules of the two purely international tribunals (*see* Fausto Pocar, *The Proliferation of International Criminal Courts and Tribunals*, 2 J. INT'L CRIM. JUST. 304, 305 (2004)).

126 Jenks, *supra* note 124, at 165.

127 *See* STL-ll-O I/I/PT J, *Commission d'office de conseils aux fins de la procédure par défaut tenue en application de l'article 106 du réglement*, 2 février 2012 (assigning lawyers to represent the suspects in their absence based upon the request of the pre-trial judge). *See also* Press Release, Assignment of Permanent Counsel (Feb. 2, 2012), *available at* http://www.stl-tsl.org/en/media/press-releases/02-02-2012-assignment-of-permanent-counsel.

as backup systems that, in the language of the ICC Statute, only come to apply in situations of inactivity and when the national jurisdiction is unwilling and or unable to prosecute.[128]

One aspect of the civil law system that the majority of international tribunals seem to have adopted is the belief that it is not always up to the defendant to protect his own rights at trial. Even though Barayagwiza, Norman and Taylor all tried to take steps that would have seriously harmed their chances at trial, the courts refused to allow them to impair the appearance of total fairness. Instead, much like in the civil law system, the court assumed a more proactive stance and required the defendants to make use of legal counsel in order to facilitate a fair and expeditious trial, as well as an international belief that both truth and justice are legitimate objectives to be achieved. On the other side of the coin, decisions such as those in *Norman* and *Barayagwiza* have become more common after the ICTY received trenchant criticism for apparently bending over backwards to accommodate Milošević. There is ample literature confirming a general feeling that Milošević's dilatory tactics were seen as having robbed his alleged victims of the chance to see justice done.

The second question that courts at both the international and national level often face is the choice between standby counsel and *amicus* counsel. The most pertinent comparison within international jurisprudence on this subject is between the aforementioned *Milošević* and *Šešelj* cases. One important principle that both of the chambers utilized and established as part of international criminal procedure is the proportionality principle.

The ICTY Appeals Chamber first invoked this idea in *Milošević* in an attempt to temper the modalities order of the Trial Chamber in their appointment of defense counsel.[129] The appeals court ruled that the appointment of counsel, while appropriate, had gone too far in completely wresting control of the trial from Milošević.[130] The proportionality principle dictated that the trial judges could only restrict his right to conduct his own defense to the minimum extent necessary to accomplish the objective of ensuring a fair and expedient trial.[131] The Appeals Chamber, therefore, ruled that anytime Milošević's health allowed him to attend a court proceeding, the judges must allow him to handle his own case.[132] The assigned

[128] Rome Statute of the International Criminal Court, U.N. Doc. A/CONF. 183/9, art. 17.

[129] *Milošević*, Decision on Interlocutory Appeal of the Trial Chamber's Decision on the Assignment of Defense Counsel, *supra* note 21.

[130] *Id.* ¶ 16.

[131] *Id.* ¶ 17.

[132] *Id.* ¶ 19.

counsel would only take over when he was unable to attend. In a sense, then, the Appeals Chamber placed the appointed defense counsel into a kind of super-standby counsel role. This decision essentially indicated that the risk of disruption was only sufficient to move from using *amicus curiae* to standby counsel, rather than stripping Milošević of the right to defend himself entirely.

The Trial Chamber in *Šešelj* referred to the same proportionality principle.[133] The court used the principle to consider the effect of his numerous pre-trial disruptions. Before requesting to proceed without counsel, Šešelj had made numerous public statements declaring his intent to cause trouble and disrupt the proceedings.[134] Due to the threat of disruption these statements provided, the ICTY Trial Chamber determined that standby counsel was a more appropriate form of restriction on Šešelj than simply appointing *amicus curiae* as the court had done for the *Milošević* trial.[135]

The more interesting decision in the *Šešelj* case came later when the Appeals Chamber *removed* standby counsel based on a complaint raised by the defendant.[136] After the trial began, the court had tried to assign defense counsel to the accused and terminated his right to conduct his own defense. When the appellate court reversed that position because it required a warning to be issued first, the trial judges re-assigned standby counsel.[137] The defendant then raised a complaint that the Appeals Chamber judgment had given him a clean slate on the right to represent himself, and standby counsel should therefore not be allowed to interfere with his exercise of that right.[138] The Appeals Chamber agreed with the defendant, and ruled that the lower court's action had undermined their previous decision reinstating his right to conduct his own defense.[139] They determined that despite his disruptions up to that point, their prior decision had wiped the slate clean. Consequently, Šešelj deserved to continue to conduct his defense without restriction until his behavior demonstrated such a restriction was necessary.[140]

---

133 *Šešelj*, Decision on Assignment of Counsel, *supra* note 32, ¶¶ 46–51.

134 *Id.* ¶ 30.

135 *Šešelj*, Decision on Prosecution's Motion Appointing Counsel, *supra* note 4, ¶ 30.

136 Prosecutor v. Šešelj, Case No. IT-03-67-AR73.4, Decision on Appeal Against Trial Chamber's Decision (No. 2) on Assignment of Counsel (Dec. 8, 2006) [hereinafter *Šešelj*, Decision on Appeal Against Trial Chamber's Decision (No. 2) on Assignment of Counsel].

137 *Id.* ¶ 3.

138 *Id.* ¶ 13.

139 *Id.* ¶ 26.

140 *Id.* ¶ 27.

This decision, if followed, appears to be favorable to self-representing defendants. However, it creates a troubling precedent for future international penal tribunals. The trial court considered his past actions in making their decision at the beginning of the trial to appoint standby counsel. Then, halfway through the trial, the appeals court ruled that his past actions up to that point were not grounds for the imposition of standby counsel upon his rights. While the Appeals Chamber judgment would usually carry significantly more weight, consideration of past behavior and the threat of disruption have generally continued to guide the appointment of standby counsel at the international level. At the national level, in both common law and civil law jurisdictions, given his previous antics, counsel would have been imposed on the defendant irrespective of what his wishes were.

These decisions reflect the widely accepted "balancing test" that courts apply in the United States to decide how much to allow a defendant autonomy in running the defense. Courts will weigh the prejudice to the defendant's legitimate interests against the potential disruption to the trial proceedings.[141] As part of that assessment, courts will consider, "the defendant's reasons for the self-representation request, the quality of counsel representing the party, and the party's prior proclivity to substitute counsel."[142]

Standby counsel is the much more widespread solution to balancing these interests in the United States when allowing a defendant to conduct his own defense. The Supreme Court in *Faretta* specifically referenced standby counsel as an allowable restriction even over the defendant's objection.[143] Then again, in *McKaskle v. Wiggins*, the highest court found the appointment of standby counsel to help guide a defendant through courtroom procedure, thereby relieving the judge of that responsibility, was legitimate.[144] It seems to have been accepted in U.S. courts that standby counsel is preferable because they are both more able to effectively assist a *pro se* defendant during the course of trial, and can also more easily step in to take over the defense should it become necessary while the trial is proceeding.

Given the influence of the civil law tradition, however, this logic is not entirely applicable within an international court. This is because in the civil law, counsel's main goal is not necessarily to defend and protect

---

141 United States v. Pickett, 387 F. App'x 32 (2d Cir. 2010).
142 *Id.* at 34.
143 Faretta v. California, *supra* note 31, 834 n.46.
144 McKaskle v. Wiggins, *supra* note 29, 196–7.

the defendant's interests, but is more directed at assisting or guiding the defendant in presenting his story to the court. Lawyers in the civil law tradition are more restricted in acting without specific instructions from a defendant. It therefore appears problematic for standby counsel to take over a case for a defendant at international law without either a mandate or instructions from the defendant on how to proceed with the defense.[145] Because of this problem, depending on the unique facts of each case, *amicus curiae* may well be a relatively better option at international law.

Amicus curiae could assist the court to avoid having the defense depend entirely on the decisions of defendants more interested in making political statements to domestic constituencies then actually refuting prosecution allegations or making their own case. Additionally, given the complexity and length of international criminal trials, having *amicus* counsel assist the court with many different issues that arise is perhaps more helpful and necessary to ensuring a fair trial than is the case in a typical criminal trial in the U.S.[146]

In a messy and disrupted international trial, there may be significant advantages to having an independent *amicus* voice helping to protect the defendant's interests rather than standby counsel, who are necessarily required to continue on behalf of the accused. In the former situation, the defendants have limited control over counsel, whereas in the latter scenario, they could choose to stop cooperating with standby counsel and use that as a trump card to undermine the actual process and its legitimacy. Whatever decision an international court makes must be proportional. This helps to ensure that any limitation or infringement on the defendant's right will only be to the extent necessary to preserve a fair and expeditious trial.

The final question faced by international criminal tribunals is what action should be taken when a defendant, either with or without representation, is so disruptive that he has to be removed, or is absent from the proceedings. The question of what to do when a defendant has representation is fairly settled. In both national and international law, with a few minor exceptions, courts usually are able to proceed with trial as long as the defendant's counsel is able to represent him. While there is a principled guarantee in the ICCPR that the defendant will be present at trial, courts

---

[145] Jarinde Temminck Tuinstra, *Assisting an Accused to Represent Himself: Appointment of* Amicus Curiae *as the Most Appropriate Option*, 4 J. INT'L CRIM. JUST. 47 (2006).

[146] *Id.* at 62–3.

have restricted this right as long as a warning is given to the defendant that the trial will proceed in his absence.[147]

In order to proceed around the right to be present, courts typically consider defendants to have waived the right.[148] The ICTR amended its RPE in May 2003 to include Rule 82*bis* to explicitly recognize this possibility.[149] The ICTY and SCSL also explicitly allow the court to remove defendants from the courtroom and continue in their absence so long as a warning has been given.[150] The notion of waiver, of course, permits a non-disruptive defendant to take a sick day or to be absent from court for good reasons such as ill health while giving his principled indication that the trial may proceed.

Similarly, Article 63(2) of the Rome Statute of the ICC also permits the Trial Chamber to order the removal of a disruptive defendant from the court as a last resort, so long as it provides alternative ways for him to observe the trial and to instruct counsel from outside the courtroom. American courts have frequently employed telecommunications technology to allow defendants who have been removed to view or listen to court proceedings, even when they are not physically present.[151] This approach has also been utilized in the tribunals. Video recordings and transcripts of proceedings are typically made available so that defendants may view them at their leisure.[152]

The more problematic situation arises when either defendant does not have defense counsel available, or when defense counsel is removed

---

[147] *Šešelj,* Decision on Prosecution's Motion Appointing Counsel, *supra* note 4, ¶ 30.

[148] Prosecutor v. Barayagwiza, Case No. ICTR-99-52-A, Appeals Chamber Judgement, ¶¶ 95–100 (Nov. 28, 2007); Prosecutor v. Gbao, Case No. SCSL-04-15-T, Ruling on the Refusal of the Third Accused, Augustine Gbao to Attend a Hearing of the Special Court for Sierra Leone on 7 July 2004 and Succeeding Days (Jul. 12, 2004); *Taylor*, Transcript of Record, *supra* note 24.

[149] Rule 82*bis*: If an accused refuses to appear before the Trial Chamber for trial, the Chamber may order that the trial proceed in the absence of the accused for so long as his refusal persists, provided that the Trial Chamber is satisfied that:

(i) the accused has made his initial appearance under Rule 62;
(ii) the Registrar has duly notified the accused that he is required to be present for trial;
(iii) the interests of the accused are represented by counsel.

[150] ICTY RPE IT/32/Rev. 45, Rule 80, adopted Feb. 11, 1994; SCSL RPE, Rule 80, amended Mar. 7, 2003.

[151] Clark v. Perez, *supra* note 30; Torres v. United States, 140 F.3d 392 (2d Cir. 1998).

[152] The requirement of a video link for defendants removed from Court is actually codified in the SCSL RPE (SCSL RPE, Rule 80, amended May 28, 2010).

from court as well for reasons of disruption. Perhaps the best international example of a *pro se* defendant simply not showing up for trial is the *Karadžić* case that came before the ICTY. The defendant in that case believed that he should be given significantly more time to prepare his defense than the court had allowed, and refused to attend court proceedings until he felt prepared.[153] The Trial Chamber ruled that the interests of justice required the court delay the beginning of trial to give appointed defense counsel time to adequately prepare. As it turned out, by the time appointed counsel was ready to continue, so was Karadžić, and the court allowed him to continue handling his own defense while maintaining the previously appointed lawyers as standby counsel.[154]

Again, a comparison with national decisions demonstrates the concern at the international level in preserving the perception of fairness in trials of those accused of heinous international crimes. The *Karadžić* court was essentially handcuffed by the defendant into delaying the trial unless they chose to proceed with no one representing the defendant. The chamber either had to succumb to the defendant's demands and delay trial so that he could prepare, or they had to delay trial to give appointed counsel time to prepare.

Defendants seemingly gain more time to prepare by refusing to come to court, than when they do, perhaps because the ad hoc tribunal judges are under different kinds of pressures to keep the trials on schedule. They thus hesitate to grant delays favoring defendants which could lead to both internal and external criticism, especially in the face of their respective completion strategies. The irony is that, in at least two instances such as the opening and closing of the *Taylor* case at the SCSL, giving the defense more time to prepare would have obviated the need for defendants to boycott proceedings. The same may have been true in the *Karadžić* case at the ICTY. It remains to be seen whether future trials, especially at the ICC which in a few years will be the last court standing, will be more sympathetic to defendant requests for more time to review the often large disclosure dumped on them by tribunal prosecutors.

Domestic courts are not comparatively equally willing to be challenged by a defendant into granting a three-month-long delay to the start of trial. Although this should not be surprising given the more narrow geographic scope of crimes at the municipal level, a good example of this is *Davis v.*

---

153 *Karadžić*, Decision on Appointment of Counsel and Order on Further Trial Proceedings, *supra* note 22, ¶ 1.

154 Prosecutor v. Karadžić, Case No. IT-95-5/18-T, Decision on Designation of Standby Counsel, ¶¶ 8–10 (ICTY Apr. 15, 2010).

Grant, argued before the U.S. Second Circuit Court of Appeals in 2008.[155] After several warnings and numerous outbursts before the jury at trial, including profanities directed at the judge and the court, the defendant was removed from court and the trial continued.

On appeal, the court upheld the decision to continue with the trial despite the fact that the defendant had no counsel to represent him after he was removed from court. Although the appellate judges affirmed the conviction, they took care to underscore that their decision turned on the specifics of that case thereby undermining arguments that it could serve as good precedent for other cases.[156] In a somewhat unconventional move, the Second Circuit Appeals Court explicitly requested in their opinion that the U.S. Supreme Court accept a case to clarify the extent to which disruptive behavior constituted a waiver of the right to appear *pro se*, and whether it was mandatory upon a lower court to appoint standby counsel for the duration of the trial.[157]

There is a stronger precedent within the U.S. for defendants choosing to represent themselves and then voluntarily remaining absent for the duration of trial. This happened twice in the Second Circuit in the cases of *Clark v. Perez* in 2008 as well as famously in *U.S. v. Torres* in 1998. In both cases, the defendant chose to leave the court in order to further political ideologies which they cited in order to deny the legitimacy of the court's authority to conduct the trial. In both cases the court proceeded without appointing *amicus curiae* or standby counsel to protect the defendant's interests, and the jury found both defendants guilty of all charges.

In both civil law and common law systems, there are typically requirements that defendants are present at trial. The European Court of Human Rights has affirmed the rights of defendants to be present at appellate proceedings in addition to the criminal trial.[158] The problem of what to do when the defendant, as well as all legal counsel, is either absent or removed from the court is difficult because of how essential representation is to the concept of a fair trial. Although, as international criminal procedures mature, there will be a swing towards the civil law which is already discernible, for its largely adversarial process at present to work, there generally needs to be two different sides opposing one another. The international criminal justice system has not yet been willing to proceed with a trial where there was no one present to represent the interests of the

---

155 532 F.3d 132 (2d Cir. 2008).

156 *Id.* at 149.

157 *Id.* at 150.

158 Helmers v. Sweden, no. 11826/85, Judgment, ECtHR (Oct. 29, 1991).

accused. However, this step has been taken in the U.S., Canada,[159] Britain, and other common law jurisdictions. The international tribunals should remain true to the "interests of justice" standard, and hold strictly to the idea that the fairness of the trial comes before all else.

V. CONCLUSION

The international criminal law has come quite a long way in the last few decades. In a recent open session at the ICTY on July 4, 2011, the Trial Chamber in the *Mladić* case, within just an hour in court, denied a request to give the defendant more time to review the indictment and supporting evidence before entering a plea, denied a request by counsel to withdraw due to a lack of communication with the accused, denied a request by the defendant to delay the trial until his counsel of choice could be assigned, removed the defendant from court for disruptive behavior, and continued entering pleas for the defendant after he was removed.[160] All this occurred without the court-appointed duty counsel, filling in until permanent defense counsel could be assigned, raising a single word of either protest or caution regarding the court's actions.[161]

This is a remarkable transformation from the decisions discussed in this chapter granting extensive delays to ensure that all of the defendant's rights were respected. The *Šešelj* Court, for example, allowed the defendant to direct its rulings regarding the assignment of counsel rather than attempting to continue the trial without him being present.[162] The approach in that case is reflective of a common recent trend in decisions issued at international tribunals. Since the heavily criticized handling of the *Milošević* trial, international courts have steadily become stricter in dealing with attempts by defendants to upset the continuity of the trial.

Earlier in the days of the international tribunals, fairness trumped expediency in nearly every decision the court issued. With trials at the ICTY and ICTR wrapping up, however, courts have learned how to deal with frivolous attempts by the accused to cause delays while at the same time acknowledging and permitting legitimate exercise of their statutory

---

159 R v. Bitternose, 2009 SKCA 54, (2009) 460 W.A.C. 19 (Saskatchewan Ct. App.).

160 Prosecutor v. Mladić, Case No. IT-09-92, Transcript of Record (ICTY Jul. 4. 2011).

161 *Id.*

162 *Šešelj*, Decision on Appeal Against Trial Chamber's Decision (No. 2) on Assignment of Counsel, *supra* note 136.

rights.[163] A much higher importance is now being placed on finishing the mission of the tribunals and completing the administration of justice for the crimes committed almost two decades ago.

There is more to the paradigm shift than simply wanting to complete the proceedings. After Milošević embarrassed the tribunal with his antics, and then his death which meant that no formal judgment could be pronounced on his guilt or innocence, there was a definite backlash against the freedom he had been granted by the ICTY. The results of this backlash may be reflected in the provisions in the statute of the STL, which allows for the trial of accused in absentia. These types of changes perhaps reflect lessons gained from learning by doing and the belief that stricter controls may be necessary during court proceedings as more and more international criminal trials are held. That has definitely been the experience with national criminal law, and speaks to the need to improve the efficiency of trial procedures and a refusal to kowtow to the whims and caprices of manipulative and clever accused persons. At the same time, the said changes also raise new concerns about the need to maintain the integrity and fairness of trials for those accused of serious international crimes.[164]

The more stringent controls, and especially the in absentia provisions of the STL Statute, are indicative of a steady rise of civil law principles within international law. This gravitational pull is perhaps also reflective of global changes in common and civil law systems. There has been scholarly documentation of the steady convergence of the two types of systems recently.[165] Many of the distinguishing features of each particular system have been slowly adopted by countries of the opposing system as a set of agreed upon best practices has emerged.[166] These developments may lead one to believe that systems of criminal justice at both the national and international level are finally "getting it right," but there is still much to learn, and future international tribunals would do well not to forget about upholding the interests of justice in each decision.

One important element that has yet to be incorporated into international justice is the principles from alternative legal systems. Both the civil and common law traditions have a largely "Western" background that excludes traditional African, Chinese, Indian, Islamic, and many

---

163 Pocar, *supra* note 33, at 8.

164 *See* Jenks, *supra* note 124, at 57; Williams, *supra* note 3, at 553.

165 Salvatore Mancuso, *The New African Law: Beyond the Differences Between Common Law and Civil Law*, *in* 14 Annual Survey of International and Comparative Law ¶¶ 9-12 (2008); Pocar, *supra* note 33, at 1.

166 Mancuso, *supra* note 165.

other legal traditions and beliefs.[167] How the major criminal justice belief systems can better adapt to situations where non-western notions of justice predominate is a question yet to be resolved. This question, like all those facing ad hoc criminal tribunals now and yet to exist, requires a careful balancing of rights and interests. Some of those systems emphasize more conciliatory and rehabilitative approaches. The jury is out on whether those are or are not appropriate for application in international criminal trials, but in a pluralist world, the question should now be attended to rather than ignored.

If nothing else, this discussion of how courts handle the role of counsel should have illuminated how many different perspectives each decision at the international court can be seen through. Courts have to consider the fundamental rights of the defendant guaranteed by the rules of the court, the interests of the victims looking to the court to quench their thirst for justice, the larger interests, including the finding of truth, fair and expeditious justice, as well as an evidence-based trial, and possibly, even contributions to national healing reconciliation.

When considering what lessons the international courts should draw from common law systems, civil law systems, and their own unique experiences that aim to balance rights may well be the key. As the international criminal law continues its lofty pursuit to "end impunity," it is unlikely that any single provision, such as allowing trials in absentia, will determine the success or failure of the provision of international justice. Provided that international tribunals apply such provisions, keeping in mind the interests of justice and the balancing of rights required, international justice will likely come out farther ahead than behind.

As evidence of this truth, consider the cases discussed in this chapter. Despite alleged gaffes in judgment at the *Milošević*, *Šešelj*, and *Barayagwiza* trials, the ICTY and ICTR have been largely successful in fairly prosecuting those responsible for persons accused of some of the most gruesome crimes in the world's recent history, and the legitimacy of those convictions is not substantially contested. It is too soon to judge how history will ultimately measure the success of the ICTR, ICTY, SCSL and the STL. What is clear is that the international community has saddled these tribunals with an exceedingly difficult task, one that requires a careful balancing of rights that no amount of rule-making or statutory provisions will easily solve.

---

[167] *Id.* ¶¶ 13–14.

6. The role of victims

Sigall Horovitz*

I. VICTIMS AND THE CRIMINAL PROCESS

This chapter addresses the role of victims in proceedings before international criminal tribunals. It mainly focuses on the relevant practices of the International Criminal Court (ICC), the first international criminal tribunal to allow victims to actively participate in criminal proceedings. Occasionally, references will be made to the approaches of other international criminal tribunals, especially where they differ from that of the ICC. The chapter will not discuss the right of victims to receive reparations, which the ICC grants them separately from the right to participate in proceedings.[1]

While the ICC is the first international tribunal to grant victims an active role in its proceedings, this approach is not uncommon in national jurisdictions that follow the civil law tradition. For example, in France, victims can become "civil parties" to the proceedings by attaching their civil claim for compensation to the criminal proceedings against the

* PhD Candidate and Transitional Justice Project Manager, Hebrew University of Jerusalem; LL.M. Columbia University (2003); formerly Legal Officer at the International Criminal Tribunal for Rwanda (ICTR) and Consultant at the Special Court for Sierra Leone (SCSL). I thank Michael Youril for his research assistance.

[1] Article 68(3) of the Rome Statute grants victims the right to participate in the proceedings. Article 75 of the Rome Statute grants them the right to receive reparation. At the time of writing, the ICC has not concluded any of its cases and has therefore not issued any decisions on reparation. Victim participation issues, however, have been the subject of numerous ICC decisions. It is noted that this chapter's discussion about the requirements for receiving "victim status" can be relevant to the right of victims to receive reparation. This is because, regardless of whether or not they seek to participate or to receive reparation, applicants must first be granted victim status by the ICC. It is also noted that participating in the trial of their perpetrators can itself have a reparative effect on victims, as discussed below.

accused.[2] Similar types of "adhesion" procedures are available in most other European states.[3] These jurisdictions allow victims to bring accusations against their perpetrators, receive legal representation during the criminal process, and obtain reparations through criminal prosecutions.[4] Some states, such as Germany and Spain, in addition to having adhesion procedures, allow victims of serious offenses to become "auxiliary" (or "private") prosecutors in the trial of their offender, alongside or instead of the public prosecution.[5] Auxiliary prosecutors have similar rights to the public prosecution and defense, including the rights to be present for the duration of the trial (even if the victim is also a witness), introduce and challenge evidence, object to judicial orders, submit statements and motions, present closing arguments, lodge appeals (although usually not on sentencing matters), and be represented by a state-funded lawyer.[6] While the main purpose of the adhesion model is to allow victims to receive compensation, victims with the status of auxiliary prosecutors enjoy rights that go beyond their right to compensation.[7] In any event,

---

[2] *See* Héctor Olásolo, *Systematic and Casuistic Approaches to the Role of Victims in Criminal Proceedings Before the International Criminal Court*, 12 NEW CRIM. L. REV.: AN INT'L & INTERDISC. J. 513, 514 (2009) (relying on Articles 89, 117, 118, 183, 186, 312, 487(3), 573, 567 and 573 of the French Code of Criminal Procedure). It is noted that in some common law national jurisdictions, such as the UK, courts may impose penal sanction in the form of a "compensation order." Still, it is up to the prosecutor to request this measure, and the victim has no voice in the matter. *See* ERNESTINE HOEGEN & MARION BRIENEN, VICTIMS OF CRIME IN 22 EUROPEAN CRIMINAL JUSTICE SYSTEMS 28 (2000).

[3] In addition to France, adhesion procedures are also available in Austria, Belgium, Denmark, Germany, Greece, Iceland, Italy, Liechtenstein, the Netherlands, Norway, Portugal, Spain, Sweden, and Turkey. *See* LORRAINE WOLHUTER ET AL., VICTIMOLOGY: VICTIMISATION AND VICTIMS' RIGHTS 193 n.10 (2009).

[4] In France, victims can initiate proceedings before criminal courts even when the public prosecutor decides not to initiate proceedings. However, in most other civil law jurisdictions, victims can seek civil damages through criminal court only if the public prosecution initiated criminal proceedings. *See* Criminal Procedure: Comparative Aspects – Prosecution, *available at* http://law.jrank.org/pages/900/Criminal-Procedure-Comparative-Aspects-Prosecution.html (last visited Oct. 18, 2011).

[5] HOEGEN & BRIENEN, *supra* note 2, at 28; Olásolo, *supra* note 2, at 514 (referring to Article 101 of the Spanish Code of Criminal Procedure).

[6] Auxiliary prosecution procedures are also available in Austria, Denmark, Portugal and Poland. *See* WOLHUTER ET AL., *supra* note 3, at 189–90.

[7] HOEGEN & BRIENEN, *supra* note 2, at 29 ("contrary to the civil claimant, the auxiliary prosecutor's participatory rights are not restricted to the reach of his civil claim for compensation"). Still, some argue that compensation claims are a major motivation for victims to participate actively in the trial even where they have additional rights. *See, e.g.*, Julio Pérez Gil, *Private Interests Seeking Punishment:*

both the adhesion and auxiliary prosecutor models allow victims to actively participate in the criminal process. By contrast, national jurisdictions that follow the common law tradition, such as the United Kingdom and the United States, limit the role of victims in criminal proceedings to that of witnesses with no active participation rights. It is noted, however, that many common law jurisdictions allow victims to submit impact statements at the sentencing stage (which is separate from the trial stage and takes place only if the accused is found guilty).[8] Impact statements contain details of the physical, emotional, psychological and financial impact of the crime on the victim. It is noted, however, that confining victim participation to the sentencing stage may limit the amount and scope of information they can provide.

In both common law and civil law jurisdictions, the idea of victim participation in criminal proceedings gained importance following the victims' rights movement of the 1960s and 1970s, which responded to the marginalization of victims and a concern with their secondary victimization by national justice systems. Secondary victimization refers to a crime victim's suffering from further victimization by the treatment he or she receives from the criminal justice system.[9] In the 1980s, international and regional legal instruments were adopted to urge states to enhance the involvement of victims in national criminal proceedings, an approach expected to minimize secondary victimization. The first (and arguably the most important) of these international legal instrument was the 1985 United Nations Declaration of Basic Principles of Justice for Victims of Crime and Abuse of Power (UN Declaration on Victims).[10] Accordingly,

---

Prosecution Brought by Private Individuals and Groups in Spain, 25 L. & POL'Y 151, 156 (2003).

[8] Countries that grant victims the right to make impact statements include Canada, Israel, New Zealand, the United States and parts of Australia and Ireland. *See* U.N. OFFICE FOR DRUG CONTROL AND CRIME PREVENTION, HANDBOOK ON JUSTICE FOR VICTIMS: ON THE USE AND APPLICATION OF THE DECLARATION OF BASIC PRINCIPLES OF JUSTICE FOR VICTIMS OF CRIME AND ABUSE OF POWER 39 (1999), *available at* http://www.uncjin.org/Standards/9857854.pdf. *See also* Paul G. Cassell & Edna Erez, *Victim Impact Statements and Ancillary Harm: The American Perspective*, 15 CAN. CRIM. L. REV. 149, 153 (2011) ("virtually all American states had laws or court rules allowing victims to provide victim impact statements to sentencing judges, either in written or oral form. These laws were aimed at fulfilling two independent but interrelated goals: first, to inform the court about the harm sustained by the victim for determining the quantum of punishment at sentencing; and second, to increase victim welfare during the sentencing process").

[9] HOEGEN & BRIENEN, *supra* note 2, at 24.

[10] United Nations General Assembly (UNGA) Resolution 40/34, UN Doc. A/RES/40/34 (1985) [hereinafter UN Declaration on Victims]. This declaration urges

states implemented a variety of measures in an attempt to give victims a voice in the criminal process. Common law states began allowing victims to make impact statements,[11] and civil law states reinforced already existing victim participation schemes.[12] Subsequent research has sustained the claim that allowing victims to participate has therapeutic effects on them.[13] It is noted that besides empowering and rehabilitating victims, additional goals attributed to victim participation include promoting the determination of truth by providing information to the court, clarifying the crime's harm to the defendant, and improving the perceived fairness and relevance of the judicial process.[14]

However, civil law jurisdictions that typically involve inquisitorial

---

states to accord victims an active role in national criminal proceedings, without specifying how this should be achieved. Accordingly, a variety of approaches were adopted by states in an attempt to give victims a voice in the criminal process. An important regional legal instrument concerning the rights of crime victims is the Council of Europe's Recommendation No. R (85) 11 of the Committee of Ministers to Member States on the Position of the Victim in the Framework of Criminal Law and Procedure, adopted by the Committee of Ministers on June 28, 1985, at the 387th meeting of the Ministers' Deputies. For a broader discussion of international and regional legal developments concerning the rights of crime victims see BRIANNE MCGONIGLE LEYH, PROCEDURAL JUSTICE? VICTIM PARTICIPATION IN INTERNATIONAL CRIMINAL PROCEEDINGS 93–130 (2011).

11 *See, e.g.*, Paul G. Cassell & Steven Joffee, *The Crime Victim's Expanding Role in a System of Public Prosecution: A Response to the Critics of the Crime Victims' Rights Act*, 105 NW. U. L. REV. 164, 183 (2011) (explaining that when the U.S. Congress passed the Crimes Victim Rights Act, "Congress was worried that '[t]oo often victims of crime experience a secondary victimization at the hands of the criminal justice system,'" referring to 150 CONG. REC. S10911 (daily ed. Oct. 9, 2004) (statement of Senator Kyl)).

12 *See, e.g.*, MCGONIGLE LEYH, *supra* note 10, at 83 (explaining that although the auxiliary prosecutor model was available in Germany since 1924, it was largely unused until the victims' rights movement gained momentum in the 1980s).

13 Edna Erez, *Who's Afraid of the Big Bad Victim? Victim Impact Statements as Victim Empowerment and Enhancement of Justice*, 1999 CRIM. L. REV. 545, 550–51 ("The cumulative knowledge acquired from research in various jurisdictions, in countries with different legal systems, suggests that victims often benefit from participation and input. With proper safeguards, the overall experience of providing input can be positive and empowering."). But also note that there are indications that the use of impact statement may not promote the goals of victim participation such as empowerment and prevention of secondary victimization. *See* WOLHUTER ET AL., *supra* note 3, at 181–2.

14 Jérôme de Hemptinne, *Challenges Raised by Victims' Participation in the Proceedings of the Special Tribunal for Lebanon,* 8 J. INT'L CRIM. JUST. 165, 168 (2010); Paul G. Cassell, *In Defense of Victim Impact Statements*, 6 OHIO ST. J. CRIM. L. 611, 648 (2009) (referring to the US practice of "victim impact statements" but relating generally to goals of victim participation).

judge-led procedures are far more accommodating to active victim participation than the adversarial proceedings of common law jurisdictions, which are premised on a competition between the prosecution and defense and where adding a third party may tilt the scale. As Professor Damaška has noted:

> Where fact-finding is court-directed, tendering evidence and participation in proof-taking need not be limited to the parties: fact-finding is like a conference at which many voices can be heard. But where two fact-finding hypotheses are advanced by the parties and are rival suitors for the judges' attention, a bi-polar force field emerges, making it difficult to include successfully a third side in the development of evidence.[15]

It is also noted that in civil law jurisdictions witnesses and victims usually testify in narrative form, whereas in common law states, lawyers typically intervene during the course of the testimony in an attempt to preclude evidence that does not specifically relate to the charges. Such interventions may have an adverse impact on victims who are trying to achieve some closure by telling their story. Victims may feel particularly harassed when cross-examined by lawyers who try to impeach their credibility, a practice characteristic to common law jurisdictions.

II. OVERVIEW OF VICTIM PARTICIPATION AT INTERNATIONAL CRIMINAL TRIBUNALS

The first modern-era international criminal tribunals adopted the adversarial approach of the common law tradition. Accordingly, the International Criminal Tribunal for the former Yugoslavia (ICTY) and the International Criminal Tribunal for Rwanda (ICTR) limit the role of victims to that of witnesses. Nonetheless, these tribunals offer certain services to testifying victims in order to prevent their secondary victimization and to help their rehabilitation. For example, specialized units at the ICTY and ICTR provide protection and support (including medical and psychological care) to victims who testify as witnesses, and to their family members, thereby promoting their rehabilitation to some degree.[16]

---

[15] Mirjan Damaška, *The International Criminal Court Between Aspiration and Achievement*, 14 UCLA J. INT'L L. & FOREIGN AFF. 19, 29 (2009).

[16] However, victims testifying before the ICTR and ICTY have complained about being disrespected by lawyers and judges. *See, e.g.*, *Kigali Unhappy with Cross-Questioning of Prosecution Witnesses*, HIRONDELLE NEWS AGENCY, (Feb. 27, 2001), http://hirondellenews.org/ictr-rwanda/404-ictr-institutional-news/17770-

Further, according to the Rules of Procedure and Evidence of the ICTY and ICTR, victims can use the judgments of these international tribunals as a basis for compensation claims before national courts.[17]

The ICC, however, set a new trend by granting victims an active role in international criminal proceedings. Established in July 2002, it was the first international criminal tribunal that allowed victims to participate actively in criminal proceedings, in particular, by allowing them to present their views and concerns during the proceedings. This victim-centered approach is considered one of the ICC's greatest innovations compared to other international criminal tribunals. As of the end of October 2011, almost 10,000 victims applied to participate in ICC proceedings. Of these, over 3,500 victims applied to participate in connection with the Central African Republic situation and over 2,500 applied in connection with the Kenyan situation.[18]

Hybrid criminal tribunals such as the Special Court for Sierra Leone (SCSL), the Extraordinary Chambers in the Courts of Cambodia (ECCC) and the Special Tribunal for Lebanon (STL) generally follow the approach of the national system they are associated with, albeit with some modifications.[19] Thus, the SCSL follows the common law approach of the Sierra Leonean justice system by limiting the role of victims to that of witnesses.[20] The ECCC and STL, hybrid tribunals which were created after the ICC, follow the approach of the Cambodian and Lebanese legal systems respectively by granting victims active participation rights. However, their approach somewhat differs from the respective national

---

en-en-kigali-unhappy-with-cross-questioning-of-prosecution-witnesses68216821 (referring to a statement made by Rwanda's Justice Minister that there had been "harassment of [ICTR] witnesses by defence lawyers" during cross-examination).

17 ICTY Rule 106; ICTR Rule 106.

18 *See* Victims' Rights Working Group, The Implementation of Victims' Rights Before the ICC – Issues and Concerns Presented by the Victims' Rights Working Group on the occasion of the 10th Session of the Assembly of States Parties, n.7 (Dec. 12-21, 2011), *available at* http://www.redress.org/downloads/publications/2011_VRWG_ASP10.pdf ("At the end of October 2011, according to Registry statistics: 9,910 victims applied to participate in proceedings (2,228 for the situation or individual cases in the Democratic Republic of the Congo; 1,028 for Uganda; 209 for Darfur; 3,873 for the Central African Republic and 2,572 for Kenya) . . .").

19 After all, what makes them "hybrid" criminal tribunals is their mixture of national and international elements, with the national elements deriving from the legal system of the state associated with the tribunal. Collective references in this chapter to "international criminal tribunals" include hybrid criminal tribunals.

20 It is noted that the constitutive instruments of the SCSL were modeled after those of the ICTR, rather than exclusively inspired by Sierra Leonean national law.

victim participation models, due to the particular characteristics of international criminal proceedings.[21]

The ICC's victim participation regime also differs in some respects from civil law approaches to victims. A fundamental difference is that the ICC does not regard victims as parties to the proceedings. Rather, like common law systems, the ICC recognizes only the prosecution and defense as parties. It regards victims, on the other hand, as "participants" who may present their views and concerns under certain conditions. The ICC furthermore subjects victim participation to the judges' discretion at each stage of the proceedings. Moreover, victims usually do not physically participate in ICC proceedings but are represented by "Legal Representatives for Victims" who are assigned by the Chamber. Unlike adhesion procedures (but similar to auxiliary prosecutor approaches) victims can participate in ICC proceedings even if they do not request compensation, and they may request compensation even if they do not participate in the proceedings.

Notwithstanding these differences, it is clear that the ICC's victim participation scheme is closer to the civil law system's approach to victims than to that of the common law system. But because the ICC is designed to address mass crimes involving mass victims, it departed from a straightforward civil law model and developed a new approach. One of the main concerns was that allowing potentially large numbers of victims to participate as parties before the ICC would significantly slow down the proceedings and violate the right of the accused to an expeditious trial. Recent developments at the ECCC illustrate this point clearly. The ECCC grants victims the status of civil parties, and accordingly, its Internal Rules (IRs) originally provided broad victim participation rights. This was manageable in the first ECCC trial, in the *Duch* case.[22] However, while that trial involved fewer than 100 civil parties, almost 4,000 victims have been granted civil party status in the ECCC's second trial.[23] In an effort to minimize trial delays, prior to the commencement of

---

[21] For example, STL Rule 86(A) prohibits victim participation before the indictment is confirmed, in contrast to the Lebanese Code of Criminal Procedure which grants victims the status of *parties civiles* and allows them to initiate criminal proceedings. *See* de Hemptinne, *supra* note 14, at 172.

[22] *See Kaing Guek Eav alias Duch, Appeal Judgement (Public), 3 February 2012, available at* Case 001AppealJudgementEn.pdf.

[23] *See 10th Regional Forum for 300 Civil Parties in Case 002 held in Chba Morn Town, Kampong Speu Province*, ECCC, VICTIM SUPPORT, LATEST UPDATE ON VICTIMS ACTIVITIES (Oct. 28, 2011, 2:24 PM), http://www.eccc.gov.kh/en/articles/10th-regional-forum-300-civil-parties-case-002-held-chba-morn-town-kampong-speu-province ("The total number of Civil Parties in Case 002 is cur-

its second trial, the ECCC has amended its IRs to restrict the number of civil parties and the scope of their participation. For example, civil parties are now required to organize themselves in one group, and to submit their civil party applications "no later than 15 days after the Co-Investigating Judges notify the parties of the conclusion of the judicial investigation," effectively precluding the ECCC from receiving victims' participation requests during the trial proceedings.[24] The STL, by contrast, has adopted a similar approach to that of the ICC, where victims are not civil parties but can still participate in the proceedings by presenting their views and concerns.[25] However, unlike the ICC, the STL rules explicitly mandate the Pre-Trial Judge to "limit the number of victims entitled to express their views and concerns in proceedings."[26] Further, victims can participate in STL proceedings only after an indictment has been confirmed,[27] so after most of the investigation has been concluded and defendants identified, as opposed to the ICC's approach of involving participating victims from very early stages of the investigation.[28] Still, relative to the ad hoc tribunals, the STL norms provide broad participation rights to victims. For example, STL Rule 87(B) allows victims to call witnesses and tender other evidence, to examine and cross-examine witnesses, and to file motions and briefs. In addition, STL Rule 87(C) allows victims to make oral or written submissions on sentencing issues, which they cannot do in many civil law jurisdictions or as civil parties at the ECCC.

In addition to slowing down the proceedings, victim participation at the ICC may give rise to difficulties stemming from the introduction of a third participant to what is predominantly an adversarial process. This is because the accused might eventually be confronted with two accusers – the prosecutor and the victims – instead of one, in violation of the principle

---

rently 3,867").

[24] See ECCC IR 23(3). These provisions were added as part of a reform undertaken by the ECCC intended to restrict victim participation in anticipation of a flood of civil party applications made in connection with the tribunal's second trial. Before this amendment, a previous version of ECCC IR 23(4) provided that "victims may submit a Civil Party application up until the opening of proceedings before the Trial Chamber."

[25] STL Statute, Article 17.

[26] STL Rule 86(C). The ICC judges have no such authority.

[27] STL Rule 86(A) ("If the Pre-Trial Judge has confirmed the indictment under Rule 68, a person claiming to be a victim of a crime within the Tribunal's jurisdiction may request the Pre-Trial Judge to be granted the status of victim participating in the proceedings pursuant to Article 17 of the Statute").

[28] STL Rule 87(B) and (C).

of equality of arms, which is fundamental to adversarial proceedings.[29] This problematic aspect has indeed occupied some of the ICC judges, who, as the discussion below illustrates, consider that the right of victims to express their views and concerns before the ICC should be interpreted in a limited manner. However, in reality, the ICC grants more possibilities to victims than merely expressing their views and concerns, including presenting evidence and cross-examining witnesses. These and other forms of victim participation at the ICC are discussed in further detail below.

While the effects of victim participation at the ICC are yet to be scientifically assessed, it has been argued that this approach "would bring the Court 'closer to the persons who have suffered atrocities' and, thus, increase the likelihood that victims would be satisfied that justice was done."[30] One advantage of victim participation may be that the ICC, in addition to allowing victims to express their views and concerns, will allow them to testify or otherwise provide evidence even when they are not called as witnesses by one of the parties.[31] For example, in *Prosecutor v. Lubanga*, the Chamber allowed victims (who were not included in the parties' witness lists) to testify under oath despite the prosecutor's objection on the ground that their anticipated testimonies would duplicate existing evidence.[32] In allowing the victims to testify, the Chamber stressed that "none of their personal histories are the same."[33] This increased participation of victims may further a restorative goal in addition to a retributive one.[34] The involvement of large groups of victims before the

---

[29] *See, e.g.*, de Hemptinne, *supra* note 14, at 168.

[30] Susana SáCouto, *Victim Participation at the International Criminal Court and the Extraordinary Chambers in the Courts of Cambodia: A Feminist Project?*, 18 MICH. J. GENDER AND L. 297, 316, sources cited in nn.93–4 (2011-12) [hereinafter SáCouto, *Victim Participation*].

[31] It is noted that, unlike the STL and ECCC, the ICC allows individuals to participate in the proceedings as victims and in parallel to testifying on behalf of a party. See related discussion in notes 84–7 *infra* and accompanying text. Some of the difficulties that arise when someone has the dual status of victim-witness are outlined in Prosecutor v. Lubanga, Case No. ICC-01/04-01/06, Decision on Certain Practicalities Regarding Individuals Who Have the Dual Status of Witness and Victim (June 5, 2008) [hereinafter *Lubanga*, Decision on Dual Status of Witness and Victim].

[32] Prosecutor v. Lubanga, Case No. ICC-01/04-01/06, Decision on the Request by Victims a/0225/06, a/0229/06 and a/0270/07 to Express Their Views and Concerns in Person and to Present Evidence During the Trial (June 16, 2009) (made public on July 9, 2009). It is interesting to note that both the prosecution and defense were united in their objection to the victims' request to testify.

[33] *Id.* ¶ 37.

[34] The *Basic Principles on the Use of Restorative Justice Programmes in*

ICC may even have a restorative impact on entire communities affected by the atrocities.

III. NORMATIVE FRAMEWORK FOR VICTIM PARTICIPATION AT THE ICC

Provisions on victim participation (or reparations) were not included in the original draft of the ICC Statute, which was largely modeled after the statutes of the ICTY and ICTR.[35] However, during the negotiations on the final version of the ICC statute, national delegations were inspired by their respective national legal systems and accordingly wanted the ICC to handle certain matters, including victim participation, differently from the ad hoc tribunals.[36] In addition, human rights organizations were present

---

Criminal Matters defines a "Restorative process" as "any process in which the victim, the offender and/or any other individuals or community members affected by a crime actively participate together in the resolution of matters arising from the crime, often with the help of a fair and impartial third party. Examples of restorative process include mediation, conferencing and sentencing circles." U.N. ECONOMIC & SOCIAL COUNCIL, BASIC PRINCIPLES ON THE USE OF RESTORATIVE JUSTICE PROGRAMMES IN CRIMINAL MATTERS (2002), *available at* http://www.unodc.org/pdf/criminal_justice/06-56290_Ebook.pdf.

[35] The point of departure for the discussions on the establishment of the ICC was the 1994 draft ICC Statute prepared by the ILC. *See Report of the International Law Commission on the Work of Its Forty-Sixth Sessions*, UNGA Doc. A/49/355 (Sept. 1, 1994), *available at* http://www.iccnow.org/documents/ILCDraftRomeStatute94.pdf. Article 43 of the 1994 draft ICC Statute, which would later develop into the present day Article 68 of the ICC Statute, merely stated that "the Court shall take necessary measures available to it to protect the accused, victims and witnesses and may to that end conduct closed proceedings or allow the presentation of evidence by electronic or other special means." In 1995, the Ad Hoc Committee on the Establishment of an International Criminal Court reported that Article 43 "was viewed by a few delegations as calling for further elaboration, particularly with regard to the protection of victims and witnesses. Also noted was the need to consider the rights of the accused in this context." *See* UNGA, *Report of the Ad Hoc Committee on the Establishment of an International Criminal Court*, ¶ 181, UNGA Doc. A/50/22, Supp. No. 22 (Sept. 6, 1995), *available at* http://www.undemocracy.com/A-50-22.pdf.

[36] For example, in 1996, France proposed an alternative draft ICC Statute, including over 150 articles, many of which reflected French criminal law and procedure. Article 50 therein proposed to allow victims to participate in the proceedings for the purpose of obtaining reparations. *See* UNGA, *Preparatory Committee on the Establishment of an International Criminal Court, Draft Statute of the International Criminal Court, Working Paper Submitted by France*, UN Doc. A/AC.249/L.3 (Aug. 6, 1996), *available at* http://www.legal-tools.org. However, the

during the negotiations at Rome and advocated for an ICC with a more victim-centered approach than that of the ad hoc tribunals.[37] As a result of these dynamics, victim-related issues gained importance during the negotiations, and proposals made by Egypt, New Zealand and Canada to allow victims to actively participate in ICC proceedings eventually led to the formulation of the present Article 68(3) of the ICC Statute.[38] Article 68(3) sets out the general framework on victim participation before the ICC, in particular, by providing that victims may present "their views and concerns" during Court proceedings and be represented by legal counsel. Its full text provides as follows:

> Where the personal interests of the victims are affected, the Court shall permit their views and concerns to be presented and considered at stages of the proceedings determined to be appropriate by the Court and in a manner which is not prejudicial to or inconsistent with the rights of the accused and a fair and impartial trial. Such views and concerns may be presented by the legal repre-

---

ICC Statute, as eventually adopted, separated the right of victims to participate from their right to receive reparations.

[37] They did so mainly to rectify the perceived failure of the ad hoc tribunals to sufficiently take into account the interests of victims. *See* SáCouto, *Victim Participation*, *supra* note 30, at 317, sources cited n.98.

[38] On August 19, 1996, Egypt proposed to add a provision to Article 43 stating that "[l]egal representatives of victims of crimes have the right to participate in the proceedings with a view to presenting additional evidence needed to establish the basis of criminal responsibility as a foundation for their right to pursue civil compensation" and suggesting that "[t]he Rules of Procedure shall include provisions giving effect to the [UN Declaration on Victims (*supra* note 10)]." *See Preparatory Committee on the Establishment of an International Criminal Court, Proposal Submitted by Egypt for Article 43*, UN Doc. A/AC.249/WP.11 (Aug. 19, 1996), *available at* http://www.legal-tools.org. On August 13, 1997, New Zealand proposed the following formulation: "The Court shall permit the views and concerns of the victim to be presented and considered at appropriate stages of the proceedings where their personal interests are affected in a manner which is consistent with the rights of the accused and a fair and impartial trial." *See* UNGA, *Preparatory Committee on the Establishment of an International Criminal Court, Amended Proposal by New Zealand on Article 43, Non-Paper/WG*, UN Doc. 4/No.19/Rev (Aug. 13, 1997), *available at* http://www.legal-tools.org. On July 6, 1998, Canada submitted a proposal which became the present day Article 68(3). *See Committee of the Whole, Working Group on Procedural Matters, Proposal Submitted by Canada*, UN Doc. A/CONF.183/C.1/WGPM/L.58 (July 6, 1998), *available at* http://www.legal-tools.org. It is noted that also the preamble of the Rome Statute reflects the Court's victim-centered approach by stressing that the States Parties created the ICC while being "[m]indful that during this century millions of children, women and men have been victims of unimaginable atrocities that deeply shock the conscience of humanity."

sentatives of the victims where the Court considers it appropriate, in accordance with the Rules of Procedure and Evidence.

Rule 68(3) is worded after the UN Declaration on Victims.[39] According to some commentators, this demonstrates that the ICC's approach to victim participation was influenced by human rights ideas.[40] It is noted that the statute of the STL includes a similar provision,[41] while the ECCC grants victims the status of civil parties.[42]

In addition to the general right of participation provided in Article 68(3), the ICC Statute grants victims specific authorization to participate in particular types of proceedings, including admissibility and jurisdiction hearings, reparations hearings, and proceedings addressing prosecution requests to open an investigation *proprio motu*.[43] Proceedings of the latter type are held very early in the criminal process, even before an investigation commences.[44] This is similar to the approach of some national civil law jurisdictions where victims can participate in the decision to open an investigation, but differs from the more restrictive approach of the STL, where victims can participate in the proceedings only after an indictment is confirmed.[45]

---

39 For a discussion concerning the UN Declaration on Victims see *supra* note 10 and accompanying text.

40 William Schabas, The International Criminal Court: A Commentary on the Rome Statute 826 (2010).

41 STL Statute, Article 17.

42 ECCC IR 23. It is noted that, under this rule, civil parties at the ECCC are considered to be "supporting the prosecution" rather than possessing an independent interest (as the ICC and STL consider them to have). Another unique feature of the ECCC's approach to victims is that it only grants them symbolic reparations ("collective and moral reparations"), as opposed to the ICC and STL which can grant material reparations to participating victims. In addition, the ECCC restricts some forms of participation that are allowed at the ICC, for example, victims at the ECCC have not been allowed to make opening statements. *See, e.g.*, Case 002, Trial Chamber Response to Lead Co-Lawyers and Civil Party Lawyers' Request to Make a Brief Preliminary Remarks on Behalf of Civil Parties (ECCC Nov. 15, 2011) (Doc. No. E131/4).

43 These specific rights of participation are granted under Articles 15(3), 19(3) and 75(3) of the Rome Statute. They can be regarded as specific cases of the general right granted in Article 68(3). It is also noted that, under ICC Rule 50(1), the ICC Prosecutor must inform victims whenever he or she intends to seek the Pre-Trial Chamber's authorization to open an investigation (unless doing so would risk the investigation or the security of victims and witnesses).

44 It is also noted that ICC Rule 93 allows (but does not require) the Chamber to seek victims' views on any issue, including regarding a review of a prosecutorial decision not to investigate.

45 In addition, as discussed in Section II above, both the STL and ECCC follow

Victim participation rights under the ICC Statute are regulated by the ICC Rules of Procedure and Evidence. Significantly, Rule 86 includes a general provision instructing the ICC judges and other Court organs to take into account, in fulfilling their functions, the needs of all victims (and witnesses) in accordance with Article 68 of the Statute. Rule 85 defines the "victims" who can participate in ICC proceedings. This rule and the related jurisprudence are discussed in more detail in the next section. Other important provisions are found in Rules 91(2) and 91(3), which grant victims the right to have their legal representatives personally attend and participate in ICC proceedings, including by questioning the witnesses and accused.[46] While these provisions are intended to facilitate the participation of victims in ICC proceedings, at the same time they aim to balance victims' rights with the rights of the accused and the need to prevent trial delays. For example, under Rule 91(2) the Chamber can make exceptions to the rule that victims can have their legal representative personally participate in the proceedings, where it considers that victims should participate through written submissions.[47] Moreover, under Rule 91(3) the victims' representatives must seek the Chamber's permission before questioning any witnesses, experts or the accused, and the Chamber may take into account the parties' related observations when considering such requests.[48] Interestingly, such balancing acts can also be seen in national jurisdictions that follow the adversarial approach but allow some forms of victim participation (even if such participation is confined to the sentencing stage). For example,

rules which aim to limit the number of participating victims (*see supra* notes 24–6 and accompanying text).

[46] Other relevant provisions are found in ICC Rule 119(3), which requires the Pre-Trial Chamber to seek the views of victims before conditionally releasing a suspect or accused (or amending the terms of a previously granted provisional release), and ICC Rule 93, which allows (but does not require) the Chamber to seek victims' views on any issue. ICC Rule 93 gives some examples of issues regarding which the Chamber may wish to seek victims' views, such as a review of a prosecutorial decision not to investigate, a decision to hold a confirmation hearing in the absence of the person concerned, an amendment of the charges, joining and separating trials, a decision on admission of guilt, and certain immunities provided by the Court to witnesses to ensure their testimony.

[47] ICC Rule 91(2).

[48] ICC Rule 91(3)(a) ("When a legal representative attends and participates in accordance with this rule, and wishes to question a witness, including questioning under rules 67 and 68, an expert or the accused, the legal representative must make application to the Chamber. The Chamber may require the legal representative to provide a written note of the questions and in that case the questions shall be communicated to the Prosecutor and, if appropriate, the defence, who shall be allowed to make observations within a time limit set by the Chamber").

in the United States, at the sentencing proceedings of the case against Moussaoui (also known as the "twentieth 9/11 hijacker"), not all but only a representative sample of victim impact statements was presented in court.[49]

When the ICC began hearing cases, and victims started seeking to participate in the proceedings, the judges had to interpret and apply the above normative framework in a manner ensuring that the participation of victims – potentially in large numbers – would not adversely affect the rights of the accused or the smooth running of the trials. As of the time of writing, the ICC has issued several guiding decisions on victim participation. The following sections will further elaborate on victim participation issues, while relying on the relevant case law.

IV. OBTAINING VICTIM STATUS

As noted above, Rule 85 of the ICC Rules of Procedure and Evidence defines the concept of "victims" for purposes of ICC proceedings. In particular, it provides the following definition:

> (a) 'Victims' means natural persons who have suffered harm as a result of the commission of any crime within the jurisdiction of the Court;
> (b) Victims may include organizations or institutions that have sustained direct harm to any of their property which is dedicated to religion, education, art or science or charitable purposes, and to their historic monuments, hospitals and other places and objects for humanitarian purposes.

On July 11, 2008, in the *Lubanga* case, the ICC Appeals Chamber rendered its first decision on the definition of "victims" for the purposes of participating in ICC proceedings.[50] Focusing on Rule 85(a), the Appeals Chamber interpreted its provisions as including two categories of victims: (i) direct victims, i.e., those who suffered harm as a result of the crimes

---

49 Cassell, *supra* note 14, at 645–6. The sample included a cross-section from each of the four flights, diversity in terms of race, religion, economic status and occupation, and relationship to the victim. In addition, to expand the participation of victims, the *Moussaoui* prosecutors also introduced into evidence a large poster with photos of decedents and four notebooks containing 408 letters from victims and survivors.

50 Prosecutor v. Lubanga, Case No. ICC-01/04-01/06, Judgement on the Appeals of The Prosecutor and The Defence Against Trial Chamber I's Decision on Victims' Participation of 18 January 2008 (July 11, 2008) [hereinafter *Lubanga*, AC Judgement of 11 July 2008].

attributed to the accused,[51] and (ii) indirect victims, i.e., those who suffered harm "as a result of the harm suffered by direct victims."[52] The *Lubanga* case involved charges of recruiting and using children under 15 years old in active hostilities. In accordance with the above interpretation, direct victims of these crimes would be the child soldiers who were recruited and used as fighters by the accused, whereas their parents could be recognized as indirect victims (having suffered trauma from their children's recruitment). The Chamber held that to qualify as victims by the ICC, the harm suffered by natural persons could be material, physical or psychological.[53] What is important is that the harm *personally* affected the individuals in question, and that it was directly or indirectly caused by the crimes attributed to the accused.[54]

The issue of indirect victims was later revisited by the Trial Chamber in the same *Lubanga* case, when certain individuals sought the Court's recognition as indirect victims on the basis that they were attacked and harmed by child soldiers who had been recruited by the accused.[55] Applying the Appeal Chamber's interpretation of "indirect victims," the Trial Chamber found that there was no causal link between the harm inflicted on the applicants and the crimes attributed to the accused (the recruitment and use of child soldiers). In other words, the harm suffered by the applicants was not caused (even indirectly) by the accused's recruitment and use of child soldiers, but rather by the later conduct of the child soldiers. Accordingly, the Trial Chamber refused to grant the applicants the status of indirect victims.[56] As *obiter dicta*, the Chamber reiterated a previous holding by the Appeals Chamber that a kinship or close personal relationship to a direct victim may be a precondition for considering an individual as an indirect victim, and added that indirect victims may also include a person who "intervenes to prevent one of the crimes alleged against the accused."[57]

---

[51] *Id.* ¶ 61. While Rule 85 merely requires that the victims' harm be linked broadly to a crime covered by the Court's jurisdiction, the Appeals Chamber considered that an interpretation of the rule in the context of the Statute and other Rules requires that the victims' harm be linked to the specific charges brought against the accused.

[52] *Id.* ¶ 38.

[53] *Id.* ¶ 35.

[54] *Id.* ¶ 38. There was a partial dissent on this issue by Judge G.M. Pikis. *See id.*, Partly Dissenting Opinion of Judge G.M. Pikis, ¶ 3 [hereinafter *Lubanga*, AC Judgment of 11 July 2008, Pikis Dissent].

[55] Prosecutor v. Lubanga, Case No. ICC-01/04-01/06, Redacted Version of "Decision on 'Indirect Victims'" (Apr. 8, 2009).

[56] *Id.* ¶ 52.

[57] *Id.* ¶ 51.

For comparison purposes, it is noted that the Rules of the ICTY and ICTR define a victim as "a person against whom a crime over which the Tribunal has jurisdiction has allegedly been committed,"[58] a definition which seems to exclude indirect victims and which does not require a showing of harm. However, these tribunals do not have to deal with active participation of victims. One reason why it may matter, however, if a person is deemed a "victim" before the ICTY or ICTR is that it can make a difference later in obtaining compensation from national courts.[59] The STL defines a victim as a "natural person who has suffered physical, material or mental harm as a direct result of an attack within the Tribunal's jurisdiction."[60] But to limit the number of victims participating in the proceedings, the STL RULES distinguish the concept of "victim" from that of "victim participating in the proceedings," defining the latter as a "[v]ictim of an attack within the Tribunal's jurisdiction who has been granted leave by the Pre-Trial Judge to present his views and concerns at one or more stages of the proceedings after an indictment has been confirmed."[61] The ECCC IRs define a victim as "a natural person or legal entity that has suffered harm as a result of the commission of any crime within the jurisdiction of the ECCC,"[62] but to participate in the proceedings a victim must receive the status of a civil party which is defined as "a victim whose application to become a civil party has been declared admissible by the Co-Investigating Judges or the Pre-Trial Chamber in accordance with these IRs."[63] Under the US Federal Crime Victims' Rights Act, the term "crime victim" is defined as "the person against whom the State offense is committed or, if that person is killed or incapacitated, that person's family member or other lawful representative."[64] A comparative study of 22 European national jurisdictions found that:

> [a] common feature of all jurisdictions is that private persons who want to act within criminal proceedings have to fulfill certain conditions. First of all, their legal rights or interests must be affected, or at least jeopardized, by an act punishable under criminal law. Secondly, the damage suffered should be caused by the criminal offence.[65]

---

58 ICTY Rule 2(A); ICTR Rule 2(A).

59 *See* discussion in *supra* note 17 and accompanying text.

60 STL Rule 2(A).

61 *Id.*

62 ECCC IR, annexed Glossary.

63 *Id.*

64 Crime Victims' Rights Act, 18 U.S.C.A. § 3771.

65 Hoegen & Brienen, *supra* note 2, at 25. However, to participate in national criminal proceedings, the victim must acquire a formal position within the criminal justice system. *Id.* at 30.

V. MODALITIES AND TIMING OF VICTIM PARTICIPATION

In addition to receiving victim status from the ICC, victims must receive the Chamber's explicit permission to participate at specific stages of the proceedings each time they wish to take part. This differs from most national civil law jurisdictions, where victims may participate in the various stages of the criminal process without having to seek the court's permission before each stage. In accordance with Article 68(3) of the ICC Statute, the Chamber will grant victims permission to become involved when two conditions are satisfied: (1) the victims' "personal interests" are affected by the issues under consideration in the particular stage of the proceedings, and (2) it is "appropriate" that they should do so at that stage. The judges determine whether these conditions are met on a case-by-case basis, in each particular stage of the proceedings where victim participation is sought.[66] Each time victims request to participate, the parties may respond to their request, raising concerns about the adverse effects that victim participation can have on the rights of the accused or the conduct of the trial at any stage of the proceedings.[67] The Chamber may consider these concerns in determining whether victim participation is appropriate at a particular stage.

This case-by-case approach to victim participation stems from the need to balance the rights of victims against those of the accused and to prevent lengthy proceedings. The ICC addresses mass crimes which affect many victims. Allowing unlimited access to large numbers of victims may cause serious delays in the proceedings and require unrealistic resources of the ICC. As noted above, the ECCC IRs were recently reformed to minimize

---

[66] Prosecutor v. Lubanga, Case No. ICC-01/04-01/06, Decision of the Appeals Chamber on the Joint Application of Victims a/0001/06 to a/0003/06 and a/0105/06 Concerning the 'Directions and Decision of the Appeals Chamber' of 2 February 2007, ¶ 28 (June 13, 2007). In this decision, the ICC Appeals Chamber articulated for the first time what has since become its rule of thumb: "any determination . . . of whether the personal interests of victims are affected in relation to a particular appeal will require careful consideration on a case-by-case basis." While that decision related to a procedure before the Appeals Chamber, the above rule of thumb has also been followed by the Trial and Pre-Trial Chambers. *See also Lubanga*, AC Judgment of 11 July 2008, *supra* note 50, ¶¶ 99–100 (holding that a decision by the Trial Chamber to permit victims to participate in the specific proceedings before it, must be based on a determination that their personal interests are affected and that this is an appropriate stage for them to participate given the effect of such participation on the rights of the accused).

[67] ICC Rule 91(2).

delays caused by mass amounts of participating victims in the tribunal's second trial. One aspect of the ECCC reform was to require civil parties to organize themselves in one group represented by one team of legal representatives.[68] The ICC judges, although not required to do so by the rules, have instructed groups of victims to choose one common legal representative in order to minimize delays caused by the participation of large numbers of victims in the proceedings. For example, in *Prosecutor v. Bemba*, approximately 2,300 victims[69] were ordered to participate through only two common legal representatives.[70] The ICC is currently considering adopting an approach where one common legal representation will be provided to all victims in a particular case.[71]

To date, victims have been allowed by the ICC to participate in numerous types of proceedings including those concerning confirmation of charges,[72] admissibility of cases,[73] trial proceedings,[74] and interlocutory appeals.[75] It is noted that for victims to participate in interlocutory

---

68 ECCC IR 23(3).

69 *See* Prosecutor v. Bemba Gombo, Case No. ICC-01/05-01/08, Case Information Sheet (ICC-PIDS-CIS-CAR-01-008/12_Eng; updated Mar. 5, 2012), *available at* http://www.icc-cpi.int/iccdocs/PIDS/publications/BembaEng.pdf (last visited Apr. 3, 2012) ("Trial Chamber III granted 2287 persons the status of victims authorised to participate in the proceeding.").

70 Prosecutor v. Bemba Gombo, Case No. ICC-01/05-01/08, Decision on Common Legal Representation of Victims for the Purposes of Trial, ¶ 10 (Nov. 10, 2010).

71 ICC, *Interim Report of the Court on Legal Aid: Legal and Financial Aspects for Funding Victims' Legal Representatives Before the Court*, ICC - ASP/8/3, (May 6, 2009).

72 *See, e.g.*, Prosecutor v. Lubanga, Case No. ICC-01/04-01/06, Decision on the Confirmation of Charges, ¶ 31 (Jan. 29, 2007) [hereinafter *Lubanga*, Confirmation Decision of 29 January 2007]; Prosecutor v. Katanga & Ngudjolo, Case No. ICC-01/04-01/07, Decision on the Confirmation of Charges, ¶¶ 59–60 (Sept. 30, 2008). The confirmation hearing takes place after the accused has made an initial appearance before the Chamber but before his or her trial begins. At the end of the confirmation hearing, the Court considers whether to validate or revoke the charges against the accused. While victims can make submissions at the confirmation hearings, as a general rule, they cannot present evidence during this stage.

73 *See, e.g.*, Prosecutor v. Katanga & Ngudjolo, Case No. ICC-01/04-01/07, Reasons for the Oral Decision on the Motion Challenging the Admissibility of the Case (Article 19 of the Statute), ¶ 4 (June 16, 2009).

74 Prosecutor v. Lubanga, Case No. ICC-01/04-01/06, Decision on Victims' Participation (Jan. 18, 2008) [hereinafter *Lubanga*, Decision on Victims' Participation] (allowing victims to present evidence and examine witnesses during the trial proceedings).

75 Prosecutor v. Lubanga, Case No. ICC-01/04-01/06, Decision, *in limine*, on Victim Participation in the Appeals of the Prosecutor and the Defence Against the

appeals proceedings, they must have already been accorded victim status in the lower-instance proceedings.[76] Still, victims must specifically seek the Appeals Chamber's permission to participate in interlocutory appeals proceedings, even if they were previously authorized to participate in the proceedings leading to the decision being appealed.[77] It is stressed that while victims may participate in ICC appellate proceedings, the ICC Statute does not explicitly grant them a right to *initiate* an appeal against ICC decisions. Rather, the Statute refers only to "parties" as the holders of such a right.[78] This is different at the ECCC (and in some national civil law jurisdictions), where the participating victims may appeal against court decisions and judgments, at least in some cases.[79]

The ICC judges decide on a case-by-case basis not only *when* the victims may present their views and concerns, but also *how* these views and concerns will be presented. In other words, once the Chamber allows victims to participate (on the basis that the "personal interest" and "appropriate

---

Trial Chamber I's Decision Entitled "Decision on Victims' Participation" (May 16, 2008) [hereinafter *Lubanga*, AC Decision of 16 May 2008].

[76] *Id.* ¶ 36.

[77] Prosecutor v. Lubanga, Case No. ICC-01/04-01/06, Judgement on the Appeal of Mr Thomas Lubanga Dyilo Against the Decision of Pre-Trial Chamber I Entitled "Décision sur la demande de mise en liberté provisoire de Thomas Lubanga Dyilo", ¶¶ 40, 46 (Feb. 13, 2007) [hereinafter *Lubanga*, AC Decision of 13 February 2007] (the Appeals Chamber considered that Article 68(3) of the Statute requires victims to actively apply for participation at the stage of the interlocutory appeal and to file such application "as soon as possible after the appeal is filed"). *See also* Prosecutor v. Bemba Gombo, Case No. ICC-01/05-01/08, Reasons for the 'Decision on the Participation of Victims in the Appeal Against the "Decision on the Interim Release of Jean-Pierre Gombo and Convening Hearings with the Kingdom of Belgium, the Republic of Portugal, the Republic of France, the Federal Republic of Germany, the Italian Republic, and the Republic of South Africa"', ¶ 14 (Oct. 20, 2009) (the Appeals Chamber explains that regulation 64(4) and (5) of the Regulations of the Court "were not understood as granting victims an automatic right to participate in an interlocutory appeal, as this would preclude a specific determination by the Appeals Chamber that participation in the particular interlocutory appeal is appropriate").

[78] One exception is found in Article 82(4) of the Rome Statute, which allows victims to appeal against reparation awards. Arguably, this unique appearance in the Statute of an explicit permission to appeal against reparation awards indicates that victims' right to appeal against reparation decisions is an exception to the general rule that they have no right to appeal ICC decisions. *See* SCHABAS, *supra* note 40, at 949.

[79] The ECCC nonetheless places some restrictions on the right of civil parties to appeal. *See, e.g.*, ECCC IR 105(1)(c) ("The Civil Parties may appeal the decision on reparations. Where the Co-Prosecutors have appealed, the Civil Parties may appeal the verdict. They may not appeal the sentence").

stage" tests were met), it will decide on the manner of participation which will be consistent with the rights of the accused and a fair and impartial trial, in accordance with Article 68(3). For example, in the *Lubanga* case, victims were allowed (through their legal representatives) to actively participate in the confirmation hearing,[80] make opening and closing statements,[81] question witnesses, and present evidence.[82] In interlocutory appeals, victims are restricted to submitting their observations in writing (similar to the manner of participation of the parties).[83]

It is noted that participating victims can also be called by one of the parties as witnesses before the ICC.[84] This differs from the approach of the ECCC and STL, as well as some national civil law jurisdictions, where participating victims cannot testify as witnesses (or can testify only with special permission).[85] Under those jurisdictions, if someone is called by a party as a witness, he or she cannot participate in the proceedings as a victim. One possible rationale for this rule is that participating victims have the right to be present for the duration of the proceedings, while witnesses are usually not permitted to attend the proceedings before they testify, to ensure that their evidence is not influenced by earlier testimony.

---

80 *Lubanga*, Confirmation Decision of 29 January 2007, *supra* note 72, ¶ 31.

81 *Lubanga*, Decision on Victims' Participation, *supra* note 74, ¶ 117.

82 *Id.* ¶ 108.

83 *Lubanga*, AC Decision of 16 May 2008, *supra* note 75, ¶ 50. The Chamber stressed that the victims must confine their written submissions to issues that are relevant both to the specific appeal and their personal interests which it affects.

84 The dual role of victim-witness was recognized by the ICC in *Lubanga*, Decision on Victims' Participation, *supra* note 73. However, the decision stressed that "when the Trial Chamber considers an application by victims who have this dual status, it will establish whether the participation by a victim who is also a witness may adversely affect the rights of the defence at a particular stage in the case." *Id.* ¶ 134.

85 ECCC IR 23(4) ("The Civil Party cannot be questioned as a simple witness in the same case and, subject to Rule 62 relating to Rogatory Letters, may only be interviewed under the same conditions as a Charged Person or Accused"); STL Rule 150(D) ("A victim participating in the proceedings may be permitted to give evidence if a Chamber decides that the interests of justice so require."). It is noted that STL Rule 150(D) was amended on Feb. 8. 2012, whereas it originally read: "A victim participating in the proceedings shall not be permitted to give evidence unless a Chamber decides that the interests of justice so require." The amendment was "aimed at reversing the presumption in favour of allowing victims participating in the proceedings to also appear as witnesses." *See Summary of Accepted Rule Amendments and Some Key Rejected Rule Amendment Proposals Pursuant to Rule 5(I) of the Special Tribunal for Lebanon's Rules of Procedure and Evidence* (Fourth Plenary of Judges, Feb. 2012), *available at* http://www.stl-tsl.org/images/rpe/12-02-21_Plenary4_Accepted_and_Rejected_Rules_Summary.pdf.

In addition, there may be a conflict of interests between the legal representative of the participating victim and the party who called him or her as a witness.[86] It is noted that, although the ICC allows a dual role of victim-witness, its judges have permitted participating victims to testify before the Court even when they were not called as witnesses by a party.[87]

Another interesting involvement of the victims in the *Lubanga* case was their ability to initiate proceedings regarding modification of the charges. Following a request by participating victims that the Trial Chamber consider modifying the legal characterization of the facts presented by the prosecution (by adding the crimes of inhuman and cruel treatment and sexual slavery to the existing characterization), the Trial Chamber notified the parties and participants that the legal characterization of the facts might be subject to change. However, the Appeals Chamber reversed the Trial Chamber's decision, finding that there was no legal basis for a modification from the child soldier offenses to the requested offenses.[88] While the charges were eventually not modified, that these proceedings were initiated by victims demonstrates that the interests of victims can sometimes differ from those of the prosecution. Indeed, both the prosecution and defense opposed the victims' request to modify the charges against the accused Lubanga. On another occasion, which is discussed above, the prosecutor objected to victims giving testimony in the *Lubanga* case. There, too, the interests of victims were in opposition to those of the prosecutor.[89] It is further noted that victims participating in the *Lubanga* case were permitted to access part of the case file,[90] much like the practice

---

[86] For an attempt by the ICC to resolve such tensions see *Lubanga*, Decision on Dual Status of Witness and Victim, *supra* note 31.

[87] *See supra* note 32 and accompanying text.

[88] *See* Prosecutor v. Lubanga, Case No. ICC-01/04-01/06, Decision Giving Notice to the Parties and Participants That the Legal Characterisation of the Facts May Be Subject to Change in Accordance with Regulation 55(2) of the Regulations of the Court (July 14, 2009); Prosecutor v. Lubanga, Case No. ICC-01/04-01/06, Judgement on the Appeals of Mr Lubanga Dyilo and the Prosecutor Against the Decision of Trial Chamber I of 14 July 2009 Entitled "Decision Giving Notice to the Parties and Participants That the Legal Characterisation of the Facts May Be Subject to Change in Accordance with Regulation 55(2) of the Regulations of the Court" (Dec. 8, 2009).

[89] *See supra* note 32 and accompanying text.

[90] Prosecutor v. Lubanga, Case No. ICC-01/04-01/06, Decision on the Arrangements for Participation of Victims a/0001/06, a/0002/06 and a/0003/06 at the Confirmation Hearing, 6–7 (Sept. 22, 2006). Note that the Pre-Trial Chamber I allowed victims, in principle, to access only public documents, but accepted that they may be granted access to confidential filings in exceptional circumstances. In the *Katanga* case, the judges adopted the principle that the victims' legal

of national civil law jurisdictions.[91]

Importantly, the victims participating in the *Lubanga* case were allowed to present and challenge evidence, for example by calling expert witnesses and by cross-examining witnesses and the accused, despite the fact that the rules are silent on these issues. The victims were allowed to present evidence even when it related to the guilt or innocence of the accused.[92] The Chamber based this approach on Article 69(3) of the ICC Statute, which allows the Court to request additional evidence to that presented by the parties. The Chamber held that such Court-requested evidence can originate from victims, even if Article 69(3) does not explicitly provide for this option.[93] The Appeals Chamber upheld this ruling, stressing that although the parties are the primary holders of the right to present evidence on the guilt or innocence of the accused, nothing in the ICC Statute precludes victims from presenting or challenging evidence, including that which goes to the guilt or innocence of the accused.[94] The Appeals Chamber added that if these modalities of participation were precluded, the victims' right to participate under Article 68(3) may not be "meaningful."[95]

However, this was a majority decision, with only three out of the five Appeals Chamber judges reaching this conclusion. The two dissenting judges opted for a more limited interpretation of the Statute's victim participation scheme, which did not include a right to present evidence on the guilt of the accused. They asserted that it was solely the prosecutor who was responsible for investigating and presenting evidence against

---

representatives (rather than the victims themselves) could generally have access to confidential information. *See* Prosecutor v. Katanga & Ngudjolo, Case No. ICC-01/04-01/07, Decision on the Modalities of Victim Participation at Trial, ¶¶ 121–3 (Jan. 22, 2010).

91 But unlike in certain national civil law jurisdictions, victims at the ICC do not have an *automatic* right of access to case documents. *See* War Crimes Research Office, Am. Univ. Washington Coll. of Law, Victim Participation Before the International Criminal Court 31 and references in n.136 (2007).

92 *Lubanga*, Decision on Victims' Participation, *supra* note 74.

93 *Id.* ¶¶ 108, 121. It is interesting to note in this context the different approach of the STL, where the Trial Chamber is explicitly mandated to call evidence that is requested by the participating victims. *See* STL Rule 146(B) ("Unless otherwise directed by the Trial Chamber in the interests of justice, evidence at the trial shall be presented in the following sequence: evidence for the Prosecutor; evidence called by the Trial Chamber at the request of victims participating in the proceedings; evidence for the defence; Prosecutor evidence in rebuttal; rebuttal evidence called at the request of victims participating in the proceedings; defence evidence in rejoinder").

94 *Lubanga*, AC Judgment of 11 July 2008, *supra* note 50, ¶¶ 93–4.

95 *Id.* ¶ 97.

the accused, since otherwise the accused would have to respond to more than one accuser, in violation of the principle of equality of arms.[96] In an earlier decision, where he also rejected broad participation rights of victims, one of the dissenting judges expressed his opinion that "[c]asting the burden of proof, as the Statute does, upon the Prosecutor confines the discharge of this burden to the Prosecutor and limits the confrontation to the parties, i.e., the Prosecutor and the defendant."[97] However, a majority of the Appeals Chamber judges did not consider that by allowing victims to present evidence they are necessarily causing the accused to face two prosecutors.[98]

The above positions expressed by the dissenting judges in the *Lubanga* case are exactly the kind of arguments made by those who oppose victim participation in national adversarial criminal systems.[99] However, some national jurisdictions, such as Italy, have attempted to achieve a balance between active victim participation and an adversarial system. The German legal system, moreover, introduced the principle of equality of arms without departing from its inquisitorial civil-law roots and active victim participation models. Adopting active victim participation schemes

---

[96] *Lubanga*, AC Judgment of 11 July 2008, Pikis Dissent, *supra* note 54, ¶¶ 7–9, 14–15; Prosecutor v. Lubanga, Case No ICC-01/04-01/06, Judgement on the Appeals of the Prosecutor and The Defence against Trial Chamber's Decision on Victim's Participation of 18 January 2008, Partly Dissenting Opinion of Judge Philip Kirsch (July 23, 2008), ¶¶ 6–15, 24, 30 [hereinafter *Lubanga*, Kirsch Dissent]. Kirsch also added that while the prosecution has a duty to disclose evidence to the defense, victims have no such obligations under the Statute, which suggests that the drafters could not have intended that victims would have a right to present evidence on the guilt of the accused. He also noted that granting victims the right to present evidence would unduly prolong the proceedings. *Id.*, Kirsch Dissent, ¶¶ 15–16, 28. But note a previous holding by the Appeal Chamber: "The Appeal Chamber also did not accept the submission of the Appellant that, by allowing the victims to participate, the Appellant was facing two prosecutors." *Lubanga*, AC Decision of 13 February 2007, *supra* note 77, ¶¶ 54–5. Also see the following holding by the Pre-Trial Chamber in the *Darfur* situation: "in situation and case proceedings before the Pre-Trial Chamber . . . the fact that one or several natural or legal persons may be entitled to the procedural status of victim is not, per se, prejudicial to the Defence." Situation in Darfur, Sudan, ICC-02/05, Decision on the Requests of the OPCD on the Production of Relevant Supporting Documentation Pursuant to Regulation 86(2)(e) or the Regulations of the Court and on the Disclosure of Exculpatory Materials by the Prosecutor (Dec. 3, 2007).

[97] *Lubanga*, AC Decision of 13 February 2007, Separate Opinion of Judge Pikis, *supra* note 77, ¶ 18.

[98] *Lubanga*, AC Decision of 13 February 2007, *supra* note 77, ¶¶ 54–5.

[99] *See, e.g.*, Damaška, *supra* note 15. *See also* WOLHUTER ET AL., *supra* note 3, at 196.

in adversarial systems may mean broadening the notion of fair trial to apply not only to defendants but also to victims.[100] This is consistent with the jurisprudence of the European Court of Human Rights, that a civil party to criminal proceedings has the right to a fair trial.[101]

VI. VICTIMS' ACCESS TO THE ICC

How do victims organize in order to participate in the proceedings? First, the ICC disseminates information through its website and outreach activities to potential victims and victims' representatives. Often potential representatives reach out to affected communities and collect victims to represent. In addition, the ICC's Victim Participation and Reparations Section, including through its field officers, communicates directly with victims to inform them of their rights under the ICC Statute, helps them complete and submit applications to the Court seeking victim status as well as participation and reparation, and assists them in obtaining legal representation.[102] The ICC's Office of the Public Counsel for Victims provides legal advice and information to victims and their representatives, and represents victims before the Court when such need arises (usually following an order by the Chamber).[103] Moreover, the ICC helps victims find a legal representative by providing them with a list of counsel authorized to act before the Court. Counsel can be admitted to the list if they meet certain threshold requirements.[104] It is also noted that the ICC's Victims and Witnesses Unit promotes the protection of victims (and witnesses), without which they would be unable to enjoy their right to participate in

---

[100] Wolhuter et al., *supra* note 3, at 196.

[101] *See, e.g.*, Perez v. France, no. 47287/99, Eur. Ct. H.R. (Feb. 12, 2004).

[102] On the ICC's Victims Participation and Reparations Section, see ICC official website at http://www.icc-cpi.int/Menus/ICC/Structure+of+the+Court/Victims/Participation/.

[103] On the ICC's Office of the Public Counsel for Victims, see ICC official website at http://www.icc-cpi.int/Menus/ICC/Structure+of+the+Court/Victims/Legal+Representation/.

[104] To be admitted to the list of counsel authorized to act before the court, candidates must satisfy the minimum quality assurance requirements set out in ICC Rule 22 and Regulation 67 of the Regulations of the Court. These prerequisites to practicing before the Court are designed to guarantee that every person in need of legal representation implicated in ICC proceedings has available to him or her a pool of highly competent counsel to ensure quality legal representation. *See* ICC official website at http://www.icc-cpi.int/Menus/ICC/Structure+of+the+Court/Victims/Legal+Representation/.

the proceedings.[105] These provisions stress that special attention must be given to the protection of victims of sexual or gender crimes and to child victims. In practice, to protect participating victims, their identities are often concealed from the public and pseudonyms are used to identify them during the proceedings and in the records. In addition, their voices and images are sometimes distorted.[106]

VII. CONCLUSION

The ad hoc tribunals and the SCSL adopted the common law approach of limiting victims' role in the proceedings to that of witnesses. By contrast, the ICC, STL and ECCC follow the civil law approach of granting victims active participation rights. It is recalled that active victim participation at the national level has restorative goals such as empowering and rehabilitating victims, and clarifying the crime's harm to the defendant. At the same time, retributive goals are promoted as the victims' information assists the court in establishing the truth, a prerequisite to holding accountable and punishing perpetrators.[107] Thus, by allowing active victim participation, international criminal tribunals could promote both retributive and restorative goals, consistent with their dual mandate of peace and justice. Given the type of atrocities and contexts addressed by international criminal tribunals, the involvement of large numbers of victims in the proceedings can have a restorative effect on entire communities. It is also recalled that the participation of victims improves the perceived fairness of the judicial process and its relevance to the victims and their communities, features which may appeal to international criminal tribunals as they build their legitimacy.

---

[105] The Victims and Witnesses Unit fulfills its task by providing the Chambers with objective information about victims and witnesses, and special advice regarding their need for protection. *See* Prosecutor v. Kony et al., Case No. ICC-02/04-01/05, Decision on the Prosecutor's Application That the Pre-Trial Chamber Disregard as Irrelevant the Submission Filed by the Registry on 5 December 2005, ¶ 38 (Mar. 9, 2006); Prosecutor v. Lubanga, Case No. ICC-01/04-01/06, Decision on Third Defence Motion for Leave to Appeal, 8 (Oct. 4, 2006). The protection of victims and witnesses is regulated by Rome Statute Articles 68(1) and 68(2), and ICC Rules 87–88.

[106] *See, e.g.*, Prosecutor v. Lubanga, Case No. ICC-01/04-01/06, Transcript, at 1–5 (Jan. 16, 2009). Victims and witnesses may even be relocated for their protection.

[107] For the goals of active victim participation, see *supra* note 14 and accompanying text.

However, when the international criminal proceedings are adversarial in nature, as is the case at the ICC, active victim participation may cause imbalances stemming from introducing a third participant to the competition between the prosecution and defense. This explains the passive role of victims in national common law jurisdictions. In civil law jurisdictions this problem does not arise, as the judge-led inquisitorial nature of the proceedings accommodates active victim participation. Furthermore, while the narrative form of testimony in civil law jurisdictions may have a rehabilitating effect on victims, the frequent lawyers' interventions in common law jurisdictions may achieve the opposite. The ICC proceedings are adversarial rather than judge-led (even if judges are more involved in the proceedings than in national common law jurisdictions), and the testimony is not given in narrative form. Thus, for the ICC to successfully incorporate an active victim participation scheme, it must carefully balance victim participation with the right of the accused to a fair trial.

In addition, while the international criminal tribunals' paradigm shift from passive to active victim participation has great potential to contribute to restorative justice goals, these tribunals must at the same time guard themselves against the hazards involved in a flood of victims demanding unrealistic resources that may threaten to paralyze the judicial proceedings (and thereby impede their retributive goals).

As illustrated above, the ICC judges are developing, through the case law, prerequisites and modalities for victim participation that aim to resolve some of the tensions arising from the participation of large numbers of victims in cases of mass atrocities before a court with adversarial proceedings. As the judges continue to face new challenges relating to victim participation issues, this case law will continue to develop.

7. Right to appeal

Magali Maystre*

I. INTRODUCTION

The appellate proceedings before international courts and tribunals are a mixture of civil law and common law approaches.[1] This blending of traditions has not always led to an overall satisfactory compromise consistent with the highest standard of a fair trial.

In the spirit of a civil law approach, appellate proceedings are broadly conceived and attribute a right to appeal against convictions and sentence to both the defendant and the prosecutor. However, the appellate proceedings under discussion tend more towards a common law approach in not allowing for a trial *de novo* and limiting the admission of additional evidence on appeal.

Given this combination, the appeal judges of international criminal courts and tribunals have faced two major issues that have been problematical in the development of the procedures in the courts. This chapter will examine them in turn. The first question concerns how to respect the fundamental right to an appeal in the case of an appeal by the prosecutor against an acquittal. Against strong dissents, the international criminal courts and tribunals confronted with this issue have so far been unable to consistently capture the best of common law and civil law traditions and

---

* Magali Maystre holds a *D.E.A.* (post-graduate degree) in international law from the *Institut universitaire de hautes études internationales* in Geneva, Switzerland. She currently works as a Legal Officer in the Appeals Chamber of the ICTY. She is also a Senior Advisor for the Case Matrix Network (CMN) (http://www.casematrixnetwork.org/) whose primary purpose is to strengthen national ability to investigate and prosecute international core crimes. The views expressed herein are those of the author and do not necessarily reflect the views of the United Nations, the ICTY or the CMN. The author would like to thank Matthew Carlson (Legal Officer in the Appeals Chamber of the ICTR) for his assistance and comments.

[1] The scope of this chapter will be limited to the right to appeal against judgments of courts of first instance. It will not examine the right to appeal against interlocutory decisions.

to reconcile them with the fundamental right to appeal. The International Criminal Court (ICC) has yet to address this issue (Section II).

The second main issue relates to the standard of appellate review to be applied in cases where additional evidence, which has not previously been considered by the trial chamber, is admitted on appeal. Specifically, the questions were: should the appeal judges hear additional evidence themselves? And if so, is the right of the appellant to a trial chamber's decision beyond reasonable doubt based on all of the evidence before it, violated if the appeals chambers use the usual appellate standard of deference to the trial chamber's findings? The International Criminal Tribunal for the former Yugoslavia (ICTY) resolved this issue in favor of the appellant's right to a trial chamber's decision beyond reasonable doubt. The ICC has yet to address this issue (Section III).

II. THE RIGHT TO APPEAL, INCLUDING AGAINST ACQUITTALS

Although the right to appeal in the context of international criminal courts and tribunals is a mixture of both systems of civil law and common law, it also presents features which are different from any national court setting. Outlining the problems, challenges and limits the Appeals Chamber of the ICTY and International Criminal Tribunal for Rwanda (ICTR) have met with respect to the right to appeal against an acquittal allows a better assessment of the best solution to be adopted in the future by the ICC (Section C). Before turning to this main issue, this chapter first describes the fundamental right to appeal, which from an international human rights law perspective should apply in all legal systems (Section A) and, subsequently, briefly discusses the divergence in procedures with respect to the right to appeal in the context of civil law and common law legal systems (Section B).

A. The Fundamental Right to Appeal

According to Article 14(5) of the International Covenant on Civil and Political Rights of 16 December 1966 (ICCPR), "[e]veryone convicted of a crime shall have the right to his conviction and sentence being reviewed by a higher tribunal according to law."[2]

---

[2] International Covenant on Civil and Political Rights (ICCPR), annexed to UN Doc. A/RES/21/2200(A) (Dec. 16, 1966).

The right of a person convicted of a crime to have his or her conviction and sentence reviewed by a higher judicial body was also recognized in other international treaties such as the Geneva Conventions of 1949.[3]

The need for a right to appeal was similarly recognized in a number of regional conventions on human rights. For example, Article 8(2)(h) of the American Convention on Human Rights of 22 November 1969 provides that:

> [e]very person accused of a criminal offense has the right to be presumed innocent so long as his guilt has not been proven according to law. During the proceedings, every person is entitled, with full equality, to the following minimum guarantees: . . . the right to appeal the judgment to a higher court.

Similarly, according to Article 2(1) of Protocol No. 7 to the Convention for the Protection of Human Rights and Fundamental Freedoms of 22 November 1984 (Protocol 7 to the ECHR), "[e]veryone convicted of a criminal offence by a tribunal shall have the right to have his conviction or sentence reviewed by a higher tribunal. The exercise of this right, including the grounds on which it may be exercised, shall be governed by law."[4]

The Human Rights Committee's (HRC) interpretation of Article 14(5) of the ICCPR has eliminated any doubt that an accused's right to appeal against conviction also entails the right to appeal a conviction entered for the first time on appeal. The HRC has held that:

> Article 14[(5) of the ICCPR] is violated not only if the decision by the court of first instance is final, but also where a conviction imposed by an appeal court or a court of final instance, following acquittal by a lower court, according to domestic law, cannot be reviewed by a higher court. Where the highest court of a country acts as first and only instance, the absence of any right to review by a higher tribunal is not offset by the fact of being tried by the supreme tribunal of the State party concerned; rather, such a system is incompatible with the [ICCPR], unless the State party concerned has made a reservation to this effect.[5]

---

[3] Geneva Convention Relative to the Treatment of Prisoners of War, Aug. 12, 1949, 75 U.N.T.S. 135. *See also* Convention Relative to the Treatment of Prisoners of War, art. 64, July 27, 1929, 118 L.N.T.S. 343.

[4] However, it is worth mentioning that, according to Article 2(2) of Protocol 7 to the ECHR, "[t]his right may be subject to exceptions . . . in cases in which the person concerned was tried in the first instance by the highest tribunal or was convicted following an appeal against acquittal."

[5] HRC, General Comment No. 32 – Article 14: Right to Equality Before Courts and Tribunals and to a Fair Trial, UN Doc. CCPR/C/GC/32 (Aug. 23, 2007), ¶ 47 (internal references omitted) [hereinafter HRC, General Comment]. *See*

With respect to the expression "according to law" in Article 14(5) of the ICCPR, the HRC has clarified that this reference is not intended to leave the very existence of the right to appeal to the discretion of States, since this right is not merely recognized by domestic law but by the ICCPR itself. Rather, this expression refers to the determination of the modalities by which the appeal by a higher tribunal is exercised, as well as which tribunal would be responsible for it.[6] In this respect, the HRC has held that "Article 14 [of the ICCPR] contains guarantees that States parties must respect, regardless of their legal traditions and domestic law" and that "it cannot be left to the sole discretion of domestic law to determine the essential content of [the ICCPR] guarantees."[7]

Thus, according to the international human rights law standard espoused by the United Nations, the right to appeal convictions and sentence, not excluding convictions – or an increase in the sentence – entered for the first time on appeal, should always be granted to an accused.

Finally, with respect to the scope of the right to appeal, the HRC has clarified that Article 14(5) of the ICCPR does not require a trial *de novo*. Instead, the provision simply imposes a duty on States Parties to review substantively the conviction and the sentence, both on the basis of sufficiency of the evidence and of the law. However, review proceedings "limited to the formal or legal aspects of the conviction without any consideration whatsoever of the facts is not sufficient."[8]

B. The Approach of Common Law and Civil Law Systems

The right to appeal a judgment of a court to a higher instance in criminal cases is found in national legal systems generally.[9]

---

also MANFRED NOWAK, U.N. COVENANT ON CIVIL AND POLITICAL RIGHTS: CCPR COMMENTARY 268 (1st ed. 1993).

6 HRC, General Comment, *supra* note 5, ¶ 45. *See also* NOWAK, *supra* note 5, at 267; Robert Roth & Marc Henzelin, *The Appeal Procedure of the ICC, in* 2 THE ROME STATUTE OF THE INTERNATIONAL CRIMINAL COURT: A COMMENTARY 1540 (Antonio Cassese et al. eds., 2002).

7 HRC, General Comment, *supra* note 5, ¶ 4.

8 *Id.* ¶ 48. *See also* NOWAK, *supra* note 5, at 266; Gómez Vázquez v. Spain, HRC, Communication No. 701/1996, UN Doc. CCPR/C/69/D/701/1996 (2000) (where the HRC found that Spain was in violation of Article 14(5) of the ICCPR because Mr. Gómez Vázquez's conviction was reviewed only by the Supreme Court on the basis of an incomplete judicial review procedure on very limited legal grounds without any consideration of the evidence).

9 Christopher Staker, *Article 81: Appeal Against Decision of Acquittal or Conviction or Against Sentence, in* COMMENTARY ON THE ROME STATUTE OF THE INTERNATIONAL CRIMINAL COURT 1450 (Otto Triffterer ed., 2d ed. 2008).

As preliminary remarks, it is important to recall that the terminology and language of appellate proceedings vary significantly between common law and civil law systems, as well as within these two groups.[10] In addition, different forms of appellate proceedings may exist in national legal systems.[11]

Generally, in common law systems, the right to appeal is strictly limited, especially if it covers not only error of law but also error of fact, while in civil law systems, the right to appeal is granted more generously to both the defendant and the prosecution.[12]

An appeal in the common law tradition is not a trial *de novo* – i.e., an entire new hearing of the case – but is usually limited to the review of the trial record in a search for the errors claimed by the appellant. However, errors found to be harmless will not result in a reversal of the judgment. Depending on the reasons for the success of the appeal, the court of appeal may annul the conviction and acquit the defendant or order a re-trial.[13] Hence appeal courts are only involved in controlling the application of the law rather than the assessment of facts. The rationale behind this approach is that appellate proceedings are tried by professional judges rather than a jury and deference must be given to findings of facts by a jury.[14]

In the common law tradition, generally, only the convicted person is vested with the right to appeal against a conviction.[15] The right of appeal

---

10 Roth & Henzelin, *supra* note 6, at 1538, 1542–3; JEAN PRADEL, DROIT PÉNAL COMPARÉ 614 (2d ed. 2002).

11 Staker, *supra* note 9, at 1455.

12 Alphons Orie, *Accusatorial v. Inquisitorial Approach in International Criminal Proceedings Prior to the Establishment of the ICC and in the Proceedings Before the ICC, in* 2 THE ROME STATUTE OF THE INTERNATIONAL CRIMINAL COURT: A COMMENTARY, *supra* note 6, at 1455–6.

13 *Id.* at 1455. *See also* GEERT-JAN ALEXANDER KNOOPS, THEORY AND PRACTICE OF INTERNATIONAL AND INTERNATIONALIZED CRIMINAL PROCEEDINGS 290 (2005); Fausto Pocar, *Common and Civil Law Traditions in the ICTY Criminal Procedure: Does Oil Blend with Water?, in* COMMON LAW, CIVIL LAW AND THE FUTURE OF CATEGORIES 454 (Janet Walker & Oscar G. Chase eds., 2010); J.R. Spencer, *The English System, in* EUROPEAN CRIMINAL PROCEDURES 203 (Mireille Delmas-Marty & J.R. Spencer eds., 2002).

14 KNOOPS, *supra* note 13, at 290; CHRISTOPH J.M. SAFFERLING, TOWARDS AN INTERNATIONAL CRIMINAL PROCEDURE 334 (2001); Mark C. Fleming, *Appellate Review in the International Criminal Tribunals*, 37 TEX. INT'L L.J. 111, 139 (2002); A.T.H. Smith, *England and Wales, in* CRIMINAL PROCEDURE SYSTEMS IN THE EUROPEAN COMMUNITY 100–1 (Christine Van den Wyngaert ed., 1993).

15 Orie, *supra* note 12, at 1455; Adolphus G. Karibi-Whyte, *Appeal Procedures and Practices, in* 1 SUBSTANTIVE AND PROCEDURAL ASPECTS OF INTERNATIONAL

against an acquittal usually does not exist in such systems.[16] In the United States, for example, prosecutorial appeals from acquittals are deemed to violate the double jeopardy clause (*ne bis in idem*) enshrined in the Fifth Amendment of the Constitution.[17] In England and Wales, save for appeals permitted in certain limited and clearly circumscribed instances,[18] the prosecutor cannot appeal against an acquittal, but can appeal against sentence.[19] It may also request the Court of Appeal's opinion on a point of law. However, the Court of Appeal does not affect the situation of the person acquitted in that case, but clarifies the law for the future.[20] In South Africa, appeals against acquittals only on questions of facts are not allowed.[21] In sum, with the exception of the Unites States, which maintains a rigid proscription against all prosecutorial appeals from acquittals, many common law systems allow prosecutorial appeals against acquittals to the extent that they concern questions of law.[22]

CRIMINAL LAW: THE EXPERIENCE OF INTERNATIONAL AND NATIONAL COURTS 645 (Gabrielle Kirk McDonald & Olivia Swaak-Goldman eds., 2000); Smith, *supra* note 14, at 100.

16 Kai Ambos, *International Criminal Procedure: "Adversarial", "Inquisitorial" or Mixed?*, 3 INT'L CRIM. L. REV. 1, 33 (2003); SAFFERLING, *supra* note 14, at 332. *See also* Pocar, *supra* note 13, at 453; Roth & Henzelin, *supra* note 6, at 1542; Mario Chiavario, *Private Parties: The Rights of the Defendant and the Victim*, *in* EUROPEAN CRIMINAL PROCEDURES, *supra* note 13, at 573; Christopher Gane, *Scotland*, *in* CRIMINAL PROCEDURE SYSTEMS IN THE EUROPEAN COMMUNITY, *supra* note 14, at 377.

17 The Fifth Amendment of the United States Constitution reads as follows: "nor shall any person be subject for the same offence to be twice put in jeopardy of life or limb . . . ." *See also* Orie, *supra* note 12, at 1455; Fleming, *supra* note 14, at 117, 127–31; Ambos, *supra* note 16, at 33; Vincent M. Creta, *The Search for Justice in the Former Yugoslavia and Beyond: Analyzing the Rights of the Accused Under the Statute and the Rules of Procedure and Evidence of the International Criminal Tribunal for the Former Yugoslavia*, 20 HOUS. J. INT'L L. 381, 411–12 (1997); Pocar, *supra* note 13, at 453–4; Rafael Nieto-Navia & Barbara Roche, *The Ambit of the Powers Under Article 25 of the ICTY Statute: Three Issues of Recent Interest*, *in* ESSAYS ON ICTY PROCEDURE AND EVIDENCE IN HONOUR OF GABRIELLE KIRK MCDONALD 477–8 (Richard May et al. eds., 2001); Helen Brady & Mark Jennings, *Appeal and Revision*, *in* THE INTERNATIONAL CRIMINAL COURT—THE MAKING OF THE ROME STATUTE: ISSUES, NEGOTIATIONS, RESULTS 297 (Roy S. Lee ed., 1999); Chiavario, *supra* note 16, at 573.

18 *See* Nieto-Navia & Roche, *supra* note 17, at 478–80; Spencer, *supra* note 13, at 203.

19 *See also* Chiavario, *supra* note 16, at 573; Spencer, *supra* note 13, at 203.

20 SAFFERLING, *supra* note 14, at 332; Staker, *supra* note 9, at 1451, n.10; Spencer, *supra* note 13, at 203. *See also* Nieto-Navia & Roche, *supra* note 17, at 479.

21 Nieto-Navia & Roche, *supra* note 17, at 479.

22 Fleming, *supra* note 14, at 127, 139.

In civil law systems, there is generally a distinction between an appeal and what is called "*cassation*" in French or "*Revision*" in German. The same distinction also appears, inter alia, in Belgium, Denmark, Italy, Spain and the Netherlands.[23] An appeal is normally from the court of first instance to a court of appeal where reconsideration of both issues of fact and of law are possible and the merits of the case may be re-determined, while "*cassation*" or "*Revision*" is an appeal to the court of highest instance where the appeal is confined essentially to questions of law.[24] In France, for example, the Court of Cassation only examines whether the rules of law have been correctly applied by the lower courts based on the facts.[25]

In the civil law tradition, an appeal to a court of appeal generally entails a full re-hearing of the case – i.e., a trial *de novo* – open to both the prosecution and the defendant with no deference given to the trial chamber's judgment.[26] Civil law systems also generally allow the possibility of appeals by the prosecutor against acquittals.[27] It follows that the sentence of the defendant might be increased on appeal. This is the case in Germany for example. However, in such a scenario, a convicted person's situation may not be worsened in the event that he appeals or that the prosecutor

---

[23] Staker, *supra* note 9, at 1455 and nn.38–9; Christine Van den Wyngaert, *Belgium*, *in* CRIMINAL PROCEDURE SYSTEMS IN THE EUROPEAN COMMUNITY, *supra* note 14, at 46–8; Brigitte Pesquié, *The Belgian System*, *in* EUROPEAN CRIMINAL PROCEDURES, *supra* note 13, at 99, 131; Antoinette Perrodet, *The Italian System*, *in* EUROPEAN CRIMINAL PROCEDURES, *supra* note 13, at 356; Piermaria Corso, *Italy*, *in* CRIMINAL PROCEDURE SYSTEMS IN THE EUROPEAN COMMUNITY, *supra* note 14, at 255–7; A.H.J. Swart, *The Netherlands*, *in* CRIMINAL PROCEDURE SYSTEMS IN THE EUROPEAN COMMUNITY, *supra* note 14, at 314–15; Enrique Ruiz Vadillo, *Spain*, *in* CRIMINAL PROCEDURE SYSTEMS IN THE EUROPEAN COMMUNITY, *supra* note 14, at 397–8. *See also* Prosecutor v. Kupreškić et al., Case No. IT-95-16-A, Appeal Judgement, ¶ 45 and references cited therein (ICTY Oct. 23, 2001) [hereinafter *Kupreškić et al.* Appeal Judgement].

[24] Staker, *supra* note 9, at 1455; Fleming, *supra* note 14, at 114; J.R. Spencer, *Introduction* to EUROPEAN CRIMINAL PROCEDURES, *supra* note 13, at 30; Chiavario, *supra* note 16, at 575–6; Rodolphe Juy-Birmann, *The German System*, *in* EUROPEAN CRIMINAL PROCEDURES, *supra* note 13, at 307, 332–3; Van den Wyngaert, *supra* note 23, at 46–8; Vagn Greve, *Denmark*, *in* CRIMINAL PROCEDURE SYSTEMS IN THE EUROPEAN COMMUNITY, *supra* note 14, at 70–1; Jean Pradel, *France*, *in* CRIMINAL PROCEDURE SYSTEMS IN THE EUROPEAN COMMUNITY, *supra* note 14, at 134–5; Hans-Heiner Kühne, *Germany*, *in* CRIMINAL PROCEDURE SYSTEMS IN THE EUROPEAN COMMUNITY, *supra* note 14, at 160–1.

[25] PRADEL, *supra* note 10, at 387; Valérie Dervieux, *The French System*, *in* EUROPEAN CRIMINAL PROCEDURES, *supra* note 13, at 232, 275.

[26] Orie, *supra* note 12, at 1456; KNOOPS, *supra* note 13, at 290; Pocar, *supra* note 13, at 454; Fleming, *supra* note 14, at 114; Karibi-Whyte, *supra* note 15, at 646.

[27] Staker, *supra* note 9, at 1451; Dervieux, *supra* note 25, at 274.

appealed on behalf of the convicted person.[28] In the civil law tradition, as the appeal is often filed without any grounds submitted, it may touch on errors of law and/or fact but there can also be an intention to obtain a more lenient sentence.[29] Thus, in addition to assessing alleged errors of law, the appeal courts are generally involved in an adjudication process on the factual merits of the case.[30] Consequently, if the court of appeal does not affirm the judgment of the lower court, it replaces it by its own judgment.

C. The Right to Appeal in International Criminal Courts and Tribunals

The right of appeal was not recognized in the Charter of the International Military Tribunal of Nuremberg[31] or in the Charter of the International Military Tribunal for the Far East.[32] The procedure of the post-WWII international military tribunals has been strongly criticized on this ground, especially because most of the accused were sentenced to death and executed.[33]

While most of the procedural rules at the international level are enshrined in the rules of procedure and evidence of the international tribunals, the drafters of the international tribunals' statutes already envisaged the scope of the right to appeal. As explained below, this right is provided for in all the statutes of contemporary international criminal tribunals and courts.[34]

---

28 Safferling, *supra* note 14, at 332. *See also supra* note 20 and accompanying text.

29 Orie, *supra* note 12, at 1491.

30 Knoops, *supra* note 13, at 290.

31 Charter of the International Military Tribunal, annexed to the London Agreement (Aug. 8, 1945) [hereinafter IMT Nuremberg Charter]. Article 16 of the IMT Nuremberg Charter on "fair trial for defendants" is silent on the right to appeal. Moreover, Article 26 of the IMT Nuremberg Charter reads as follows: "The judgment of the Tribunal as to the guilt or the innocence of any Defendant shall give the reasons on which it is based, and shall be final and not subject to review."

32 Charter of the International Military Tribunal for the Far East (Jan. 19, 1946) [hereinafter IMT Tokyo Charter]. Article 17 of the IMT Tokyo Charter reads as follows: "The record of the trial will be transmitted directly to the Supreme Commander for the Allied Powers for his action thereon. A sentence will be carried out in accordance with the order of the Supreme Commander for the Allied Powers, who may at any time reduce or otherwise alter the sentence except to increase its severity."

33 Roth & Henzelin, *supra* note 6, at 1535 and n.1.

34 For an overview of the historical development of the right of appeal from

When proposing the Statute of the ICTY to the Security Council in his report pertaining to the establishment of the ICTY, the UN Secretary-General explicitly referred to the ICCPR and observed that the right to appeal is "a fundamental element of individual civil and political rights." For this reason, he suggested a two-level jurisdiction and, therefore, the creation of an appeals chamber.[35] Moreover, the Secretary-General asserted that "[i]t is axiomatic that the [ICTY] must fully respect internationally recognized standards regarding the rights of the accused at all stages of its proceedings" and that "such internationally recognized standards are, in particular, contained in [A]rticle 14 of the [ICCPR]."[36]

Before examining the practice of the ICTY and ICTR Appeals Chamber (ICTY and ICTR Appeals Chamber or Appeals Chamber)[37] with respect to appeal against acquittals and request to increase sentence (section 2) and, subsequently, the prospective attitude of the ICC in this regard (section 3), this chapter first discusses the grounds for appeal and the appellate standards of review (section 1).

1. Grounds of appeal and standards of appellate review

The appellate proceedings before the ICTY and ICTR Appeals Chamber are, by nature, corrective and, therefore, do not give rise to a *de novo* review of the case.[38] Rule 108 of the ICTY and ICTR Rules of Procedure and Evidence (RPE) further confirms that the appellate proceedings are not a trial *de novo*, as this rule specifies that a party seeking to appeal a judgment shall file a notice of appeal setting forth the grounds for appeal. The ICTY Appeals Chamber has stated clearly that it "does not operate as

---

the Committee of the UN General Assembly set up after WWII to examine the feasibility of creating an International Criminal Court until the adoption of the Rome Statute, *see id.* at 1536–7; Staker, *supra* note 9, at 1451, 1453, 1455.

[35] Report of the Secretary-General Pursuant to Paragraph 2 of Security Council Resolution 808 (1993), UN Doc. S/25704 (May 3, 1993), ¶ 116 [hereinafter Secretary-General Report].

[36] *Id.* ¶ 106. Various States and organizations provided proposals to the UN Secretary-General with respect to the right to appeal. Most of the proposals envisioned only a limited right of appeal from acquittals. For an overview of these proposals, *see* Fleming, *supra* note 14, at 118 and references cited therein.

[37] *See* note 44 in the introductory chapter, *supra*.

[38] Prosecutor v. Furundžija, Case No. IT-95-17/1-A, Judgement, ¶ 40 (ICTY July 21, 2000) [hereinafter *Furundžija* Appeal Judgement]; *Kupreškić et al.* Appeal Judgement, *supra* note 23, ¶ 22; Prosecutor v. Krnojelac, Case No. IT-97-25-A, Judgement, ¶ 5 (ICTY Sept. 17, 2003) (the English translation of the French original was filed on Nov. 5, 2003) [hereinafter *Krnojelac* Appeal Judgement]; Prosecutor v. Akayesu, Case No. ICTR-96-4-A, Judgment, ¶¶ 17, 177 (June 1, 2001) [hereinafter *Akayesu* Appeal Judgement].

a second Trial Chamber"[39] and, therefore, "an appeal is not an opportunity for the parties to reargue their cases."[40] This is more in line with the common law tradition and has an impact on the nature of the submissions that a party may legitimately raise on appeal, as well as the standard of appellate review that will be exercised.[41]

Thus, an appellant cannot simply repeat on appeal arguments that did not succeed at trial, unless it can demonstrate that the rejection of those arguments by the trial chamber constituted an error warranting the intervention of the Appeals Chamber.[42]

Moreover, according to the "waiver" principle, "a party should not be permitted to refrain from making an objection to a matter which was apparent during the course of the trial and to raise it [on appeal] only in the event of an adverse finding against that party."[43] Because of the corrective nature of the appellate proceedings, the parties are in general under an obligation to raise all the relevant arguments at trial. Otherwise the party is to be taken as having waived its right to adduce the matter as a valid ground of appeal.[44] Nevertheless, in exceptional circumstances, the ICTY and ICTR Appeals Chamber has not applied this principle.[45]

---

39 *Furundžija* Appeal Judgement, *supra* note 38, ¶ 40.

40 *Kupreškić et al.* Appeal Judgement, *supra* note 23, ¶ 22.

41 *Krnojelac* Appeal Judgement, *supra* note 38, ¶ 5. *See also* Staker, *supra* note 9, at 1456.

42 *See, e.g.*, Bagosora & Nsengiyumva v. The Prosecutor, Case No. ICTR-98-41-A, Judgement, ¶ 19 (Dec. 14, 2011) [hereinafter *Bagosora & Nsengiyumva* Appeal Judgement].

43 Prosecutor v. Delalić et al., Case No. IT-96-21-A, Judgement, ¶ 640 (ICTY Feb. 20, 2001) [hereinafter *Čelebići* Appeal Judgement]. *See also* Prosecutor v. Tadić, Case No. IT-94-1-A, Judgement, ¶ 55 (ICTY July 15, 1999) [hereinafter *Tadić* Appeal Judgement]; *Furundžija* Appeal Judgement, *supra* note 38, ¶ 174; Kambanda v. The Prosecutor, Case No. ICTR-97-23-A, Judgement, ¶¶ 22–28 (Oct. 19, 2000) [hereinafter *Kambanda* Appeal Judgement]; Prosecutor v. Kayishema & Ruzindana, Case No. ICTR-95-1-A, Judgment (Reasons), ¶ 91 (delivered orally on June 1, 2001 and filed on July 19, 2001) (the English translation of the French original was filed on Dec. 4, 2001).

44 Staker, *supra* note 9, at 1457.

45 *See, e.g.*, *Kambanda* Appeal Judgement, *supra* note 43, ¶ 55 ("The Appeals Chamber notes that the Appellant had several opportunities to raise any issues of fact on the basis of which he now alleges that his guilty plea was invalid, but failed to do so until after receiving a life sentence for the guilty plea. In the absence of a satisfactory explanation of his failure to raise the validity of the guilty plea in a timely manner before the Trial Chamber, the Appeals Chamber could find that the Appellant has waived his right to later assert that his guilty plea was invalid. However, as this is the Chamber of last resort for the Appellant facing life imprisonment on the basis of his guilty plea, and as the issues raised

In line with the civil law tradition, Article 25 of the ICTY Statute and Article 24 of the ICTR Statute empower both the convicted person and the prosecutor to appeal against a trial judgment on grounds of both error of law and error of fact. These articles provide that:

> 1. The Appeals Chamber shall hear appeals from persons convicted by the Trial Chambers or from the Prosecutor on the following grounds:
>   (a) an error on a question of law invalidating the decision; or
>   (b) an error of fact which has occasioned a miscarriage of justice.
> 2. The Appeals Chamber may affirm, reverse or revise the decisions taken by the Trial Chambers.

Article 20 of the Special Court for Sierra Leone Statute (SCSL and SCSL Statute, respectively) is broader in theory[46] than the above-mentioned provision as it also encompasses "a procedural error" as one of the grounds for appeal.[47] This is similar to the provision of the Rome Statute on the right to appeal discussed below.[48]

While not explicitly included in the ICTY or ICTR Statutes, the ICTY Appeals Chamber has clarified that, in exceptional circumstances, it will also hear appeals in which a party has raised a legal issue that would not lead to the invalidation of the trial judgment, but is nevertheless of general significance to the Tribunal's jurisprudence.[49] The ICTR

---

in this case are of general importance to the work of the Tribunal, the Appeals Chamber deems it important to consider the question of the validity of the guilty plea.").

[46] It seems that some procedural errors are partly included into errors of law at the ICTY. *See Krnojelac* Appeal Judgement, *supra* note 38, ¶ 10 ("With regard to the alleged errors of law, the Appeals Chamber recalls that, as arbiter of the law applicable before the International Tribunal, when a party raises such an allegation, it is bound in principle to determine whether an error was in fact committed on a substantive or procedural issue."); Prosecutor v. Kunarac et al., Case No. IT-96-23 & IT-96-23/1-A, Judgement, ¶ 38 (ICTY June 12, 2002) ("Where a party contends that a Trial Chamber has made an error of law, the Appeals Chamber, as the final arbiter of the law of the Tribunal, must determine whether such an error of substantive or procedural law was in fact made.").

[47] *See* Article 20(1)(a) of the SCSL Statute.

[48] *See infra* note 151 and accompanying text.

[49] *See, e.g.*, *Tadić* Appeal Judgement, *supra* note 43, ¶¶ 247, 281, 315–16; *Akayesu* Appeal Judgement, *supra* note 38, ¶¶ 19, 23–4; *Čelebići* Appeal Judgement, *supra* note 43, ¶ 221; *Kupreškić et al.* Appeal Judgement, *supra* note 23, ¶ 22; *Krnojelac* Appeal Judgement, *supra* note 38, ¶ 6; Prosecutor v. Stakić, Case No. IT-97-24-A, Judgement, ¶ 59 (ICTY Mar. 22, 2006) [hereinafter *Stakić* Appeal Judgement]; Prosecutor v. Brđanin, Case No. IT-99-36-A, Judgement, ¶¶ 8, 361 (ICTY Apr. 3,

Appeals Chamber has further clarified that, although it has no advisory power,[50] the rationale behind the approach taken to the development of the Tribunal's jurisprudence is justified by the Appeals Chamber's role in unifying the applicable law and providing guidance to the trial chambers in interpreting it.[51] The ICTR Appeals Chamber has further explained in part its willingness to decide such issues because of the special *ad hoc* and temporary nature of the Tribunal and that clarification of the law at an early stage of the Tribunal development would "ensure an effective and equal administration of justice"[52] and contribute "to the overall development of international humanitarian law and criminal law."[53] Nonetheless, the ICTR Appeals Chamber indicated that not all issues of general significance would be considered and that its examination of such issues will be limited to questions of law with a nexus with the case in question and of interest to the legal practice of the Tribunal.[54] Moreover, even when these requirements are fulfilled, the exercise of this power by the Appeals Chamber is discretionary.[55]

With respect to errors of law, the ICTY and ICTR Appeals Chamber has specified that it is not any error of law that leads to a reversal of the trial chamber's decision; rather the appealing party alleging an error of law must further demonstrate that the error renders the decision invalid.[56]

The ICTY and ICTR's Appeals Chamber has previously stated:

> Where a party alleges that there is an error of law, that party must advance arguments in support of the submission and explain how the error invalidates the decision. However, if the appellant's arguments do not support the contention, that party does not automatically lose its point since the Appeals Chamber

---

2007); Nahimana et al. v. The Prosecutor, Case No. ICTR-99-52-A, Judgement, ¶ 12 (Nov. 28, 2007) (the English translation was filed on May 16, 2008).

50 *Akayesu* Appeal Judgement, *supra* note 38, ¶ 23.

51 *Id.* ¶¶ 21–2. *See also Krnojelac* Appeal Judgement, *supra* note 38, ¶ 7; *Stakić* Appeal Judgement, *supra* note 49, ¶ 59.

52 *Akayesu* Appeal Judgement, *supra* note 38, ¶ 21. *See also Krnojelac* Appeal Judgement, *supra* note 38, ¶ 7.

53 *Akayesu* Appeal Judgement, *supra* note 38, ¶ 22.

54 *Id.* ¶ 24.

55 *Id.* ¶ 23. *See, e.g.*, Prosecutor v. Blagojević & Jokić, Case No. IT-02-60-A, Judgement, ¶¶ 316–18 (ICTY May 9, 2007) and Kanyarukiga v. The Prosecutor, Case No. ICTR-02-78-A, Judgement, ¶ 267 (May 8, 2012) (where the ICTY and ICTR Appeals Chamber declined to exercise its discretionary power to consider legal issues of general significance to the Tribunal's jurisprudence).

56 *Furundžija* Appeal Judgement, *supra* note 38, ¶ 36; *Akayesu* Appeal Judgement, *supra* note 38, ¶ 18.

> may step in and, for other reasons, find in favour of the contention that there is an error of law.[57]

Contrary to errors of fact, the Appeals Chamber does not accord any particular deference to determination of law made by trial chambers, since trial chambers are not more capable than the Appeals Chamber of determining what the law is.[58] Indeed, "[e]rrors of law do not raise a question as to the standard of review as directly as errors of fact" as "the Appeals Chamber, as the final arbiter of law of the Tribunal, must determine whether there was such mistake."[59]

However, a party who submits that a trial chamber made an error of law "must at least identify the alleged error and advance some arguments in support of its contention."[60] Finally, the ICTY and ICTR Appeals Chamber has further explained that where the Appeals Chamber finds that there is an error of law in a trial judgment arising from the application of the wrong legal standard, it may articulate the correct legal standard and review the relevant factual findings of the trial chamber accordingly. In so doing:

> the Appeals Chamber not only corrects a legal error, but applies the correct legal standard to the evidence contained in the trial record, in the absence of additional evidence, and must determine whether it is itself convinced beyond reasonable doubt as to the factual finding challenged by the Defense, before that finding is confirmed on appeal.[61]

Regarding errors of fact, it is not every error of fact which will cause the Appeals Chamber to overturn a decision of the trial chamber, but only

---

57 *Bagosora & Nsengiyumva* Appeal Judgement, *supra* note 42, ¶ 16. This was first articulated by the ICTY and ICTR Appeals Chamber in the *Furundžija* and the *Akayesu* cases. *See Furundžija* Appeal Judgement, *supra* note 38, ¶ 35; *Akayesu* Appeal Judgement, *supra* note 38, ¶ 179.

58 Staker, *supra* note 9, at 1465.

59 *Furundžija* Appeal Judgement, *supra* note 38, ¶ 35.

60 *Kupreškić et al.* Appeal Judgement, *supra* note 23, ¶ 27. The ICTY Appeals Chamber has clarified, in this respect, that: "[a]n appeal cannot be allowed to deteriorate into a guessing game for the Appeals Chamber. Without guidance from the appellant, the Appeals Chamber will only address legal errors where the Trial Chamber has made a glaring mistake. If the party is unable to at least identify the alleged legal error, he or she should not raise the argument on appeal. It is not sufficient to simply duplicate the submissions already raised before the Trial Chamber without seeking to clarify how these arguments support a legal error allegedly committed by the Trial Chamber." *See id.*

61 Prosecutor v. Blaškić, Case No. IT-95-14-A, Judgement, ¶ 15 (ICTY July 29, 2004) [hereinafter *Blaškić* Appeal Judgement]. *See also, e.g.*, *Bagosora & Nsengiyumva* Appeal Judgement, *supra* note 42, ¶ 17.

one which has led to a miscarriage of justice. A miscarriage of justice has been defined by the ICTY Appeals Chamber as "a grossly unfair outcome in judicial proceedings, as when a defendant is convicted despite a lack of evidence on an essential element of the crime."[62]

Assessment of facts is primarily[63] a prerogative of the trial chamber. Trial judges have the task of hearing, assessing and weighing the evidence presented at trial.[64] In *Tadić*, with respect to challenges to factual findings of a trial chamber, the ICTY Appeals Chamber held that:

> [it] must give a margin of deference to a finding of fact reached by a Trial Chamber. It is only where the evidence relied on by the Trial Chamber could not reasonably have been accepted by any reasonable person that the Appeals Chamber can substitute its own finding for that of the Trial Chamber. It is important to note that two judges, both acting reasonably, can come to different conclusions on the basis of the same evidence.[65]

The reason why the Appeals Chamber will not lightly disturb findings of fact made by trial chambers is because trial chambers have the advantage of observing witness testimony in person and, therefore, are in a better position than the Appeals Chamber to assess the reliability and credibility of the evidence.[66]

In sum, the standard of appellate review with respect to alleged errors of fact is one of reasonableness.[67] In the case of an appeal against a conviction, instead of determining whether it is *itself* satisfied beyond reasonable doubt of the guilt of the accused like in civil law tradition, the Appeals Chamber applies a deferential standard of review, under which it must decide whether no reasonable trier of fact *could* have reached

---

62 *Furundžija* Appeal Judgement, *supra* note 38, ¶ 37, *citing* BLACK'S LAW DICTIONARY (7th ed. 1999).

63 In case of additional evidence on appeal, this task may also be exercised by the Appeals Chamber. *See infra* notes 185–7 and accompanying text.

64 *See also, e.g.*, Karibi-Whyte, *supra* note 15, at 656.

65 *Tadić* Appeal Judgement, *supra* note 43, ¶ 64. *See also Furundžija* Appeal Judgement, *supra* note 38, ¶ 37; Prosecutor v. Aleksovski, Case No. IT-95-14/1-A, Judgement, ¶ 63 (ICTY Mar. 24, 2000) [hereinafter *Aleksovski* Appeal Judgement]. In *Aleksovski*, the ICTY Appeals Chamber added that it may also overturn the trial chamber's finding of fact "where the evaluation of the evidence is wholly erroneous." *Aleksovski* Appeal Judgement, ¶ 63.

66 *Furundžija* Appeal Judgement, *supra* note 38, ¶ 37; *Aleksovski* Appeal Judgement, *supra* note 65, ¶ 32; *Kupreškić et al.* Appeal Judgement, *supra* note 23, ¶ 32.

67 Prosecutor v. Kvočka et al., Case No. IT-98-30/1-A, Judgement, ¶ 18 (ICTY Feb. 28, 2005) [hereinafter *Kvočka et al.* Appeal Judgement].

the conclusion of guilt beyond reasonable doubt. If a reasonable Trial Chamber could have reached such a conclusion, the Appeals Chamber will then affirm the finding of guilt.[68] This strict deferential standard of review to the trier of fact's assessment of the evidence is clearly more in line with the common law approach.

In the case of a prosecution appeal against an acquittal, the same deferential standard of reasonableness applies to factual findings of the Trial Chamber.[69] However, because the prosecution bears the burden of proving the guilt of the accused beyond reasonable doubt at trial, the ICTY and ICTR Appeals Chamber has held that:

> the significance of an error of fact occasioning a miscarriage of justice is somewhat different for a Prosecution appeal against acquittal than for the defence appeal against conviction. An accused must show that the Trial Chamber's factual errors create a reasonable doubt as to his guilt. The Prosecution faces a more difficult task. It must show that, when account is taken of the errors of fact committed by the Trial Chamber, all reasonable doubt of the accused's guilt has been eliminated.[70]

This unique feature of a prosecutorial appeal against an acquittal on questions of facts is not consistent with the common law tradition.

Finally, according to Article 25(2) of the ICTY Statute, Article 24(2)

---

[68] *Kupreškić et al.* Appeal Judgement, *supra* note 23, ¶ 41; *Blaškić* Appeal Judgement, *supra* note 61, ¶¶ 22, 24(a). In *Čelebići*, the ICTY Appeals Chamber articulated the standard of appellate review regarding errors of facts as follow: "The test to be applied in relation to the issue as to whether the evidence is *factually* sufficient to sustain a conviction is whether the conclusion of guilt beyond reasonable doubt is one which *no* reasonable tribunal of fact *could* have reached. If an appellant is *not* able to establish that the Trial Chamber's conclusion of guilt beyond reasonable doubt was one which no reasonable tribunal of fact could have reached, it follows that there must have been evidence upon which such a tribunal could have been satisfied beyond reasonable doubt of that guilt. Under those circumstances, the latter test of legal sufficiency is therefore redundant, and the appeal must be dismissed. Similarly, if an appellant *is* able to establish that no reasonable tribunal of fact could have reached a conclusion of guilt upon the evidence before it, the appeal against conviction must be allowed and a judgement of acquittal entered. In such a situation it is unnecessary for an appellate court to determine whether there was evidence (if accepted) upon which such a tribunal could have reached such a conclusion." *Čelebići* Appeal Judgement, *supra* note 43, ¶¶ 434–5.

[69] Prosecutor v. Bagilishema, Case No. ICTR-95-1A-A, Judgement (Reasons), ¶ 13 (delivered orally on July 3, 2002 and filed on Dec. 13, 2002) (the English translation of the French original was filed on June 16, 2003) [hereinafter *Bagilishema* Appeal Judgement]. *See also Krnojelac* Appeal Judgement, *supra* note 38, ¶ 14.

[70] *Bagilishema* Appeal Judgement, *supra* note 69, ¶ 14. *See also Krnojelac* Appeal Judgement, *supra* note 38, ¶ 14.

of the ICTR Statute, and Article 20(2) of the SCSL Statute, the Appeals Chamber of these international tribunals may affirm, reverse or revise the decisions taken by the Trial Chambers. The appeal may result in an order for re-trial,[71] but usually the Appeals Chamber will be able to decide on the issues raised without a new trial being held.

2. The ICTY and ICTR Appeals Chamber's practice on appeals against acquittals and requests to increase sentences

As noted previously, a unique aspect of the appellate jurisdiction of the ICTY and ICTR partly unknown to the common law tradition is the ability of the prosecution to appeal from an acquittal or an inadequate sentence entered at trial.[72]

Thus, one of the major issues with respect to the right to appeal from an international human rights law perspective is the question of whether the entering of a new – or more serious – conviction or the increasing of a sentence on appeal by the ICTY and ICTR Appeals Chamber deny the accused his right to appeal.

As discussed below in more detail, the ICTY and ICTR Appeals Chamber has taken three distinct, but at times overlapping, approaches where the prosecution, on appeal, has successfully demonstrated an error with respect to an acquittal or an inadequate sentence entered at trial. Most often, the ICTY and ICTR Appeals Chamber has re-evaluated the factual and legal circumstances surrounding the overturned acquittal or sentence and then entered a new conviction or an increased sentence on appeal. This approach has been taken despite frequent vigorous dissents,[73] arguing in particular that entering a new conviction or increasing a sentence on appeal violates an accused's fundamental right to appeal as set forth in Article 14(5) of the ICCPR (section a). In a limited number of cases, the ICTY and ICTR Appeals Chamber has adopted a different approach and simply identified the error in the trial chamber's reasoning without entering a new conviction or increasing the sentence on appeal (section b). On occasion, the ICTY and ICTR Appeals Chamber has also ordered a new trial on the overturned allegation or remitted the case to a

---

71 *See* Rule 117(C) of the ICTY RPE; Rule 118(C) of the ICTR RPE; Rule 118(C) of the SCSL RPE. *See also, e.g.*, Muvunyi v. The Prosecutor, Case No. ICTR-2000-55A-A, Judgement, ¶¶ 148, 171 (Aug. 29, 2008); Prosecutor v. Haradinaj et al., Case No. IT-04-84-A, Judgement, ¶¶ 50, 377 (ICTY July 19, 2010) [hereinafter *Haradinaj et al.* Appeal Judgement].

72 This is more in line with the civil law tradition. *See, e.g.*, Nieto-Navia & Roche, *supra* note 17, at 481.

73 *See infra* note 116 and accompanying text.

trial chamber for a reassessment of the sentence (section c). These three approaches will be examined and their varying justification and criticism considered.

a. The practice of reversing an acquittal and entering a conviction or increasing a sentence without any avenue of appeal The ICTY and ICTR Appeals Chamber has entered new or more serious convictions on appeal in a number of cases. It has done so in three different scenarios: when it found that the Trial Chamber failed to enter cumulative convictions; when it concluded that the Trial Chamber improperly characterized the form of the accused's responsibility; or when it characterized a particular course of conduct as criminal for the first time on appeal. The ICTY and ICTR Appeals Chamber has also imposed a higher sentence in various cases.

Under the *first scenario*, it must be noted that many of the convictions entered on appeal involve situations where a trial chamber has convicted an accused on a given count in an indictment based on certain criminal acts, but acquitted him under other counts cumulatively charging the same conduct as a different crime. In this situation, a trial chamber has either concluded that the threshold elements of the additional charges had not been met, the additional charges were impermissibly cumulative,[74] or simply did not consider entering the additional conviction. In the three cases mentioned below, the Appeals Chamber granted prosecutorial appeals against acquittals on an error of law, a right recognized in many civil and common law jurisdictions other than the United States.[75]

In the *Tadić* case, the ICTY Appeals Chamber granted the first ground of the prosecution's appeal and considered that the Trial Chamber applied an incorrect legal test in assessing the applicability of Article 2 of the ICTY Statute concerning grave breaches of the Geneva Conventions of 1949. The Appeals Chamber articulated the correct legal test, applied it on the basis of the Trial Chamber's own factual findings, found Tadić guilty of

---

[74] In the *Čelebići* Appeal Judgement, the Appeals Chamber held that "reasons of fairness to the accused and the consideration that only distinct crimes may justify multiple convictions, lead to the conclusion that multiple criminal convictions entered under different statutory provisions, but based on the same conduct, are permissible only if each statutory provision involved has a materially distinct element not contained in the other. An element is materially distinct from another if it requires proof of a fact not required by the other." The Appeals Chamber added that, where this test is not met, only the conviction under the more specific provision will be entered, because it entails the commission of the less specific one. *Čelebići* Appeal Judgement, *supra* note 43, ¶¶ 412–13.

[75] *See supra* notes 15–22, 26–28 and accompanying text.

grave breaches of the Geneva Conventions of 1949 and entered convictions on the six related counts of the indictment, therefore overturning several acquittals entered by the Trial Chamber.[76]

In the *Semanza* case, the Trial Chamber, by majority, concluded that the accused could be held criminally responsible for war crimes.[77] However, one of the judges of this majority considered that it would be impermissibly cumulative to convict the accused of these crimes since he was already convicted of crimes against humanity and complicity to commit genocide for the same acts.[78] The ICTR Appeals Chamber concluded that these crimes were not impermissibly cumulative and, by majority, entered convictions on appeal for war crimes.[79]

In the *Setako* case, the Trial Chamber held an accused responsible for his role in two distinct sets of killings which occurred at a military camp.[80] For the first larger set of killings, the Trial Chamber convicted the accused of genocide, extermination as a crime against humanity, and war crimes.[81] The genocide conviction also encompassed the second set of killings.[82] Although the prosecution also sought to hold the accused responsible of war crimes for this second set of killings, the Trial Chamber did not assess whether a conviction was warranted under that count.[83] The ICTR

---

[76] *Tadić* Appeal Judgement, *supra* note 43, ¶¶ 146–71, 327. *See also* Fleming, *supra* note 14, at 121–3. A similar scenario happened in the *Rutaganda* case. *See* Prosecutor v. Rutaganda, Case No. ICTR-96-3-T, Judgement and Sentence, 163 and ¶¶ 442, 444–5 (Dec. 6, 1999); Rutaganda v. The Prosecutor, Case No. ICTR-96-3-A, Judgement, 168 and ¶¶ 558, 574–84 (May 26, 2003) (the English translation of the French original was filed on Feb. 9, 2004) [hereinafter *Rutaganda* Appeal Judgement]. *See also id.*, Dissenting Opinion of Judge Pocar, 1–4.

[77] Prosecutor v. Semanza, Case No. ICTR-97-20-T, Judgement and Sentence, ¶¶ 535, 551 (May 15, 2003) [hereinafter *Semanza* Trial Judgement]. *See also* Semanza v. The Prosecutor, Case No. ICTR-97-20-A, Judgement, ¶ 367 (May 20, 2005) [hereinafter *Semanza* Appeal Judgement].

[78] *Semanza* Trial Judgement, *supra* note 77, ¶¶ 536, 552–3. *See also Semanza* Appeal Judgement, *supra* note 77, ¶ 367.

[79] *Semanza* Appeal Judgement, *supra* note 77, at 126 and ¶¶ 368–71. *See also id.*, Dissenting Opinion of Judge Pocar, ¶¶ 1–4. A similar scenario happened in the *Kupreškić et al.* case. *See* Prosecutor v. Kupreškić et al., Case No. IT-95-16-T, Judgement, ¶¶ 821–4, 831–3 (ICTY Jan. 14, 2000); *Kupreškić et al.* Appeal Judgement, *supra* note 23, at 172 and ¶¶ 386–8.

[80] Prosecutor v. Setako, Case No. ICTR-04-81-T, Judgement and Sentence, 131 and ¶¶ 368, 474, 482, 491 (delivered orally on Feb. 25, 2010 and filed on Mar. 1, 2010) [hereinafter *Setako* Trial Judgement].

[81] *Id.*

[82] *Id.* at 131 and ¶¶ 368, 474.

[83] Setako v. The Prosecutor, Case No. ICTR-04-81-A, Judgement, ¶ 256 (Sept. 28, 2011) [hereinafter *Setako* Appeal Judgement].

Appeals Chamber concluded that the Trial Chamber erred in not doing so. After considering various findings made by the Trial Chamber, the Appeals Chamber concluded that they would support a conviction for war crimes and, by majority, entered one on appeal.[84]

The ICTY Appeals Chamber has previously concluded that additional cumulative convictions would not in themselves warrant an increase in the existing sentence imposed by the trial chamber.[85] The other types of convictions entered on appeal, however, usually have much more serious implications for a convicted person and frequently result in a more serious sentence, as will be described below.

The *second category of convictions entered on appeal* involves scenarios where the ICTY and ICTR Appeals Chamber has concluded that the Trial Chamber improperly characterized the form of the accused's responsibility. In these cases, the ICTY and ICTR Appeals Chamber has generally determined that a Trial Chamber erred in limiting its consideration of the modes of responsibility or in making its factual findings related to the various forms which were charged. After identifying the error, the ICTY and ICTR Appeals Chamber has then revised or entered a new conviction entailing a more serious form of liability, always resulting in an increase in the sentence.

For example, in the *Krnojelac* case, the ICTY Appeals Chamber concluded that the trial chamber erred in characterizing the accused's conduct as aiding and abetting persecution as a crime against humanity and cruel treatment as a war crime and entered convictions against him as a co-perpetrator based on his participation in a joint criminal enterprise for these two crimes.[86] In the *Semanza* case, the ICTR Appeals Chamber

---

84 *Setako* Appeal Judgement, *supra* note 83, ¶¶ 256, 258–62, 301. *See also id.*, Partially Dissenting Opinion of Judge Pocar, ¶¶ 1–6.

85 *See, e.g.*, *Aleksovski* Appeal Judgement, *supra* note 65, ¶ 153(iii).

86 *Krnojelac* Appeal Judgement, *supra* note 38, at 113–14. The Appeals Chamber held that the Trial Chamber erred in going beyond the intent criterion for establishing the second category of joint criminal enterprise set by the Appeals Chamber in the *Tadić* case. The application of the correct intent criterion should have led the Trial Chamber to find Krnojelac guilty as a co-perpetrator and not as an aider and abetter. *See id.* ¶¶ 95–7, 107–13. Moreover, the Appeals Chamber further expanded his conviction for persecution as a crime against humanity based on forced labour, deportation and expulsion as a co-perpetrator of the joint criminal enterprise. *See id.* at 113–14 and ¶¶ 193–6, 199–203, 205–7, 214–47. Finally, the Appeals Chamber found Krnojelac guilty, as a superior under Article 7(3) of the ICTY Statute, of four counts of torture and murder as crimes against humanity and war crimes; charges that he was originally acquitted of by the Trial Chamber. *Id.* at 113–14 and ¶¶ 154–6, 166–72, 177–80. Accordingly, the Appeals Chamber imposed a new sentence of 15 years of imprisonment to Krnojelac. *Id.* at 115 and ¶ 264.

found that the Trial Chamber erred in finding that the accused merely aided and abetted a certain category of perpetrators during a particular attack and instead – by majority – entered a conviction against him on the basis of ordering, a more direct and serious form of responsibility.[87] Finally, in the *Seromba* case, the ICTR Appeals Chamber, by majority, concluded that the Trial Chamber erred in characterizing an accused's conduct as aiding and abetting and entered a conviction against him for committing the crimes as a principal perpetrator.[88]

A *third category of convictions entered on appeal* involves situations where the ICTY and ICTR Appeals Chamber characterized a particular course of conduct as criminal for the first time on appeal and entered a corresponding conviction. This occurred in the *Tadić* case mentioned above.[89] In relation to the second ground of the prosecution's appeal, the ICTY Appeals Chamber considered that the Trial Chamber in the *Tadić* case misapplied the burden of proof in assessing the circumstantial evidence surrounding the killings of five men from the village of Jaskići.[90] The Appeals Chamber reassessed the factual findings made by the Trial Chamber and determined that "the only reasonable conclusion the Trial Chamber could have drawn is that the armed group to which [Tadić] belonged killed the five men."[91] The Appeals Chamber then proceeded to assess the appropriate form of criminal liability for the crimes, developing the doctrine of joint criminal enterprise in the process, which it then applied in convicting Tadić under three counts of the indictment for the killings.[92]

In addition, the ICTR Appeals Chamber in the *Gacumbitsi* case also overturned an acquittal for murder as a crime against humanity after determining that no reasonable trier of fact could have found, as the Trial Chamber did, that the accused's actions in evicting his tenants would not have resulted in their death. Accordingly, after examining the Trial

---

[87] *Semanza* Appeal Judgement, *supra* note 77, at 126 and ¶¶ 362–4. *See also id.*, Dissenting Opinion of Judge Pocar, ¶¶ 1–4.

[88] Prosecutor v. Seromba, Case No. ICTR-01-66-A, Judgement, ¶¶ 206, 240 (Mar. 12, 2008) [hereinafter *Seromba* Appeal Judgement].

[89] *See supra* note 76 and accompanying text. *See also* Rafael Nieto-Navia, *The Application by the ICTY/ICTR Appeals Chamber of Article 14(5) of the International Covenant on Civil and Political Rights in Sentencing Proceedings*, *in* LIBER FAUSTO POCAR—INDIVIDUAL RIGHTS AND INTERNATIONAL JUSTICE 617 (Gabriella Venturini & Stefania Bariatti eds., 2009).

[90] *Tadić* Appeal Judgement, *supra* note 43, ¶¶ 183, 233–4. *See also* Fleming, *supra* note 14, at 132–5.

[91] *Tadić* Appeal Judgement, *supra* note 43, ¶ 183.

[92] *Id.* ¶¶ 185–237, 327.

Chamber's findings, the ICTR Appeals Chamber, by majority, entered a conviction on appeal for aiding and abetting murder as a crime against humanity.[93]

Notably, as discussed below, the ICTY Appeals Chamber ultimately concluded in the *Tadić* case that it would be preferable for the sentencing of these new convictions to be conducted by a trial chamber in the first instance, thereby allowing an appeal on the new sentence.[94] With this bifurcated approach, the ICTY Appeals Chamber appeared to underscore the importance of having a trial chamber in the first instance impose a more significant sentence, which would then be subject to appellate consideration. The approach, however, was short-lived.

The *fourth scenario involves higher sentences imposed on appeal.* In the *Aleksovski* case, the ICTY Appeals Chamber granted a prosecution's sentencing appeal after concluding that the Trial Chamber erred in assessing the gravity of Aleksovski's crimes and aggravating circumstances.[95] After concluding that the sentence entered by the Trial Chamber was "manifestly inadequate," the Appeals Chamber imposed a higher sentence.[96] In doing so, the Appeals Chamber noted the impact of the element of double jeopardy since Aleksovski was forced to appear for sentencing twice, in particular after he had already been released at the conclusion of his initial sentence. The Appeals Chamber observed that this factor prevented it from imposing an even higher sentence.[97]

This consideration was also mentioned in the *Čelebići* case following a successful prosecution sentencing appeal where the ICTY Appeals Chamber expressed its view on an appropriate increase in the sentence of one of the appellants, whose sentencing had been remitted to a trial chamber for reassessment on other grounds. Although a separate matter from an accused's right to appeal, the consideration of double jeopardy implicitly provided an additional reason for remanding the matter to the Trial Chamber to consider the effect of its errors on the sentence.[98] This principle, however, has not been taken into account by the

---

93 Gacumbitsi v. The Prosecutor, Case No. ICTR-2001-64-A, Judgement, ¶¶ 124, 207 (July 7, 2006) [hereinafter *Gacumbitsi* Appeal Judgement].

94 *See infra* note 117 and accompanying text. *See also* Nieto-Navia & Roche, *supra* note 17, at 482.

95 *Aleksovski* Appeal Judgement, *supra* note 65, ¶¶ 183, 186–7. *See also* Nieto-Navia & Roche, *supra* note 17, at 485; Nieto-Navia, *supra* note 89, at 615–6.

96 *Aleksovski* Appeal Judgement, *supra* note 65, ¶¶ 187, 191–2.

97 *Id.* ¶ 190. *See also* Nieto-Navia & Roche, *supra* note 17, at 485; Nieto-Navia, *supra* note 89, at 617.

98 *Čelebići* Appeal Judgement, *supra* note 43, ¶ 853.

Appeals Chamber in subsequent cases where it has decided to increase a sentence.

A successful prosecution sentencing appeal can at times result in severe consequences for a convicted person.[99] Specifically, after identifying errors in the Trial Chambers' consideration of the gravity of the accuseds' respective offences,[100] the Appeals Chamber increased to life imprisonment the 30-year sentence imposed by the Trial Chamber in the *Gacumbitsi* case and the 20-year sentence imposed in the *Galić* case.[101] Other cases involving sentencing appeals have resulted in more modest increases.[102]

Turning now to the *justification and criticism for entering new or more serious convictions or imposing higher sentences on appeal*, the ICTY and ICTR Appeals Chamber has not extensively discussed the propriety of entering convictions or increasing sentences on appeal. Specifically, there was no discussion about the ICTY Appeals Chamber's authority to do so in the *Tadić* case, which was both its first judgment on the merits and the first case in which convictions were entered on appeal.[103] One of the judges, however, discussed the matter briefly in a Declaration appended to the judgment, but limited his consideration only to whether entering a conviction on appeal violated the principle of *ne bis in idem*.[104] This judge reviewed the practice of appeals against acquittals in civil law and common law jurisdictions and concluded that "there is no general principle of law that would prohibit prosecution appeals against

---

99 *See also* Nieto-Navia & Roche, *supra* note 17, at 483 (qualifying the consequences for the accused of being "immense").

100 *Gacumbitsi* Appeal Judgement, *supra* note 93, ¶¶ 204–6; Prosecutor v. Galić, Case No. IT-98-29-A, Judgement, ¶ 455 (ICTY Nov. 30, 2006) [hereinafter *Galić* Appeal Judgement].

101 *Gacumbitsi* Appeal Judgement, *supra* note 93, ¶¶ 206–7; *Galić* Appeal Judgement, *supra* note 100, 185. *See also id.*, Partially Dissenting Opinion of Judge Pocar, ¶¶ 1–5; *id.*, Separate Opinion of Judge Shahabuddeen, ¶¶ 7–58; *id.*, Separate and Partially Dissenting Opinion of Judge Meron, ¶¶ 3–13. Notably, in the *Galić* case, the ICTY Appeals Chamber had not otherwise altered Galić's criminal liability found at trial. *Galić* Appeal Judgement, 185. In the *Gacumbitsi* case, although the ICTR Appeals Chamber had entered new and more serious convictions, the success of the sentencing appeal appears to be the main factor in its increase. *Gacumbitsi* Appeal Judgement, *supra* note 93, ¶¶ 204–6.

102 *See, e.g.*, Prosecutor v. Šljivančanin, Case No. IT-95-13/1-R.1, Review Judgement, ¶¶ 33–7 (Dec. 8, 2010) [hereinafter *Šljivančanin* Review Judgement] (five-year increase); *Aleksovski* Appeal Judgement, *supra* note 65, ¶¶ 191–2 (four-and-a-half-year increase).

103 *See also* Fleming, *supra* note 14, at 113, 117, 121.

104 *Tadić* Appeal Judgement, Declaration of Judge Nieto-Navia, *supra* note 43, ¶¶ 1–11. *See also* Nieto-Navia & Roche, *supra* note 17, at 483.

acquittals."[105] This separate declaration did not consider, however, whether entering a conviction on appeal – as opposed to remanding the matter to a trial chamber for reassessment under a correct test – would infringe an accused's right to appeal as enshrined in Article 14(5) of the ICCPR.

In addition, in the *Aleksovski* case, after identifying several errors in the Trial Chamber's assessment of the sentence, the ICTY Appeals Chamber examined very briefly the practice in four civil and common law jurisdictions to satisfy itself that it had the authority to review sentences. While answering this question in the affirmative, the Appeals Chamber did not consider the key question of whether, after identifying an error, it was the appropriate body to increase the sentence.[106] Indeed, the authority to review is significantly different from the authority to revise without the opportunity for appellate review.

The most extensive justification of the ICTY and ICTR Appeals Chamber's authority to enter convictions or to increase sentences on appeal appears in the Separate Opinions of a judge appended to the *Rutaganda* and *Galić* Appeal Judgments.[107] In his Separate Opinions, this judge primarily justifies the Appeals Chamber's authority by pointing to the provisions in the Statute and RPE that allow the prosecution to appeal, the judges understanding of these provisions as granting such authority, as well as the prior cases where the Appeals Chamber exercised that authority in entering convictions or increasing sentences on appeal.[108]

His Separate Opinions acknowledge the general guarantee in Article 14(5) of the ICCPR of the right of review by a higher tribunal of convictions and sentences, as well as the reservations made to this provision and the related case law of the HRC interpreting this right.[109] However, according to the judge's analysis, "a reservation in respect of a requirement for the provision of a right of appeal from a conviction made on appeal is not incompatible with the object and purpose of the

---

105 *Tadić* Appeal Judgement, *supra* note 43, Declaration of Judge Nieto-Navia, ¶¶ 3–9. *See also* Nieto-Navia & Roche, *supra* note 17, at 477–81.

106 *Aleksovski* Appeal Judgement, *supra* note 65, ¶ 186.

107 *Rutaganda* Appeal Judgement, *supra* note 76, Separate Opinion of Judge Shahabuddeen, ¶¶ 1–40; *Galić* Appeal Judgement, *supra* note 100, Separate Opinion of Judge Shahabuddeen, ¶¶ 6–29.

108 *Rutaganda* Appeal Judgement, *supra* note 76, Separate Opinion of Judge Shahabuddeen, ¶¶ 2–10; *Galić* Appeal Judgement, *supra* note 100, Separate Opinion of Judge Shahabuddeen, ¶¶ 7–17, 27.

109 *Rutaganda* Appeal Judgement, *supra* note 76, Separate Opinion of Judge Shahabuddeen, ¶¶ 11–29; *Galić* Appeal Judgement, *supra* note 100, Separate Opinion of Judge Shahabuddeen, ¶¶ 10, 18, 25–6.

ICCPR."[110] Thus, according to this judge, international criminal tribunals are exceptional and "particular provisions of internationally recognised human rights instruments do not apply to the Tribunal lock, stock and barrel."[111] In particular, he also notes that a number of states have expressed reservations to this particular guarantee and that the tribunal's "Statute may be treated as having the effect of one."[112]

On one occasion, the ICTY Appeals Chamber questioned its authority to enter convictions on appeal in relation to a conviction for contempt related to the *Tadić* appeal which was tried by the Appeals Chamber ruling in the first instance.[113] This arose in the *Vujin* Appeal Judgment issued not long after the first conviction was entered on appeal in the *Tadić* case and the first sentence was increased in the *Aleksovski* case. Specifically, in the *Vujin* Appeal Judgment, the Appeals Chamber acknowledged that Article 14(5) of the ICCPR guarantees an accused's right to appeal a conviction or sentence by a higher tribunal and that Article 14 of the ICCPR reflects "an imperative norm of international law to which the Tribunal must adhere." In view of this, the Appeals Chamber then considered that "the preferred course in this case would have been for the contempt trial to have been initially referred to a Trial Chamber, thereby providing for the possibility of appeal, rather than being heard by the Appeals Chamber, ruling in the first instance." The Appeals Chamber further stressed that "a person found guilty of contempt by the Appeals Chamber must have the right to appeal the conviction."[114] As a result, the Appeals Chamber allowed the convicted person to appeal his conviction to a separately constituted bench. However, as illustrated above, the *Vujin* Appeal Judgment

---

110 *Rutaganda* Appeal Judgement, *supra* note 76, Separate Opinion of Judge Shahabuddeen, ¶ 20.

111 *Galić* Appeal Judgement, *supra* note 100, Separate Opinion of Judge Shahabuddeen, ¶ 19.

112 *Id.* ¶ 26. *See also Rutaganda* Appeal Judgement, *supra* note 76, Separate Opinion of Judge Shahabuddeen, ¶¶ 15–21. For a response to Judge Shahabuddeen's arguments, *see id.*, Dissenting Opinion of Judge Pocar, at 2; Prosecutor v. Mrkšić & Šljivančanin, Case No. IT-95-13/1-A, Judgement (ICTY May 5, 2009) [hereinafter *Mrkšić & Šljivančanin* Appeal Judgement], Partially Dissenting Opinion of Judge Pocar, ¶ 6.

113 Prosecutor v. Tadić, Case No. IT-94-1-A-AR77, Appeal Judgement on Allegations of Contempt Against Prior Counsel, Milan Vujin (ICTY Feb. 27, 2001) (the correct English translation of the French original was filed on Apr. 6, 2001) [hereinafter *Vujin* Appeal Judgement]. Milan Vujin was originally found guilty of contempt by the Appeals Chamber, ruling in the first instance. *See* Prosecutor v. Tadić, Case No. IT-94-1-A-R77, Judgement on Allegations of Contempt Against Prior Counsel, Milan Vujin (ICTY Jan. 31, 2000).

114 *Vujin* Appeal Judgement, *supra* note 113, at 3–4.

has not tempered the Appeals Chamber's willingness to enter convictions or to increase sentences on appeal in any later case, nor has there been a subsequent appeal of one of its convictions by a separately constituted bench.

Only one judge, a member of the bench in the *Vujin* case, has maintained a consistent[115] objection to the entry of convictions or increased sentences on appeal through his Dissenting Opinions in the *Rutaganda, Semanza, Galić, Mrksić and Šljivančanin*, and *Setako* cases.[116] In the first of this series of Dissenting Opinions in the *Rutaganda* case, which is illustrative of his approach, the dissenting judge reviewed the ICTY Appeals Chamber's prior practice in the *Tadić, Aleksovski*, and *Čelebići* cases. In particular, he noted that, in the *Tadić* case, the ICTY Appeals Chamber found it preferable to remit sentencing to a trial chamber and that, in the *Čelebići* case, it held that "a new matter of such significance should be determined by a Chamber from which an appeal is possible."[117]

In particular, the dissenting judge emphasized the right to appeal to a higher tribunal enshrined in Article 14(5) of the ICCPR as well as the report of the UN Secretary-General pertaining to the establishment of the ICTY recognizing the importance of this right. He also highlighted the ICTY Appeals Chamber's pronouncement in the *Vujin* Appeal Judgment that this provision was "an imperative norm of international law."[118] The dissenting judge further challenged the contention that this right was not universal by observing that only ten of 149 states parties to the ICCPR had

---

[115] Judges Meron and Jorda appended a Separate Opinion in the *Rutaganda* case in which they acknowledge that "the absence of any right whatsoever to appeal such a conviction [entered on appeal], save in the case where the matter is remitted to the Trial Chamber, is likely to infringe upon the fundamental principle of fairness recognized both in international law and many national legal systems." *See Rutaganda* Appeal Judgement, *supra* note 76, Separate Opinion of Judges Meron and Jorda, at 1. However, Judges Meron and Jorda were not convinced that this principle was infringed where a conviction handed down on appeal was already covered by other convictions entered by the Trial Chamber and the sentence was not increased. *Id.*

[116] *See id.*, Dissenting Opinion of Judge Pocar, at 1–4; *Semanza* Appeal Judgement, *supra* note 77, Dissenting Opinion of Judge Pocar, ¶¶ 1–4; *Galić* Appeal Judgement, *supra* note 100, Partially Dissenting Opinion of Judge Pocar, ¶¶ 1–5; *Mrkšić & Šljivančanin* Appeal Judgement, *supra* note 112, Partially Dissenting Opinion of Judge Pocar, ¶¶ 1–13; *Šljivančanin* Review Judgement, *supra* note 102, Partially Dissenting Opinion of Judge Pocar, ¶¶ 1–4; *Setako* Appeal Judgement, *supra* note 83, Partially Dissenting Opinion of Judge Pocar, ¶¶ 1–6.

[117] *Rutaganda* Appeal Judgement, *supra* note 76, Dissenting Opinion of Judge Pocar, at 1–2 (quoting *Čelebići* Appeal Judgement, ¶ 711).

[118] *Id.* at 2–3 (quoting *Vujin* Appeal Judgement, at 3).

entered reservations to Article 14(5).[119] He also emphasized that judicial economy should not be an excuse to derogate from a fundamental right. Finally, the dissenting judge observed that entering a conviction on appeal was not the only option and highlighted the Appeals Chamber's alternative practice, discussed below, of simply acknowledging an error in the trial chamber's reasoning, but leaving an acquittal otherwise undisturbed.[120]

b. The Appeals Chamber's practice of simply acknowledging an error In the *Aleksovski* case, its second judgment on the merits, the ICTY Appeals Chamber granted several grounds of a prosecution appeal.[121] However, it took a different approach from that in the *Tadić* case in terms of entering convictions on appeal. With respect to the first ground of the prosecution appeal, the Appeals Chamber, as in the *Tadić* case, concluded that the Trial Chamber had applied an incorrect legal test in determining the applicability of Article 2 of the ICTY Statute. However, unlike in the *Tadić* case, the Appeals Chamber declined to reverse the acquittals entered by the trial chamber on the relevant counts of the indictment.[122] The Appeals Chamber reasoned that no useful purpose would be served for either it or a Trial Chamber to re-examine the facts under the appropriate legal test since Aleksovski had already been convicted under a different cumulative charge in the indictment for the "material acts" underlying the charges under Article 2 of the ICTY Statute. Accordingly, the Appeals Chamber reasoned that, even if a finding of guilt were entered, it would not be appropriate to increase his sentence.[123]

In relation to the second ground of the prosecution's appeal, the ICTY Appeals Chamber determined that the Trial Chamber erred in limiting its findings on a particular count to superior responsibility and in failing to consider whether Aleksovski also aided and abetted the crime.[124] After

---

119 *Id.* at 2. See also Mrkšić & Šljivančanin Appeal Judgement, supra note 112, Partially Dissenting Opinion of Judge Pocar, ¶ 6.

120 Rutaganda Appeal Judgement, supra note 76, Dissenting Opinion of Judge Pocar, at 3–4.

121 *Aleksovski* Appeal Judgement, *supra* note 65, ¶¶ 154, 172, 183, 192.

122 *Id.* ¶¶ 153–4, 192.

123 *Id.* ¶ 153(iii).

124 *Id.* ¶ 171. In the practice of the ICTY, when an Indictment charges an accused cumulatively under both Articles 7(1) and 7(3) of the ICTY Statute for a specific count and the same set of facts, the Trial Chamber is required to make factual and legal findings with respect to both articles. If the accused could be found guilty under both articles, the Trial Chamber should enter a conviction under Article 7(1) of the ICTY Statute alone and consider the superior position of the accused as an aggravating factor for the purpose of sentencing. A trial cham-

identifying this legal error, the Appeals Chamber re-examined the Trial Chamber's factual findings and concluded that Aleksovski could be held responsible for aiding and abetting. Nonetheless, the Appeals Chamber was not convinced that this error invalidated the existing guilty verdict on the relevant count and did not enter a new conviction based on aiding and abetting. Instead, the Appeals Chamber stated that the additional finding was "strictly" a matter to be taken into account in entering a revised sentence. It ultimately concluded that the additional finding alone did not warrant a heavier sentence.[125]

In the *Jelisić* case, the ICTY Appeals Chamber granted several grounds of a prosecution appeal against an acquittal entered by a trial chamber, pursuant to Rule 98*bis* of the ICTY RPE, at the conclusion of the prosecution case.[126] The Appeals Chamber, by majority, concluded that the Trial Chamber applied an incorrect legal standard in prematurely terminating the accused's trial on genocide-related counts.[127] The Appeals Chamber further considered that, at the conclusion of the prosecution case, a reasonable trier of fact could have found the evidence sufficient to sustain a conviction, beyond reasonable doubt, for genocide.[128] Notwithstanding this finding, the Appeals Chamber, by majority, declined to remit the case for a new trial on the genocide count.[129] In particular, the Appeals Chamber noted that Jelisić had already pleaded guilty to the underlying criminal conduct under other counts and had received a significant sentence.[130]

In similar cases in which a trial chamber erred in not entering a cumulative conviction, the ICTY Appeals Chamber has simply identified the error and observed that the individual could have been held criminally responsible on an additional basis. This occurred in the *Krstić*, *Stakić*, and

ber's failure to make such a finding constitutes an error of law. *See, e.g.*, *Setako* Appeal Judgement, *supra* note 83, ¶ 268.

125 *Aleksovski* Appeal Judgement, *supra* note 65, ¶¶ 172–3, 189.

126 Prosecutor v. Jelisić, Case No. IT-95-10-A, Appeal Judgement, 41 and ¶¶ 29, 40, 55, 72 (ICTY July 5, 2001) [hereinafter *Jelisić* Appeal Judgement]. Rule 98*bis* of the ICTY RPE states as follows: "At the close of the Prosecutor's case, the Trial Chamber shall, by oral decision and after hearing the oral submissions of the parties, enter a judgement of acquittal on any count if there is no evidence capable of supporting a conviction."

127 *Jelisić* Appeal Judgement, *supra* note 126, ¶¶ 39–40, 55, 72. *See also id.*, Partial Dissenting Opinion of Judge Pocar, ¶¶ 1–7.

128 *Id.* ¶¶ 56–72.

129 *Id.* at 41 and ¶ 77. *See also id.*, Partial Dissenting Opinion of Judge Shahabuddeen, ¶¶ 1–29; *id.*, Partial Dissenting Opinion of Judge Wald, ¶¶ 1–15.

130 *Id.* ¶¶ 73–7.

Naletilić and Martinović cases.[131] This practice of simply acknowledging a legal error without affecting the situation of the person acquitted in the first instance is similar to the practice of England and Wales where the Court of Appeal can clarify the law without affecting the verdict to the detriment of the person acquitted.[132] This approach stands in stark contrast to the entry of convictions by the ICTY and ICTR Appeals Chamber in the *Kupreškić et al.*, *Rutaganda*, *Semanza*, and *Setako* cases which presented nearly identical scenarios.[133] Notably, the time frame during which these sets of judgments were issued overlaps, highlighting an inconsistency in the approach of the ICTY and ICTR Appeals Chamber on this issue and raising the question of whether convictions must be entered on appeal in order to fully capture an accused's criminality.

c. The Appeals Chamber's practice of ordering a re-trial or remanding a case to a Trial Chamber Finally, in a very limited number of cases, the ICTY Appeals Chamber has remitted an erroneous acquittal or a sentencing matter to a trial chamber. Specifically, during the course of the appeal proceedings in the *Tadić* case, the ICTY Appeals Chamber accepted the necessity, which was advanced by both parties, of having a separate sentencing procedure in the event that it overturned any of the acquittals and entered convictions.[134] Thus, the Appeals Chamber deferred assessing an appropriate sentence for the new convictions in the disposition of its judgment.[135] Following its delivery, the Appeals Chamber sought written and oral sentencing submissions from the parties. During the presentation of their oral arguments, the parties agreed that the Appeals Chamber had the authority to pronounce a sentence in relation to the new convictions, but considered it preferable in the circumstances of the case that the matter be remitted to a trial chamber. The Appeals Chamber agreed and remitted

---

131 Prosecutor v. Krstić, Case No. IT-98-33-A, Judgement, 87 and ¶¶ 219–27, 229 (ICTY Apr. 19, 2004); *Stakić* Appeal Judgement, *supra* note 49, 141–2 and ¶¶ 359–60, 362, 364, 366–7; Prosecutor v. Naletilić & Martinović, Case No. IT-98-34-A, Judgement, 207 and ¶¶ 588-91 (ICTY May 3, 2006) [hereinafter *Naletilić & Martinović* Appeal Judgement]. *See also Stakić* Appeal Judgement, *supra* note 49, Partly Dissenting Opinion of Judge Shahabuddeen, ¶ 1; *id.*, Joint Separate Opinion of Judges Vaz and Meron, 171.

132 *See supra* note 20 and accompanying text.

133 *See supra* notes 76–84 and accompanying text.

134 Prosecutor v. Tadić, Case No. IT-94-1-A, Order Remitting Sentencing to a Trial Chamber, 1 (ICTY Sept. 10, 1999) [hereinafter *Tadić* Order of 10 September 1999]. *See also* Prosecutor v. Tadić, Case No. IT-94-1-A, Judgement in Sentencing Appeals, ¶ 8 (ICTY Jan. 26, 2000) [hereinafter *Tadić* Sentencing Appeal Judgement].

135 *Tadić* Appeal Judgement, *supra* note 43, ¶ 327.

the case to a trial chamber to consider sentencing on the new convictions. A new trial chamber was subsequently composed for this purpose.[136] Following its sentencing judgment, Tadić was given the opportunity to appeal the sentences imposed on the new convictions.[137]

In the *Čelebići* case, the ICTY Appeals Chamber also remanded a case for a new sentencing procedure after identifying errors in the Trial Chamber's assessment of the gravity of one of the appellants' crimes, which would have warranted an increase in sentence.[138] However, the Appeals Chamber's principal reason for remanding the sentencing appears to be based on its decision to overturn several impermissibly cumulative convictions entered at trial. The Appeals Chamber acknowledged that there may have been a different outcome in the sentence had the Trial Chamber not imposed the cumulative convictions. It further emphasized that sentencing matters lie within the discretion of a trial chamber and, thus, concluded that a remand was necessary.[139]

This approach was reminiscent of the course of action taken in the *Tadić* case mentioned above and ostensibly reinforced the view that, at least with sentencing, the Trial Chamber was best placed to pronounce a revised sentence in the first instance. Notably, however, in relation to the prosecution's successful sentencing appeal against one of the accused in the *Čelebići* case, the Appeals Chamber gave a clear indication of the increased sentence that should be imposed to the extent that the reversed cumulative convictions indeed had no impact on the original sentence.[140] However, the specific increase, based on the error identified by the Appeals Chamber in relation to the gravity of the crime, would equally be a matter most appropriately dealt with in the first instance by a trial chamber applying the correct standard.

The ICTY Appeals Chamber has only ordered a new trial following the overturning of an acquittal in one instance, in the *Haradinaj et al.* case. That case differs significantly from the other acquittals overturned by the ICTY and ICTR Appeals Chamber. In particular, the ICTY Appeals Chamber did not simply conclude that the Trial Chamber applied an incorrect legal test or made erroneous factual findings which resulted in it acquitting the accused. Rather, the Appeals Chamber considered that the Trial

---

[136] *Tadić* Order of 10 September 1999, *supra* note 134, at 1–2. *See also Tadić* Sentencing Appeal Judgement, *supra* note 134, ¶¶ 9–10.

[137] *See generally Tadić* Sentencing Appeal Judgement, *supra* note 134. *See also* Nieto-Navia & Roche, *supra* note 17, at 482.

[138] *Čelebići* Appeal Judgement, *supra* note 43, 306–7 and ¶¶ 851–4.

[139] *Id.*: ¶ 431.

[140] *Id.* at 306–7 and ¶ 853.

Chamber "failed to take sufficient steps to counter the witness intimidation that permeated the trial and, in particular, to facilitate the Prosecution's requests to secure the testimony of [two prosecution witnesses]."[141] It concluded that this error of law undermined the fairness of the proceedings and thus ordered a new trial.[142] In quashing the decision of the Trial Chamber and sending it back for re-trial, the ICTY Appeals Chamber acted in a similar way to a court of cassation in civil law systems.

d. Conclusion on the ICTY and ICTR Appeals Chamber's practice This review of the ICTY and ICTR Appeals Chamber's jurisprudence and practice related to overturning acquittals, entering convictions, and increasing sentences on appeal reveals significant inconsistencies[143] and concerns. As has been correctly noted:

> The case law of the Tribunal could have promptly clarified the borders of the Appeals Chamber's powers in the case of the Prosecution's appeals against acquittals, based on the Statute, the [RPE], international human rights standards and general principles of law. However, to this date, the Appeals Chamber has omitted to do so, thus leaving room for an oscillating jurisprudence on this crucial issue.[144]

There are compelling arguments grounded in fundamental fair trial rights, which indicate that the ICTY and ICTR Appeals Chamber should not enter convictions or increase sentences without providing any avenue for appeal. The suggestion that the Appeals Chamber has the authority to do so simply because the ICTY and ICTR Statutes allow for prosecution's appeals fails to appreciate the distinction between identifying an error and correcting it in a manner detrimental to a fundamental right.[145] Moreover,

---

141 *Haradinaj et al.* Appeal Judgement, *supra* note 71, ¶ 49.

142 *Id.* ¶¶ 49–50, 377

143 *See also* Bing Bing Jia, *The Right of Appeal in the Proceedings Before the ICTY and ICTR*, *in* Liber Fausto Pocar—Individual Rights and International Justice, *supra* note 89, at 425. Given the ICTY and ICTR Appeals Chamber's inconsistent practice, it is not entirely surprising that the SCSL Appeals Chamber has followed an oscillating practice on this crucial issue as, according to Article 20(3) of the SCSL Statute, the SCSL Appeals Chamber shall be guided by the decisions of the ICTY and ICTR Appeals Chamber. *See* Prosecutor v. Brima et al., Case No. SCSL-04-16-A, Judgement, 105 (Feb. 22, 2008); Prosecutor v. Fofana & Kondewa, Case No. SCSL-04-14-A, Judgment, 187–92 (May 28, 2008); Prosecutor v. Sesay et al., Case No. SCSL-04-15-A, Judgement, 465–6 (Oct. 26, 2009).

144 Pocar, *supra* note 13, at 454–5 (internal references omitted).

145 *See also* Fleming, *supra* note 14, at 117 ("the fact that Article 25 facially *permits* appeals from acquittals in a positive sense does not necessarily *justify* them normatively").

the fact that the ICTY and ICTR Appeals Chamber has entered convictions or increased sentences in the past does not provide compelling justification since the issue was not in fact considered from a human rights perspective in the early jurisprudence. The exceptional nature of international criminal tribunals should also not justify its derogation from the fundamental principles enshrined in Article 14 of the ICCPR. Instead, given the nature of the institution, these principles should be their touchstone, as recognized in the *Vujin* Appeal Judgment.

The fact that, in many cases, the imposition of the additional conviction has no overall impact on the sentence raises additional questions about the necessity of doing so. This is particularly the case where there is a contemporaneous and competing practice of the ICTY Appeals Chamber simply to acknowledge the error as guidance for future cases without altering the verdict.[146] Finally, given that at least on one occasion, in the *Šljivančanin* case, the ICTY Appeals Chamber reversed a conviction entered on appeal through review proceedings underscores the necessity of appellate review for any conviction or increase in sentence.[147] Although this type of proceeding may offer some avenue of relief in these instances, review is exceptional, and it has only been granted with respect to a convicted person in one case.[148] The best practice is for the ICTY and ICTR Appeals Chamber to avoid entering convictions or increasing sentences on appeal and to

---

146 Judge Nieto-Navia criticized this alternative as falling outside the scope of the ICTY Statute and becoming "simply academic exercises, whereby the Prosecution could appeal against an acquittal but solely with a view to obtaining a ruling from the Appeals Chamber on an issue of law, for guidance in future cases." *See* Nieto-Navia & Roche, *supra* note 17, at 486. However, this criticism is misplaced given that the ICTY and ICTR Appeals Chamber has accepted the possibility, in exceptional circumstances, to hear appeals in which a party has raised a legal issue that would not lead to the invalidation of the trial judgment, but is nevertheless of general significance to the Tribunal's jurisprudence. *See supra* notes 49–55 and accompanying text.

147 In the *Mrkšić & Šljivančanin* Appeal Judgement, the Appeals Chamber reviewed the relevant circumstantial evidence and concluded that, contrary to the Trial Chamber's findings, it showed that Šljivančanin possessed the necessary *mens rea* for aiding and abetting murder as a violation of the laws and customs of war. Accordingly, it entered a conviction for that crime on appeal and increased Šljivančanin's sentence in part on that basis. Subsequent evidence called that inference into question and the Appeals Chamber quashed the conviction during review proceedings. *See generally Šljivančanin* Review Judgement, *supra* note 102, ¶¶ 23–32, 37.

148 *See generally id. See also* Prosecutor v. Šljivančanin, Case No. IT-95-13/1-R.1, Decision with Respect to Veselin Šljivančanin's Application for Review, 4 (July 14, 2010).

remit matters to an appropriate trial chamber in those few cases where re-trial is necessary to avoid a miscarriage of justice or, in other cases, to simply correct the error on appeal but without entering a new conviction or increasing the sentence.[149]

3. The prospective attitude of the ICC with respect to appeal against acquittals and increase of sentences

As will be described below, the Rome Statute of the ICC is a blend of civil law and common law approaches. In line with the civil law tradition, the Statute follows the appellate standard set by the ICTY and ICTR Appeals Chamber in granting generous scope of the right to appeal to both parties. However, in line with the common law approach, it does so without allowing a trial *de novo*.[150] Articles 81 and 83 of the Rome Statute govern the right to appeal against a verdict or a sentence.

Article 81(1) of the Rome Statute empowers both the convicted person and the prosecutor to appeal as of right on grounds of procedural error, error of fact or error of law. Moreover, the appellant exclusively may appeal on any other ground that affects the fairness or reliability of the proceedings or decision.[151] The enumeration of grounds for appeal is

---

149 *See also* Nieto-Navia, *supra* note 89, at 633; Karibi-Whyte, *supra* note 15, at 659.

150 Orie, *supra* note 12, at 1490–1. *See also* Brady & Jennings, *supra* note 17, at 299, stating that Article 81 of the Rome Statute reflects a compromise between civil and common law jurisdictions.

151 Article 81(1)(b)(iv) of the Rome Statute. This catch-all ground for appeal seems to add little to the other specified grounds. As pointed out by one scholar, "[t]he apparent intention was to include a 'catch-all' provision in the case of appeals by or on behalf of the convicted person, to ensure that any miscarriage of justice would be capable of correction on appeal. The addition may have been out of an abundance of caution, since it is likely that any valid grounds of appeal would fall within one of the other categories . . . . In particular, anything occurring within the context of the trial itself that affects the fairness or reliability of the proceedings could be regarded as a procedural error on the basis that a fair trial is a procedural requirement under article 67, para. 1. Because this ground of appeal is somewhat amorphous, there is probably no one standard of review that governs. The standards of review of one of the other grounds of appeal is likely to be applied by analogy, depending on the particular circumstances of the case." *See* Staker, *supra* note 9, at 1466. However, other scholars have stated that "it is important to know exactly how Article 81(1)(b)(iv) relates to 'procedural error' and 'errors of fact or law', because the Prosecutor is debarred from appealing on this fourth ground, as these two issues are very close in their substance. In principle, 'procedural errors' ought to include any formal violations of the Statute or the Rules of Procedure and Evidence, whereas 'grounds that affect the fairness or reliability of the proceedings or decision' should be substantive . . . . These 'grounds'

more in accordance with the common law tradition than with the civil law tradition.[152]

Similar to the practice in some civil law systems, one aspect of the right to appeal in the Rome Statute is that, according to Article 81(1)(b), the prosecutor may also make an appeal on the convicted person's behalf. However, Rule 152(2) of the ICC RPE requires that the prosecutor inform the convicted person if he or she intends to discontinue the appeal in order to give him or her the opportunity to continue the appellate proceedings. The prosecutor's ability to appeal on the convicted person's behalf is disconcerting. This unique feature of the prosecutor's authority is not consistent with an adversarial approach and relativizes the "accusatory" role of the prosecutor.[153] However, as noted by some scholars, this provision requires the prosecutor to serve the interests of abstract justice and underscores the office's non-partisan duty to truth and justice.[154] In other words, "the Prosecutor's role in the trial ceases to be purely dialectic, in the 'accusatory' tradition of UK and American courts: he must help to guarantee the proper administration of justice" in the case where "the convicted person has no counsel of his own, or – in exceptional and alarming cases – his counsel has failed to represent him adequately, forcing the Prosecutor to assume the task."[155] This is in line with some civil law systems such as Germany.[156]

---

may relate to the trial in open court, equality of arms, or self-incrimination; to the accused's right to be legally represented and to cross-examine prosecution witnesses; or to the publication of, and grounds for, the judgment . . . . In theory, then, it seems doubtful, in light of Article 81(1)(b)(iv), that the ICC Appeals Chamber can voluntarily and in general restrict its own powers to examine the grounds for an appeal. Rather, it seems that the Appeals Chamber *must* examine the grounds for any appeal that is brought to it against a conviction or sentence handed down by a Trial Chamber, before deciding whether or not that appeal is admissible." *See also* Roth & Henzelin, *supra* note 6, at 1544–5.

[152] Orie, *supra* note 12, at 1490. *See also* Helen Brady, *Appeal*, *in* THE INTERNATIONAL CRIMINAL COURT—ELEMENTS OF CRIMES AND RULES OF PROCEDURE AND EVIDENCE, *supra* note 17, at 585.

[153] Orie, *supra* note 12, at 1490; Roth & Henzelin, *supra* note 6, at 1543.

[154] Roth & Henzelin, *supra* note 6, at 1543; Staker, *supra* note 9, at 1453. *See also* Barayagwiza v. The Prosecutor, Case No. ICTR-97-19-AR72, Decision (Prosecutor's Request for Review or Reconsideration) (Mar. 31, 2000) (the English translation was filed on Apr. 7, 2000), Separate Opinion of Judge Shahabuddeen, ¶ 68 ("The Prosecutor of the ICTR is not required to be neutral in a case: she is a party. But she is not of course a partisan . . . . The implications of that requirement suggest that, while a prosecution must be conducted vigorously, there is room for the injunction that prosecuting counsel 'ought to bear themselves rather in the character of ministers of justice assisting in the administration of justice'." (internal reference omitted)).

[155] Roth & Henzelin, *supra* note 6, at 1543.

[156] Staker, *supra* note 9, at 1453 and n.25.

Both the prosecutor and the convicted person may appeal as of right against the sentence on the ground of disproportion between the crime and the sentence.[157] It is surprising that no other grounds for appeal – such as procedural error, error of fact or error of law – were included in this provision as such errors can clearly arise in the sentencing process. In fact, if the ICC Appeals Chamber finds that the "sentence appealed from was materially affected by error of fact or law or procedural error," Article 83(2) of the Rome Statute empowers it to grant an appropriate remedy. Thus, it seems that an appeal alleging "disproportionality" of sentence within the meaning of Article 81(2)(a) encompasses any appeal seeking to have the sentence itself reduced or increased on appeal on any of these grounds.[158] Moreover, a characteristic of the right of appeal in the Rome Statute is that, according to Article 81(2)(b) and (c), the ICC Appeals Chamber may initiate a conversion – or broadening – of an appeal on sentence into an appeal on conviction and vice versa by inviting the parties to submit additional grounds for the appeal. However, if the ICC Appeals Chamber considers an appeal on conviction, it can only convert it to an appeal on sentence in order to reduce it.[159] The ICTY Appeals Chamber exercised a similar power of conversion in one case, although the ICTY Statute and RPE do not contain a similar provision.[160] Erdemović, who had pled guilty, appealed his sentence and the ICTY Appeals Chamber, *proprio motu*, raised the issue of the validity of his guilty plea. The ICTY Appeals Chamber held:

> The Appeals Chamber has raised preliminary issues *proprio motu* pursuant to its inherent powers as an appellate body once seised of an appeal lodged by either party pursuant to Article 25 of the Statute. The Appeals Chamber finds nothing in the Statute or the Rules, nor in practices of international institutions or national judicial systems, which would confine its consideration of the appeal to the issues raised formally by the parties. The preliminary issues revolve around the question of the validity of the plea of guilty entered by the Appellant.[161]

---

157 Article 81(2)(a) of the Rome Statute.

158 Staker, *supra* note 9, at 1454.

159 Article 81(2)(c) reads as follows: "The same procedure applies when the Court, on an appeal against conviction only, considers that there are grounds to *reduce* the sentence under paragraph 2(a)" (emphasis added). *See also* Roth & Henzelin, *supra* note 6, at 1546–7; Brady, *supra* note 152, at 576.

160 Prosecutor v. Erdemović, Case No. IT-96-22-A, Judgement (ICTY Oct. 7, 1997) [hereinafter *Erdemović* Appeal Judgement].

161 *Id.* ¶ 16. *See also Akayesu* Appeal Judgement, *supra* note 38, ¶ 17: "Article 24 of the Statute seeks to circumscribe the scope of review on appeal. On this point, the Appeals Chamber endorses the statement by ICTY Appeals Chamber that

This blurring distinction between appeal against conviction or acquittal and against sentence is more in accordance with the civil law approach.[162]

With respect to the possibility of an appeal against an acquittal, the title of Article 81 of the Rome Statute itself – "Appeal against decision of acquittal or conviction or against sentence" – sets the tone.[163] Article 81(1)(a) of the Rome Statute allows for an appeal of the prosecutor against acquittal. This point is clearly more in line with the civil law tradition.[164]

However, the ICC has yet to address the issue of whether the ICC Appeals Chamber can enter a new conviction on appeal and/or increase the sentence to the detriment of the defendant. For the time being, the ICC Appeals Chamber has issued no appeal judgment. A critical analysis of how this issue will play out in practice must therefore await its first appeal judgment dealing with this issue. However, some tentative remarks on the possible attitude of the ICC Appeals Chamber in this regard can be made on the basis of the Rome Statute.

Article 83 of the Rome Statute deals with the powers of the ICC Appeals Chamber and proceedings on appeal. *A priori*, the Rome Statute does not seem to forbid the possibility for the ICC Appeals Chamber to enter new conviction(s) on appeal and/or increase the sentence of the defendant as, according to Article 83(2) of the Rome Statute, it may reverse or amend the trial judgment or sentence or order a re-trial before a different trial chamber.[165] Moreover, according to Article 83(2) of the Rome Statute, a trial judgment or a sentence cannot be amended to the convicted person's detriment when it was appealed only by that person or by the prosecutor on that person's behalf.[166] Thus, Article 83(2) of the Rome Statute *a contrario* would allow the ICC Appeals Chamber to substitute a conviction

---

'the role of the Appeals Chamber *is limited,* pursuant to Article 25 of the Statute, to correcting errors of law invalidating a decision, and errors of fact which have occasioned a miscarriage of justice' (emphasis added). Nevertheless the Appeals Chamber underscores that within the framework predefined by the Statute, the Appeals Chamber may consider issues *proprio motu,* as previously held by ICTY Appeals Chamber in the *Erdemović* case." (internal references omitted); Staker, *supra* note 9, at 1454, 1468.

162 Orie, *supra* note 12, at 1490–1.

163 *See also* Roth & Henzelin, *supra* note 6, at 1541, 1543.

164 Orie, *supra* note 12, at 1490.

165 With respect to the sentence, the power of the ICC Appeals Chamber to vary it is spelled out in Article 83(3) of the Rome Statute. Article 83(3) of the Rome Statute reads as follows: "If in an appeal against sentence the Appeals Chamber finds that the sentence is disproportionate to the crime, it may vary the sentence in accordance with Part 7."

166 *See also* Roth & Henzelin, *supra* note 6, at 1556.

for an acquittal or to amend a sentence to the convicted person's detriment when an appeal is brought by the prosecutor.[167]

However, the Rome Statute also directly encourages resort to human rights law in its section on applicable law. Article 21(3) of the Rome Statute provides that "[t]he application and interpretation of law pursuant to this article must be consistent with internationally recognized human rights."[168] The ICC Appeals Chamber has itself confirmed that the Rome Statute must be interpreted and applied consistently with internationally recognized human rights.[169] With respect to the issue at stake, the reference to "*internationally recognized* human rights" would clearly mean that the Rome Statute must, first and foremost, be interpreted and applied consistently with the ICCPR[170] and, therefore, its Article 14(5). Moreover, in this regard, the ICC Appeals Chamber should prefer referring to Article 14(5) of the ICCPR rather than to Article 2(2) of Protocol 7 to the ECHR for two reasons.[171] First, "*internationally recognized*" should be primarily understood as favoring the higher standard of human rights given by an international instrument espoused by the United Nations rather than the lower standard of human rights enshrined in a regional instrument,[172]

---

167 Staker, *supra* note 9, at 1483.

168 According to one scholar, "[t]here was virtual unanimity among delegations as to the desirability of stipulating that the interpretation of law 'must be consistent with internationally recognized human rights'." *See* Margaret McAuliffe de Guzman, *Article 21: Applicable Law*, *in* COMMENTARY ON THE ROME STATUTE OF THE INTERNATIONAL CRIMINAL COURT, *supra* note 9, at 712.

169 *See, e.g.*, Prosecutor v. Lubanga, Case No. ICC-01/04-01/06 OA 13, Judgment on the Appeal of the Prosecutor Against the Decision of Trial Chamber I Entitled "Decision on the Consequences of Non-Disclosure of Exculpatory Materials Covered by Article 54(3)(e) Agreements and the Application To Stay the Prosecution of the Accused, Together with Certain Other Issues Raised at the Status Conference on 10 June 2008", ¶ 46 (Oct. 21, 2008); Prosecutor v. Lubanga, Case No. ICC-01/04-01/06 OA 4, Judgment on the Appeal of Mr. Thomas Lubanga Dyilo Against the Decision on the Defence Challenge to the Jurisdiction of the Court Pursuant to Article 19(2)(a) of the Statute of 3 October 2006, ¶¶ 36–7 (Dec. 14, 2006).

170 *See also* Gerhard Hafner & Christina Binder, *The Interpretation of Article 21(3) ICC Statute, Opinion Reviewed*, 9 AUSTRIAN REV. INT'L AND EUR. L. 163, 178–85, 188–9 (2004).

171 *See supra* note 4 and accompanying text. *See also* Hafner & Binder, *supra* note 170, at 187.

172 In this regard, it has been held that "the ICCPR and the ECHR provisions as to right of appeal are not in conflict, but rather present two different standards of protection of fair trial rights. One of the key principles in the international protection of human rights is that when there are diverging international standards, the highest should prevail. In addition, the difference in the scope of the obligations accepted by

especially if the case on appeal before the ICC is part of a non-European situation. Second, such interpretation is more advantageous to the defendant and should be preferred, according to the principle that the interpretation favoring the defendant must be chosen.

In light of Article 21(3) of the Rome Statute, the prospective attitude of the ICC with respect to the right to appeal should be for the ICC Appeals Chamber not to enter convictions on appeal or to increase the defendant's sentence in light of the fundamental right to an appeal as articulated in the ICCPR and interpreted by the HRC. However, Article 83(2) of the Rome Statute "does not spell out the principles for determining which of the possible courses of action under this paragraph should be adopted by the ICC Appeals Chamber in the event of a successful appeal."[173] Accordingly, with respect to an appeal against an acquittal or the increase of a sentence, the only avenues opened to the ICC Appeals Chamber in order to respect the fundamental right to an appeal would be to either correct the error on appeal but without entering a new conviction or increasing the sentence, or to remand the matter back to the Trial Chamber for a re-trial or for its determination. It is important to note, in this regard, that the Rome Statute explicitly allows the ICC Appeals Chamber to "remand a factual issue to the original Trial Chamber for it to determine the issue and to report back accordingly."[174]

It may be appropriate for the ICC Appeals Chamber to choose the first option when there is no need to determine additional facts in order to reach a final verdict. Similarly, if as a result of the appeal, the final verdict depends only on one or more narrow issues of fact, it may be appropriate for the Appeals Chamber to use the mechanism available . . . to remand those issues of fact back to the Trial Chamber. If wide-ranging new fact-finding is necessary, a new trial may be more appropriate.[175]

States under the ICCPR and ECHR is explained by the different enforcement mechanisms attached to those instruments. In ratifying the ECHR, States must accept the compulsory jurisdiction of the European Court of Human Rights, the decisions of which are binding on those States. Accordingly, the fact that States parties to the ECHR have ratified an instrument wherein the scope of certain rights is limited, cannot be read as evidence that those States only recognise such rights within the specified limits. Rather, it means that those States have only accepted the *jurisdiction* of the European Court of Human Rights to that limited extent." *See Mrkšić & Šljivančanin* Appeal Judgement, *supra* note 131, Partially Dissenting Opinion of Judge Pocar, ¶ 7. *See also* Hafner & Binder, *supra* note 170, at 187.

[173] Staker, *supra* note 9, at 1483.

[174] Article 83(2) of the Rome Statute.

[175] Staker, *supra* note 9, at 1483 (internal references omitted).

III. THE STANDARD OF REVIEW ON APPEAL IF ADDITIONAL EVIDENCE IS CONSIDERED AND A JUDGMENT RENDERED

This second part highlights the divergence in civil law and common law systems with respect to the possibility to admit additional evidence on appeal (Section A). Outlining the different approaches allows for a better understanding of the challenges faced by the ICTY Appeals Chamber when admitting additional evidence on appeal (Section B). This, in turn, may provide some guidance to the options available to the ICC when it will be confronted with a similar scenario in the future (Section C).

A. The Approach of Common Law and Civil Law Systems

In civil law systems, admission of additional evidence on appeal that was not before the court of first instance is generally allowed without any restriction.[176] This is a corollary to the fact that an appeal, in civil law tradition, generally consists in a full re-hearing of the case, *i.e.*, a trial *de novo*, and that the appeal courts are involved in an adjudication process on the factual merits of the case.[177]

By contrast, in common law systems, because appeal courts are only involved in controlling the application of the law rather than the assessment of facts, there is no automatic entitlement to adduce new evidence on appeal and new evidence is generally not considered.[178] Moreover, in such systems where there is a right to a jury, it would be an infringement of this right to allow the appeals court to admit further evidence and weigh it. In such a situation, a complete re-trial would be mandatory; otherwise the judges would usurp the function of the jury.[179] In the United States, for example, new evidence is not admitted on appeal.[180]

---

176 *Kupreškić et al.* Appeal Judgement, *supra* note 23, ¶ 45.

177 *See supra* note 26 and accompanying text. *See also* Linda E. Carter, *The Importance of Understanding Criminal Justice Principles in the Context of International Criminal Procedure: The Case of Admitting Evidence on Appeal*, *in* LIBER FAUSTO POCAR—INDIVIDUAL RIGHTS AND INTERNATIONAL JUSTICE, *supra* note 89, at 132; Yvonne M.O. Featherstone, *Additional Evidence in the Appeals Proceedings and Review of Final Judgement*, *in* ESSAYS ON ICTY PROCEDURE AND EVIDENCE IN HONOUR OF GABRIELLE KIRK MCDONALD, *supra* note 17, at 497.

178 SAFFERLING, *supra* note 14, at 334. *See also Kupreškić et al.* Appeal Judgement, *supra* note 23, ¶ 46.

179 SAFFERLING, *supra* note 14, at 334.

180 Carter, *supra* note 177, at 133. *See also Kupreškić et al.* Appeal Judgement, *supra* note 23, ¶ 46 and references cited therein.

Other common law systems, however, do allow for the admission of additional evidence on appeal, but in limited circumstances.[181] In such systems, statutory provisions generally govern the admission of additional evidence on appeal.[182] In England and Wales, the Court of Appeal can admit additional evidence on a limited basis.[183] In Canada, additional evidence can be admitted if it is in the interests of justice and is of sufficient strength that it might reasonably affect the verdict. Similar possibilities exist in Australia and South Africa.[184]

B. The ICTY and ICTR Appeals Chamber's Practice to Admit Additional Evidence on Appeal

Since, on the one hand, the ICTY and ICTR Appeals Chamber is authorized to correct errors of facts but that, on the other hand, an appeal is not a trial *de novo*, the question arises as to whether the parties should be allowed to present additional evidence on appeal.

Usually, in accordance with Rule 109 of the ICTY RPE and 109(A) of the ICTR RPE, the Appeals Chamber will be able to decide on the issues raised without a new trial being held and on the basis of the trial record.[185] However, according to Rule 115 of the ICTY and ICTR RPE,[186] the parties may apply for leave to present additional evidence on appeal. In that case, the Appeals Chamber shall deliver its judgment on the basis of the record on appeal together with the admitted additional evidence.[187]

As previously explained,[188] according to the deferential standard of appellate review, the ICTY and ICTR Appeals Chamber may overturn a trial chamber's factual finding only where the evidence relied on could not

---

[181] Carter, *supra* note 177, at 133.

[182] *Kupreškić et al.* Appeal Judgement, *supra* note 23, ¶ 46.

[183] Smith, *supra* note 14, at 101–2; Carter, *supra* note 177, at 133. *See also Kupreškić et al.* Appeal Judgement, *supra* note 23, ¶ 46.

[184] *Kupreškić et al.* Appeal Judgement, *supra* note 23, ¶ 46.

[185] Rule 109 of the ICTY RPE and Rule 109(A) of the ICTR Rules read as follows: "The record on appeal shall consist of the trial record, as certified by the Registrar."

[186] Rule 115(B) of the ICTY and ICTR RPE reads as follows: "If the Appeals Chamber finds that the additional evidence was not available at trial and is relevant and credible, it will determine if it could have been a decisive factor in reaching the decision at trial. If it could have been such a factor, the Appeals Chamber will consider the additional evidence and any rebuttal material along with that already on the record to arrive at a final judgement in accordance with Rule 117 [of the ICTY RPE and Rule 118 of the ICTR RPE]."

[187] *See* Rule 117(A) of the ICTY RPE; Rule 118(C) of the ICTR RPE.

[188] *See supra* notes 62–68 and accompanying text.

have been accepted by any reasonable tribunal or where the evaluation of the evidence is wholly erroneous.[189]

However, one issue which has arisen with respect to the right to appeal from an international human rights law perspective is the question of which standard of appellate review should apply if additional evidence is admitted on appeal that has not been considered by the trial chamber. Is the right of the appellant to a trial chamber's decision beyond reasonable doubt, based on all of the evidence before it, violated if the Appeals Chamber uses the usual appellate standard of deference to the trial chamber's findings?

When additional evidence is admitted on appeal pursuant to Rule 115 of the ICTY and ICTR RPE, the identification of the criteria regulating the application of this standard is not so obvious and the ICTY Appeals Chamber has adopted different positions over time. These various approaches may be considered as reflecting the different understandings of lawyers from common law and civil law traditions on the role and meaning of an appeal.[190]

During the *Kupreškić et al.* appellate proceedings, the appellants filed 26 motions pursuant to Rule 115 of the ICTY RPE, seeking to admit a wide range of additional evidence, including witnesses' testimonies, written evidence and video-recordings.[191] After having admitted some additional evidence on appeal, the ICTY Appeals Chamber had to assess whether the additional admitted evidence actually revealed an error of fact which had occasioned a miscarriage of justice.[192]

One of the appellants, Josipović, submitted on behalf of all the appellants that the Appeals Chamber should adopt the test applicable in most common law systems, namely: "might or could the additional evidence have caused the Trial Chamber to have arrived at a different verdict?" If the answer were affirmative, the Appeals Chamber would allow the appeal, quash the conviction and consider whether to order a re-trial.[193]

The prosecution responded that the ICTY Appeals Chamber is not bound by jurisprudence of national jurisdictions and that the correct standard to be applied in the case where additional evidence has been admitted at trial should be that "[t]he additional evidence must be sufficiently compelling that when assessed in light of all the evidence in the record on appeal, and if believed, it would have tilted the balance in favour

---

189 *Aleksovski* Appeal Judgement, *supra* note 65, ¶ 63.
190 Pocar, *supra* note 13, at 456–7.
191 *Kupreškić et al.* Appeal Judgement, *supra* note 23, ¶ 42.
192 *Id.* ¶ 72.
193 *Id.* ¶ 73.

of another verdict if it was made available before the Trial Chamber."[194] In reply, the appellants warned that accepting this standard could result in injustice in cases that were not crystal clear.[195]

After refusing to import tests from national jurisdictions, the Appeals Chamber articulated the test to be applied in deciding whether or not to affirm a conviction where additional evidence has been admitted in the following terms: "has the appellant established that no reasonable tribunal of fact could have reached a conclusion of guilt based upon the evidence before the Trial Chamber together with the additional evidence admitted during the appellate proceedings"[196] (*Kupreškić* test). The *Kupreškić* test was subsequently adopted by the ICTR Appeals Chamber.[197]

In *Blaškić*, however, the ICTY Appeals Chamber considered that the peculiarities of the case required a further examination of the existing standard of appellate review in case additional evidence is admitted.[198]

During the appellate proceedings, the ICTY Appeals Chamber heard six witnesses and admitted 108 pieces of evidence.[199] The Appeals Chamber faced the dilemma of trying to reconcile two conflicting principles. The first is that a trier of fact's decision beyond reasonable doubt on guilt should be based on a consideration of all the evidence presented. The second is that an appellate court should give deference to a trial chamber's factual findings.[200]

Different options were open to the ICTY Appeals Chamber. One of them was to remand the case to the Trial Chamber to hear the additional evidence and to make any necessary adjustments in the trial judgment. The benefit of this option would have been to keep the fact-finding and appellate functions separate.[201] However, the wording of Rule 115(B) of

---

194 *Id.* ¶ 74.

195 *Id.*

196 *Id.* ¶ 75. *See also id.* ¶ 76.

197 Musema v. Prosecutor, Case No. ICTR-96-13-A, Judgement, ¶ 185–6 (Nov. 16, 2001) (the English translation of the French original was filed on Aug. 14, 2002); *Rutaganda* Appeal Judgement, *supra* note 76, ¶ 473.

198 *Blaškić* Appeal Judgement, *supra* note 61, ¶ 8; Pocar, *supra* note 13, at 458.

199 *Blaškić* Appeal Judgement, *supra* note 61, ¶ 6 and Partial Dissenting Opinion of Judge Weinberg de Roca, ¶ 5.

200 Carter, *supra* note 177, at 131–2.

201 It seems that the ICTY Appeals Chamber considered this option in the *Blaškić* case. "[G]iven the sheer volume of clearly admissible evidence, the possible submission of rebuttal evidence and the recalling of witnesses who testified at trial, as well as the potential of the additional evidence to bring about a re-determination of the facts of the case," the ICTY Appeals Chamber considered that "it would be more appropriate for any re-determination of the facts in the particular circumstances of this case to be made by a Trial Chamber." Thus, the Appeals Chamber

the ICTY RPE[202] suggests that the task of considering additional evidence is incumbent upon the Appeals Chamber itself as it clearly states that "the Appeals Chamber will consider the additional evidence and any rebuttal material along with that already on the record to arrive at a final judgement in accordance with Rule 117."[203] The Appeals Chamber rejected the option to remand the case to the Trial Chamber and, instead, considered the additional evidence itself.[204]

However, the Appeals Chamber in *Blaškić*, by majority, did not apply the standard articulated in the *Kupreškić et al.* Appeal Judgment but set forth four scenarios and indicated the standards that would apply in each case.[205]

In so doing, the Appeals Chamber first reiterated that an appeal is not a trial *de novo* and confirmed the validity of the *Kupreškić* test. It further noted that, because the outcome in the *Kupreškić et al.* case was that no reasonable trier of fact could have reached a finding of guilt, the Appeals Chamber did not need to determine whether it was satisfied *itself*, beyond reasonable doubt, as to the conclusion reached.[206] However, it pointed out that if, in a given case, the outcome was that a reasonable trier of fact could reach a conclusion of guilt beyond reasonable doubt, the Appeals Chamber "should, in the interests of justice, be convinced itself, beyond reasonable doubt, as to the guilt of the accused, before confirming a conviction on appeal."[207] Thus, the Appeals Chamber – by majority – recognized that, when additional evidence is admitted on appeal, the standard of review could not be deferential in all circumstances.[208] The Appeals Chamber justified its choice by explaining that:

> if it were to apply a lower standard [*i.e.* the normal 'deferential' standard of review], then the outcome would be that neither in the first instance, nor on appeal, would a conclusion of guilt based on the totality of evidence relied upon

---

ordered "the parties to present oral argument limited to the issue of whether the above-mentioned clearly admissible evidence justifies a new trial by a Trial Chamber, on some or all of the counts." Prosecutor v. Blaškić, Case No. IT-95-14-A, Scheduling Order, 3 (Oct. 31, 2002).

202 *See supra* note 186.

203 *See also* Carter, *supra* note 177, at 128–9, 134.

204 Prosecutor v. Blaškić, Case No. IT-95-14-A, Decision on Evidence, 6–7 (Oct. 31, 2003).

205 *Blaškić* Appeal Judgement, *supra* note 61, ¶ 24. *See also id.*, Partial Dissenting Opinion of Judge Weinberg de Roca, ¶¶ 1–9.

206 *Id.* ¶¶ 13, 21–2.

207 *Id.* ¶ 23.

208 *See also* Carter, *supra* note 177, at 136.

> in the case assessed in light of the correct legal standard, be reached by either Chamber beyond reasonable doubt.[209]

In light of this reasoning, the Appeals Chamber articulated the two-step standard to be applied when the Appeals Chamber is confronted with an alleged error of fact and that additional evidence is admitted on appeal and that there is no error in the legal standard:

> (i) The Appeals Chamber will first determine, on the basis of the trial record alone, whether no reasonable trier of fact could have reached the conclusion of guilt beyond reasonable doubt. If that is the case, then no further examination of the matter is necessary as a matter of law.
> (ii) If, however, the Appeals Chamber determines that a reasonable trier of fact could have reached a conclusion of guilt beyond reasonable doubt, then the Appeals Chamber will determine whether, in light of the trial evidence and additional evidence admitted on appeal, it is itself convinced beyond reasonable doubt as to the finding of guilt.[210]

In other words, in the case of an appeal against a conviction, if the Appeals Chamber determines that it would reverse a conviction on the basis of a deferential standard, the additional evidence on appeal would then become irrelevant as the reversal would be exclusively based on the trial record. This is the *Kupreškić et al.* case scenario. On the other hand, if the Appeals Chamber would uphold a conviction on the basis of the trial record, then the additional evidence would need to be considered. In this latter scenario, the Appeals Chamber would no longer apply a deferential standard but determine whether it is itself convinced beyond reasonable doubt as to the finding of guilt (*Blaškić* test).[211]

The Appeals Chamber further envisaged the scenario where the Appeals Chamber is confronted with an error in the legal standard applied in relation to the factual finding and an error of fact and that additional evidence is admitted on appeal. In that case, the two-step standard is the following:

> (i) The Appeals Chamber will apply the correct legal standard to the evidence contained in the trial record, and will determine whether it is itself convinced beyond reasonable as to the finding of guilt, on the basis of the trial record. If it is not convinced, then no further examination of the matter is necessary as a matter of law.

---

209 *Blaškić* Appeal Judgement, *supra* note 61, ¶ 23. *See also* Staker, *supra* note 9, at 1464.

210 *Blaškić* Appeal Judgement, *supra* note 61, ¶ 24(c). *See also id.*, Partial Dissenting Opinion of Judge Weinberg de Roca, ¶¶ 1–9.

211 *See also* Carter, *supra* note 177, at 136.

(ii) If, however, the Appeals Chamber, applying the correct legal standard to the evidence contained in the trial record, is itself convinced beyond reasonable doubt as to the finding of guilt, it will then proceed to determine whether, in light of the trial evidence and additional evidence admitted on appeal, it is itself still convinced beyond reasonable doubt as to the finding of guilt.[212]

The rationale of the Appeals Chamber was that, although the assessment of the evidence by the Trial Chamber judgment was based on the beyond reasonable doubt standard, it was incomplete as it did not examine the additional evidence. Thus, if the Appeals Chamber would have applied a deferential standard of appellate review, the appellant would not have the benefit of a finding of guilt beyond reasonable doubt based on *all* the evidence.

The *Blaškić* test of review when additional evidence is admitted on appeal was reiterated by the Appeals Chamber in the *Kvočka et al.* Appeal Judgment. In this case, the Appeals Chamber explained that the *Blaškić* test answered the question left open in the *Kupreškić et al.* case, further developing the standard first articulated therein.[213] However, in a separate opinion appended to the *Kvočka et al.* Appeal Judgment, one judge explained that the standard developed in *Blaškić* was in contradiction with the one articulated in *Kupreškić et al.*,[214] and that "the approach of the Appeals Chamber in this case effectively makes the Appeals Chamber a Trial Chamber, causes a trial to be held before the Appeals Chamber, requires the Appeals Chamber to make a finding as to whether it is 'itself convinced' that the guilt of the appellant has been proved beyond reasonable doubt, and in these and other ways misapprehends the appellate process of the Tribunal."[215] This vigorous dissent does not seem to have affected the position of the Appeals Chamber, which reiterated that the *Blaškić* test is not in contradiction with the *Kupreškić* test, but further develops the latter.[216]

Finally, in the *Haradinaj et al.* case, although the prosecution did not file a motion to admit additional evidence on appeal pursuant to Rule

---

212 *Blaškić* Appeal Judgement, *supra* note 61, ¶ 24(d).

213 *Kvočka et al.* Appeal Judgement, *supra* note 67, ¶ 426. *But see id.*, Separate Opinion of Judge Weinberg de Roca, ¶¶ 1–8, and Separate Opinion of Judge Shahabuddeen, ¶¶ 1–107.

214 *Id.*, Separate Opinion of Judge Shahabuddeen, ¶¶ 1–107.

215 *Id.* ¶ 104.

216 *See, e.g.*, *Naletilić & Martinović* Appeal Judgement, *supra* note 131, ¶¶ 11–12 and n.49*bis*; Prosecutor v. Krajišnik, Case No. IT-00-39-A, Judgement, ¶ 15 (ICTY Mar. 17, 2009).

115 of the ICTY RPE, it argued on appeal that the Trial Chamber erred when it refused its request for additional time to exhaust all reasonable steps to secure the testimony of two crucial witnesses and order the close of the prosecution's case before such reasonable steps could be taken. The prosecution further contended that the Trial Chamber's error invalidated the verdict by precluding it from presenting crucial evidence of two witnesses, who possessed direct evidence relating to the guilt of the three defendants. Rather than requesting to hear the testimonies of these two witnesses on appeal as additional evidence, the prosecution requested the Appeals Chamber to quash the defendants' acquittals and to remand the matter to a trial chamber for a re-trial, asserting that such a course of action would provide the reasonable possibility of hearing these crucial witnesses.[217] The prosecution justified its choice for a re-trial – rather than for requesting additional evidence to be admitted on appeal – by arguing that:

> Given that the Accused elected not to call a case in defence, and may have done so had the Trial Chamber heard the evidence of these witnesses, the Appeals Chamber should remit the matter back to a trial chamber for a re-trial to determine the[ir] liability.[218]

Moreover, it added that such re-trial should include the two crucial witnesses' testimonies.[219]

Different options were available to the ICTY Appeals Chamber. Because the prosecution stated that they did not intend to apply to the Appeals Chamber for the statements of the two witnesses to be admitted pursuant to Rule 115 of the ICTY RPE,[220] this option was therefore not a real possibility. Another alternative would have been for the ICTY Appeals Chamber to summon these witnesses itself pursuant to Rules 54, 98 and 107 of the ICTY RPE. This approach had previously been used at the ICTY in the *Krstić* case and in the *Stakić* case[221] for example

---

[217] *Haradinaj et al.* Appeal Judgement, *supra* note 71, ¶¶ 14–15.

[218] Prosecutor v. Haradinaj et al., Case No. IT-04-84-A, Prosecution's Notice of Appeal, ¶ 7 (ICTY May 2, 2008) (public with confidential annex) [hereinafter *Haradinaj et al.* Prosecution Notice of Appeal]. *See also* Prosecutor v. Haradinaj et al., Case No. IT-04-84-A, AT, 158-59 (ICTY Oct. 28, 2009) (appeals hearing) [hereinafter *Haradinaj et al.* Appeals Hearing].

[219] *Haradinaj et al.* Prosecution Notice of Appeal, *supra* note 218, ¶ 7.

[220] *Haradinaj et al.* Appeals Hearing, *supra* note 218, at 158–9.

[221] Prosecutor v. Krstić, Case No. IT-98-33-A, Decision to Summon a Witness *Proprio Motu* (ICTY Nov. 19, 2003); Prosecutor v. Stakić, Case No. IT-97-24-A, Decision to Summon a Witness *Proprio Motu* (ICTY Sept. 20, 2005).

and was later adopted by the ICTR Appeals Chamber in the *Bagosora and Nsengiyumva* case.[222] However, in the special circumstances of the *Haradinaj et al.* case, hearing witnesses may have involved complex procedures and required calling additional witnesses, which would have further complicated the appellate proceedings. Moreover, in the case that the Appeals Chamber would have convicted the defendants based on the additional evidence, they would not have been able to appeal their convictions.

Avoiding these scenarios, the Appeals Chamber decided to remand the matter to a trial chamber and have the defendants retried.[223] This option definitely has the benefit of keeping the fact-finding and appellate functions separate and to fully respect the right to appeal. The reason why the Appeals Chamber was not limited in this case by the wording of Rule 115(B) of the ICTY RPE to consider the additional evidence itself[224] was because the prosecution did not request the admission of the witnesses' testimonies as additional evidence on appeal pursuant to Rule 115 of the RPE.

The question of the appropriate standard of review when the Appeals Chamber admits and considers additional evidence on appeal was a novel issue that needed to be addressed, given the silence of the ICTY Statute and RPE on this point and the restriction of the wording of Rule 115 of the ICTY RPE on remanding the case to the trial chamber. In balancing between a deferential standard and the right of the accused to

---

222 *Bagosora & Nsengiyumva* Appeal Judgement, *supra* note 42, ¶ 531. *See also* Bagosora & Nsengiyumva, Case No. ICTR-98-41-A, Decision on Théoneste Bagosora's Motion for Admission of Additional Evidence, ¶¶ 8–10 (Feb. 7, 2011) (where the Appeals Chamber held that the purpose of Rule 115 of the RPE is to deal with the situation where a party *is in possession of material* that was not before the court of first instance and which is additional evidence of a fact or issue litigated at trial but that this rule does not permit a party to merely request a particular person to be summoned as a witness to give evidence at the appellate stage without providing a statement or other documentation of the potential witness's proposed evidence, which the Appeals Chamber may admit as additional evidence pursuant to Rule 115 of the RPE and on the basis of which it may determine whether calling the witness to testify on appeal is necessary. Given that Bagosora did not provide the Appeals Chamber with any statement or documentation from the witness to be called on appeal that may be admissible as additional evidence and the contents of which would have prompted it to call the witness to testify in person, the Appeals Chamber dismissed Bagosora's request for an order to call Gatsinzi as a witness pursuant to Rule 115 of the RPE but, *proprio motu*, summoned Gatsinzi pursuant to Rules 98 and 107 of the RPE).

223 *Haradinaj et al.* Appeals Hearing, *supra* note 218, at 50–51, 377.

224 *See supra* note 186 and accompanying text.

a judgment beyond reasonable doubt based on all of the evidence, the ICTY Appeals Chamber concluded that the latter was paramount to the former. The solution reached by the Appeals Chamber is sound because the four scenarios of the *Blaškić* test preserve a right balance between the respect of the right of the accused, while – at the same time – respecting as much as possible the usual distinction between appellate and trial proceedings.[225]

C. The Options Available to the ICC

A critical analysis of how, in practice, the ICC Appeals Chamber will deal with the admission of additional evidence on appeal must wait for the first appeal judgments to be issued. However, some tentative remarks on the possible attitude of the ICC Appeals Chamber in this regard can be conducted on the basis of the Rome Statute.

As explained above, the appellate proceedings at the ICC are not a trial *de novo*.[226] The ICC Appeals Chamber will therefore face similar issues to the ones which occurred at the ICTY.

Like the ICTY and ICTR Appeals Chamber, the ICC Appeals Chamber may hear additional evidence.[227] However, the ICC Appeals Chamber has options that are not available to the ICTY Appeals Chamber. It is important to note, in this regard, that the Rome Statute explicitly allows the ICC Appeals Chamber to "remand a factual issue to the original Trial Chamber for it to determine the issue and to report back accordingly" or "may itself call evidence to determine the issue."[228]

Accordingly, the first option would be for the ICC Appeals Chamber to remand the issue back to the trial chamber that heard the evidence and ask that chamber to determine a factual issue.[229] This option would have the advantage of keeping the assessment of facts and witnesses' credibility within the purview of the trial chamber, which originally heard the rest of the evidence in the case. Moreover, it would preserve the right of the appellant to a trial chamber's decision beyond reasonable doubt based on all of the evidence before it.[230]

The second option would be for the ICC Appeals Chamber to hear the additional evidence itself over and above that brought before the

225 Carter, *supra* note 177, at 139–40.
226 *See supra* note 150 and accompanying text.
227 Article 83(2) of the Rome Statute.
228 *Id.*
229 *See also* Roth & Henzelin, *supra* note 6, at 1553.
230 *See also* Carter, *supra* note 177, at 141.

trial chamber.[231] The ICC Appeals Chamber would thus face the same dilemma as the ICTY Appeals Chamber with respect to the appropriate standard of appellate review.[232] This extensive power of the ICC Appeals Chamber would – apparently or at least potentially – contradict the principle that the most competent chamber with respect to findings of facts is the trial chamber which originally heard the evidence.[233]

It remains to be seen which approach the ICC Appeals Chamber adopts to the issue of the admissions of additional evidence on appeal.

IV. CONCLUSION

While the ICTY Appeals Chamber succeeded in finding an adequate solution with respect to the standard of appellate review to be applied in case of admission of additional evidence on appeal, the right to appeal against acquittal before international criminal tribunals and courts is a notable exception to the generally good compromise of the mixture of civil law and common law approaches in international criminal procedure. Arising from the difficulty to reconcile common law and civil law traditions, the right to appeal represents a problem, which remains open to debate.[234] With respect to the possibility to appeal against an acquittal, while different avenues were opened to the ICTY and ICTR Appeals Chamber, its practice has been inconsistent and, in some cases, has resulted in an undue dilution of the rights of the accused. From a strict international human rights law point of view, the ICTY and ICTR Appeals Chamber's practice – as well as the SCSL's practice – of entering convictions or increasing sentences on appeal is in clear violation of Article 14(5) of the ICCPR.

Reconciliation between the approaches of the civil law and common law systems would have been possible if due weight had been given to the need for the ICTY and ICTR Appeals Chamber to respect the fundamental right to appeal, as enshrined in Article 14(5) of the ICCPR.[235] The ICTY and ICTR Appeals Chamber could have respected this international recognized human right standard by interpreting the respective provisions of the ICTY and ICTR Statutes in the sense the most favorable to the accused and recognizing that two alternatives are open in the case of a prosecution's appeal against an acquittal or against the sentence. The

231 *See also* Roth & Henzelin, *supra* note 6, at 1553.
232 Carter, *supra* note 177, at 142.
233 Roth & Henzelin, *supra* note 6, at 1553.
234 *See also* Pocar, *supra* note 13, at 444.
235 *See also id.* at 455–6.

first avenue would be for the ICTY and ICTR Appeals Chamber to remit the matter to a trial chamber in those few cases were re-trial is necessary. In case of an appeal against an acquittal on an error of fact, this option would further have the merit for the Appeals Chamber to give deference to the trial chamber and not to abuse its role in entering a conviction based on the record of the trial without observing witness testimony or evidence presentation, which may be important in assessing witness credibility. The second avenue would be to simply acknowledge the error on appeal, noting that the trial chamber incorrectly disallowed the convictions, but without entering a new conviction or increasing the sentence.

The fact that the international criminal courts and tribunals have thus far followed a third avenue of entering convictions or increasing the sentence on appeal is problematic. However, as Justice Robert Jackson stated in the last sentence to his report to the President of the United States on the performance of the International Military Tribunal of Nuremberg, "many mistakes have been made and many inadequacies must be confessed" but one might take consolation in the fact that, "in proceedings of this novelty, errors and missteps may also be instructive to the future."[236] Accordingly, outlining the problems, challenges and limits the international criminal courts and tribunals have faced with respect to the right to appeal might be instructive to the ICC, which has yet to address this issue, in order to find a better solution without contravening the fundamental right to appeal.

[236] Robert H. Jackson, United States Representative to the International Conference on Military Trials, *Report to the President* (Oct. 7, 1946).

Index